MW00997602

CHINA'S LEADERS

Previous Books by David Shambaugh

Where Great Powers Meet: America & China in Southeast Asia (2021)
China & the World (edited, 2020)
The China Reader: Rising Power (edited, 2016)
China's Future (2016)
International Relations of Asia (co-edited, 2008 and 2014)
China Goes Global: The Partial Power (2013)
Tangled Titans: The United States and China (edited, 2012)
Charting China's Future: Domestic & International Challenges (edited, 2011)
China's Communist Party: Atrophy & Adaptation (2008)
China–Europe Relations: Perceptions, Policies, and Prospects (co-edited, 2008)
China Watching: Perspectives from Europe, Japan, and the United States (co-edited, 2007)
Power Shift: China & Asia's New Dynamics (edited, 2005)
The Odyssey of China's Imperial Art Treasures (co-authored, 2005)
Modernizing China's Military: Progress, Problems, and Prospects (2002)
Making China Policy: Lessons from the Bush and Clinton Administrations (co-edited, 2001)
The Modern Chinese State (edited, 2000)
Is China Unstable? (edited, 2000)
The China Reader: The Reform Era (co-edited, 1999)
China's Military Faces the Future (co-edited, 1999)
Contemporary Taiwan (edited, 1998)
China's Military in Transition (co-edited, 1997)
China and Europe: 1949–1995 (1996)
Greater China: The Next Superpower? (edited, 1995)
Deng Xiaoping: Portrait of a Chinese Statesman (edited, 1995)
Chinese Foreign Policy: Theory & Practice (co-edited, 1994)
American Studies of Contemporary China (edited, 1993)
Beautiful Imperialist: China Perceives America, 1972–1990 (1991)
The Making of a Premier: Zhao Ziyang's Provincial Career (1984)

CHINA'S LEADERS

From Mao to Now

David Shambaugh

polity

First published in 2021 by Polity Press

Internal silhouettes designed by Steve Leard

Polity Press
65 Bridge Street
Cambridge CB2 1UR, UK

Polity Press
101 Station Landing
Suite 300
Medford, MA 02155, USA

ISBN-13: 978-1-5095-4651-0

A catalogue record for this book is available from the British Library.

Library of Congress Cataloging-in-Publication Data

Names: Shambaugh, David L., author.
Title: China's leaders : from Mao to now / David Shambaugh.
Description: Cambridge ; Medford, MA : Polity, 2021. | Includes bibliographical references and index. | Summary: "A world-renowned Sinologist explores China's modern history through the lives of its leaders"-- Provided by publisher.
Identifiers: LCCN 2021008012 (print) | LCCN 2021008013 (ebook) | ISBN 9781509546510 (hardback) | ISBN 9781509546527 (epub)
Subjects: LCSH: Zhongguo gong chan dang. Zhong yang wei yuan hui--Biography. | Heads of state--China--Biography. | Statesmen--China--Biography. | China--Politics and government--1949- | China--History--1949-
Classification: LCC DS734 .S43 2021 (print) | LCC DS734 (ebook) | DDC 951.05092/2--dc23
LC record available at https://lccn.loc.gov/2021008012
LC ebook record available at https://lccn.loc.gov/2021008013

Typeset in 11 on 15 pt Dante by
Servis Filmsetting Ltd, Stockport, Cheshire
Printed and bound in Great Britain by TJ Books Ltd, Padstow, Cornwall

For further information on Polity, visit our website:
politybooks.com

Dedicated Admiringly to the Memory of

Roderick MacFarquhar

The Doyen of Chinese Leadership Studies

CONTENTS

BOXES, TABLES, & FIGURES

Boxes

Tables

Figures

PREFACE AND ACKNOWLEDGMENTS

Ever since I first started studying China and its politics in 1973 I have focused on a variety of aspects and dimensions of the Chinese political system, but none more consistently than its senior leaders and leadership. My first book in 1984 was in fact about a Chinese leader (Zhao Ziyang); it traced his life and career path from being a sub-provincial official in Guangdong province to becoming the national Premier and then General Secretary of the Chinese Communist Party,[1] and other Chinese leaders have played a central role in many of my subsequent publications. Of course, leaders matter a great deal in the life and politics of all nations, but their impact is greater in certain autocratic systems—of which China is one. I have long been interested in the different dimensions of how Chinese communist leaders rule—their individual idiosyncrasies, how they interact with each other, what strategies and tactics they adopt, how they use the institutional levers of power and control at their disposal, how they impact Chinese society, and how they interact with the other leaders from other countries.

This book about China's leaders has thus been percolating in my mind for many decades. As I have taught my own university courses on Chinese politics during the past three decades, I have always adopted a leader-centric approach, and would assign individual biographical books and articles on different leaders, but I always wished that there was a single volume that covered China's main leaders and their periods of rule from 1949 to the present. The one that does successfully do this was edited by the eminent Harvard professor Roderick MacFarquhar;[2] in this volume and all others that he authored during his distinguished career, Chinese leaders played *the* central role in his analysis. Rod unfortunately recently passed away in February 2019, but during his scholarly career he was truly the doyen of the study of Chinese communist "elite politics." Rod was always most kind and mentoring to me (although I was never his student), I hold him in extremely high esteem, and therefore I admiringly dedicate this book to his memory and to all that he contributed to the scholarly study of Chinese politics. During the period 1991–1996 when I served as the Editor of *The China Quarterly*, the leading journal in contemporary China studies, which Rod founded in 1960, Rod was also very supportive and mentoring from across the Atlantic and his professorial position at Harvard.

While China has many leaders at any given time, who populate the approximately 25-member Political Bureau (Politburo) and the 7-member Standing Committee, there has always been one dominant "paramount leader" (much more than a *primus inter pares*). This book is about the five main individuals who have been in this position (Mao Zedong, Deng Xiaoping, Jiang Zemin, Hu Jintao, and Xi Jinping)—but it also definitely considers others who held the top institutional portfolios as party leader (Hua Guofeng, Hu Yaobang, Zhao Ziyang) as well as a variety of other Politburo members who have been significant political players in their own rights.

While the book is centered on the lives of these individual Chinese communist leaders it is also very much focused on their times as well. It is thus simultaneously a survey of the evolution of the People's Republic of China (PRC) over the past seven decades. Taken together, I hope that the combined focus on leaders and their times will serve as a good overview and introductory text for students and readers who seek a comprehensive survey of the PRC. In trying to make this an accessible and readable account that keeps the narrative moving along, inevitably I have had to make numerous judgments along the way concerning certain facts and events—providing sufficient detail but not so much as to bog the reader down. This has been a fine balance to strike—providing lots of detail but not too much. As Chinese politics (like all systems but perhaps more than most) are filled with lacunae, specialists and scholars of Chinese politics will inevitably ask, "What about this or what about that?" But I have intended this book to be more for the general public and students than for my scholarly colleagues, so I hope they will remember this when they read it.

Although I have been teaching this material for a long time and thought

I had a pretty thorough grasp of the intricacies of different leaders' careers and their periods in power, once I got into the research and writing I realized that there was still a great deal that I either had forgotten or did not know. I have done my very best to check, double-check, and be very careful about all the events and actors covered in this study—but any errors or oversights are, of course, my own. For certain periods and leaders I have sought the advice and expertise of some of my close and respected colleagues, who were generous enough to read over the draft text to help catch any errors and offer suggestions for improvement. Stanford University Professor Andrew Walder is truly one of the world's leading experts on Mao and the Maoist era,[3] and he was most gracious in reading and reviewing that chapter, as well as the introductory chapter. Robert Suettinger—now an independent scholar who had a distinguished career in the US Government as one of the CIA's chief analysts of Chinese politics, as National Intelligence Officer for East Asia, and as Senior Director of Asian Affairs on the National Security Council—was kind enough to read the Mao chapter and parts of the Deng Xiaoping and Hu Jintao chapters. Professor Ezra Vogel of Harvard University (recently deceased), who himself wrote *the definitive* biography of Deng Xiaoping,[4] was kind enough to read and improve the draft of my Deng chapter. Robert F. Ash, my former colleague at the University of London's School of Oriental & African Studies (SOAS), was extremely generous with his time and carefully read *all* of the chapters in draft—his careful eye and "blue pencil" caught countless things that merited revision. Bob also was a particular help with the sections in each chapter on China's economy, and helped to design some of the graphics in the book. I am enormously grateful to all four individuals—Andy, Bob, Ezra, and Bob—each of whom have been close personal friends as well as much-respected professional colleagues. I am also grateful to Harry Harding for steering me to broader studies of leadership (he too has been a close China colleague and friend for many years). I am also in debt to the two anonymous reviewers arranged by Polity Press—I do not know who you are, but I am sincerely grateful for your eagle eyes and constructive suggestions. Lastly, I am grateful to my student Miles Ogden-Peters for his research assistance on the Hu Jintao and Xi Jinping chapters.

I am also indebted to the great team at Polity Press in Cambridge,

England, for their highly professional support throughout the writing process. This is the second book I have published with Polity,[5] and I cannot recommend the press more highly. Louise Knight, editor for politics and international relations, is an absolute joy to work with. Editorial assistant Inès Boxman has also been superbly helpful and hardworking on many logistical dimensions of the book, most notably tracking down photographs and permissions reproduced in this book. Evie Deavall has been a first-rate and efficient production editor, shepherding the manuscript through to publication. I am also grateful to Ann Klefstad for expert copyediting and to Elizabeth Ball for compiling the Index. One of the great things about Polity as a publisher is their speed of production—this volume went from final draft manuscript to published book in six months! It was truly a team effort by all of these individuals. Altogether, working and publishing with Polity has been a very enjoyable experience.

While this book has been brewing in my brain for a long time and I have been teaching it for many years, I actually wrote it over a brief nine-month period (May 2020–January 2021) during the COVID pandemic (it was one positive side effect of hibernating at home). Like all of my previous books over the past quarter century, it was written mainly at our summer home near Traverse City, Michigan and at our winter home in Arlington, Virginia. I am most fortunate to have such wonderful domiciles in which to live and be creative.

Last, but not least, I must again thank my wonderful wife Ingrid Larsen for her love and support throughout our four decades of marriage, as well as her patience and tolerance during the writing of this book. Our two wonderful sons Christopher and Alexander, now young professionals in their own right, are a constant source of pride and love for me. Our faithful golden retriever Ollie once again lay by my side and kept me company as I wrote this book, although sadly she passed away just before its conclusion. One could not ask for a better canine companion. Such family support has been critically important for me personally and professionally for decades, including during this project. I cannot be more grateful to them.

January 2021
Arlington, Virginia USA

CHAPTER 1

ON CHINA'S LEADERS AND LEADERSHIP

LEADERS MATTER IN ALL POLITICAL SYSTEMS—BUT IN SOME THEY MATTER much more. Leaders in totalitarian systems, or authoritarian leaders in single-party systems, are unconstrained by the checks and balances of democracies, and thus their actions are more determinative and have an outsized impact on their societies and the world beyond their borders. China is such a case.

This book assesses and contrasts the five main leaders that the People's Republic of China (PRC) and the Chinese Communist Party (CCP) has had over its first seven decades: Mao Zedong, Deng Xiaoping, Jiang Zemin, Hu Jintao, and Xi Jinping. While a number of other leaders have served as President of the People's Republic of China (PRC) and as Premiers (heads of government), this study focuses on the five principal Party leaders (Hua Guofeng, Hu Yaobang, and Zhao Ziyang will be folded into the Deng chapter, as their brief tenures at the top were not really long enough to merit separate chapters). The book is about the leadership styles of these five individuals, as well as about these men's times and records as paramount leaders. Each had a distinctive leadership style: I characterize Mao as a *populist tyrant*, Deng as a *pragmatic Leninist*, Jiang as a *bureaucratic politician*, Hu as a *technocratic apparatchik*, and Xi as a *modern emperor*. These descriptions tell us not only about the individual leaders' styles of rule, but also about different aspects of the Chinese political system itself. The main analytical approach is therefore to explore the intersection between each individual's persona and style of rule with China's developments domestically and internationally. Readers will therefore not only gain an (admittedly compressed) survey of the last 70 years, but one seen principally through the lens of the leader's visions and actions during each period in power (Mao Zedong 1949–1976; Deng Xiaoping 1977–1989; Jiang Zemin 1989–2002; Hu Jintao 2002–2012; Xi Jinping 2012—). This book is primarily intended for students and readers who wish to gain an overview of the past seven decades of Chinese politics—in itself quite a task—but it is also a study for specialists who wish to dig inside the persona of each leader and try to understand how their socialization shaped their particular styles of rule.

One might assume that there has been much continuity of leadership style in a Leninist political system such as communist China. Actually, I find that there has been a considerable degree of *discontinuity* of style among these five leaders. This can be seen in particular in the different ways they each approached institutional bureaucracies of party and state, as well as varying differences over policies. Their differences are also evident in the manner that each performed their public roles, in how each approached the mass public, how each used the language of propaganda and ideology, and how each dealt with their contemporaries and subordinates. Each leader also approached the outside world and China's foreign relations in different ways.

Of course, each ruled at a different period of time—and thus confronted differing sets of policy challenges at home and abroad. Each was born, reared, and matured professionally during different decades; this is why each is said to have represented five different generations of leaders (五代的零售价). They also therefore faced different tasks: only Mao had to build a regime and country from scratch—all the others inherited a system and nation-state, to which their efforts can be said to have been additive and supplemental. Even though the system and country that Deng inherited from Mao had been deeply traumatized by the late Maoist era, the anarchy of the Cultural Revolution, and had to be rebuilt, the CCP and PRC nonetheless were well solidified by that time (1977). Deng's reforms did nonetheless constitute significant qualitative changes, albeit within the existing systemic framework. The post-1989 (Tiananmen massacre) China that Jiang Zemin inherited from Deng, and the policy adjustments he made, were also a significant departure from the 1980s—yet these changes were more to the superstructure rather than the foundation of the CCP operating system. Hu Jintao made minimal incremental changes to the system, although he (and his Premier Wen Jiabao) did launch a number of social policy initiatives (which largely went unrealized). Xi Jinping has certainly been a strong leader—the strongest since Deng (some judge since Mao)—but, again, the changes he has made to the system have been largely additive rather than fundamental and original.

They have certainly shown commonalities as well. As with *all* Chinese leaders since the "self-strengtheners" of the late Qing dynasty (1870s–1890s), they sought to build China economically, make it "wealthy and powerful" (富强), to maintain its territorial integrity and sovereignty, to protect its national security, to recover its lost dignity and respect, and to strengthen the country's position in Asia and the world.[1] All also sought to continually strengthen the Chinese Communist Party institutionally (Mao and the Cultural Revolution being the major exception, although it can be argued that Mao too was trying to remake and thus reinvigorate the Party). As leaders of "new (socialist) China" (post-1949) they had the common vision of reducing poverty and social inequalities, increasing literacy and education, reducing the rural–urban gap, eliminating social vices, and maintaining social stability (the Cultural Revolution again being the exception). Yet the *means* and *approaches* for achieving many of these goals varied considerably among the five leaders. Thus, when conceptualizing the similarities and differences among these five leaders it may be analogous to think of a house or building where the foundation, walls, and roof remain the same—but the interior rooms and wiring were constantly being altered.

Perspectives on Leadership

It is also useful to view Chinese leaders through different prisms and paradigms that have been developed to analyze leadership and authority. When doing so, we also see differences. Max Weber famously distinguished between three types of political authority: *charismatic*, *traditional*, and *legal-rational*.[2] By Weber's criteria, all five leaders exhibited elements of each. All five were "traditional" in that they operated in—and continued—the patrimonial male-dominant, hierarchical political system that had characterized China since its inception. All five (to differing extents) were "legal-rational" in that they all were comfortable with and sought to build strong institutional hierarchies to administer both the state and society, and the decision bases for policy were taken more or less rationally and meritocratically within these institutions. Mao's post-1966 attack on bureaucracy could also be interpreted as a deviation—but, again, he was trying to *remold* the bureaucracy, not destroy it altogether. Mao was not an anarchist. Concerning Weber's third type of leadership, only Mao and Xi can be said to have been "charismatic" leaders—motivating the masses through personal populist appeal—the other three (including Deng) were not. Jiang Zemin was certainly extroverted and gregarious, but that is not the same as being charismatic.

Another popular paradigm is of "transformational" versus "transactional" leadership, as famously put forth by the American political scientist James MacGregor Burns in his classic book *Leadership*.[3] Transformational leaders, Burns argued, seek to transform society through ideas; they are generally intellectuals who pursue an ideological agenda. Three of our five Chinese leaders—Mao, Deng, and Xi—can be said to have been the former, as they all truly had a qualitatively transformative impact on society and institutions. Burns also defined four specific sub-categories of transformational leaders, into which I would place each leader: *ideational* leaders (Mao, Deng, Xi), *reform* leaders (Deng, Xi), *revolutionary* leaders (Mao), *heroes* (Mao), and *ideologues* (Mao, Xi). He also noted that transformational leaders "recognize and exploit an existing need or demand of a potential follower."[4] In this regard as well, Mao, Deng, and Xi all tapped into popular needs of the mass public—all three through deep nationalist yearnings as well as preference for "strongman" leaders, Mao through the appeal of egalitarian socialism, Deng through the opportunity of economic empowerment, and Xi through a preference for social order and crackdown on privileged corruption. Jiang and Hu were transactional leaders, "exchanging" the right to rule for incremental improvements in people's lives and patronage of specific bureaucracies (what Burns described as "bargains with bureaucrats"). Jiang and Hu also acted more in what Burns describes as a "managerial style" (similar to a corporate boss), and were "consensus builders" rather than transformative proactive leaders. Jiang and Hu were also the most comfortable of the five operating within "groups" and "collective" leadership, both typical of the transactional style of leadership.

The academic field of "leadership studies" in the United States has burgeoned since the 1960s and has produced a vast literature as well as dedicated leadership schools on university campuses. One leading scholar of leadership (and practicing psychologist), Daniel Goleman, who is known particularly for his pioneering work on emotional intelligence, has identified six distinct leadership styles: *coercive* (demands immediate compliance), *authoritative* (mobilizes people toward a vision), *affiliative* (builds personal relationships with colleagues), *democratic* (forges consensus through participation), *pacesetting* (sets high standards for performance), and *coaching* (develops successors for the future).[5] Mao, Deng, and Xi distinctly exhibited coercive tendencies. Mao and Xi, to a lesser extent Deng, were authoritative. Deng, Jiang, and Hu were affiliative. Deng, Jiang, and Hu were democratic. Deng, Jiang, Hu, and Xi were all pacesetters. Only Mao and Deng can be said to have been concerned with fostering (coaching) their successors.

Of course, leadership is also very culturally and system dependent.[6] Leaders who would succeed in Europe would not likely succeed in the Middle East, for example, and those who are successful in autocratic systems are not appropriate for democratic systems (and vice versa). Nonetheless, it is interesting to consider leadership skills comparatively, as certain ones do transcend different political systems. Take, for example, the seven core leadership qualities identified by the American politics scholar Fred Greenstein for successful American presidents: vision, political skill, organizational capacity, public communicator, cognitive style (how a leader acquires and processes information), emotional intelligence, and moral character.[7] If we were to apply these to China's leaders, I would judge that Mao, Deng, and Xi all possessed vision. Mao, Deng, Jiang, and Xi all possessed political skill (defined by Greenstein as being motivational and able to forge political coalitions). Deng, Jiang, and Xi all excelled at organizational capacity. Mao and Deng were poor public speakers, while both Jiang and Hu were rather robotic in their public presentations (Jiang was just the opposite in private). Only Xi was a good public communicator. Each had their own distinct cognitive style of processing information. So-called emotional intelligence—the ability to read and channel others' emotional needs—is a key ingredient noted in many studies of leadership, as it naturally creates "followership." The best leaders inspire and incentivize followers, and thus do not need to rely on other forms of inducement. I would say that only Mao and Xi, among our five leaders, possessed this skill. Finally, what about moral character? Here, all five strike out if measured by the repressive system they presided over and the personal use of arbitrary power each wielded. But, if measured on the basis of the behavioral type of Chinese Communist Party members and society's citizens that each sought to foster—then we can say that all five advocated policies encouraging honesty, clean living, noncorruption, frugality, and other traditional communist values. There has been an additional expectation that China's leaders should embody the traditional Confucian archetype of the caring, benevolent, and patriarchal figure (all five fit this paradigm).

Some leaders exhibit the character trait of narcissism (excessive interest in or admiration of oneself), and this has been extensively studied by political psychologists.[8] When it occurs in leaders this personality disorder usually leads to a compulsive desire of the leader for mass adulation and the creation of a "cult of personality." Among the five leaders in this study, it is clear that Mao had a severe case of narcissism, Xi Jinping has a very strong case, and Jiang Zemin had a mild case. Deng Xiaoping and Hu Jintao were self-effacing individuals who were not so inclined (although in Deng's case the propaganda apparatus nonetheless still tried to create such a cult of personality).

An individual leader's lifelong socialization is also critical to understanding their behavior. It is well established in the fields of psychiatry, psychology, social psychology, psychohistory, political psychology, and psychopathology that pre-adult and early adult socialization are critical formative periods that do much to shape how a person behaves throughout their life. In particular, at least the following experiences and relationships have been identified as key influences: where one grows up and their standard of living; relationships with mothers and fathers; degree of maternal nurturing (or lack thereof); experiences in school and relationships with teachers; and relationships with peers. All of these encounters usually have far-reaching impacts on subsequent personality development. For example—for boys—maternal nurturing, a secure home environment, interactive siblings, financial stability, supportive primary and secondary school teachers, and inclusivity with a network of peers can all lead to a secure ego, confidence, and an outgoing adult personality. Conversely, antagonistic relations with fathers, a sense of neglect from mothers or abandonment by parents (even if they are away from home working), bickering with siblings, financial instability, harsh discipline from teachers, exclusion by peers—these experiences can all lead to an alienated, frustrated, angry, repressed, aggressive, insecure, insular adult personality type. This latter type is frequently associated with the development of strong anti-authoritarian and frequently narcissistic adult personality types. These two sets of general pre-adult characteristics have also been found across multiple national-cultural environments and are not simply characteristics of modern Western societies. Indeed, in pre-modern agrarian or early industrialized societies they are quite common.

To what degree do these early family rearing and socialization features shed light on the five leaders covered in this study? One interesting commonality is that only one of the five (Jiang Zemin) grew up in a close-knit and stable nuclear family environment. All the others had very disrupted youths with absent or deceased parents.

Mao and his father had very strained relations, they clashed frequently, and Mao's anti-authority persona has been attributed to his deep antagonistic relationship with his father.[9] His father made Mao work in the fields beginning at age six, something he resented. As Mao described his father in an interview with Edgar Snow in Yanan in 1937 (his only known reflection on his youth and family): "He was a hot-tempered man and frequently beat both me and my brothers."[10] Mao told Snow that he grew to "hate" his father. Being unfilial toward his father, in such a patriarchal traditional culture, gave Mao an "Oedipus complex" (a Freudian reference to Greek King Oedipus, who unknowingly killed his father and married his mother), in the view of Sinologist and social scientist Richard H. Solomon, who authored a comprehensive psychocultural biography of Mao.[11] In sharp contrast to his father, Mao's mother was very nurturing and indulgent of her first son—thus providing him with a strong sense of self-confidence and a self-assured ego. As he described her to Snow: "My mother was a kind woman, generous and sympathetic, and ever ready to share what she had."[12] Mao was also very protective of his mother (sometimes physically) when she clashed with his father. There was much acrimony in the Mao family household. Mao's anti-authority trait deepened in primary school, where his teacher frequently punished and beat him. Mao described his teacher as belonging to the "stern treatment school; he was harsh and severe."[13] After five years in this school and one too many beatings Mao ran away, never to return. These early childhood experiences proved pivotal for Mao—producing resentment of his father and authority figures, and instilling "revolutionary" traits in him at an early age.

In Deng Xiaoping's case, his father was absent for long periods from the family residence in rural Sichuan, and thus Deng did not have much of a relationship with his father. His mother, like Mao's mother, was loving, and doted on her first-born son. But she died when Deng was only 14. Deng then left home for middle school in Chongqing, also never to return. At just age 16 Deng had the wrenching experience of being sent on a long steamship trip to France for an overseas work-study program (which turned into much work and little study). Altogether Deng spent a total of six years abroad in France and one year in Moscow before returning to China at age 23. These early experiences on his own certainly bred a certain self-reliance in Deng. While in France Deng developed a liking for French food, liquor, and a passion for croissants. He found a series of odd jobs and factory work, but his schooling only lasted three months. Deng did find a peer group in relationships with other young Chinese and Vietnamese (including Ho Chi Minh) then studying and working there, many of whom were active in socialist politics following the Bolshevik Revolution (1917). One of these individuals who did play an important mentoring role in Deng's life was Zhou Enlai, who was six years Deng's senior and who brought him into the nascent Chinese Communist Party Socialist Youth League. Deng's main job in the League was to produce propaganda pamphlets, for which he became known as "Monsieur Mimeograph."

Hu Jintao was also deprived of parents early. His mother died when he was only 7, and because his father (a merchant) was often away on business traveling throughout the lower Yangzi delta region, Hu and his three sisters were raised by an aunt. While the aunt was a good provider, Hu never had the security and familiarity of a close nuclear family. This likely contributed to his own self-reliance, and possibly also to the aloofness he displayed as an adult.

Jiang Zemin is the only one of the five leaders in this study to have had a fairly normal nuclear and extended family life, growing up in Yangzhou, Jiangsu province. His father was a writer and part-time electrician, and Jiang recalled later that his mother was doting and loving.[14] The Jiang family was well-to-do and well-known in Yangzhou, an important cultural and commercial center for centuries. Jiang was one of five children. His uncle Jiang Shangqing and his wife were second parents to Jiang Zemin, essentially raising him. Jiang Shangqing was a leftist intellectual who was active in communist underground activities, arrested and rearrested by the Nationalists' police, and who had just joined the communist Red Army when he was killed in an ambush during the Japanese occupation in 1939, thus becoming a CCP martyr (giving the extended Jiang family a communist pedigree). Following his death Jiang Zemin's natural father Jiang Shijun offered their son to his brother's widow, as the couple had no male children of their own.[15] This was not as disruptive for young Jiang Zemin as it might seem, as he had been living mostly with the aunt and uncle from an early age. Other than this anomaly, as described in Chapter 4, Jiang's upbringing was quite normal and quite intellectual—which may have given him a secure self-confidence.

Xi Jinping was also thrust into the world at the tender age of 14, when he was sent from Beijing to rural Shaanxi province during the Cultural Revolution. His father had been imprisoned five years earlier and his mother was sent to a rural cadre school. The Xi family household thus broke apart early in Xi's young life—he was just 9 when his father was imprisoned— Xi was thereafter sent to a boarding school on the outskirts of Beijing.

Thus, if self-confidence and independence born of adversity at an early age is a characteristic of individuals who become leaders, all five leaders in this study had their youths and home life disrupted and had to learn to cope on their own in their mid-teens. Only Jiang Zemin had the semblance of a normal family life, although he grew up in split households between his birth parents and his aunt and uncle.

Of course, leaders—like all humans—are not static creatures. Despite the important impact of childhood and early adult socialization, we all learn and change as we grow older. Certain learned "lessons" from the past are assimilated and applied to the future—or at least they should be ("those who do not remember the past are condemned to repeat it," famously observed philosopher George Santayana). So, a leader at one stage of his or her career may act differently at another. It is thus relevant to consider mid-life and late-life experiences. As individuals approach death, paranoia and irrationality grip some leaders. However, it is not only that people pass through identifiable stages in the life cycle, but psychologists observe that the *transitional* periods from one stage to the next can be particularly unpredictable and unsettled (like "power transitions" in international relations). Three key transitions are distinguishable: adolescence to young adulthood (ages 17–22); the young adult to middle adulthood transition (ages 40–45); and mid-life to late adulthood transition (ages 60–65).[16] The literature in psychology generally argues that one's political orientations are formed by stage 1, habits of decision-making and leadership emerge by stage 2, increasing decisiveness occurs by stage 3, but that "decisional sclerosis" can set in after age 65, with increasing unpredictability, irrationality, and dogmatism frequently apparent (which fear of death only exacerbates).[17]

In the case of the five leaders in this study, it does not seem to me that these transition points were very influential (the exception being Mao, who certainly grew quite irrational, unpredictable, and dogmatic in his sixties). Rather, I would argue, more significant in shaping the personas and leadership styles of the five were experiences they all had during their twenties and thirties, prior to the mid-life transition point noted above. As is described in detail in their individual chapters, it was primarily during these two decades of their lives that each really began to form a distinct leadership style and modus operandi.

While it is important to analyze leaders in their adult years, psychologists have long established that people are actually creatures of habit, and are quite resistant to change and adaptation. People's essential personalities are fairly firmly established by early adulthood—absent profound experiences (such as war, natural calamity, or life-altering events). Their basic belief systems and worldviews (*weltanschauungen*) are predominantly determined by one's twenties—and they are determined by a combination of family, school, community, and peer group socialization influences. Thereafter, as the psychological theory of *cognitive dissonance* (expounded most thoroughly by Leon Festinger)[18] tells us, adults go through life selectively accepting evidence that *confirms* pre-existing beliefs and images while rejecting (dissonant) information that contradicts the core belief systems established by their twenties.

With respect to our five Chinese leaders, I would argue that the theory of cognitive dissonance and the argument that their worldviews were strongly formed *prior to* their thirties applies really only to Mao. Deng, Jiang, Hu, and Xi all forged their professional personas during their thirties and forties—through working in and managing CCP institutions. All three were strong institutionalists, and I would argue that this was an outgrowth of their work experience rather than their childhoods, teenage years, twenties, or revolutionary activities (in the case of Deng).

All of these features of human development and behavior should be kept in mind when reading this book, as Chinese leaders are not unique human beings—they are susceptible to many of the behavioral patterns that psychologists, political scientists, and other researchers have discovered across multiple countries and cultures. Recognizing this, individual countries and cultures also exert their own specific influences on individual leaders. In this context, the next two sections discuss, respectively, the unique impacts of Chinese traditional political culture and that of Leninist-type communist parties.

The Influences of Chinese Political Culture

CCP leaders are, of course, communist (Marxist-Leninist) in their orientation. In the next section we examine the unique aspects of communist party systems and how that institutionally and normatively shapes the environment in which the CCP leaders examined in this book must operate. They are also *Chinese* leaders and are thus deeply shaped by historical and cultural traditions of politics and rule. As far back as Plato's *Republic* it has been recognized that the cultural socialization of politicians is determinative of their orientation and behavior. There are limits to the political culture approach, of course, as criticisms tend to take aim at the level of (over)generalization of alleged influences, but I nonetheless am one political scientist who finds this analytical approach extremely insightful and valuable. Below I list a number of the most salient residual elements and built-in assumptions from Chinese historical political culture that have continued to influence post-1949 CCP leaders:

- Leaders should inherently be benevolent (王道) and look out for the best interests of the people. Rulers should set a moral example (道德) through their behavior. Legitimacy is based on benevolent and benign morality.
- While benevolence is preferred, coercion against usurpers is justified to maintain stability and the sanctity of the regime; excessive coercion, however, is considered hegemonic (霸道) and thus illegitimate.
- The physical core (内心) of China is ethnically Han; other ethnic groups on the periphery, as well as further away, are "outsiders" (外人) or "barbarians" (夷人).
- Other powers are predatory, foreigners have ulterior motives to take advantage of China, and thus are not to be trusted.
- China is a global great power with over 3,000 years of history and a highly accomplished civilization and is deserving of respect from all others on this basis. Restoring China to global status as a respected great power is the primary mission of all Chinese leaders.
- China is the leading power in Asia and should be treated deferentially by all neighbors (the "tribute system").
- Beginning in the late eighteenth century until 1949 China experienced external aggression and plundering by foreign (mainly European) powers—leading to the "century of shame and humiliation" (百年国耻). China must never again be subjected to such physical dismemberment, social exploitation, and psychological trauma.
- Japan's aggression during the Sino-Japanese War (1894–1895) and atrocities in China (1937–1945) are unforgivable.
- A strong national identity and patriotic nationalism must be inculcated in all Chinese.
- To the greatest extent possible, China must remain as autonomous and self-reliant (自力更生) as possible vis-à-vis other nations; (inter)dependency is a recipe for manipulation.

- Avoid open confrontation with others, but use deception and a variety of Sun Zi-like tactics to neutralize and overcome adversaries.
- A strong state is the best defense against both internal and external threats.
- Disorder (乱) is an ever-present possibility, but to be avoided at all costs. Consequently, a premium is placed on maintaining "stability" (稳定) and order (秩序).
- Regional and local centrifugal forces are always strong and pull against the centripetal power of the Center. As a result, there is a tendency for the periphery to feign compliance with the Center (a phenomenon known as "the sky is high and the emperor is far away": 天高皇帝远).
- Elite politics can be a zero-sum game of "tigers eating tigers." Never trust others, as they likely are seeking to subvert your power and position.
- Maintenance of "face" (面子) and avoiding embarrassment is essential not only in Chinese society, but also in dealings with foreigners. Elaborate lengths are gone to in order to avoid public embarrassment and maintain appearances of confidence and grandeur.
- The people of China are a "loose sheet of sand" who need to be led through the tutelage of enlightened elites.
- Maintain flexibility and avoid dependence in foreign relations.
- Play the long game and keep a clear eye on end goals. Time is always an asset. Do not be impatient. Maneuver is a constant tactical feature, as all relationships are eternally fluid.
- Vigilantly safeguard China's territories and claimed sovereignty.

These are many of the operative assumptions I believe China's leaders are inculcated with. They are subliminal assumptions, which individual Chinese may not even be conscious of, but these assumptions all are inherited from the past and have real impact on people's behavior. Additionally, China's leaders have in common with leaders of other developing countries their nation's historical encounters with Western imperialism and colonialism, the strong mission to gain independence and autonomy, and thus the imperative to undertake modernization and nation-building.[19]

The Influences of Chinese Leninist Culture

In addition to these historical and cultural influences, all Chinese Communist Party leaders must operate within, and are deeply influenced by, the fact that the CCP is a Leninist-type party. This has both institutional and normative dimensions and consequences.

Institutional Imperatives

The former involves the institutional structures and policy processes that are unique to communist parties: the Central Committee and its departments, the Politburo and Politburo Standing Committee, Leading Small Groups (领导小组), Party committees (党委), Party groups (党组), and Party teams (党班子) that are embedded within the vast majority of institutions in society (factories, schools, neighborhoods, media, the military, all provinces, all cities, all counties, all villages, etc.). Leninist communist parties are like cellular organisms that permeate *all* elements of a society—they penetrate into the society and thereby control from the inside. The embedded institutional structure of the CCP is pervasive throughout China. China's leaders must operate within this institutional framework. Among other manifestations this means that there are built-in mechanisms of constant surveillance among Party members and by the Party vis-à-vis all levels of government and throughout society.

Party congresses are held every five years (since 1982). In between, plenary sessions (or plenums) are held—usually once or twice per year. It is customary that each plenum focuses on a specific policy area (third plenums are about the economy, fourth plenums about the Party and ideology, fifth plenums usually about legal and administrative affairs, sixth plenums are about culture, and so on). While there is no fixed requirement, and it has fluctuated a great deal over time, the Politburo (政治局) usually convenes only for plenums, while the Politburo Standing Committee (政治局常委) usually meets once or twice per month. The state (government) structure is entirely separate (although also penetrated by the CCP at all levels). It includes the State Council and all of its ministries, commissions, bureaus, and agencies. It is headed by the Premier—who is also a senior leader, but not the preeminent one (technically the Chairman of the National People's Congress outranks the Premier). Also on the government side is the state (PRC) President and Vice-President, but both are simply titles and do not come with attached institutions. The national judiciary is similarly a separate system (also referred to as the *political-legal system*, 政法系统) from the Party and government, but national leaders rarely interface with it. Finally, the preeminent leader is also normally Chairman of the Central Military Commission (CMC, 中央军委), a Party institution (although there has been a separate state CMC since 1982, with identical membership).

There has been fluctuation in these positions, their occupants, and their terms of occupation over time. The evolution of the five principal Chinese leaders of this study, as well as other top leaders, can be found in Table 1.1. With the exception of Hua Guofeng, prior to the 1990s those leaders who held these Party, military, and government positions were divided—but since Jiang Zemin's tenure (1989–2002) China's preeminent leader has held the trifecta of positions: CCP General Secretary, CMC Chairman, and PRC President. Only two leaders (Hua Guofeng and Zhao Ziyang) served both as CCP leader and State Council Premier (Hua simultaneously, Zhao consecutively), while "normally" the Premier has not held another position. Similarly, some served only as state President.

In China power does not always correlate directly with institutional positions. While the table below lists no fewer than eighteen individual leaders over the past seven decades, it is fair to say that only the five analyzed in this book have been the "paramount leader." Some readers may question why I have not included Hua Guofeng, Hu Yaobang, and Zhao Ziyang as "paramount leaders" worthy of their own individual chapters. The reasons vary in each case. Hua Guofeng was certainly China's preeminent leader following Mao's death and the arrest of the Gang of Four in 1976, but his authority over the military was certainly constrained by Marshal Ye Jianying—and by mid-1977 Deng Xiaoping had returned to the senior leadership and immediately and progressively began to whittle away at Hua's institutional positions and authority. By September 1990, Hua was stripped of the premiership in favor of one of Deng's chosen disciples, Zhao Ziyang. Less than a year later, in June 1981, Deng himself seized the CMC chairmanship from Hua, while inserting his other disciple Hu Yaobang as

Table 1.1: China's Principal Leadership Positions and Leaders Since 1949

	CCP Chairman	CCP General Secretary	CCP CMC Chairman	PRC President	State Council Premier
MAO ZEDONG	3/1943–9/1976		9/1954–9/1976	1950–1959	
HUA GUOFENG	10/1976–6/1981		10/1976–6/1981	*(position abolished 1975–1982)*	2/1976–9/1980
DENG XIAOPING		4/1954–9/1956	6/1981–11/1989		
HU YAOBANG	6/1981–9/1982 *(position abolished in 9/1982)*	12/1978–2/1980			
ZHAO ZIYANG		1/1987–6/1989			9/1980–11/1987
JIANG ZEMIN		6/1989–11/2002	11/1989–9/2004	3/1993–3/2003	
HU JINTAO		11/2002–11/2012	9/2004–11/2012	3/2003–3/2013	
XI JINPING		11/2012—	11/2012—	3/2013—	
LIU SHAOQI			4/1959–10/1968	4/1959–10/1968	
DONG BIWU				2/1972–1/1975	
LI XIANNIAN				6/1983–4/1988	
YANG SHANGKUN				4/1988–3/1993	
ZHOU ENLAI					10/1949–1/1976
LI PENG					11/1987–3/1998
ZHU RONGJI					3/1998–3/2003
WEN JIABAO					3/2003–3/2013
LI KEQIANG					3/2013—

CCP Chairman. Thus, Hua Guofeng's tenure was really too short and too constrained to merit a separate chapter and consideration as one of China's principal leaders. While there is a better case to make for Hu Yaobang and Zhao Ziyang, each of them very much operated under Deng's preeminent status and each only possessed a single portfolio (and neither served as President or CMC Chairman). Hu and Zhao certainly played significant roles, and we will consider them in Chapter 3, but I do not feel that either merits inclusion among the principal leaders of the PRC.

Normative Imperatives

Another, perhaps more important, set of characteristics of the CCP as a Leninist party, which influences its senior leaders, are *normative* elements. There are a number of these—all unseen—which constitute the "operating software" of the CCP.[20]

Regulate everything. The CCP and its leaders carry out their work according to an enormous number of rules and statutes, as embodied in the Party and state constitutions,[21] as well as a plethora of internal (内部) regulations. Official rules and regulations are certainly important, particularly in a party that is so extraordinarily characterized by formally specified procedures. The CCP is an extremely "scripted" party that leaves little to chance. Thousands of handbooks are published for Party committees and members (党员手册) which specify everything from who sits where at a meeting to precise procedures for all activities. There is likely no more formally organized political party on the planet. These voluminous stipulations and imperatives really do guide the behavior of Party institutions and members on a daily basis, and thus it is important to appreciate just what an excessively regulated environment China's leaders have to operate in. These regulatory and behavioral stipulations have *increased* significantly since 1989, and notably under Xi Jinping.

Hierarchy, discipline, and factionalism. As a Leninist party, within which leaders and rank-and-file members alike must operate, three elements are notable: *hierarchical organization, maintaining discipline,* and *constraining* *factionalism*. They are all interrelated. Hierarchical command is one essential characteristic of a Leninist party. In real ways, both before Xi Jinping but certainly under him, the CCP operates a lot like a military—orders and directives are given and are to be followed. Those who do not do so are punished. The CCP is a hierarchical vertical institution with horizontal mechanisms that penetrate throughout society. Leninist parties like the CCP are not voluntary organizations, where members participate out of their own free will and make their own decisions about what to say and do—there is rigid and strict *discipline*. This is what is variously referred to as the "dictatorship of the proletariat," the "people's democratic dictatorship," or "democratic centralism." The concept underlying all three terms is that the Party is the "vanguard" of the "masses" and "people," and legitimately acts on behalf of the populace. So, where does the aforementioned term "democratic" come in? This harkens back to Mao's concept of the "mass line," first developed by him in Yanan (the Communists' revolutionary stronghold after 1937) whereby the Party floats a policy idea to the masses, gets feedback from them, and then it makes a policy decision—after which strict adherence is required during policy implementation. This "down-up-down" process of policy formulation and implementation is meant to (theoretically at least) give the veneer of mass participation in the system. Related to the need to maintain strict hierarchy and discipline is the corollary of checking *factionalism*. Factionalism is an endemic feature of Chinese political culture. Rooted in interpersonal *guanxi* and the belief that there is safety in personal networks, Chinese citizens, cadres, and leaders alike have a long history of factionalism. It is hard-baked into the DNA of Chinese politics. There are a variety of factional types in the PRC: institution-based, locality-based, patron/client-based, "line"-based, issue-based, school-based, and more.[22] The past seven decades (and before the CCP seized power) have been rife with factional struggles and power plays. Some losers find themselves in Qingcheng Prison (the facility outside of Beijing reserved for elite prisoners). But factionalism runs exactly counter to hierarchical Leninism. Hence there has been a longstanding attempt by the CCP to quell factionalism within its ranks and particularly at the top of the system. This has particularly been the case since the leadership split on the eve of the June 4, 1989, massacre.

The nomenklatura. The CCP may portray itself as a mass political party, representing the vast peasantry and working class of China, but in fact it is very much an elite party. Its current 94 million Party members only represent approximately 6 percent of the population of 1.5 billion people. Because of this obvious asymmetry of leaders and led, and the popular perception that the Party is a class in itself,[23] the CCP goes to extensive lengths to promote the propaganda narrative that the Party "cherishes the people," "puts people first" (以人为本), and otherwise is not detached from the masses. But not only is the Party a small percentage of broader society, but there is a "Party within the Party." This is known as the *nomenklatura*—a Soviet term to identify the list of official positions in the Party and throughout the country that must be staffed by Party members. The most recent data we have on the CCP nomenklatura is from 2003, when there were 525,000 individuals identified as "leading cadres" (领导干部), essentially the *nomenklatura* corps. These elites not only run the Party—they run all major institutions in society (media, major universities, state-owned enterprises, and many companies, and so on).[24] There is a list of 3,800 institutional positions (编制 in Chinese) that require the appointment of a "leading cadre" selected by the CCP Organization Department. The *nomenklatura* system is thus not only a prime example of Party penetration of the entire society, but also of all the key organs of institutional power. Such penetration, and thereby control, is the essence of how Leninist parties exercise control.

"The Party controls the gun." In addition to controlling socioeconomic entities, the CCP has always kept a tight grip on the internal security services and the military. As Chairman Mao memorably said in 1938, "Political power grows out of the barrel of a gun. Our principle is that the Party commands the gun, and the gun shall never be allowed to command the Party."[25] The People's Liberation Army is thus a "party-army" that is 100 percent under the control of the CCP and *not* the government or the nation per se. The military is, moreover, an instrument for *domestic* security (as well as external security). The PLA has used force *repeatedly* during the People's Republic to backstop and rescue the Party—most notably during the Cultural Revolution and in 1989. It is therefore imperative that the leader of the CCP simultaneously control the Central Military Commission.

In addition to the PLA and its various service branches, China's "armed forces" include the paramilitary People's Armed Police, the national militia, and a variety of local self-defense units. The internal security services also include the Ministry of Public Security (police) and Ministry of State Security (internal and external intelligence and counter-intelligence organ similar to KGB). The security apparatus available to the CCP and its leaders is thus sprawling and enormous, and it is another key instrument of the Party's power.

Constantly under siege by internal and external enemies. A second related concept concerns the "people"—as distinct from the "enemy." Early on Mao made this distinction in his 1949 essay "On the People's Democratic Dictatorship."[26] The CCP represents the "people," who are primarily drawn from the "working class" plus other "united front" elements in society (essentially any social elements who were willing to submit to CCP hegemony). In his essay Mao asked: "Who are the people? At the present stage in China, they are the working class, the peasantry, the urban petty bourgeoisie and the national bourgeoisie."[27] At that time, Mao distinguished the "people" from "reactionaries," but later he would broaden the latter into a wide variety of "class enemies." As noted below and discussed at length in the next chapter, the Maoist era was one extended series of attacks and persecutions of different groups of society not deemed to be part of the "people." At one point in 1957, in his speech "On the Correct Handling of Contradictions Among the People," Mao deemed that 98 percent of Chinese constituted the "people" while 2 percent were "enemies." Do the math: China in 1957 had a population of 646.5 million = 32.3 *million* "enemies of the people"! In this hallmark speech Mao explained at great length which social elements comprised each category as well as how to handle "contradictions" (矛盾) in each. The point here is not so much that the CCP legitimizes repressive methods toward elements of the domestic population—but that the CCP has a "siege mentality" whereby domestic enemies always are assumed to exist and seek to undermine hegemonic Party rule. Moreover, Mao insisted, *external* enemies also exist in large numbers, and similarly seek to undermine and subvert CCP rule—often in collaboration with *internal* enemies. Ever since the CCP came to power, every single day over the past 70 years, the CCP has operated on the assumption that the West and the noncommunist world (particularly the United States) seeks to usurp and overthrow CCP rule and the PRC. This is an axiomatic belief of all Chinese communist leaders.

The United Front. The concept of the "united front" arose during the Communists' rise to power. There were two ways the CCP adopted "united front" tactics.[28] The first was to cooperate with the Nationalists (Guomindang or KMT). This occurred twice: the first beginning in 1924 on the Soviet Comintern directive to infiltrate the KMT (the "bloc within"), which ended in the bloody April 12, 1927, Shanghai massacre by the Nationalists against the Communists; a second CCP–KMT united front was formed in 1937–1941 to fight together against Japan. This was one definition of *united front* in CCP history: to collaborate with the KMT. A second definition was for the CCP to enlist and *co-opt* various social groups in support of the CCP cause. This was extended to foreigners as well.[29] The tactic was also applied to most domestic opponents. Some who could not be co-opted must be unremittingly resisted, but the CCP theorizes that a majority segment of people inside and outside of China can be "won over" through various inducements—and thereby neutralized and effectively controlled.

Inside the CCP there is an entire department in the Central Committee (one of only five), the United Front Work Department (中央统战部), charged with this task domestically and abroad. Externally, there are also other CCP and PRC departments and agencies devoted to co-optation of foreign elites (so-called "elite capture") and sectors of foreign societies. In both cases the operative normative assumption is that the CCP and PRC must neutralize and co-opt various groups at home and abroad.

Reeducation and Rectification. In addition to co-optation, another set of CCP norms for dealing with deviant behavior are the twin methods of reeducation and rectification. Early in the 1950s, when the CCP was actively dealing with the 2 percent of "enemies" that were remnants of the "old regime," Mao put forward the instruction to "cure the disease but save the patient." In other words, through "reeducation" (brainwashing and indoctrination), deviant tendencies could be "corrected," "proper" behavior inculcated, and many "enemies of the people" could be remolded so that they could rejoin society. Mao said this was the appropriate way to deal with "non-antagonistic contradictions among the people." The same principle was applied to deviant Party members—the practice of "rectification" (整风). Yet not all rectification movements in CCP history (and they have been numerous) practiced reeducation and rehabilitation. Chinese Communist history has been replete with *purges*. Tens of millions of Party members have been purged from the Party, stripped of their membership and "rights," usually incarcerated for periods, and subject to lifelong stigmatization.

Ideology and Correct Thought. Another core operative norm for the CCP and all Chinese leaders is the imperative of ideology and enforcement of "correct thought" (正确思想) among Party members and all citizens.[30] To be sure, this is not unique to the PRC, as it has deep roots in imperial and republican Chinese history. Ever since Confucius and his orthodoxy, one of the principal responsibilities of all subsequent emperors was to *reinterpret* the original doctrine for contemporary times. The orthodoxy therefore was supposed to evolve with the times. Today's core doctrinal orthodoxy is known as "Socialism with Chinese Characteristics," which of course is based on Marxism-Leninism but Sinicized over time. Each leader adds his own element to the canon. According to the CCP Constitution, the current liturgy is as follows: "The Communist Party of China uses Marxism-Leninism, Mao Zedong Thought, Deng Xiaoping Theory, the Theory of Three Represents [Jiang Zemin], the Scientific Outlook on Development [Hu Jintao], and Xi Jinping Thought on Socialism with Chinese Characteristics for a New Era as its guides to action."[31] The CCP, principally via its Propaganda Department (中央宣传部), is the principal enforcer of "correct thought," conformity of narrative (提法), and "unifying thinking" (统一思想) among Party members and the public.

Secrecy. The CCP thrives and operates on secrecy. All policy decisions are made in secret by Party leaders and cadres, and many are implemented via secret internal (秘密内部) channels. Internal Party deliberations and procedures are obscure, if known at all. The personal lives, families, and health of senior leaders are not known in any detail. One manifestation of this system is that information is highly prized and compartmentalized. There is limited freedom of information in China. Much information about official decision-making that is normally made public in democracies remains secret in China. Divulging such information brings heavy punishment, discipline is enforced, and as a result leaks do not occur. Consequently, leadership dynamics and normal policy deliberations remain out of public view, and no other institutional checks and balances exist to scrutinize leaders' decisions and actions. The CCP's Central Secrets Bureau (中央机密局), the Central Discipline Inspection Commission (中央纪委), and National Supervisory Commission (中国人民共和国国家检查委员会) are the principal internal monitors to enforce secrecy.

Oscillation Between Hard versus Soft Leninism and the "Fang-Shou Cycle." The final normative feature of the CCP as a Leninist party has been the repetitive oscillation between tight control and loosened control and modest liberalization. As the great Sinologist and political scientist Lucian Pye astutely observed in his book on Chinese political culture more than 30 years ago, "The rhythm of Chinese politics is not the left-right swings of Western systems, but the up and down motion of tightening and loosening controls, of centralization and decentralization; any increase in anxiety on the part of the leadership is likely to translate into a greater degree of repression."[32] All communist parties have experienced periods where they have experimented with allowing modest liberalization and personal freedoms—only to be followed by periods of retrenchment and enhanced repression. These periods of brief liberalization are usually the result of a combination of two factors: built-up pressure from below combined with more liberal-minded leaders who decide to relatively relax the draconian controls over society. Thus, what I call "hard Leninism" (or hard authoritarianism) is the main pattern, but these periodic bursts of relaxation represent reformist "soft Leninism" (or soft authoritarianism).[33] In Chinese this is known as the *fang-shou cycle* (放-手周期). Think of Ulbricht's East Germany in 1953, Khrushchev's Soviet Union in 1956, Nagy's Hungary in 1956, Dubček's Czechoslovakia in 1968, and so on. In China, Mao flirted with such a liberalization during the Hundred Flowers Movement of 1956 (prior to the ensuing crackdown), but otherwise the Mao era was one long totalitarian period of

Table 1.2: China's Political Orientation Since Mao

Period/Leader	Political Orientation
1978–1983 Deng Xiaoping/Hu Yaobang	Democracy Wall & Political Relaxation
1984 Deng Xiaoping/Hu Yaobang	Anti-Spiritual Pollution Campaign
1985–1986 Deng Xiaoping/Hu Yaobang	Neo-Authoritarianism
1987 Deng Xiaoping/Zhao Ziyang	Anti-Bourgeois Liberalization Campaign
1988–1989 Deng Xiaoping/Zhao Ziyang	Neo-Authoritarianism
1989–1992 Deng Xiaoping/Jiang Zemin/Li Peng	Neo-Totalitarianism
1993–1997 Jiang Zemin	Soft Authoritarianism
1998–2008 Jiang Zemin/Hu Jintao	Soft Authoritarianism & Political Reform
2009–present Hu Jintao/Xi Jinping	Hard Authoritarianism/Neo-Totalitarianism

hard Leninism. Post-Mao, however, we have witnessed repeated periods of liberalization oscillating with tightened controls. These are depicted in Table 1.2.

Thus, it is not so simple as to describe the Chinese political system as Leninist, because there has been a repetitive pattern of oscillation back and forth between periods of relative relaxation followed by periods of tightening and repression. Beginning three years *before* Xi Jinping came to power in 2012, the CCP has entered its longest stretch of repression and tightened control since the aftermath of the 1989 Tiananmen massacre.

Keeping these cultural and systemic characteristics that affect all Chinese leaders in mind, let us now move sequentially to five successive chapters on individual Chinese leaders since 1949. In Chapter 7 we will consider them together as a group and offer concluding observations on China's leaders from 1949 to 2020.

CHAPTER 2

MAO ZEDONG

(毛泽东)

Populist Tyrant

A revolution is not a dinner party, or writing an essay, or painting a picture, or doing embroidery. . . . A revolution is an insurrection, an act of violence by which one class overthrows another.

—Mao Zedong, "Report on an Investigation of the Peasant Movement in Hunan," March 1927[1]

BEING A RULER IS VERY DIFFERENT FROM BEING A REVOLUTIONARY. To preside over a handful of rural Soviet base areas with (at most) ten million inhabitants is far different from trying to rule half a billion people (China's population at the time). Knowing what you are against (the Nationalist regime) is different from knowing what kind of society you want to build. A whole different set of challenges and responsibilities confront revolutionaries once they become rulers. Most revolutionaries-turned-rulers make various practical and tactical adjustments to their political modalities after coming to power, even if they continue their revolutionary rhetoric.

Not Mao. He saw no such division between revolting and ruling. Indeed, Mao recognized the tendency of revolutionary regimes to become bureaucratized and bogged down in inertia and self-interests (known as the "Thermidorian Reaction," a description of Robespierre's usurpation of the French Revolution). Thus, throughout his entire reign, Mao consistently fought against this unrevolutionary tendency. Of all of his many

Figure 2.1 Mao Zedong (1893–1976)
Source: Photo 12 / Alamy

hallmarks, Mao's signature commitment to keep the revolution alive may have been the most consistent[1] and notable. He thus constantly stoked the fires of "continuous revolution" at home and sought to export it abroad. The most notable example was his full-scale assault on bureaucracy and the Communist Party itself during the Great Proletarian Cultural Revolution (1966–1976), but the pre-Cultural Revolution period was also replete with Mao's repeated attacks on institutions, established customs, and multiple groups he deemed to be "revisionist" or "counterrevolutionary." Mao had a true *transformative* mission to thoroughly remold Chinese society, and he sought to spread his revolutionary ideology and practices to other societies. He was not just another emperor in a long line of Chinese dynasties. His rule was diametrically *opposed* to China's past. The iconoclastic campaign that kicked off and morphed into the Cultural Revolution was known as "destroy the four olds" (破 四旧): old customs, old culture, old habits, old ideas. Mao saw the 3,000 years of Chinese history as *the problem* and he sought to overturn it.

Mao had a vision for a very different kind of society for China: a communist society. He saw socialism as a mere mid-step on the transition from capitalism to pure communism. Mao was a true believer in communism and Marxism-Leninism, although closely aligned with its Trotskyite variety of permanent revolution. He thought that communism was entirely realizable, and during his lifetime (he was 56 when he gained power). That is one reason why he launched the Great Leap Forward in 1958—to "telescope the revolution" and fast-forward from the preliminary stage of socialism to advanced communism (with full industrialization) in a mere fifteen years. His initiative of the same year to move all rural Chinese into "people's communes" of between 5,000 to 10,000 people was intended for everyone to "eat out of the same big pot" (大锅饭), money was to be abolished, and other social-leveling policies were instituted. Instead of a compressed shortcut to communism, Mao's utopian scheme created the second worst famine in human history (after the Ukraine famine of 1932–1933) with between 30 and 45 million people perishing in a mere three years.

Mao had other goals for a "new China" as well. Central to his vision was to restore territorial unity and sovereignty to the country, following more than a century of physical dismemberment and exploitation by foreign powers—which included "extraterritorial" "treaty ports," colonies (Shandong, Macao, Hong Kong, Taiwan), and several invasions and occupations. Concomitantly, the goal was also to bring the borderlands of Tibet, Xinjiang, and Mongolia back into the national fold (Mao's regime also initially claimed huge tracts of Siberia and Central Asia, originally claimed by the Qing dynasty, before abandoning them quietly).[2] Accompanying the physical reunification of China, importantly, was the restoration of Chinese dignity. Physical dismemberment had created a parallel collective national psychological depression. China itself faced a seeming existential precipice by the late Qing, when the national rallying cry literally became "save the nation from extinction" (救国). While this existential psychological perception in a country with 3,000 years of continuous history may seem exaggerated in retrospect, there is no disputing the fact that a once-powerful China had lost its way and had been subjected to what the Chinese Communist Party describes as the "century of shame and humiliation" (百年国耻).

This is what Mao and the communists sought to reverse—to restore China's sense of pride, dignity, independence, and nationalism free from encumbrance by exploitative foreigners. These powerful emotive forces contributed a great deal to the palpable excitement among urbanites when People's Liberation Army forces rolled into and "liberated" (解放) the major cities of China during 1949, and it was no accident that Mao began his address proclaiming the establishment of the People's Republic of China with the famous sentence "The Chinese people have stood up!" (我们中国人站起来了!) Yet, this restoration of sovereignty was not an end goal—it was viewed as only an initial step on the road to restoring China's status as one of the great powers in the world. These forces that motivated Mao and animated the communist revolution—sovereign independence and nationalism, restored dignity and respect, and identity as a great power—are all deeply ingrained in the Chinese Communist Party to this day. All foreign analysts would do well not to forget these animating drivers of contemporary China's behavior.

There were, of course, other goals that Mao and the Chinese communists carried with them into power: ridding the society of criminals, beggars, itinerants, peddlers, hawkers, prostitutes, gamblers, drug (mainly opium) users, and other social vices. Establishing gender equality and emancipating women from centuries of discriminatory practices (including foot binding) was another priority. Working toward universal literacy and schooling, while eliminating abject poverty, were also priorities. So too was eliminating chronic unemployment and providing full employment for all able-bodied citizens. Restoring the physical health of the nation was a pressing problem (with a life expectancy in 1949 of an average of 37 years). This included building hospitals and sanitoriums for the indigent, reducing infant mortality, establishing a free and ostensibly universal healthcare system, restocking medicines, and training an army of paramedics to penetrate deep into the countryside. As is commonplace under socialism, other cradle-to-grave social provisions were also envisioned.

These are some of the primary ambitions that the communists brought with them to power when Mao proclaimed the establishment of the People's Republic of China on October 1, 1949 (Fig. 2.2).

Figure 2.2 Mao Zedong Proclaiming Founding of People's Republic of China, October 1, 1949
Source: World History Archive / Alamy

Mao's Inheritance and Immediate Challenges

If these were their aspirations, what kind of nation did Mao and the CCP inherit in 1949 and what were the immediate challenges that they faced? These can be grouped in four categories and can be discussed in the context of the first three years after the CCP came to power. Generally speaking, these three years were preoccupied with four aspects of rule: establishing it, consolidating it, organizing it, and extending it spatially across the country and in different domains functionally.

The Economic Situation

The Chinese economy inherited by the communists had been battered by years of war. Many factories had been destroyed, and those that had not were barely operating. At the time of the communist takeover, state statistics reported that only 250,000 tons of pig iron and 160,000 tons of rolled steel were produced in the entirety of the country.[3] Following Stalin's eleventh-hour entry into the Second World War against Japan in August 1945, the Soviet forces had dismantled many factories in Manchuria and removed their parts back to the Soviet Union. Physical and transport infrastructure were severely damaged. Nearly 80 percent of China's 14,700 miles of railways in 1937 had been disrupted or destroyed by 1949, and rolling stock sat idle. Telephone lines were fragmentary at best and electricity was intermittent. The currency had collapsed (multiple times, most recently in August 1948) and hyper-inflation was out of control. By the time the CCP came to power, the wholesale price index in Shanghai had reached a level 6.6 *million* times that of 1937![4]

The situation in rural China was little better. Grain output in 1949 was a mere 113.18 million tons, far from sufficient to feed a population of half a billion people (541.67 million in 1949), even at a subsistence level.[5] Total agricultural output had plummeted 30 percent below its pre-war (1937) level, although it still accounted for about 60 percent of national GDP (with 80 percent of the population engaged in it). Most people lived close to the margin of subsistence. Because per capita income was so low, household consumption was dominated by spending on food, which absorbed 60 to 80 percent of total expenditure. The balance was allocated to clothing, housing, and fuel, with hardly anything left for other goods and services. Food consumption was overwhelmingly dominated by coarse grains (wheat and rice), with little meat, eggs, or vegetables in the average diet. Rural cultivation was very uneven throughout the country, with much farmland damaged or idle. Irrigated land was actually less than during the last years of the Qing dynasty.

The output of major industrial products in 1949 ranged between 15 and 80 percent of the peak levels of the 1930s.[6] Light industry and the handicraft sector accounted for only 10 percent of economic output (and was thus not much of an alternative source of employment). Production in a number of other sectors was also operating only at fractions of pre-war levels.[7] Total GDP was only in the neighborhood of $25 billion, with a per capita income around 66 yuan in 1949.[8] Even India had slightly higher per capita income and industrial output than China in 1952.[9]

All in all, Mao and the CCP inherited a broken and poorly functioning national economy. It would take three years to stabilize, before reorienting and rebuilding could begin in 1953.

The Social Situation

Chinese society was also in a state of chaos and exhaustion after eight years of brutal occupation by the Japanese military,[10] followed by four years of civil war between the Communists and the Nationalists. The country was awash in refugees. The propertied classes and those affiliated with the Nationalist government were attempting to flee to the island of Taiwan, to British Hong Kong, or over the border into Burma. The cities were filled with vagrants, beggars, common criminals, prostitutes, drug addicts, and legions of unemployed. In 1949 life expectancy was only 43.3 years, with an infant mortality rate of 20 per thousand births. Various infectious diseases were rampant: tuberculosis, cholera, hepatitis, typhoid, smallpox, encephalitis, and leprosy. Only 20 percent of the population was literate (illiteracy for women was over 90 percent), with primary and secondary schooling intermittent in the cities and almost completely absent in the countryside. In the countryside, domination of landholding by the landlord class left China's 400 million peasants disenfranchised and landless. Various rural bandits roamed the countryside, particularly in Anhui and mountainous central China, while religious sects and secret societies operated in cities and rural areas alike. Those who belonged to such underground social groups were not minimal—an estimated one-fifth of the population of Tianjin, 15 percent of Beijing, 11 percent of Sichuan were allegedly members of secret societies in 1950–1951.[11] As we will see, all of these groups quickly became targets of the CCP and the new regime.

Not everything had fallen apart by 1949. For example, universities were still functioning in the major cities and graduating classes of students. Foreign companies continued to operate as well. But, by and large, Chinese society had become a basket case by the late 1940s—making it ripe for revolution and regime change.

The National Security Situation

On the eve of the communist takeover, China's national security situation was totally preoccupied with the domestic civil war. The defeat of Nationalist forces by the communist Red Army in eastern China went stunningly quickly after the northeastern Manchurian provinces fell in October 1948: Beijing was captured in January 1949, followed by Tianjin in February, Nanjing in April, Shanghai in May. However, the "liberation" of the south, southeast, southwest, northwest, and Tibet was much more protracted and complicated, and did not occur until *after* Mao proclaimed the establishment of the PRC on October 1, 1949. It would take two more years for these provinces to be subdued and brought fully under control.

Externally, China at this juncture did not face threats. Japan was defeated, following the atomic attacks and surrender of August 1945, and was under occupation by the United States. Hong Kong remained a British colony and Macao a Portuguese one. The Korean peninsula had been divided into two rival regimes. South and Southeast Asia, however, were very unsettled—with independence being wrested from European colonial states by Burma, India, Indonesia, Malaya, Pakistan, and the Philippines (a former American colony), while war against the French still raged in Indochina. On the eve and at the time of the founding of the People's Republic of China, the Cold War had not yet taken shape in Asia. That would soon change after June 1950. The Americans, however, were still unfailingly backing Mao's arch-rival Chiang Kai-shek and the Nationalists.

So, generally speaking, this was the situation facing Mao and the Chinese Communists when they began their reign. How did they deal with these challenges?

Consolidation of Rule, 1949–1953

Mao had five main immediate priorities in the wake of the establishment of the PRC. First, he had to consolidate the CCP's physical control over the country and eliminate all vestiges of resistance from Nationalist forces and groups that resisted the new regime. Second, he needed to ensure national security for his new country. Third, he had to stabilize and begin the rebuilding process of the fractured national economy. Fourth, he needed to establish a nationwide system of political governance. Fifth, Mao wanted to begin the process of socialist transformation of society. There were linkages between these priorities. For example, the second, third, and fourth priorities had one thing in common: the Soviet Union.

By visiting Moscow and meeting with Stalin between December 1949 and February 1950, Mao was able to negotiate a security alliance and large aid package. Embedded in both was a systemic organizational model for organizing both China's political system and its economy. But negotiating the Treaty of Friendship, Alliance, and Mutual Aid was by no means easy for Mao, and it was really Zhou Enlai who managed the negotiations on the Chinese side and brought them to fruition. It was not an easy visit or set of encounters with Stalin and their Soviet counterparts.

Chairman Mao had never been outside of China before, but a mere six weeks after proclaiming his new state he boarded a special armor-plated train for the long trek across the frozen Siberian tundra to Moscow. The entourage arrived at noon on December 16, 1949.[12] The welcome extended by Soviet Politburo members Vyacheslav Molotov and Nikolai Bulganin was almost as frigid as the winter weather. Breaking protocol, Stalin was not at the station to greet Mao. After a brief perfunctory reception at the Kremlin that evening, the two communist leaders sat down for an initial talk. The transcript of this conversation has subsequently been declassified from the former Soviet archives. It reveals a fairly lengthy discussion in which Mao raises his specific desire for a large economic and technical assistance package in addition to a military treaty. For his part, Stalin asked for a variety of concessions for the Soviet Union in Port Arthur (Dalian) and with respect to Manchurian railroads.[13] Yet, after believing that the treaty and aid negotiations would be quickly concluded, Mao was made to wait . . . and wait . . . and wait. Stalin snubbed and stalled China's new leader for nearly six weeks, leaving Mao to fume in an isolated dacha outside Moscow. The two communist titans did meet at the Bolshoi Theatre December 21 on the occasion of Stalin's 71st birthday (Fig. 2.3), but at this encounter Stalin and his colleagues were again aloof toward their Chinese counterparts.

Stalin's snub was indeed puzzling to Mao. He was not being overtly rebuffed, but he was being toyed with by Stalin. Subsequently declassified

Figure 2.3 Mao and Stalin in Moscow, December 1949
Source: Helsingin Sanomat / Public Domain

Soviet archival records make clear that Stalin and the Soviet leadership were sizing Mao up (fearing he might be a "second Tito" who was disloyal to the Kremlin) and had intentionally orchestrated the stalling tactics. Following the Bolshoi encounter, Mao was sent off on a trip to Leningrad (St. Petersburg) and the Gulf of Finland. He did not see Stalin again for a month. Mao became increasingly agitated. He had a new country to build at home, and here he was languishing in Russia. Stalin would on occasion dispatch lower-ranking officials to "liaise" with Mao at his dacha. One such intermediary was Ivan Kovalev, a distinguished general who Stalin had selected as his personal envoy to China in 1948. Mao repeatedly asked Kovalev to arrange another meeting or meal with Stalin in order to begin serious negotiations for concluding the treaty and aid package. On one visit in mid-January, Mao exploded at Kovalev: "You invited me to Moscow and you do nothing! Why have I come? Why have I come here to spend whole days just eating, sleeping, and shitting?"[14] Still no meetings with Stalin were arranged. Again, Mao exploded at Kovalev: "I cannot stand it anymore. I am in such a state that I cannot control myself."[15] After Premier and Foreign Minister Zhou Enlai, who had joined Mao in Moscow for the sole purpose of negotiating the treaty, made known to Kovalev and other Soviet leaders that Mao had reached the end of his patience and was preparing to leave and return to Beijing, the Kremlin relented and negotiations quickly commenced. On February 14, 1950, two months after Mao had first arrived in

Moscow, the Treaty of Friendship, Alliance, and Mutual Aid was concluded and Mao and his team returned to Beijing.

The extended nine-week stay had been a long, frustrating, and humiliating experience for Mao and the senior CCP leaders who had accompanied him to the cradle of world communism. But the way the visit had unfolded was no accident. Now Stalin had shown Mao who was the real boss. Despite some Comintern (Communist International) advisors, in fact Stalin and the CPSU (Communist Party of the Soviet Union) had never really been supportive of Mao and his rural revolution—instead working with rival Chiang Kai-shek's Nationalist government to the bitter end. In their initial discussions in Moscow, Stalin had even questioned Mao's military tactics during the closing days of the civil war. These discussions and the relationship that emerged were illustrative of the actual asymmetric inequality between the supposedly egalitarian communist comrades. Even the economic aid package (equivalent to $300 million in rubles to be paid in equal installments over five years) came in the form of interest-bearing loans rather than grants. Just as symbolically, following the final banquet at the Kremlin to commemorate the conclusion of the treaty, the Chinese side was shocked and humiliated to receive a bill for the cost of the banquet![16] All of these symbolic Soviet snubs were harbingers of things to come in Sino-Soviet relations.

Adopting the Soviet Model

Returning to Beijing, Mao brought back more than just a treaty—he returned with a template for the entire organization of the country: for the political system, organization of the military, the national economy, the educational system, for everything.[17] *China was to become Sovietized.* The importance of this cannot be overemphasized, as many core structural elements and procedures *to this day* were drawn directly from the Soviet Union. Bureaucratically, this meant that the entire government and country were organized into vertical hierarchies of functional sectors (called "systems," 系统, in Chinese). This is how the Stalinist Soviet Union was organized.[18]

The Soviet leadership and Chinese leadership may not have agreed on revolutionary tactics (they didn't, as Moscow counseled a traditional urban-based strategy while Mao and the CCP pursued a rural strategy after 1927), but organizationally they were cut from the same Leninist cloth. Since its founding in 1921, the Chinese Communist Party was organized as an exact clone of the Communist Party of the Soviet Union: the Central Committee and its separate departments for propaganda, organization, international liaison, and united front: the Secretariat of the Central Committee; the ruling Politburo and the elite Politburo Standing Committee; the system of Party congresses, plenary sessions, Party committees and cells, and so on. Make no mistake: organizationally, the CCP is (to this day) a Soviet byproduct.

The same applied to the Chinese military. Until it was reorganized by Xi Jinping in 2015–2016, the People's Liberation Army (renamed from the Red Army in 1945) was also an exact organizational clone of the Soviet Red Army. Most important, as noted in Chapter 1, both are "party-armies"—that is, they are entirely beholden to their ruling communist parties. They therefore do *not* answer to the government, the parliament, or the nation—they are entirely an armed instrument of the ruling Communist Party. The PLA answers to the Party's Central Military Commission, which is headed by the CCP leader. Moreover, as in all other institutions throughout society, the Party penetrates the military in China—with embedded Party committees, political commissars, and a "political work system" centered on the General Political Department.[19] When Mao returned from Moscow, Soviet military advisors followed soon thereafter and were placed in the PLA; they were responsible for reorganizing the PLA along Soviet organizational lines (via a series of "general departments").

The same occurred to the higher education system. Western-style universities and curricula were abolished in 1950. Most social science departments were closed, and those that remained were Sovietized. Soviet textbooks were translated into Chinese across a range of disciplines and subjects, while Western textbooks were physically destroyed. With the small exception of a handful of special government and intelligence training schools for interpreters and diplomats, all foreign languages *except Russian* were banned in schools and universities. About 10,000 Chinese students were dispatched to the Soviet Union to study (altogether about 40,000 personnel, including many post-graduates and technical personnel, were trained in the USSR during the 1950s), and several thousand Soviet professors came to teach in China. Additionally, during the decade, 11,000 Soviet scientific and technical personnel came to work as "experts" in China, advising on many of the 156 "turn-key" factories that the USSR agreed to build. A new Chinese Academy of Sciences (replacing the Nationalists' Academia Sinica, which moved to Taiwan) was established and modeled exactly on the Soviet Academy of Sciences. Its director, Sergei Vavilov, served as an advisor, and his *Thirty Years of Soviet Science* was translated into Chinese. A national sports system was created and modeled on the Soviet system (although the PRC was banned from the Olympics). The PRC medical system was also remodeled on the Soviet system (after decades of American funding and training). The media were put under the control of the Central Committee Propaganda Department, itself modeled on the Soviet Department of Agitation and Propaganda. The CCP Investigation Department and Social Affairs Department, along with elements of the new Ministry of Public Security, were reconstituted into a KGB-like structure for internal security and counter-intelligence (in 1982 a new Ministry of State Security was established).

The entire "people's government" structure that was created after Mao's return from Moscow was also very similar to the Soviet system.[20] A Central People's Government was created with Mao as the Chairman. Underneath this umbrella organ was a Government Administration Council, which included a variety of functional ministries and Soviet-style "commissions" (委员会) that coordinated plans within various functional spheres (such as education, finance, trade, industry). The State Planning Commission (国家计委) oversaw all individual commissions, ministries, departments, and bureaus, and was responsible for all long-term planning and coordination. The Supreme People's Court and the Supreme People's Procuratorate were also under the Central People's Government, as was the Central Military Commission. Outside of Beijing, the provinces and country were divided up into six overarching regional bureaus. In terms of a parliament, Mao had established the Chinese People's Political Consultative Conference (CPPCC) in 1948 as a "united front" organ to mobilize and give voice to various sectors of society. The CPPCC operates to this day, although some of its functions were replaced in 1954 when the National People's Congress (NPC) was created and the six regional bureaus were dissolved. The Potemkin

NPC parliament was similar to the USSR Supreme Soviet, and its Standing Committee to the Soviet Presidium. And so on. The PRC's *entire* bureaucratic system was modeled on a transplanted Soviet model.[21]

Perhaps most important, the national economy was reconfigured along Soviet lines. Soviet-style planning had a number of features. First and foremost was The Plan—actually all kinds of plans: annual plans, five-year plans, ten-year plans, twenty-five-year plans, provincial plans, individual enterprise plans, and so on. Atop the entire system sat the ubiquitous State Planning Commission, which was established in 1952 and modeled exactly on the Soviet Gosplan. Next, these plans set *quotas* and *targets* to be met by all producers. Quality was not the goal, quantity was. As long as the numerical output targets were met or the quotas fulfilled, that was all that mattered. Since targets and quotas were usually fulfilled or over-fulfilled (often through doctored statistics, in order to please higher-level cadres), there was an inbuilt bias toward increasing the targets/quotas year by year. This further created disequilibrium and exaggerated inputs and outputs in the system. Unlike capitalist economies, enterprises did not operate according to profit and loss or supply and demand; any losses were written off, creating further perceptual distortions that gave the appearance of all being financially solvent. In fact, once the process of nationalization was complete (1955) and thousands of state-owned enterprises (SOEs) were created, government subsides (another feature of the Soviet planned economy) flowed into these entities—keeping them artificially afloat. Under this system any profits are entirely ploughed back into the enterprise, with no dividends accruing (the Stalinist euphemism of enterprise "reinvestment"). Moreover, in such a system, produced goods were not priced by market forces of supply and demand, but rather were arbitrarily fixed by the state. Inflation was kept low to nonexistent, but it was a subterfuge because of state-set price ceilings and subsidies. Workers' wages were similarly arbitrarily fixed by the state. Workers enjoyed full employment, and that was certainly a good thing given the past, but there was no labor market or mobility. Everyone's physical residence was determined by the newly created household registration (*hukou*) system and everyone had to work in their assigned "work unit" or *danwei* (单位). *Hukou* constraints were very restrictive, essentially locking down the population, with no mobility. The work units provided all housing, healthcare, primary education, medicines, and other features of daily life. All of this collectively became known as the "command" or "planned" economy. This was the Soviet-style national economic system that Mao brought back with him from Moscow.

Social Campaigns

The early 1950s also witnessed a number of directed attempts to reorder specific sectors of Chinese society. These efforts were characterized by another hallmark of Maoism that would be repeated multiple times during his rule: the "campaign" or *yundong* (运动). During the first three years there were five main campaigns launched: the "suppress counterrevolutionaries" campaign of 1950–1953 (肃反运动); the "thought reform" movement for intellectuals (思想改造运动), which began in 1951 and continued through 1956; the land reform movement of 1949–1952 (土地改革运动); the "three anti" campaign of 1951–1952 (三反运动); and the "five anti" campaign of 1952 (五反运动). In addition, there were other targeted efforts to "mop up bandits," eradicate secret societies and religious sects, root out underground urban gangs, eliminate vice, affix "class labels" to all citizens, create the nationwide household registration system, and (as discussed separately below) the "resist America, aid Korea" (抗美援朝) campaign, which accompanied the Korean War from 1950 to 1953. The early years of the PRC were awash in campaigns—which would become the hallmark of Mao's own style of rule: mass mobilization against selected targets. Let us briefly describe the five noted above.

The campaign against counterrevolutionaries kicked off in February 1951 and lasted into 1953. While this chilling term would assume an all-encompassing connotation throughout the Mao era (anyone supposedly opposed to the CCP and regime could be so labeled, and then criticized, attacked, punished, incarcerated, or killed), during the initial period it was used to round up and eliminate those opposed to the new regime. This included a large number of former Nationalist military officers, police, and internal security agents (those who were unfortunate enough not to get on the boats to Taiwan), but it was also broadened to include members of secret societies, underground criminal gangs, religious sects, and "spies, saboteurs, and members of underground resistance organizations."[22] Quotas were set for counterrevolutionaries to be rounded up in each of these sub-categories. It was an urban campaign, normally involving mass denunciation rallies and kangaroo courts, followed by executions. Official statements at the time indicated that 800,000 counterrevolutionary cases had been dealt with in the first six months of 1951 alone, with Premier Zhou Enlai stating that 16.8 percent had been sentenced to death (that works out to 135,000 executions in just the first six months of the campaign).[23] Data from Minister of Public Security Luo Ruiqing in 1952 indicated that only 301,800 in total had been executed, with provincial breakdowns as follows: Henan 56,700; Hubei 45,500; Hunan 61,400; Jiangxi 24,500; Guangxi 46,200; Guangdong 39,900. In 1954, Liu Shaoqi, Chairman of the Standing Committee of the new National People's Congress, reported that a total of 710,000 had been killed during the movement.[24] Those who were not executed were imprisoned or sent to another new Maoist invention: the labor camp. By the end of 1951, more than two million had been imprisoned, with an additional 670,000 incarcerated in labor camps (by 1955 this number had reached 1.3 million).[25] As it unfolded, the campaign became a killing frenzy. Welcome to Maoist rule. Mao apparently took personal pleasure and interest in the campaign, monitoring it closely from his residence inside the Zhongnanhai leadership compound (an expansive site adjacent to the Forbidden City and used by the imperial family prior to 1911 but commandeered by the CCP for their headquarters in 1949).[26]

The "thought reform" campaign was a natural counterpart to the counterrevolutionaries campaign, but was more specifically targeted at intellectuals, university professors, and some middle school teachers.[27] Referred to by its targets as "brainwashing reform" (洗脑改造), it was most intense during 1951 but percolated all the way through 1955, only to have a brief respite during the Hundred Flowers movement of 1956—and then was reignited in the form of the 1957–58 Anti-Rightist Movement (see below). The campaign actually had a precursor in the 1942–1944 CCP "rectification" (整风) movement in Yanan. Indeed, it is fair to say that for Chinese intellectuals, the entire nearly eight-decade period from Yanan to the present has been one long persistent persecution and experience in thought reform, censorship, and repression. Mao himself emphasized its importance in a speech in October 1951: "Thought reform, especially thought reform of all categories of intellectuals, is one of the important conditions for the thoroughgoing democratic transformation and industrialization of our country."[28] But rather than kill intellectuals, as Mao did to several other categories of "class enemies," he at least feigned to practice his aphorism to "treat the disease, but save the patient."

The thought reform campaign ran simultaneously with the Sovietization of Chinese education. In order to implant the new system and way of thinking, the old roots had to be pulled out. This meant that several thousand university faculty had to "learn the revolutionary standpoint of serving the people, the viewpoint of materialism, and the method of dialectics."[29] This, in turn, required abandoning and denouncing Western pedagogy, curricula, and languages. The United States, and those trained either in the US or in American missionary colleges in China (of which there were many prior to 1949) were particular targets. By 1951 almost all American academics had left the country, but those few that stayed behind were imprisoned and also subject to thought reform. Such was the case with my former Chinese teacher (at the University of Michigan) Harriet Mills, who had been a Fulbright student and was arrested in 1951 and subjected to four years in prison before being released to Hong Kong in 1955.[30] After her release and return to the United States Professor Mills wrote about her experience.[31] So too did Allyn and Adele Rickett, although their account was more positive (the brainwashing worked on them, where it did not on Mills).[32] But the thousands of Chinese faculty who were forced to undergo thought reform had no escape valve, as did the foreigners. Many were incarcerated for years, and precious few were permitted to teach and do research again.

The "three anti" and "five anti" campaigns can be discussed together, as they were carried out in succession in 1951 and 1952. The "three antis" were aimed at local officials who were attacked for corruption, waste, and bureaucratism. The "five antis" were targeted at the urban bourgeoisie, and attacked those accused of bribery, tax evasion and embezzlement, theft of state property, cheating on government contracts, and stealing state assets. Some were also held for hoarding of labor or material supplies. Many were simply arrested, while some were subjected to the same mass denunciation sessions used in other campaigns. Others were sent to labor camps for "reform through labor," and an unknown number were executed (estimated in the tens of thousands).

Meanwhile, as these vicious campaigns were sweeping the cities, in the countryside the even more draconian land reform campaign was unfolding. Transforming the rural sector was a protracted and complicated process which would last a decade, but one that was absolutely central to Mao's revolutionary agenda. His revolution had been rooted in the 80 percent of China who lived in barely subsistence conditions in the countryside. Mao was determined to break the back of the centuries-old "feudal" landholding system. In fact, land confiscation and redistribution had already proceeded in the "liberated" areas of rural China prior to 1949. Once in power, though, the communists intensified and expanded the movement nationwide. In general, it passed through two phases: "soft" land reform in 1949–1950 and then "harsh" land reform from the spring of 1951 through 1952 (and until the spring of 1953 in Guangdong). The former was premised on a somewhat voluntary approach whereby landlords would voluntarily see the evils of their ways, recant their transgressions, and hand over their land to peasants. This did not last long, and the approach was inconsistent at best. By mid-1951, and especially as the CCP extended its physical control over the southern provinces of Fujian, Guangdong, and Guangxi, things turned very harsh and violent.[33] Countless "struggle sessions" (斗争会) were carried out across the country, with peasants humiliating and torturing their landlords. Executions were widespread, with perhaps 1 to 2 million killed.[34] But land reform did result in 43 percent of cultivated land being redistributed to about 60 percent of the rural population.[35] As the landlords were stripped of their holdings, CCP cadres moved in—and began the reorganization of villages into "mutual aid teams" (MATs). This was the first step of the four-stage process of collectivization of agriculture during the 1950s: in 1955 MATs gave way to so-called lower Agricultural Producers' Cooperatives, then in 1956 to Higher Agricultural Producers' Cooperatives, and finally in 1958 to full-blown people's communes (人民公社).[36]

As all of these Maoist campaigns were unfolding during the early 1950s, there was one other significant challenge that Mao and his comrades faced: the Korean War against the United States. The history of the war is well known and need not be recounted here.[37] All available evidence (especially

Soviet archives) strongly indicates that Mao did *not* specifically know in advance of Kim Il-Sung's plans to invade South Korea. The story of how China got involved, and how Mao made the decision for China to enter the war by sending 200,000 "people's volunteers" (actually battle-hardened main force PLA units) across the Yalu River and the China–North Korean border into direct combat with American forces on October 19, 1950 is also well known, in part based on declassified Chinese archives.[38] The Chinese intervention sent American forces reeling backwards before recouping and counterattacking after the Inchon Landing. Over the next two years the war stalemated around the 38th parallel until an armistice was reached on July 27, 1953. The war had cost China almost 400,000 casualties, including 148,400 dead.[39] One of the deceased Chinese soldiers was Mao's eldest son Mao Anying.

There were two other notable consequences of the Korean War for China. The first was that the wartime mobilization under the "Resist America, Aid Korea" campaign gave great stimulus to rebuilding China's heavy industrial infrastructure. China was on a war footing. This in turn also accelerated the CCP's organization of urban society into work units, thus accelerating control over China's cities and urban population more quickly than otherwise would have been the case.[40] The other consequence was not so positive for Mao and the CCP. With the outbreak of the war, the United States Navy dispatched ships from its Seventh Fleet into the Taiwan Strait and effectively sealed the island off from the mainland (thus also protecting the rump Republic of China regime on the island of Taiwan). On the eve of North Korea's attack on South Korea Mao was, in fact, massing his armies in Zhejiang and Fujian provinces for an all-out final assault to conclude the civil war against Chiang Kai-shek's remnant forces on Taiwan and the offshore islands of Quemoy and Matsu. President Truman's actions to dispatch the Seventh Fleet and effectively seal the strait served as a sufficient deterrent, and Mao had to abort the invasion. In 1954, just after the Korean War armistice, the United States concluded a Mutual Defense Treaty with the Republic of China on Taiwan. Although the treaty was abrogated in 1979, when the US and PRC established formal diplomatic relations, the island remains autonomous from the PRC to this day.

Building the Nation, 1953–1957

By 1953, the territory of China and outlying regions had been brought under the communist's physical control, CCP political power had been consolidated, various sectors (described above) had been repressed and domestic opposition had been quelled, the economy had recovered, the Korean War had ended, and now Mao and the Party leadership were ready for a new phase—which they officially designated as the "build the nation era" (建国时期).

Box 2.1 Chinese Political Names

The term *jianguo* (build the country) was a specific reference to the First Five-Year Plan (FFYP) of 1953–1957. Thus, male children born during this period were frequently given the name of *Jianguo*, e.g. Build the Nation Wang, Zhang, etc., together with their surnames. Indeed, it became a common practice in the Maoist era to name children after the political campaign of the time. Those born during the Korean War were often named *Yuanchao* (Aid Korea), those born during the Great Leap Forward were *Yuejin* (Leap Forward), those born in 1955 were *Ya-Fei* (Asia-Africa to commemorate the Asian-African conference in Bandung, Indonesia of that year), those born in the early years of the Cultural Revolution were often *Hong* (Red) or *Xiaobing* (Little Soldier), and so on.

The First Five-Year Plan

During the mid-1950s the national focus shifted entirely to economic development. What type of economic development? *Soviet* economic development. This was the heyday of the Soviet model and Soviet influence over the PRC. As noted above, thousands of Soviet technicians came to China to oversee the reconfiguration of bureaucracies and the transformation of the economy along Soviet lines. For the economy this meant central planning (described above) with a priority emphasis on heavy industry. As economist Nicholas Lardy observed about the First Five-Year Plan: "The strategy of the FFYP rested squarely on the belief in the Marxist law of expanded reproduction that identifies the industries producing capital goods as the major source of growth."[41] Whole plants were planned for construction with Soviet support (156 in total) and the entire urban landscape was reorganized for development of new industrial factories (700 were planned for construction). Centralized planning was made easier by the nationalization of enterprises that had occurred during the 1949–1952 period. By the end of 1952, 70 to 80 percent of heavy industry and 40 percent of light industry had become state-owned.[42] The *danwei* system was also fully in place,[43] as was the national *hukou* residency system. These controls on the labor market made central planning far easier. Within the Five-Year Plan there were separate annual plans, and specific plans for certain produced goods with fixed output quotas and targets set. The allocation and distribution of key inputs—like ores—were pegged to industrial factories according to their fixed output goals. By 1956 the list of such key controlled commodities reached 200. This was certainly an efficient way of allocating inputs for those industries that benefitted, but it also caused shortages for those not so privileged. Of course, heavy industry needed and produced steel—lots of it. Steel ingots output (measured in millions of metric tons) more than quintupled between 1953 and 1957. This rate of growth in production was not unusual. During this period, as Figure 2.4 and Table 2.1 show, the output of many goods and commodities enjoyed spectacular growth. This

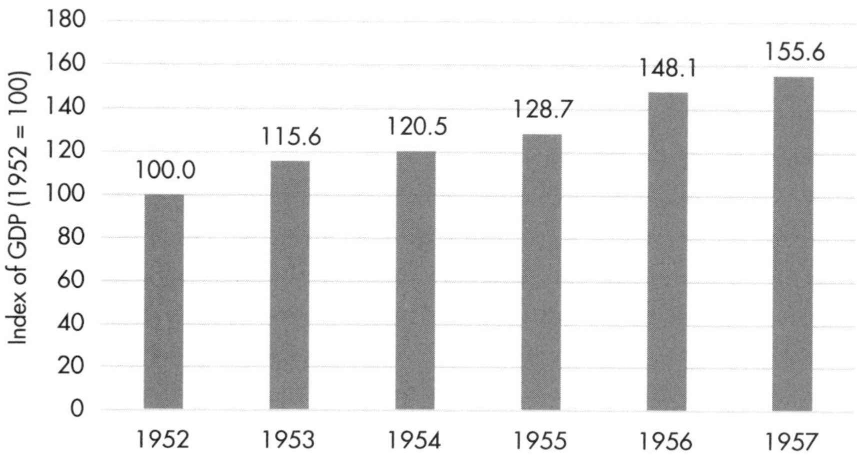

Figure 2.4 GDP Growth During First Five-Year Plan
Source: Xin Zhongguo Liushi Nian Tongji Ziliao Huibian, 1949–2008 [China Compendium of Statistics] (Beijing: Zhongguo tongji chubanshe, 2010).

Table 2.1: Output of Selected Goods During the First Five-Year Plan

	1952 Actual	1957 Target	1957 Actual	1957 Actual as % Target
		HEAVY INDUSTRY		
Coal (mmt)	66.0	113.0	131.0	115.9
Oil ('000 mt)	440.0	2,012.0	1,460.0	72.6
Steel (mmt)	1.35	4.12	5.35	129.9
Cement (mmt)	2.86	6.00	6.86	114.3
Electric generators ('000 kw)	29.7	227.0	284.0	125.1
Electric power (b. kwh)	7.3	15.9	16.6	104.4
Chemical fertilizers ('000 tons)	181.0	578.0	631.0	109.2
Locomotives (units)	20.0	200.0	124.0	62.0
Trucks (units)	0.0	4,000.0	7,500.0	187.5
		LIGHT INDUSTRY		
Cotton yarn ('000 bales)	3,618.0	5,000.0	4,650.0	93.0
Cotton cloth (mn. metres)	3,830.0	5,375.0	5,050.0	94.0
Sugar ('000 tons)	451.0	1,100.0	864.0	78.5
Salt ('000 tons)	4,945.0	7,544.0	8,277.0	109.7
Cigarettes ('000 cases)	2,650.0	4,700.0	4,456.0	94.8

mmt = million metric tons

Source: All 1957 targets from Choh-Ming Li, *Economic Development of Communist China; An Appraisal of the First Five Years of Industrialization* (University of California Press, 1959), pp. 44–45. 1952 and 1957 data from China National Bureau of Statistics, *Xin Zhongguo Liushi Nian Tongji Ziliao Huibian, 1949–2008*; and Nai-Ruenn Chen, *Chinese Economic Statistics: A Handbook for Mainland China* (Edinburgh: Edinburgh University Press, 1966). I am indebted to Robert F. Ash for compiling these data.

was considerably due to Soviet-aided projects. Such spectacular industrial growth also led to excessive, exaggerated expectations—which would have disastrous effects within a few years.

Not surprisingly, the explosive growth in industrial output had implications for other sectors. Agricultural growth was slow. Grain output rose only 2.5 percent in 1953–1954, far below the 9 percent target, which produced shortfalls in available foodstuffs.[44] By 1955 the shortages were acute. This set off an intense debate within the CCP leadership. Mao's answer to the laggard rural sector was to *accelerate* the collectivization of agriculture—while on the other side of the debate stood Deng Zihui, a toughened cadre who had overseen land reform and was head of the Central Committee Rural Work Department. Deng not only wanted to relatively slow-walk collectivization, he also favored giving peasants some leeway in what crops they planted, how agricultural produce was priced, and the level of harvest quotas they were forced to meet (these tactics later became the foundation of the "agricultural responsibility system" of the 1960s and 1980s). The two men (Mao versus Deng Zihui) engaged in a showdown over the pace of collectivization during the spring and summer of 1955. Liu Shaoqi and other senior leaders seemingly backed Deng. But, being the leader, Mao prevailed. Deng was consequently censured as a "rightist empiricist" at the Sixth Plenum of the Seventh Central Committee in October 1955, and the expansion of Agricultural Producers Cooperatives (APCs) was stepped up. In fact, Mao proclaimed that a "high tide" had been reached in agricultural output and the entire economy could accelerate and produce "greater, faster, better."[45] The problem was that actual agricultural output did not match Mao's rhetoric. To the contrary, agricultural output was actually *falling*. 1956 and 1957 were both slow-growth years, with agricultural output actually shrinking as a percentage of GDP (from 46.6 percent in 1955 to 43.5 percent in 1956 to 40.6 percent in 1957). By the end of the FFYP, agriculture as a percentage of GDP had actually *shrunk* fully 10 percent between 1952 and 1957, according to official statistics.[46] By 1957 a severe grain supply crisis loomed and, dissatisfied with being forced into collectives and increasingly hungry, peasants (particularly in southern provinces) were actively seeking to leave—rather than join—the APCs. Premier Zhou Enlai and Vice Premier Chen Yun both tried to counter Mao's exuberance with the slogan "oppose rash advance" (反冒进), but to no avail.

Undeterred by these realities, Mao's zeal for the statistical successes of urban industrial output taken together with his impatience with the pace of rural agricultural collectivization were harbingers for what was to come during 1958: the Great Leap Forward (GLF).[47] Mao sought to will reality into being simply by proclaiming it to be so. Mao's excessive optimism, divorced from reality, led him directly into the GLF. But before Mao launched the GLF, he had two other matters to take care of.

The Gao Gang Affair

The first was an intra-Party purge in 1954, the first major one since the CCP came to power. The victims were two senior cadres named Gao Gang and Rao Shushi. Gao was a senior Politburo member, head of the State Planning Commission, and the senior official in northeastern China (东北), where he had built a strong political power base (including independent ties with Stalin and other Soviet leaders). Rao was the Director of the CCP Organization Department in Beijing, which put him at the epicenter of the Party personnel appointments system nationwide. They made for an odd couple, but they needed each other and found common cause in their opposition to Liu Shaoqi and Zhou Enlai. Gao Gang apparently had a very inflated sense of his importance in the Party hierarchy and, it was alleged, sought to oust Liu and Zhou from the No. 2 and 3 positions in the Party hierarchy (after Mao). Gao worked through Rao and his deputy An Ziwen to develop a draft list of Politburo members for upcoming Party meetings which promoted the idea of "rotating" senior leaders—with the de facto sidelining of Liu and Zhou (who, under Gao Gang's scheme, were to rotate off the Politburo), thus opening space for Gao to catapult himself to the No. 2 or 3 position in the Party.

Such a conspiratorial coup to undermine such senior leaders was sure to be found out and fail. And it did. Gao's and Rao's maneuverings came to the attention of Deng Xiaoping and Chen Yun, both of whom alerted Mao. A February 1954 Party plenum, overseen by Liu Shaoqi, clearly sidelined Gao. Thereafter an investigation into his and Rao's conspiratorial activities unfolded. Knowing that his plotting had been discovered, Gao committed suicide in September. Rao was arrested and jailed for twenty years. A sweeping purge of other Party cadres involved in the "Gao Gang–Rao Shushi anti-Party alliance" took place over the next year.[48] Mao authorized the purge. Perhaps the significant aspect of this case was that there had been a factional struggle at the apex of the CCP leadership just a few years into the new republic. But it was far from the last.

The Hundred Flowers Movement and Anti-Rightist Campaign

The second matter Mao dealt with in these years concerned the intelligentsia. In 1955 he launched a searing campaign against the writer Hu Feng—a senior literary figure who served on the executive board of China's Writers Association and was a delegate to the newly formed National People's

Congress. Despite his positions (or perhaps because of them), Hu Feng felt the need to speak out against troubling trends he perceived in the cultural and educational spheres. Indeed, most intellectuals were deeply disturbed by the Sovietization of intellectual life. But Hu Feng had the temerity to write a lengthy report to the Central Committee criticizing ideological dogmatism, censorship, socialist realism and he called for the maintenance of professional and literary standards in the national journal *People's Literature* (人民文学). Zhou Yang, a senior Party cadre and doctrinaire ideologue himself, was the first to attack Hu Feng's "300,000 Word Letter" as a "counterrevolutionary" document. Mao also denounced him. Hu Feng himself was arrested and incarcerated for 24 years (he was released in 1979 but was found to suffer from mental illness and required hospitalization until his death in 1985). The Party's attacks quickly broadened thereafter, going after "elements of the Hu Feng counterrevolutionary clique"—a nationwide campaign unfolded with 18.6 million intellectuals investigated, 257,551 found guilty of being counterrevolutionaries or "bad elements," and 1,717 driven to commit suicide.[49] The Hu Feng affair was a chilling attack on China's intelligentsia—the first since 1949, but by no means the last.

The next step in Mao's and the Party's approach to the intelligentsia came only a year later with the Hundred Flowers campaign (百花运动) of 1956. Mao launched the movement on May 2, 1956, with his famous speech calling for "a hundred flowers to bloom and a hundred schools of thought to contend." The ostensible idea behind the initiative was that the PRC had now been in existence for seven years, much had been accomplished (and indeed Mao was very positive about economic development), but no doubt mistakes had also been made and there were things that required further work. Intellectuals were deemed important to the modern development of the country. This was the Party's logic. As such, a special Central Committee conference on intellectuals was convened in January 1956, with Premier Zhou Enlai presiding. Zhou's keynote speech asserted that the intelligentsia should be given greater autonomy and authority, their views were to be respected, their professional knowledge sought, their living conditions improved, their salaries raised, and their role in nation-building valued.

This was the background and ostensible rationale for Mao's Hundred Flowers speech in May 1956, and he sounded many of the same themes as Zhou had—calling on intellectuals to critique the work of the Party and government and raise suggestions for the future. But Mao's call was met with resounding silence. No intellectuals spoke up. And little wonder, given what had just happened to Hu Feng the previous year and the still-unfolding investigations into millions of intellectuals. That month Lu Dingyi (Director of the CCP Propaganda Department) also gave a follow-up speech to Mao's, claiming that the Party's outreach was genuine and it welcomed constructive criticisms of all kinds. Lu particularly reached out to university professors: "Unless independent thinking and free discussion are encouraged, academic life stagnates—and conversely when they are encouraged, academic life speeds up."[50] More generally Lu claimed: "The overwhelming majority of the intellectuals have become government workers in the service of socialism and are already part of the working class . . . a fundamental change has taken place among Chinese intellectuals in the past six years."[51]

Gradually, little by little, by mid-1956 a variety of intellectuals (mainly scientists and writers at first) hesitantly began to speak up, and during the second half of the year the criticisms gained momentum. Essentially, their critiques fell into these six categories:[52]

- blind copying of the Soviet model in education and the economy;
- forced conformity in art;
- the ideologization of literature;
- censorship in journalism and academia;
- bureaucratism and overzealous Party cadres in work units and neighborhoods;
- the insistence on Marxist dogma in academic research.

As the bottled-up criticisms gained momentum during the fall and winter of 1956–1957,[53] Mao and the Party leadership convened the 8th Party Congress during September and October. It was the first such national Party congress in eleven years (in those years, unlike now, it was not stipulated that Party congresses should be held every five years). The conclave convened in Beijing with an air of triumphalism, accomplishment, and unity. With the difficulties of the transition and consolidation years (1949–1952), the Korean War (1950–1953), the Gao Gang factional struggle all behind them, and the economy showing strong growth under the First Five-Year Plan, the CCP leadership exhibited an air of confidence. As such, they decided it was an appropriate time to take stock of their achievements and look to the future.[54] The Congress proclaimed that "socialist transformation had been achieved," a reference to the nationalization and collectivization of the urban and rural sectors, and speeches by Liu Shaoqi, Deng Xiaoping, and other leaders were generally upbeat. Mao's own address was too—but buried within it came the chilling warning: "We still have our shortcomings. Among many of our comrades there are still standpoints and styles of work which are contrary to Marxism-Leninism—namely, subjectivism in their way of thinking, bureaucracy in their way of work, and sectarianism in organizational questions. . . . Such serious shortcomings in our ranks must be vigorously corrected by strengthening ideological education in the Party."[55]

Then on February 27, 1957, Mao weighed in again. Speaking in front of 1,800 Party and non-Party attendees at a specially convened Supreme State Conference, Mao gave his famous speech "On the Correct Handling of Contradictions Among the People." It lasted four hours. This speech and its contents had been percolating in the Chairman's mind for over a year, ever since Soviet leader Nikita Khrushchev had given his "secret speech" denouncing Stalin's crimes and his "cult of personality" at the 20th Congress of the Communist Party of the Soviet Union a year earlier. The timing of Mao's speech was also animated by the Hungarian uprising and its forcible suppression by Soviet forces in October and November of 1956. Poland experienced a similar uprising in October (suppressed by Polish security forces) and discontent was brewing in other Eastern European Soviet satellite states as well. These events made Mao increasingly wary of creeping liberalization in the Soviet bloc, and also within his own society. Nikita Khrushchev had also announced a new initiative of "peaceful coexistence" with the United States and the West, which Mao deeply opposed.

The "Contradictions" speech was one of the longest Mao ever gave (the text runs to a full 43 pages in his *Selected Works*) and it was a summation of various issues confronting the CCP, but also other communist parties, at the time. The main element of the speech (as noted in Chapter 1) was Mao's distinction between the "people" and the "enemy" in socialist society, and the way that ruling communist parties should deal with "contradictions" in each category. Mao clearly distinguished between the two categories: "The contradictions between ourselves and the enemy are antagonistic contradictions. Within the ranks of the people, the contradictions among the working people are non-antagonistic."[56] But how should the Party deal with "contradictions" in each category? Mao was direct: "Dictatorship does not apply within the ranks of the people." Instead, he argued that differences in opinion "among the people" should be handled "democratically."[57] He elaborated:

> What should our policy be toward non-Marxist ideas? As far as unmistakable counterrevolutionaries and saboteurs of the socialist cause are concerned, the matter is easy: we simply deprive them of their freedom of speech. But incorrect ideas among the people are quite a different matter. Will it do to ban such ideas and deny them any opportunity for expression? Certainly not. . . . You may ban the expression of wrong ideas, but the ideas will still be there. . . . Mistakes must be criticized and poisonous weeds fought wherever they crop up. . . . We are against poisonous weeds of any kind, but we must carefully distinguish between what is really a poisonous weed and what is really a fragrant flower.[58]

Mao was thus clearly continuing to welcome the intellectuals' criticisms (at least superficially), while obliquely laying down a marker that the borderline between "non-antagonistic" and "antagonistic" contradictions was a fine one. Intellectuals could thus be forgiven for believing that the Chairman continued to welcome their feedback, and without retribution. Such criticisms thus continued to flow forth (mainly through published articles) during the spring of 1957, including the pasting up of "big character" wall posters (大字报) for the first time on the campus of famous Beijing University (北大).[59] These articles and posters became more and more bold and critical of CCP policies in the six categories noted above. Some even boldly called for an "end to Party dictatorship." Wall posters and student discussion forums began to mushroom around the country—reaching 31 campuses by the end of May. More ominously for the CCP regime, urban workers then began to protest conditions imposed under the new planned economy, while rural protests against forced collectivization also ignited.[60] A true flowering of diverse opinions was occurring, but by May 1957 it had moved beyond words and wall posters as protesters began to organize themselves.

This was too much for Mao. The outpouring of opposition was gaining momentum and beginning to simulate similar outbreaks in East Germany, Poland, and Hungary. Whether Mao and the regime were honestly taken aback by the deluge of criticism and opposition, which they had not anticipated—or whether they sensed the existence of discontent and wanted to flush it out—remains a question debated by Sinologists to this day. *Why* had Mao initiated the Hundred Flowers movement in the first place? Was his olive branch to the intelligentsia sincere—or was it a trap? While the CCP leadership may have been surprised by the pent-up ferocity of dissent and protest, it does seem in retrospect that it was a trap that had been laid to expose residual opposition to communist rule and policies.

This openness abruptly changed on May 15 when Mao published an article in the *People's Daily* entitled "Things Are Changing," in which he alleged: "In recent days some have shown themselves to be most rabid through alleged efforts to seize the leadership of various cultural and educational fields and instigate the masses against the Party and the government."[61] Mao went further and revealed: "Some say they are afraid of being hooked like a fish, and others say they are afraid of being lured into the deep, rounded up and annihilated. Now that large numbers of fish have come to the surface by themselves, there is no need to bait the hook."[62]

Then, on June 8, 1957, the *People's Daily* published an editorial entitled "What Is This For?" Over the next ten days further condemnatory editorials in the *People's Daily* were published.[63] On June 18 a revised version of Mao's "contradictions" speech was published, but this version was doctored to eliminate the references in the original that these "non-antagonistic contradictions among the people" could be resolved through an "open door" airing of their grievances. Mao had distinguished two alternative ways to deal with "contradictions": those within the Party should be dealt with using "closed door" methods (only among Party members), while contradictions in society should be dealt with using "open door" methods, whereby the masses are mobilized. Clearly, the airing of Hundred Flower grievances had gone much too far in terms of both organized dissent and direct criticisms of CCP rule. Several senior leaders blamed Mao for allowing and encouraging the dissent to pour forth throughout the spring. As noted above, it remains unclear if Mao was genuinely surprised by the outpouring of opposition—or if, as he later put it, that he was "trying to lure the snakes out of their holes."[64]

At any rate, the political tide had turned and Mao and the Party pressed ahead with the Anti-Rightist Campaign (反右倾运动). This campaign lasted for about half a year and involved many mass arrests, interrogations, torture, public denunciations, ransacking of homes, and other coercive tactics.[65] Party committees in many work units were given quotas of rightists per capita who had to be ferreted out. Jiang Zemin, China's leader who we will consider in Chapter 4, was one such local Party cadre, and he had to quite arbitrarily fulfill his quota.[66] Mao assigned none other than Deng Xiaoping to oversee the campaign. By the time the campaign concluded in early 1958, a total of 550,000 people had been "capped" (a euphemistic term for wearing a dunce cap) as "rightists."[67] Some estimates range between 1 and 2 million. All lost their professional jobs, a large number were remanded to prison or labor camps, some were executed, and those who were not were put under house arrest. The brunt of the repression fell on intellectuals of various stripes, but also included the workers who had attempted to organize strikes.

Some "rightists" were "rehabilitated" during the early 1970s, under Zhou Enlai's aegis, but the vast majority lived with the stigma and loss of work all the way until 1978 when Hu Yaobang (who headed the CCP Organization Department at the time) is credited with instituting Central Committee Document No. 55, which formally "uncapped" 547,000 rightists.[68] Following this official "reversal of verdicts," as the CCP calls them, various Party organs began to renounce Mao's actions and the campaign. For example, the Party History Research Center of the Central Committee maintained (in a 1991 official history of the CCP on its 70th anniversary): "[Mao] overestimated the attacks by a tiny number of rightists. . . . Yes, it was necessary to repulse the attacks of a handful of rightists, but it was not necessary to launch such a nationwide, large-scale mass movement for the purpose. . . . Unjustifiably labeled 'rightists' suffered tragic consequences from the mistake."[69]

With the Anti-Rightist Campaign and the sudden stoppage of the "blooming and contending" period of dissent and debate, the CCP and China were turning a page into another new era.

Leaping Forward, Backward, and Forward Again: 1958–1965

The about-face on the Hundred Flowers opening, followed by the Anti-Rightist crackdown, was a pivotal moment for Mao personally and the CCP institutionally. From 1958–1961 Mao doubled down on his radical utopian vision for China achieving communism. This produced the Great Leap Forward (1958–1960), a major leadership factional fracture (1959), a massive famine (1959–1961), and the rupture of relations with the Soviet Union (1960–1962). During 1961 and 1962 Mao temporarily stepped back and relatively withdrew from day-to-day rule, ceding leadership of the country to a handful of other senior leaders who overturned the Chairman's radical policies. This, in turn, incensed Mao—who reasserted himself in the fall of 1962 with a series of critical speeches. In 1964 he launched the Socialist Education Movement, a forerunner to the ten-year Cultural Revolution (1966–1976). Before getting to that catastrophic mass movement, though, let us first examine the seven years between 1958 and 1965 in order to understand the whipsaw nature of Chinese politics and economic development during this pivotal transitional time.

In order to understand the origins of the Great Leap Forward (a nationwide mass movement of rural industrialization, collectivization, and manual labor) recall, first of all, that Mao had argued in 1955 that the Chinese economy had reached a "high tide" and should be sped up to achieve "greater, faster, better" results. This revealed the Chairman's impatience with the methodical Soviet planning model of development (no matter that it was achieving very impressive results, as described in Table 2.1). Fundamentally, Mao was a "voluntarist" (the philosophical principle that human will is the fundamental factor in society and the universe). This viewpoint was evident in many of his writings, but perhaps best captured in his 1945 essay "The Foolish Old Man Who Removed the Mountains."[70] Second, like Trotsky, Mao was also a believer in *permanent revolution* and was ever fearful that his revolution would bog down in a sea of bureaucratism if not constantly renewed.[71] He further believed that revolutionary change was a process in which political, economic, social, and cultural transformations are carried out *simultaneously*.[72] Third, Mao further feared that capitalist tendencies are deeply rooted in society and would, like weeds, constantly crop up to compromise or overtake the planted crops of socialism. Beginning sometime during 1956 and 1957 the second and third of these fears began to fuse together in Mao's mind, and he began to worry and warn about the dangers of creeping "revisionism" (修正主义) that he perceived to be occurring in the Soviet Union under Nikita Khrushchev. This trifecta of Maoist worries is fundamental to understanding why he launched both the Great Leap Forward and the Cultural Revolution. They also had much to do with why Mao decided to break with the Soviet Union.

Launching the Great Leap Forward

The initial steps of the GLF came in four meetings during the first half of 1958: a Central Committee work conference in Nanning in January, a Politburo meeting in Chengdu in March, the second plenum of the Eighth Central Committee in May in Beijing, and a Central Committee meeting at its August 1958 annual summer retreat at the seaside resort Beidaihe. The last meeting authorized the further collectivization of agriculture and rural residents into "people's communes" (人民公社). These were huge amalgamations of people, land, animals, and farm implements into conglomerates of approximately 5,000 to 10,000 households. Whole villages became communes. These organs were seen to be the very embodiment of communism—in which all inhabitants shared everything, had no individual belongings, lived together in close proximity, ate together in mass mess halls, and worked together on mass projects. Money and wages were to be abolished and compensation for work was now based on a system of egalitarian "work points" (公分). The same Beidaihe meeting discussed production goals for the Second Five-Year Plan (1958–1962), establishing very high, unachievable targets.

The aforementioned spring CCP leadership meetings all catalyzed the Great Leap Forward. Mao himself had presaged it during his brief visit to Moscow in November 1957 for a meeting of world communist parties (his second and last trip abroad). While there, he made the famous statement that "The Soviet Union can surpass the United States in 15 years, while China can overtake Great Britain in 15 years" (Mao had also made a similar statement in 1955 and again in 1958). It is unclear if Mao was speaking about economic output in general or steel production in particular. This goal thus became enshrined in official policy in December 1957 when the National Planning Conference adopted the document "Plan to Overtake and Surpass Great Britain in the Output of Steel and Other Major Industrial Products." Mao added fuel to the fire when he told the CCP Second Plenum in May to "Go all out, aim high, and achieve greater, faster, better and more economical results in building socialism."[73] The summer Beidaihe meeting set specific output targets for steel at 10.7 million metric tons for 1958 alone, itself a doubling of the 1957 output figure, but then announced the stunning goal of *tripling* production to 27 to 30 million tons in 1959.

Exactly how were such exaggerated targets to be met? Herein lies the essence and tragedy of the Great Leap. There were essentially two means to achieve such unrealistic targets: *exaggerated statistics* and *mass mobilization of labor*. Throughout the next two years the statistics for output (for everything from grain to steel) were simply faked and passed up the line to the authorities in Beijing (with a kind of inflationary multiplier effect added at each bureaucratic level)—providing the false impression that targets were being met (even exceeded). An example of this statistical inflation was the regime reporting that the output for grain in 1958 had more than doubled from 1957 (from 195 metric tons to 450 tons). The second method—which captures the voluntarist essence of the GLF as a movement—was the mass mobilization of the entire Chinese countryside to smelt down all metal objects (utensils, farm implements, bicycles, and household objects) in "backyard furnaces" (土法炼钢) in attempts to forge steel (see Fig. 2.5). The quality of the "steel" was worthless.

In addition to the backyard furnaces (which literally made the Chinese countryside glow at night), the rural population was mobilized into a variety of mass digging and construction projects (in the Maoist vision of the "Foolish Old Man Who Removed the Mountains"). Reservoirs, dams, irrigation canals, roads, and other infrastructure were dug and made—*by hand*.

Figure 2.5 Great Leap Forward (1958–1960) Rural Steel Furnace Movement
Source: Everett Collection Historical / Alamy

The other collateral—and catastrophic—effect of the rural steel and mass digging movements was that time invested by peasants on these projects was net time not spent in agricultural cultivation. Few were tending the fields. Moreover, Mao (in another of his harebrained ideas) launched a nationwide campaign against the "four pests": rats, flies, mosquitos, and sparrows. The real problem came with the killing of sparrows (which was mainly accomplished by people banging gongs and metal objects loudly 24/7 to frighten the birds to continually fly and then literally drop from the sky from exhaustion). However, unbeknownst to Mao, sparrows performed the useful task of eating locusts and other insects that preyed on crops. The result was a massive insect infestation during the summers of 1959 and 1960. On top of these factors, during these two summers China experienced two consecutive serious droughts.

All the while that this man-made (Mao-made) human catastrophe was unfolding, national statistics for grains and foodstuffs showed *faux* bumper harvests. Yet not all CCP leaders were fooled. Several (including Liu Shaoqi, Peng Dehuai, and Chen Yun) undertook inspection trips to the countryside (in Liu's case he disguised himself in hopes of seeing the real situation rather than a Potemkin show put on by local cadres eager to please).

Showdown at Lushan

During the summer of 1959 the leadership was scheduled to convene for a plenum atop 5,000-foot-high Mount Lu (Lushan) in Jiangxi province, where the cool weather and beautiful scenery belied what was to unfold. On the eve of the conference, Marshal Peng Dehuai (Minister of Defense, Long Marcher and decorated Red Army officer, commander of troops in the Korean War, and battle-hardened veteran) decided to write Mao a "letter of opinion" (意见信) about conditions in the countryside based upon his own reconnaissance inspection trips. Peng enjoyed extremely high standing and reputation in the Party, the military, and the nation. He was said to possess "the body of a bull and face of a bulldog."[74] Peng obviously thought that his standing in the Party and personal comrade-in-arms relationship with Mao warranted his right to voice his opinion. Peng delivered his letter in person on July 14, the eve of the conference, by barging past Mao's personal guard into his bedroom where the Chairman was resting (on this occasion not *in flagrante delicto*) to personally hand-deliver his letter. In it Peng specifically mentioned that there had been "shortcomings and errors experienced in the Great Leap Forward" and he blamed these on "leftism," saying that "Petty bourgeois fanaticism renders us liable to commit 'left' mistakes." He also pinned blame on the "arbitrary and excessive setting of output targets." While pointed, the letter also was quite balanced and spoke of the need for unity, and the need to rectify the economic and social problems facing the country. Nor did he mention Mao in a negative light, saying in fact: "On the whole, there should be no investigation of personal responsibility."[75]

Mao read Peng's letter on July 17, had it printed and circulated to the conference participants, but said nothing about it . . . until six days later, on July 23, when the Chairman exploded in a venomous diatribe against Peng before the assembled cadres.[76] Mao's persona and language were visceral. He lambasted Marshal Peng in searing, sarcastic, and crude language, shocking all those present. When the Chairman's tirade had ended the room sat in stunned silence. Among the accusations he hurled at Peng was that of being a "right opportunist." Mao also said: "In my days when I was a young man and later attained middle age, I used to get angry at hearing bad remarks against me. I never attack others if I am not attacked. If others attack me first, I attack them later. This principle I have never given up to this day."[77] Mao's speech also offered a detailed defense of the Great Leap.

It is reported that Peng did not sleep for nights afterward, lost his appetite, and (not surprisingly) became despondent, although he was permitted to continue attending the daily meeting sessions. Two weeks later, the *dénouement* took place when the CCP formally convened its Eighth Plenum. Mao put a resolution before the plenum to condemn "the anti-Party clique headed by Peng Dehuai." Peng was finished. He was stripped of his position as Defense Minister (replaced by Lin Biao). Upon his return to Beijing, he was banished to house arrest under armed guard and was moved from his Zhongnanhai quarters to a dilapidated dwelling on the northern outskirts of the city.[78] He was stripped of his battle decorations and military rank as one of the PLA's eleven Marshals. While confined to his home, Peng was allowed to garden and read (and even continued to receive some Party documents). His only permitted visitor was apparently his niece. In 1962 Peng decided to pen a long 80,000-character letter of "self-criticism" to the Central Committee, asking for forgiveness and reinstatement. The leadership did not act on Peng's request, but he was allowed a brief visit to Hunan. Finally, three years later, in September 1965 Peng was assigned (with Mao's approval) to Sichuan province where he would oversee the "third line" project of relocating defense industries to the interior of the country. It was not to last long. The next year as the Cultural Revolution broke out, Peng was physically attacked by Red Guards in Chengdu, who put him in chains, hung a wooden placard around his neck denouncing his "crimes," forced him to make a "self-confession," and subjected the former Marshal to repeated "struggle sessions." He was then moved to Beijing for more such kangaroo court sessions. Peng was "interrogated" by Red Guards 260 times, "airplaned" (a practice whereby one's arms are held behind the back at upward angle for extended periods), and beaten repeatedly until his ribs were broken and legs paralyzed.[79] Finally, in August 1967, following a mass struggle session before 40,000 PLA soldiers, Peng was remanded to Qincheng prison, where he remained until his death from (untreated) colon cancer on November 29, 1974. During this period he was kept in solitary confinement most of the time.[80] When he contracted tuberculosis he was also denied medical treatment (apparently on the directive of Mao's wife Jiang Qing). Even Peng's wife, Pu Anxiu, did not learn of her husband's death until her own release from a labor camp in 1978. Such was the fate of someone who dared to confront and criticize Chairman Mao.

The Lushan Plenum and the Peng Dehuai affair was a pivotal event, for three reasons. First, it marked a turning point in Mao's own approach to his colleagues. Previous to this time, with the exception of the 1954 Gao Gang purge, Mao had operated basically as *primus inter pares* (first among equals) and had generally upheld the collegial institutional procedures of decision-making. But with his attack on Peng he clearly placed himself above *all* other senior leaders—and he unambiguously signaled to all what could happen if they crossed the Chairman. He also revealed his explosive temper. Second, Mao openly rejected criticisms of "leftist" (左派) policies, de facto identifying himself with them and thus signaling the beginning of the "two line struggle" against those more moderate leaders like Liu Shaoqi, Deng Xiaoping, and Chen Yun. On the day that the Lushan Plenum adjourned, Mao wrote a commentary in which he boldly declared: "The struggle at Lushan is a class struggle, a continuation of the life-and-death struggle between the two antagonistic classes, the proletariat and the bourgeoisie, in the course of the past ten years of socialist revolution."[81] Third, Mao defended his Great Leap policies and instead of abandoning or adjusting them, he ordered them to proceed full steam ahead.

It produced *widespread and catastrophic famine*, the second worst in world history. An estimated 30 million (the official figure) to 45 million (more recent foreign estimates based on Chinese archival and demographic data) perished during the three years 1959, 1960, and 1961—what the CCP subsequently and euphemistically refers to as the "three bitter years" (三苦年), an understatement if there ever was one. Peasants prowled the dystopian barren landscape in search of anything to eat. They ate the leaves and bark off of trees, they ate husks of grains, they ate anything they could get their hands on—there are even valid reports of cannibalism in several provinces. Official national mortality rates (undoubtedly underreported) soared to 14.59 percent in 1959, 25.43 percent in 1960, and 14.24 percent in 1961.[82] The national population actually *declined* by 14.5 million between 1959 and 1961 (from 673.1 million to 658.6 million).

Then in early 1960, Mao stunned everyone again—this time by declaring that he was going to "retire to the second line" (推到第二线) of leadership. Mao had actually floated the idea of stepping back from day-to-day rulership as early as 1955. But on this occasion, the timing was propitious—it was a convenient way for him to walk away from the mess he had created, both within the leadership and in the country, to let others clean it up. The Chairman offered multiple explanations for his decision to step aside (although he gave up no official positions). He claimed he was tired and needed rest; he claimed he had spent too much time in the capital and needed to "go to the countryside" and see conditions first-hand; and he claimed he needed more time for his "philosophical" writings.

The sometimes salacious, but first-hand, biography of Mao's life published by his doctor Li Zhisui, also argues that Mao wanted more private time with his harem of "nurses" (one of whom he reportedly impregnated while in Shanghai).[83] According to Dr. Li's account, Mao was constantly worried about his virility and impotence; thus, he fed the Chairman a continuous cocktail of different Chinese herbal aphrodisiacs and Western pharmaceuticals throughout his life. Ironically, Mao contracted syphilis from one of his paramours, which eventually reached his brain and was one of the causes of his death. He also contracted another (unspecified) venereal disease that he passed to all of his partners, which required their own treatment with antibiotics provided by Dr. Li; yet, Mao himself refused treatment. Mao's liaisons were widely known among the leadership, although efforts were taken to hide his actions. Some were not very secretive. Dr. Li describes twice-weekly dances (usually held in the Beijing Hotel ballroom) attended by many young women, during which Mao would "adjourn" to an adjacent room to "rest with them."[84] The adjacent room had an enormous bed in it. A similar room in the Great Hall of the People (designated Room 118) was set aside for similar purposes. Various photos also exist of Mao on his private train surrounded by a dozen or so eager young women fawning over the Chairman. As Dr. Li observed of Mao's harem of modern concubines:

"To be brought into the service of Mao was, for the young women who were chosen, an incomparable honor beyond their most extravagant dreams."[85] Nor did Mao engage sexually with his lovers one at a time. He preferred orgies, according to Dr. Li: "He was happiest and most satisfied with several young women simultaneously sharing his bed. He encouraged his sexual partners to introduce him to others for shared orgies, allegedly in the interest of his longevity and strength."[86] Although Mao had stopped cohabitating with his third wife Jiang Qing sometime in the early 1950s, she was a particularly jealous and venomous spouse. But by 1958, Dr. Li recalls, all efforts to hide Mao's affairs from Jiang Qing stopped, and Jiang Qing even began to befriend some of Mao's "nurses"—because they controlled physical access to the Chairman. If Jiang Qing wanted to see Mao, she had to get past the bodyguards and nurses. For Jiang Qing, political power was her aphrodisiac—and without Mao she was nothing.

After his "retirement to the second line," Mao spent the next two years (1960–1962) out of the limelight, shuttling in and out of Beijing. His residence (the Spring Lotus Chamber) in the Zhongnanhai was renovated and, according to Dr. Li, Mao "spent most of his time in bed."[87] He would leave the capital city unannounced for weeks at a time, traveling in his armor-plated personal train (specially built by the East Germans). Other senior leaders were thus never sure if Mao was in or out of town and if or when he might reinject himself back into the life of the nation. Mao's withdrawal was, after all, voluntary—and he could reappear at any time.

Even when Mao was in Beijing he was not very accessible throughout his career. Mao's work style was erratic, to say the least. He normally worked at night and slept most of the day. As time went on, he devoted his reading to Chinese history and literary classics rather than contemporary government documents. When he wanted to communicate with aides or other senior officials, he always preferred face-to-face meetings rather than the telephone; because of his stature and physical location inside the Zhongnanhai, this meant that few saw him in person. Premier Zhou Enlai was, by some measure, his most frequent political interlocutor. To accommodate Mao's nighttime work habits, but still run the government by day, throughout his life Zhou only slept a few hours per night (generally from about 4:00 to 8:00 a.m.). Mao was also frequently curt and dismissive of other aides. As one of his main interpreters, Ji Chaozhu, noted in his memoir: "In the [next] dozen or so years that I frequently interpreted for him, never did Mao acknowledge me as anything other than a talking machine. He was not cruel, but he was as oblivious to my presence as Premier Zhou had been attentive."[88] Mao was also impulsive, deciding spontaneously to leave the capital on an inspection tour in the hinterland (which would cause no end of security concerns for his bodyguards). His eating habits were also odd. He preferred greasy Shanghai style and spicy Hunan style dishes and would order them to be brought to him at any hour of the night. He had no regular mealtimes and generally did not eat with others, and he certainly did not have a balanced diet (which contributed to his heart and other conditions).

The Sino-Soviet Split

During this period China's relationship with the Soviet Union came fully apart. Multiple problems had been brewing ever since Nikita Khrushchev's famous 1956 "secret speech" denouncing Stalin and his crimes. There was no single event that triggered the Sino-Soviet Split (中苏分列), although the Kremlin's decision to abruptly withdraw all 1,390 advisors from China in July 1960 is considered the symbolic breakpoint. The advisors, who had done so much over the previous decade to literally build China and turn it into a modern socialist state, suddenly were ordered home, taking all of their blueprints with them, leaving factories unfinished and many bureaucratic relationships ruptured. But this abrupt action was a manifestation of multiple incidents that had been accumulating in the relationship, and irritating both sides, since 1956. These included:

- Khrushchev's denunciation of Stalin and his "cult of personality" (which Mao felt was aimed at him);
- Khrushchev's criticisms of Mao's accelerated pace of rural collectivization, the "people's communes," and the Great Leap Forward;
- The poor personal chemistry between Khrushchev and Mao;
- Mao's belief that, following Stalin's death, he was the natural heir as the leader of the international communist movement;

- Growing Chinese discomfort with strictures of the Soviet economic model, and difficulties encountered with Soviet experts working in China;
- Khrushchev's pursuance of a policy of "peaceful coexistence" with the United States and his visit there in 1958;
- Moscow's failure to support a PRC "liberation" of Taiwan, especially during the 1958 Taiwan Strait crisis;
- Khrushchev's delaying promised assistance to China to build its own atomic bomb, and reneging on the promise to supply a whole sample bomb;
- Khrushchev's demands during his July 31–August 3, 1959 visit to Beijing that the two sides set up a joint naval fleet and that the Soviet Union be permitted to establish a long-wave radio station on Chinese territory for military communications;
- There were also multiple festering Marxist-Leninist ideological differences, which Party theoreticians on both sides debated.

By April 1960 the subterranean differences that had been simmering erupted into the public domain on the occasion of the anniversary of Lenin's 90th birthday, with the publication of an editorial in the CCP's theoretical journal *Hongqi* (Red Flag) labeled "Long Live Leninism!"[89] A parallel editorial appeared in the *People's Daily*. These articles began a series of searing critiques of what the Chinese side called "modern revisionism." This led to a polemical war of words between the two communist parties over the ensuing years,[90] all couched in arcane Marxist-Leninist vocabulary. For them, the ideological war was deadly serious. But the two sides did not immediately sever ties (and never did break diplomatic relations). They continued to air their grievances and make their cases against the other as "revisionists" from true Marxism-Leninism in print and at international communist conclaves (most notably in Bucharest, Romania, in June 1960, in Moscow in October 1961, and in Moscow in July 1963). By then the "split" between the world's two communist powers was official and widely in the open for the world to see. In the course of a mere decade the two communist titans went from being close allies engaged in a common enterprise to build socialism and combat imperialism to being estranged and bickering ex-partners squabbling over who was at fault for the fallout.[91] Within another decade they would be fighting with conventional weapons and threatening nuclear attacks against each other. For Mao's China, in terms of its foreign relations, this not only meant that its main security partner and alliance was gone, its main external source of economic assistance had been severed, and that the PRC stood virtually alone in the world. Beijing did have relations with, and support from, some developing countries—but hardly any diplomatic relations with developed Western or many Asian states. The United States continued to be a genuine danger to China's national security, especially as the American war in Vietnam was escalating. As a result of the rupture with Moscow, China now practiced a de facto "dual adversary" strategy against both the USA and USSR.

Post–Great Leap Recovery

Meanwhile, as Mao remained largely off the national stage, there was the urgent question of how to overcome the famine and piece the national economy back together. Not only had between 30 and 45 million people perished during the famine, the overall economy had also contracted.[92] Total grain output had fallen from 197.65 million metric tons (mmt) in 1958 to 136.5 mmt in 1961.[93] Other crops showed even greater shrinkage. Total industrial output declined from 41.45 mn. RMB in 1958 to 32.54 mn. in 1962.[94] The top leaders remaining in Beijing (principally Zhou Enlai, Liu Shaoqi, Deng Xiaoping, Chen Yun, Peng Zhen) went to work developing a systematic set of policies—aimed not only at alleviating and overcoming the economic and human havoc that Mao had wrought, but also systematically addressing a wide range of policy areas. This is a period (1961–1965) during which moderate and pragmatic leaders instituted policies at direct variance with Mao's and the Party's left-wing utopian ideas. This was done primarily through the issuance of a series of official documents, each of which addressed a different functional sphere but collectively also added up to a comprehensive reform program.[95] This indicated that the PRC was moving into its third distinct stage of development in the mere twelve years of its existence: first came the Soviet model; second was Mao's utopian "leftist" policies following the Hundred Flowers movement through the Great

Leap; and, now, a new stage of less rigid socialism that permitted moderate freedoms in multiple policy areas.

Taken together, these official documents and policies captured the basic program for economic recovery from the GLF, but they went *much further*, to constitute a comprehensive blueprint for "moderate" and pragmatic policies that gave great scope to quasi-private economic production (material incentives and lease-holding), dismantling communes, giving much greater tolerance and freedoms in higher education and the arts, a commitment to light industrial production of consumer goods and handicrafts, a relative de-emphasis on heavy industry, a stress on developing modern science and technology, and other reforms that fundamentally departed from both the Soviet model and the utopian leftism of Mao.

This was precisely what bothered the Great Helmsman. Mao had been brooding and observing all of this for almost two years now. Although he attended and spoke at the "7,000 Cadres Conference" of January–February 1962, he remained generally out of view until the late summer. In August 1962 the leadership retreated (per their custom) to the beach resort of Beidaihe on the Bohai Gulf about two hours east of Beijing. There they have a sanctuary of secluded villas nestled among pine trees by the sea. Normally the leadership uses these late-summer retreats to relax and discuss the state of the nation in generalized terms. This one, though, had a particular purpose: to set and discuss the agenda for the upcoming Tenth Plenum of the Eighth Central Committee in September. It was to take stock of the successful economic recovery and progress made in all of the aforementioned fields. But Chairman Mao had other ideas. After his lengthy absence from the spotlight, Mao reasserted himself with a vengeance by giving a blistering extemporaneous speech criticizing many of the aforementioned policies—saying they amounted to "capitalist restoration," "restoration of the reactionary classes," "Chinese revisionism," and that "correct verdicts were being reversed" unless another Yanan-style "rectification" was undertaken.[96] He also specifically criticized the "individual plots" permitted farmers. Moreover, perhaps most puzzling and alarming to those present, Mao said that he had learned during his various "inspection tours" of the country over the previous two years that "*class struggle still exists*, and it must be stressed every year, every month, and every day."[97]

Mao was back! And he was not happy with what he saw taking place across China or in the leadership in Beijing. Mao then reinserted himself to preside over the Tenth Plenum in September (instead of Liu Shaoqi), at which he did not repeat the themes of his fiery Beidaihe speech but he again did denounce Soviet "revisionism"—which many present took to be a codeword for similar revisionists inside the CCP. Nonetheless, the plenum concluded by affirming the general moderate policy lines of the previous three years. Mao's only other act of that autumn—which was little noticed at the time but in retrospect had great significance for what was to come (the Cultural Revolution)—was a December article criticizing "feudal and capitalist trends" in the arts. This cast a chill over the intelligentsia, once again, and led to a mini-purge ("rectification") in the All-China Federation of Literature and Arts.[98]

The next year, in 1963, Mao plotted a more assertive pushback against what he saw as "revisionism" and "capitalist restoration." This went by the moniker of the ""Socialist Education Movement" (社会主义教育运动), also known as the "Four Cleans" (四清) campaign: to clean up four aspects of rural cadres' behavior pertaining to economic accounting, state and collective properties, and work point assessment. These all seemed innocuous enough, but they in turn quickly morphed into the document "Draft Resolution of the Central Committee on Some Problems in Current Rural Work" (a.k.a. the "First Ten Points"), issued in May 1963. This document broadened out the Four Cleans, assigning the principal role in carrying out the clean-ups *not* to the Party but rather to the "masses." This was a classic Maoist tactic used repeatedly throughout his reign—to "leapfrog" over the bureaucracy (because he didn't trust it) and appeal directly to the masses for collective action. But by the fall Mao had been undercut again, by precisely the bureaucrats whom he distrusted. In September 1963 CCP General Secretary Deng Xiaoping revised and reissued the "Later Ten Points." This new version was intended to reclaim responsibility for implementing the Four Cleans for Party cadres and special "work teams"—thereby taking the movement out of the hands of the rural masses.[99] This shift in carrying out the Socialist Education Movement—from the masses to Party cadres—was further consolidated in September 1963 when Liu Shaoqi redrafted and reissued the "Revised Later Ten Points."

All of this may seem arcane to the reader, but the gist of it was an intensifying struggle, and not just between Mao on the one hand and Deng and Liu on the other. It was very much about who was going to run the country: the masses (Mao's preference) or the party-state (the moderates' preference). The battle over the Ten Points was another skirmish in this intensifying subterranean struggle. By this time Mao was like a bomb waiting to explode. In fact, the previous three years had witnessed several precursor detonations, with his exhortation to "Never forget class struggle!", his attacks on "revisionism," and now "capitalist roaders" in the Party. But the biggest metaphorical bomb had still not gone off (although, in the midst of an economic crisis, the government did find the resources to detonate its first real atom bomb in October 1964). There was to be one more mini political explosion before the big one, and it included several of the key themes that presaged the full explosion of the Cultural Revolution the next year (1966). This was a national "work conference" (a kind of miniature Party plenum) on rural work, convened by the Central Committee from December 1964 to January 1965. Mao insisted on presiding over the meeting. After heated debate, the conference adopted the "Twenty-Three Articles on Rural Work." It was a quintessential Maoist document. After stating that the "principal contradiction" remained between socialism and capitalism, it went on to call out "those people in positions of authority *within the Party* who take the *capitalist road*."[100] In closing the meeting Mao exhorted: "We must boldly unleash the masses!" This was, in effect, Mao's declaration of political war against his opponents in the leadership and the bureaucracy. The new document also shifted—and elevated—the focus of the Four Cleans from rather rudimentary questions of rural management to four "New Cleans": clean politics, clean economics, clean organization, and clean ideology.[101] Mao was drawing the battle lines for the Cultural Revolution.

Meanwhile, another seemingly unrelated event also fed into the brewing maelstrom: the "Learn from the PLA" campaign of 1963–1964. It was aimed not at the army but at the whole of society. The PLA was to be a national role model for the society to emulate. But *what kind* of role model? A highly politicized military loyal specifically to the "Great Helmsman" (大舵手). The campaign was launched by Defense Minister Lin Biao (who had replaced Peng Dehuai after Lushan). After taking over from Peng, Lin had redirected the PLA away from a model (which had been supported by the Soviet advisors) that emphasized modern weapons, technology, and battlefield tactics—to a model that emphasized man over machine, guerilla tactics over technology, political commissars making decisions, and a doctrine of mass "people's war." When Lin (who was also a decorated Marshal) launched the movement it was to make "everyone a soldier" in the country. What this meant in practice was the formation of mass militias. A part of the campaign was also to "study Lei Feng"—an ordinary soldier known for doing selfless deeds before he was accidentally struck and killed by a falling telephone pole in 1963. There were also three key themes promoted in the "Learn From the PLA" campaign: to "combat modern revisionism," "train a new generation of revolutionary successors," and "reform leadership style." These three themes would also become the core elements of the Cultural Revolution. Finally, Lin Biao and the "Learn From the PLA" campaign were responsible for introducing the "Little Red Book" (a pocket-size red-covered special edition of *Quotations from Chairman Mao*) in May 1964. Literally tens of millions of copies were printed and distributed not only throughout the military but also into society, with soldiers leading citizens in "study sessions."

With these events in the 1962–1965 timeframe the scene was set for perhaps Mao's most impactful act.

The "Great Proletarian Cultural Revolution" and the End of the Maoist Era, 1966–1976

Mao's frustrations with "capitalist restoration," "revisionism," and "bureaucratism" had been increasingly percolating in the Chairman's mind and he had become increasingly outspoken about these alleged tendencies since 1962. But in early 1966 Mao turned his frustrations into concerted action by launching the Great Proletarian Cultural Revolution (GPCR, 无产阶级文化大革命). By the official CCP accounting of the event, it lasted ten years, from 1966 to 1976, when Mao died and the so-called Gang of Four were arrested.

The GPCR is an extraordinarily complicated event, or series of events, about which much has been written. Probably the single best account is

Roderick MacFarquhar's and Michael Schoenhals' *Mao's Last Revolution*.[102] Their nearly 700-page magnum opus traces in enormous detail all of the intricate ins-and-outs and ups-and-downs of this extremely complex movement and period. Several other book-length accounts and countless articles also exist outside of China.[103] Inside of China and the CCP, the event has become almost a nonevent, accounts of it heavily censored, and rarely mentioned in publications even in cursory fashion. One notable recent exception is Yang Jisheng's *The World Turned Upside Down*, which was published in Hong Kong in 2016 and subsequently translated and published in the West in 2020 (but is banned in mainland China).[104]

In essence, the GPCR involved a sweeping political and physical attack on leaders led by vigilante youth—the Red Guards (红卫兵)—the institutional decimation of the CCP and government and replacement of the latter at the local level by new organs called "revolutionary committees." It was economically disruptive, and it was an exercise in mass terror that traumatized members of urban society. It was initiated and led by none other than Mao Zedong, but was directed by several radical leaders designated as the Central Cultural Revolution Group.[105] It took shape over the summer of 1966 with Mao's invocations to the Red Guards: "to rebel is justified," "bombard the headquarters," and "drag out those within the Party who are in authority and are taking the capitalist road." With these three instructions the country exploded into an orgy of violence and persecution until Mao put an end to it by calling in the army to restore order in the summer of 1968. Technically, these two years constituted the Cultural Revolution—or what the CCP referred to as its "active phase" (积极阶段). The following eight years leading up to Mao's death and the arrest of the Gang of Four were hardly a passive phase, but the violence had subsided, even if the persecutions had not.

Given the extensive scholarship and first-hand accounts available,[106] it is only necessary here to sketch out the main parameters and impact of the movement. Readers are referred to these other studies for the actual chronology and unfolding of events—but below I offer my own assessments of the main elements of the Cultural Revolution, which can be seen as comprising a number of distinct movements within the Movement.

An ideological movement. The movement was triggered by Mao's own interpretation of Marxism-Leninism and particularly his belief that restoration of capitalism was a constant danger in socialist systems. If not checked and overturned, he believed that capitalism would be restored by "revisionists"—both in the Party-state apparatus but also in society at large. Economically, Mao did not believe in a "hybrid" system of proto-capitalist methods that operated alongside socialist methods. This is what he perceived Liu Shaoqi, Deng Xiaoping, and others to have instituted with the post-Great Leap reforms of 1961–1965. Mao further believed that communism was not some distant stage of societal development that would take an indeterminant period of time to reach—he believed that it was imminently achievable.

An exercise in continual revolution. Per his belief that revolutions inevitably bog down in a kind of Thermidorian reaction, Mao (like Trotsky) believed that the revolutionary fire had to be constantly stoked and rekindled in post-revolutionary society. In his view, revolution was not a process

Figure 2.6 Cultural Revolution Propaganda Poster
Source: Author's personal collection

that culminated in the seizure of power, a one-time event—it had to be continually reinvigorated lest it bog down and be overtaken by a combination of revisionist policies, traditional practices, bureaucracy, and inertia.

A cultural and iconoclastic movement. For Mao, culture was class-based. Culture contained and transmitted values. Bourgeois classes practiced bourgeois art, literature, and other cultural mediums that worshiped individualism and other capitalist values. By contrast, socialist art was made by and for the proletarian masses and collective. Moreover, Mao was convinced that thousands of years of Chinese culture was precisely the *greatest* impediment keeping China from becoming both modern and socialist. What he identified as China's "feudal" past had to be destroyed and replaced by new socialist culture and values. This is why the August 1966 "smash the four olds" (四旧) campaign was integral to the entire GPCR: smash old customs, old culture, old habits, and old ideas. Among other destructive impacts of the GPCR, countless historical artifacts and statues were destroyed, museums were ransacked,[107] ancient paintings and texts were burned, temples were destroyed and monasteries burned to the ground, Confucius and other ancient sages were criticized, and other icons of China's 3,000 years of history were wrecked.

An anti-Western xenophobic movement. The GPCR was also a profoundly xenophobic (anti-foreign) and particularly anti-Western movement. All kinds of Western items (books, art objects, clothes) were burned (those that had not previously been confiscated), Western leaders and historical figures were denounced, demonstrated against, and burned in effigy. The British Embassy in Beijing was ransacked and burned to the ground by Red Guards. Remaining foreigners in China feared for their lives.

An international movement. Beginning even before the outbreak of the GPCR, Maoist foreign policy began to externalize his promotion of revolution through supporting—in rhetoric, money, and arms—foreign communist parties, notably those that followed a "Maoist" rather than Soviet orientation. In 1964 Zhou Enlai toured Africa and proclaimed it "ripe for revolution." Beginning in 1966, once the GPCR had kicked off, China started to provide training, weapons, funds, and beamed propaganda to communist parties in *every* single Southeast Asian country (except newly independent Singapore).[108] In South Asia, the PRC/CCP sent similar support to the Maoist Naxalites in northeastern India and the Communist Party of Nepal (Maoist). That was followed in 1967 with expanded support for revolutionary movements in Latin America, like the Shining Path Maoist guerrilla movement in Peru. But the export of revolution also extended into the developed world, with Maoist follower-advocates in France, Germany, Italy, Canada, and the United States. As Julia Lovell's definitive study traces, Maoism became a truly global movement.[109] Ironically, this was a period when China enjoyed "soft power" abroad and its ideology had some universal appeal (unlike today).

A cross-generational and cross-gender mass movement. Mao was concerned that the generation of young Chinese born since the regime had come to power in 1949 had no first-hand revolutionary experience. Without actually experiencing what it was like to "make revolution" (作革命) the youth of China would also be subject to absorbing the revisionist tendencies of their parents, he believed. Thus, a key part of the GPCR was to create millions of "revolutionary successors." On August 18, 1966, Mao appeared atop Tiananmen Gate in front of thousands of delirious Red Guards filling Tiananmen Square, himself symbolically wearing a green military uniform with a Red Guard armband. "Bombard the headquarters!" Mao exhorted the assembled masses. Following his invocation, for the next two years Red Guards roamed the country like vigilantes—"making revolution" and "exchanging revolutionary experiences"—which involved incalculable physical destruction, humiliation, and torture of those citizens they denounced as "capitalist roaders," "feudal elements," "running dogs," and other epithets. The Red Guards were also composed of many young females, thus politically activating a whole new generation of young Chinese women. The Red Guards were by no means monolithic—to the contrary, they splintered into countless rival factions, which engaged in armed warfare against each other during 1967–1968.[110] Mao also believed that urban youth needed to experience the hardships of rural life, so from 1967 to 1979 a total of 16,470,000 urban youth were dispatched to the countryside for "rustication."[111] This included China's current leader Xi Jinping (see Chapter 6).

An anti-intellectual and anti-elite movement. Particular targets of the Red Guards during the GPCR were intellectuals, technical experts, former bourgeoisie, and other "bad class elements." All of these cohorts of people were "dragged out," "struggled against," publicly humiliated before mass denunciation sessions, physically tortured, sometimes killed, while many committed suicide. "Experts" of all kinds were denounced and replaced by "reds." Universities were closed for three years (1966–1969), research institutes were similarly shuttered, and most secondary schooling was suspended as well. Many government ministries and organs ceased functioning. Many of those targeted were sent to the countryside for manual labor in so-called May 7 Cadre Schools (五七干校), so named after the date in 1968 when they were created (one source reports three million were sent to these labor camps[112]). Many were not so fortunate and were incarcerated or executed.

A cult of personality by a totalitarian despot. Throughout it all, Mao became a demi-god. He was sycophantically worshiped with mass adulation. He presided over gatherings of millions of ecstatic youth and citizens shouting "Long Live Chairman Mao" (毛主席万岁) in Tiananmen Square (these sessions were reminiscent of mass rallies held by other dictators).[113] Everyone carried, read, and quoted from the *Little Red Book*, which was printed and distributed in hundreds of millions of copies nationwide. Icons of the Great Helmsman were everywhere. People were required to wear buttons with his image (Mao badges). Revolutionary posters and art with Mao's image were mass-produced (see Fig. 2.6). Big characters of Mao's words and revolutionary slogans were painted on walls across the country. Twice per day, no matter where you were, citizens were obliged to turn toward Beijing and communicate with the Chairman: at 10:00 every morning they were supposed to "ask the Chairman for instructions" and "report back" to the Chairman in the afternoon.[114] Many danced the daily "loyalty dance" to Mao.[115] It was all a mass exercise in blind sycophantic followership—that produced an anarchic frenzy and orgy of violence and destruction.

A purge of other leaders. The GPCR threw out of power just about every moderate CCP leader except Zhou Enlai and Li Xiannian. The list is long: Liu Shaoqi, Peng Zhen, Deng Xiaoping, Chen Yun, Yang Shangkun, Xi Zhongxun, Tao Zhu, and many, many others. All were subjected to mass "struggle sessions" and were imprisoned or sent to do manual labor. Liu Shaoqi, China's president and senior leader, was branded a "renegade, traitor, and scab," subjected to mass denunciation sessions and beatings at the hands of Red Guards before being banished to a 4 x 8 foot solitary cell in Kaifeng, denied food and medical treatment, and left to die under a blanket on a concrete floor on November 12, 1969.[116] Liu's wife was dressed as a prostitute and paraded before a frenzied crowd of 10,000 in Beijing, accused of being an American spy, and incarcerated in the notorious Qincheng prison. Mao had launched a wholesale purge of those he considered "revisionists" or "capitalist roaders." In their place he promoted security and intelligence czar Kang Sheng, his wife Jiang Qing, and her three Shanghai henchmen Zhang Chunqiao, Yao Wenyuan, and Wong Hongwen (designated the "Cultural Revolution Small Group"). He also promoted Defense Minister Lin Biao, and even selected him as his designated successor in 1969, before Lin and his family and military allies died in a fiery plane crash in September 1971 following an alleged *coup d'état* attempt (see discussion below).

An attack on government bureaucracy and the Party. Commensurate with Mao's belief that government and CCP institutions were filled with "revisionist" officials and cadres, and his idea that the institutions themselves were an impediment to empowering the masses to rule the country, Mao decimated them. Most government and Party organs at the national level were simply disbanded and their staff sent to May 7th Cadre Schools for manual labor and thought reform. At the provincial and municipal levels, Party committees and local governments were overthrown during the January 1967 "power seizure," and were replaced by new "revolutionary committees" composed of workers, peasants, and soldiers (the "three-in-one combination"). This situation lasted until some purged local officials were "rehabilitated" and returned to office in the early 1970s.

A disruption to the economy. Viewed in its totality, the GPCR did not have an outsized negative impact on the national economy,[117] which is quite surprising given the extent of political chaos, social ferment, and disruption of rail transport. Annual national income growth continued to average 5.66 percent over the ten-year period.[118] However, there was significant disruption during 1967 and 1968. It particularly affected industrial production, with manufacturing contracting 15.1 percent in 1967 and another 8.2 percent in 1968. Agricultural output also dropped by 1.6 percent in 1968.[119] Since the Red Guards were riding the rails, it caused a significant backlog of immediate goods (coal, steel, cement, lumber, minerals, etc.) from reaching factories and urban areas. Coal deliveries, the main source of energy at the time, were particularly affected—which had a collateral impact on electricity generation, domestic heating, and factories. The slowdown also temporarily affected Mao's "third front" initiative to relocate and build military industries deep in the interior of the country (a plan launched in 1964) where they would theoretically be less vulnerable to attack by the United States and Soviet Union.[120] If the Great Leap Forward was more of a rural phenomenon, then the impact of the Cultural Revolution was more on the urban sector.

An example of inhumane punishment. Literally millions of people were subjected to inhumane physical and psychological cruelty, humiliation, torture, and punishment. An unknown number were killed (consensus estimates are in the range of 3 million).[121] While considerably lower than foreign and subsequent Chinese estimates, the indictment against the Gang of Four—who were held largely responsible for the movement following Mao's, Lin Biao's, and Kang Sheng's deaths—indicated that "729,511 people were framed and persecuted, of whom 34,800 were persecuted to death."[122] Of these, the trial indictment listed by name 420 "victims of frame-ups and persecution," including 38 leaders of the Party and state; 93 members of the Central Committee; 36 members of the Standing Committee of the National People's Congress; 84 high-ranking cadres of the Party, state, and army; and 37 other well-known personages. The emotional and psychological devastation wrought on millions of families is also incalculable. Spouses were forced to denounce and sometimes beat one another, children denounced parents, neighbors and fellow workers denounced each other, families were

Figure 2.7 Red Guards Denouncing "Counterrevolutionary Revisionist Element" During the Cultural Revolution
Source: Everett Collection Inc / Alamy

physically broken up for years, people did not know if their loved ones were even alive or where they were. Even Mao's interpreter Ji Chaozhu, himself a victim of persecution and subjected to multiple stints of physical labor, observed: "The ways in which people were tortured and killed was limited only by the most sadistic of imaginations."[123] This was Mao's idea of permanent revolution.

One typical account of such torture concerned the famous playwright Lao She:[124]

> One of the early victims of the Cultural Revolution was an eminent 67-year-old writer Lao She, who, with more than two dozen other intellectuals, was dragged from his Beijing home by mobs of teenagers wearing Red Guard armbands. These Red Guard victims were taken to a former Confucian temple, where they received the customary yin-yang haircut administered to

those deemed enemies of the cause: half the head was shaved, the other not. Throughout this humiliating process, Lao She and the others were beaten, punched, and screamed at. Their faces were smeared with black ink, another common indignity ("black capitalist"). They were made to wear signs identifying them as demons and spirits, then beaten literally to a pulp. When Lao She was finally sent home, his wife had to cut off his clothes, they were so caked with congealed blood. Medical treatment was out of the question. No hospital would dare admit him; no doctor would dare treat him. The next day, he managed to walk to a lake near the Forbidden City, where he drowned himself.

An example of the important role of the military in Chinese politics. Finally, following two years of anarchy that had turned into civil war with Red Guards battling Red Guards (with weapons stolen from PLA arsenals and trains ferrying weapons across China from the Soviet Union to North Vietnam), and two unsuccessful attempts to restore order, in August 1968 the PLA was finally ordered by Mao to intervene and disarm the Red Guards. This time the army was successful. What this meant in practice was essentially nationwide martial law and military rule through 1974. Military dominance was reflected from the national level down to local levels. Trying to turn triumph out of tragedy, Mao convened the 9th Party Congress in April 1969 (the first Party congress in thirteen years). Mao and Minister of Defense Lin Biao presided, and the PLA was much in evidence: fully 50 percent of the new Central Committee and 14 of 28 full Politburo members were active-duty military. Throughout the system the military was in control.

The Long Transition to the Post-Mao Era

With physical and political order restored by the military, some semblance of stability was returned to the country. But it was tenuous and ephemeral. Beneath the new calm, the society remained profoundly traumatized. Families remained separated. Victims remained in prisons, labor camps, or under house arrest. The Party and state leadership remained decimated, while the radical faction around Mao's wife Jiang Qing wielded power. All hell had broken loose for three years, and it was going to take a long time to heal and restore functionality to both state and society. Eventually, following Mao's death, the CCP issued a document in 1982, *On Certain Questions in Our Party's History*, which addressed the entire Maoist era and the multiple "mistakes" made. Concerning the Cultural Revolution, the Resolution said the following:[125]

> The history of the "Cultural Revolution" has proved that Comrade Mao Zedong's principal theses for initiating this revolution conformed neither to Marxism, Leninism nor to Chinese reality. They represent an entirely erroneous appraisal of the prevailing class relations and political situation in the Party and state. . . . The "Cultural Revolution" negated many of the correct principles, policies and achievements of the seventeen years after the founding of the People's Republic. In fact, it negated much of the work of the Central Committee of the Party and the People's Government, including Comrade Mao Zedong's own contribution. It negated the arduous struggles the entire people had conducted in socialist construction.
>
> The confusing of right and wrong inevitably led to confusing the people with the enemy. The "capitalist-roaders" overthrown in the "Cultural Revolution" were leading cadres of Party and government organizations at all levels, who formed the core force of the socialist cause. The so-called "bourgeois headquarters" inside the Party headed by Liu Shaoqi and Deng Xiaoping simply did not exist. . . . The criticism of the so-called reactionary academic authorities in the "Cultural Revolution" during which many capable and accomplished intellectuals were attacked and persecuted also badly muddled up the distinction between the people and the enemy. . . . Practice has shown that the "Cultural Revolution" did not in fact constitute a revolution or social progress in any sense, nor could it possibly have done so. It was we and not the enemy at all who were thrown into disorder by the "Cultural Revolution". . . . Chief responsibility for the grave "Left" error of the "Cultural Revolution," an error comprehensive in magnitude and protracted in duration, does indeed lie with Comrade Mao Zedong. But after all it was the error of a great proletarian revolutionary. . . . In his later years, however, far from making a correct analysis of many problems, he confused right and wrong and the people with the enemy during the "Cultural Revolution."

The Early 1970s: The Lin Biao Affair, Opening to the West, and Reemergence of Factionalism

Marshal and Defense Minister Lin Biao emerged from the 9th Party Congress as Mao's designated successor and Vice-Chairman of the CCP. All of Lin's sycophancy had paid off. With the PLA now in charge of the country, it made some sense to elevate the commander of the military to the No. 2 position in the Party as well. Otherwise he had little to qualify himself for the honorific position—as Lin was a gaunt, bald, paranoid individual who was afraid of daylight, was heavily medicated, and lived in his darkened residence in western Beijing (Maojiawan,毛家湾) with the curtains drawn.[126] Maojiawan was connected to the Zhongnanhai leadership compound, the Great Hall of the People, and the Western Hills military complex by underground tunnels large enough to drive trucks through (as Lin was uncomfortable in natural light, that is how he mainly got around the city).

Seventeen months later, however, Lin was dead. He was killed along with his wife, son, and several senior military officers in a plane crash in the outer Mongolian tundra as a result of one of the most bizarre events (among many) of the entire Maoist era.[127] The plane (a British Trident) crashed when it ran out of fuel apparently en route to the Soviet Union, following an alleged failed assassination attempt against Mao! That's right: the No. 2 leader and designated successor-in-waiting had allegedly tried to kill the No. 1 leader, allegedly because he feared that time was not on his side and Mao would never permit a peaceful transfer of power.

The apparent plot was allegedly hatched by Lin, his wife Ye Qun, his son Lin Liguo, and a small group of leftist officers in the air force and navy. The alleged plan was for affiliated military units to blow up the Chairman's train as it crossed the Yangzi River near Nanjing. But Mao reportedly had caught wind of the plotters' plan and abruptly changed his travel route, bypassing Nanjing and returning directly from Shanghai to Beijing. The coup plotters, meanwhile, were holed up at the Beidaihe beach resort—awaiting word of the successful execution of the assassination. Instead, Lin's daughter Lin Liheng (a.k.a. *Doudou*, or bean curd) tipped off the Central Guards Unit, which in turn alerted Premier Zhou Enlai on the evening of September 12, 1971. Zhou immediately issued a nationwide grounding of all aircraft (civilian and military) and specifically called the control tower at the Shanhaiguan military airfield (which served Beidaihe) not to permit any aircraft to depart. Zhou then went to the Chairman's quarters in the Zhongnanhai around midnight to alert him to the situation. A half hour later, at 00:32 a.m., the Trident hastily took off, but without time to fuel up. Lin Biao, his wife, son, and six others were on board. Now together in his living quarters, Zhou Enlai asked Mao for his orders. Should the aircraft be intercepted and shot down? According to Chinese sources, Mao replied philosophically: "Rain has to fall, women have to marry, these things are immutable; let them go."[128]

The plane's flight path was due north toward Mongolia and the Soviet Union. It did not have enough fuel to head south to Guangzhou, where Lin's co-conspirators were apparently waiting to set up a rival regime. Flying east toward Taiwan, South Korea, or Japan (all American allies at the time) was not an option, as the plane was susceptible to being shot down without clearance to enter the airspace of China's adversaries. There was probably enough fuel to reach North Korea, but then what? North Korea was China's ally and would likely arrest the escapees and return them to China. So the aircraft headed due north toward the Soviet Union and Soviet satellite state, the Mongolian People's Republic. But this option makes even less rational sense, as the USSR was China's erstwhile enemy at this juncture, having just fought a border war two years earlier. The calculations of Lin Biao and the pilot will never be known. What is known is that the aircraft ran out of fuel and fell from the sky onto the Mongolian desert near Undur Khan at 2:30 a.m., killing eight men and one woman (Lin's wife Ye Qun) on board. Soviet military forces tracked the aircraft on radar and were the first to reach the crash site within a few hours. The remains of Lin (who had previously visited the Soviet Union on several occasions for medical treatment) were sent to Moscow so that his dental records could be checked for confirmation. So ended one of the most bizarre incidents in PRC history,[129] and another one of Mao's many victims.

Just two months prior to Lin Biao's demise, Mao took another of his huge initiatives: the opening to the United States. We now know in retrospect that Lin opposed the opening—which perhaps was one reason why Mao came to suspect him of disloyalty during the summer of 1971. At any rate, after two years of oblique mutual signaling between the Chinese side and the Nixon administration, President Nixon's special personal envoy, National Security Advisor Henry Kissinger, paid a secret visit to Beijing on July 9–11. This and subsequent (non-secret) visits by Kissinger paved the way for the famous visit by President Nixon in February 1972, which became known as "the week that changed the world."[130] When Mao first met Nixon in his private residence in the Zhongnanhai, Nixon tried to flatter the Chairman, which Mao returned with false modesty of his own: [131]

> President Nixon: The Chairman's writings moved a nation and have changed the world.
>
> Chairman Mao: I haven't been able to change it. I've only been able to change a few places in the vicinity of Beijing.

The Sino-American *rapprochement* is another historical event that is extremely well chronicled.[132] The animating impetus was the mutual threat felt from Moscow by both China and the United States. For China's part, following the Soviet invasion of Czechoslovakia in 1968 and the Sino-Soviet border clashes of 1969, Mao had become extremely concerned (and with good cause) that the Soviet Union was conceivably contemplating a military invasion of and/or nuclear attack on China. So concerned was Mao that, at the height of the Cultural Revolution, he nonetheless instructed four PLA Marshals (Chen Yi, Ye Jianying, Xu Xiangqian, and Nie Rongzhen) to undertake a careful assessment of China's national security threats. The Marshals delivered their report on July 11, 1969.[133] Their assessment led Mao and Zhou Enlai to conclude that the Soviet military threat to China was indeed dire, but the American threat less so, and therefore that there was some strategic utility in exploring whether Washington might be interested in forging a united front against their common enemy. The rest, as they say, is history.

Mao indeed micro-managed the delicate signaling of Beijing's possible interest over the next two years, despite dealing with the equally delicate post–Cultural Revolution domestic situation, the 9th Party Congress, and after September 1971 the fallout from the Lin Biao affair. But as Nixon's visit drew near, the Chairman was also experiencing increasingly declining health.[134] According to Mao's doctor Li Zhisui, Mao was increasingly experiencing the symptoms of congestive heart failure, a chronic lung infection, bronchitis and emphysema, edema and other manifestations of what would later be diagnosed in 1974 as Lou Gehrig's disease (amyotrophic lateral sclerosis, ALS). Just three weeks before Nixon's arrival Dr. Li thought that Mao was perhaps at death's door following an apparent stroke on top of these other maladies. In January 1972, just a month before Nixon's arrival, he could barely stand when attending Marshal Chen Yi's funeral and, according to eyewitnesses, told Premier Zhou Enlai, "I don't think I can make it. Everything depends on you now. . . . You take care of everything after my death. Let's say this is my Will."[135] But Mao insisted that Dr. Li make him better in order to receive Nixon. This required round-the-clock intensive administering of antibiotics and steroids to control his lung infection and edema, oxygen to help his breathing, acupuncture to stimulate his reflexes, and other therapies to cope with the increasing dysfunctionality of his motor skills. The treatments had produced positive results, although Mao's edema still made him bloated and he had lost strength in his legs and arms.[136] He needed help from nurses to stand, move, sit, and use the bathroom. Sleeping pills helped him sleep. Just prior to Nixon's arrival they gave Mao a shave and haircut—the first in more than five months—and propped him up (literally) in his overstuffed chair in the study adjacent to his bedroom. It all worked. Mao was able to meet Nixon and change the global strategic order.

Despite rallying to meet Nixon, Mao was clearly in physical and mental decline. As such, Mao deputized and authorized his loyal lifelong lieutenant Premier Zhou Enlai to try and put back the pieces of the party-state, stabilize the country, and work toward modernizing the economy. In order to do this Zhou needed help, lots of it. Beginning in 1972 he began to politically "rehabilitate" some of the purged "moderate" leaders. This included Deng Xiaoping, who had just spent five years working in a tractor factory in Jiangxi province. The process of bringing these former leaders and officials back from purgatory to Beijing was complicated and protracted. One principal reason is that Jiang Qing and her radical political allies (later to become known as the Gang of Four) saw this effort and these individuals, correctly, as a direct threat to their own political power, influence, and hopes of succeeding Mao upon his death. They used whatever means they could to frustrate and block Zhou Enlai's efforts. This included launching a campaign in 1974 to "Criticize Lin Biao and Confucius" (批林批孔), two unlikely bedfellows if there ever were.

The rehabilitation of previously purged leaders was necessitated by two main factors. First, like the aftermath to the Great Leap Forward, there was a need following the height of the Cultural Revolution to put the economy back on track. This required expertise and leaders who knew how to manage different spheres of policy. The second factor was that Zhou Enlai had himself been diagnosed with bladder cancer in May 1972. Zhou received treatments (including surgeries) and was in and out of the hospital over the next three and a half years. During the intervening three years Zhou did all he could to bring former leaders (those who had not been killed) back to power and put them in charge of the "four modernizations" program—modernization of agriculture, industry, science and technology, and national defense (in that order). From his rehabilitation in 1973 until he was purged again in the spring of 1976, Deng Xiaoping was deputized by Zhou and put in charge of overseeing the running of the government. However, Zhou's actions ran exactly contrary to the interests and policies of Mao's wife Jiang Qing and her radical allies in the leadership. As a result, during these years the leadership was bifurcated into two distinct contending factions: Zhou and the moderate "Cultural Revolution returnees" versus Jiang Qing and the radical "Cultural Revolution beneficiaries." This bifurcation resulted in never-ending political trench warfare between the two factions, who bitterly hated each other.

During this period Mao's health continued to deteriorate.[137] His degenerative ALS continued to progress—taking an increasing toll on the Chairman's nervous system and motor skills. The muscles of Mao's throat and larynx were noticeably affected, which made it increasingly difficult for him to speak. The syphilis had reached his brain. He also suffered one or two more strokes, which resulted in partial paralysis of his left side. Muscular atrophy affected use of both his arms and legs. As he had great difficulty swallowing, Mao sometimes had to be fed intravenously and was given oxygen on a regular basis. Mao's eyesight was also failing and he could not easily read (even with a magnifying glass). "In July 1974 we learned that Mao was going to die," Dr. Li recalled. "He could not see a finger in front of his face and could only tell light from dark." He was having increasing difficulty talking, his tongue didn't move, and he would often grunt in barely discernible words that seemingly only his nurse aide (and former lover) Zhang Yufeng could understand and render into intelligible Chinese. Despite his deteriorating condition, Mao did continue to meet with the occasional visiting foreign leader, but these were perfunctory and embarrassing encounters (including US President Gerald Ford in 1975). The state of the Chairman's health was certainly withheld from the public.

Under these conditions and at this juncture, an obscure Hunan official named Hua Guofeng began his bureaucratic ascent in Beijing; this would ultimately lead him to become Mao's successor. Mao had actually met Hua several years earlier when he visited his home prefecture of Xiangtan in Hunan province, where Hua was the Party secretary. Hua had been made a member of the Central Committee at the 9th Party Congress in 1969. In February 1971 Hua was unexpectedly catapulted up to Beijing and put to work primarily on agricultural and forestry policy in the State Council directly under Zhou Enlai. In 1973 he was selected as a member of the ruling Politburo. The next important step in Hua's elevation came at the January 1975 National People's Congress when he was appointed Vice-Premier of the State Council and simultaneously Minister of Public Security. In this former capacity Hua gained oversight over science and technology policy and began interacting with foreign delegations.

Hua's sudden climb through the ranks introduced an important third dynamic into high-level elite politics in Beijing at the time—as he was neither tied to the Gang of Four nor a rehabilitated Cultural Revolution cadre.[138] But he was tied to both Mao and to Zhou Enlai, which gave him political protection as well as some autonomy (particularly vis-à-vis the Gang of Four). Jiang Qing and her allies viewed Hua as a political threat to them and their (her) desire to succeed Mao, and they did try to undermine Hua during these years, while at the same time maneuvering against Deng Xiaoping and the rehabilitated moderates. This too is a very complicated period (1975–1976),[139] with both Zhou's and Mao's health simultaneously and rapidly deteriorating. Zhou finally succumbed to his cancer on January 8, 1976. Deeply revered, he was mourned by the whole nation.[140] With

Figure 2.8 Chairman Mao Anoints Hua Guofeng as His Successor
Source: World History Archive / Alamy

Zhou's passing there were four contenders for his position as Premier: Deng Xiaoping, Wang Hongwen and Zhang Chunqiao (Jiang Qing's associates), or Hua Guofeng. Mao chose Hua—or so it is alleged (Fig. 2.8).[141]

Hua was only given the title of Acting Premier, but this nevertheless strengthened his hand vis-à-vis Jiang Qing and her henchmen. Deng Xiaoping, meanwhile, was somewhat left in the lurch—although he did what Deng always did: get on with his practical work in the State Council. Even after Hua's appointment, Deng actually ran the apparatus of state . . . at least through April 1976. Then another twist in this long-running and confusing plot occurred.

April 4, 5, or 6 is the fifteenth day of the Spring Equinox and is commemorated in China as the annual Qingming festival, when Chinese honor the dead. This is always an occasion to visit gravesites, sweep the graves of ancestors, and to remember the deceased. But on this particular occasion, in the days leading up to April 5, 1976, there was a spontaneous mass outpouring of grief and commemoration in honor of Zhou Enlai around the Monument to the People's Heroes right in the middle of Tiananmen Square. The base of the monument was piled high with commemorative wreaths by the end of the day on April 4th. But when people returned to the square on April 5 all of the wreaths had disappeared! Overnight, on the orders of the Politburo, the wreaths had been removed by public security forces. Hua Guofeng was Minister of Public Security (PSB), but it remains unclear if he played a role in ordering the wreaths to be removed. What is now clear is that even though the order to do so had gone out in the name of the Politburo, many members had not actually participated in the meeting that took the decision. It was undertaken solely by Jiang Qing and her allies. By 4:00 a.m. the wreaths had been cleared and Wang Hongwen was seen in the square at 5:00 instructing PSB forces to deploy around the square. After daylight dawned, citizens began returning to the square on the actual day of Qingming. Finding that their wreaths and other commemorations around the Monument to the People's Heroes had all been removed, a spontaneous large-scale riot broke out. It went on all day, with citizen-demonstrators burning cars and filling the square.[142] By evening PSB units were reinforced by main force units of the PLA Beijing Garrison and the square was cleared completely by 21:45 p.m.[143] The Politburo met that evening and ruled that the "Tiananmen incident" of 1976 was a "counterrevolutionary riot." Two days later, on April 7, Mao ordered that Hua Guofeng should have his "acting" title removed and made full Premier, and perhaps just as importantly, Deng Xiaoping should be relieved of all of his positions for alleged complicity with the Tiananmen events.

Then three weeks later, on April 30, Mao reportedly met with Hua Guofeng in his residence.[144] On this occasion, Mao apparently famously told Hua, "With you in charge, I am at ease" (你办事,我放心), thus designating Hua as his successor.

The next jolt in the Maoist saga was a geologic one of mammoth proportions: on July 28 at 3:42 a.m. the ground of north China shook violently. An earthquake registering 7.6 on the Richter scale had erupted, with the epicenter in the city of Tangshan in Hebei province east of Beijing. Nearly a quarter of a million people were killed (242,000) and 164,000 were injured, with widespread damage for hundreds of miles around. Such natural disasters portend dynastic change in Chinese mythology and belief. The end of the Maoist era was coming.

Throughout the month of August 1976 Mao's condition was "precarious," in the words of Dr. Li: "He could only breathe lying on his left side, the tremors in his hands and feet were pronounced. His arrhythmia grew more severe."[145] On September 2 Mao suffered yet another heart attack, his third in three months. Finally, at 12:10 a.m. on September 9, in the words of Dr. Li, "Mao's heart stopped beating and the electrocardiograph went flat. The Chairman was dead."[146]

Mao may have physically died, but the Maoist era was not finished, and the struggle over his succession was not over. An argument among surviving leaders ensued over what to do with the Chairman's body before it was decided to embalm and preserve it, pending the construction of a memorial hall in the center of Tiananmen Square (with wax body double). Following a state funeral (see Fig. 2.9) and after almost a month of official

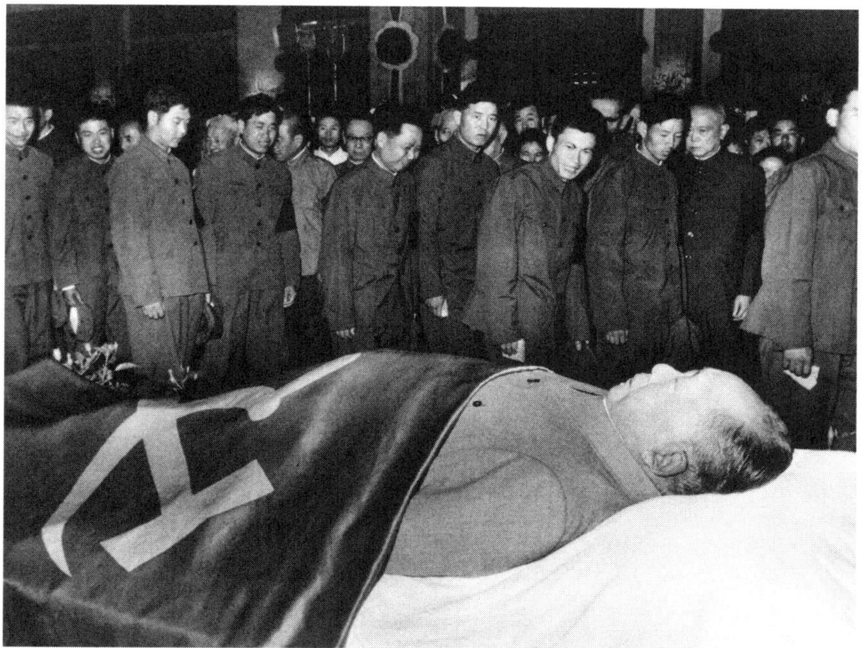

Figure 2.9 Mao Zedong Lying in State, September 1976
Source: Associated Press

mourning, during which there was intense factional maneuvering, on the orders of Hua Guofeng and Marshal Ye Jianying, in a lightning political strike, Mao's wife Jiang Qing and her three henchmen were taken into custody on October 6 by the Central Guards Unit 8341 detachment under the command of General Wang Dongxing.

Thus closed the era of Mao Zedong—but it opened the era of Deng Xiaoping, following the "interregnum" period of Hua Guofeng's tutelage. Mao's legacy is, of course, extremely complicated. He assumed multiple roles as China's leader. I reflect on them (and the other leaders covered in this book) in the concluding Chapter 7. Suffice it to merely note here, though, that Mao's greatest accomplishment was to unify the nation—but his greatest failure was to tear it apart.

CHAPTER 3

DENG XIAOPING (邓小平)

Pragmatic Leninist

"It doesn't matter whether the cat is black or white, as long as it catches mice."

—Deng Xiaoping, Speech to Communist Youth League, July 7, 1962[1]

IF MAO HAD AN INORDINATELY LARGE AND IMPORTANT IMPACT ON CHINA, so too did Deng Xiaoping. But it also can be said that Deng did more in his ten years in power to change China than Mao did in his nearly three decades of rule.[2] While Mao sought to transform the people of China, Deng allowed the people to transform China. Rather than stubbornly try to change 5,000 years of deeply entrenched beliefs and behaviors, as Mao did, Deng had the simple genius to tolerate and tap into ancient traditions to achieve modern ends. Deng's regime, which lasted for only a decade—from 1979 to 1989—tapped into the commercial entrepreneurship deep in the DNA of all Chinese. This alone unleashed bottled-up entrepreneurial activity across China's countryside and cities, stimulating the dramatic national economic boom that continues to this day and has made China into the world's second largest economy. But Deng's reforms, which transformed China, leading to what became known as its "second revolution,"[3] went far beyond the economy.

Mao bequeathed to Deng a totalitarian state characterized by highly personalized and concentrated power, an expansive and intrusive Leninist organizational apparatus that employed commandist, coercive, and

Figure 3.1 Deng Xiaoping (1904–1997)
Source: Keystone Press / Alamy

mobilization techniques of rule, with autarkic approaches to development and foreign affairs. The state under Mao was totalitarian and all-pervasive, playing multiple roles normally left to the private sector in most countries: employer, saver, investor, manager, economic planner, price setter, social provider, and redistributor of social and economic resources. All of these formerly totalistic functions performed by the Maoist state were fundamentally changed and decentralized under Deng Xiaoping.

Rather than try to suppress and eliminate various traditional religious and cultural practices in society, as Mao had done, Deng's regime permitted them. Rather than forcing people to live in Mao's communist collectives, Deng dismantled them and allowed private lease-holding of homes and land (thus private farming). Deng initiated private enterprise, private markets, and private space for individual life and expression. Although certain constraints continued, Deng restored the dignity and professional role of intellectuals in society, universities, and laboratories. In a society where the intelligentsia has traditionally been venerated, this was not unimportant. Deng also understood that intellectuals were critical to the overall modernization of the country, and he even indulged those intellectuals who were political critics.

I bore personal witness to the second revolution under Deng throughout the 1980s. I made my first visit to China in 1979, as part of a student-faculty group during my MA studies. Among other places we visited was Yanan, the historical revolutionary base area for the CCP during the 1930s and 1940s. In 1980 I returned for summer language study at Nankai University in Tianjin. The physical destruction left by the devastating 1976 Tangshan earthquake was still plainly evident in Tianjin (just 68 miles west of the epicenter), with building rubble a common sight and many people still living in makeshift outdoor dwellings. The other destruction that was still evident were pockmarks on buildings on Nankai's campus left over from Red Guards' dueling artillery battles twelve years before during the Cultural Revolution (a potent visual reminder of how violent the Cultural Revolution had been). I returned in 1981 on another delegation visit, traveling to a number of cities. In 1982 I went back for more language study, this time at Fudan University in Shanghai. The following two academic years (1983–1985) I was part of the official US scholarly exchange program with China, this time as a graduate student at Peking University (北大) carrying out my PhD dissertation research. These years were an extraordinary period, both in terms of the seesaw approach of Deng's reforms—in which advances in reforms were countered by conservative counterattacks (against what they perceived to be the dismantling of socialism)—but also in personal terms. I traveled all over the country by rail, visiting many provinces (including newly opened Tibet and Xinjiang), and rode my bicycle all over Beijing. I met a variety of intellectuals and officials, and even played on the university basketball team. I returned for short visits each year from 1986 to 1988, before returning in 1990–1991 for most of another sabbatical year (from the School of Oriental & African Studies in London, where I was then teaching) as a visiting scholar at the Chinese Academy of Social Sciences. This, of course, came in the aftermath of the June 4, 1989, Tiananmen massacre and, needless to say, the heady atmosphere that had prevailed throughout the 1980s had ground to a crashing halt. I could go on at some further length about my experiences and observations of these and subsequent years (I have visited China almost every year from 1979 through 2019), but that will have to await my memoirs. What I did bear witness to, though, was the awakening of an entire country and population that had been in a long Maoist slumber and a Cultural Revolution nightmare.

Deng was very much an institutionalist—he believed in running the country through institutions, beginning with the Communist Party. Yet, Deng also clearly understood that overly intrusive institutions were counterproductive to society's development and growth—and he thus rolled back the totalitarian dominance of the Maoist party-state and internal security services. One institution that Deng knew was in need of overhaul was the People's Liberation Army. Following the failed war that he unleashed on Vietnam in February 1979, Deng began the decades-long process (still ongoing) of streamlining, upgrading, and modernizing the armed forces. Other institutions in need of overhaul and rebuilding were the Party and government themselves—which had not only been decimated during the Cultural Revolution but had also become partially ossified institutions prior to 1966. Deng's decade of rule during the 1980s was really preoccupied with purging the Party and state of incompetence and inefficiencies, replacing older uneducated cadres with better-educated younger ones, reestablishing organs within each institution (CCP and State Council), and putting in place regularized procedures for decision- and policy-making. He also deconstructed Mao's cult of personality and one-man dictatorship by reestablishing a collegial and collective leadership system.

Deng also grasped geopolitics and understood the intricacies of world affairs. Unlike Mao, who never left China until he was 57 years old, Deng spent a decade abroad in France and the Soviet Union beginning in his late teens (Fig. 3.2).

Once in power in the late 1970s, Deng not only worked to forge a broad global coalition against the Soviet Union, but, beginning in 1983, he also initiated the process of *rapprochement* with Moscow after he deemed the Soviet threat to be waning (a perception strengthened with the rise of Mikhail Gorbachev). Most important, Deng was responsible for opening domestic China to the world—bringing traders, investors, students, teachers, and other expatriates into a previously insular and xenophobic country. It was

Figure 3.2 Deng Xiaoping in Montargis, France, 1920
Source: Historic Collection / Alamy

on Deng's watch that China established bilateral relations with many countries and began the process of integration into international multilateral institutions. There were other features of Deng's leadership style and rule, which I summarize in Chapter 7, but these were among the most notable ones.

Deng's Comeback and Power Play

Deng Xiaoping was in no immediate position to succeed Chairman Mao, as he was in political purgatory when the Chairman died, having been purged for the third time in his career. On April 7, 1976, two days after the uprising in Tiananmen over commemoration of Zhou Enlai, Deng was abruptly removed from all of his official positions (but was not expelled from the Party). Among other things, Deng was blamed for this alleged "counter-revolutionary incident." We now know, as discussed in Chapter 2, that it was principally the Gang of Four that manufactured this action in the name of Mao and the Central Committee. The degree to which Hua Guofeng was involved in the decision remains unclear, but it is unlikely that Deng's purge could have occurred without Hua's (perhaps) tacit assent. Getting rid of Deng had been a longstanding goal of the Gang, as he was one of the few senior leaders who commanded widespread respect among the Old Guard (who had all been victims of the Cultural Revolution) and had deep roots and strong support in the armed forces—and thus at a minimum could undermine the Gang's own play for power and, at a maximum, could make one himself.

Thus, the Gang succeeded in sidelining Deng in April 1976—and it would be fifteen months before he was reinstated and began his own campaign to undermine and replace Hua Guofeng as China's supreme leader. This interim period (1976–1980) is known in the China Studies field as the "Hua Guofeng interregnum." It was a transitional period in contemporary Chinese political history, between one momentous era and another. Deng's reinstatement and power play against Hua played out in several mini-phases, but collectively his seemingly independent moves revealed instead a master strategist and tactician (although Deng certainly had allies in the upper echelons of the Party and military who helped him in the cat-and-mouse game versus Hua). Throughout the next two years, before Hua was completely sidelined at the end of 1980, Deng used Hua's greatest vulnerability against him: Mao. Quite simply, everyone in the Party-army-state apparatus knew full well that Hua would not even be in the position of supreme power were it not for Mao's deathbed (supposed) anointment of him as successor. Moreover, Hua's rise was generally viewed as Mao's doing, as Hua hailed from Mao's home county. His sudden elevation from county Party secretary to State Council vice-premier was widely viewed as illegitimate, as was his rapid ascent to the Politburo. All of this gave Hua an air of illegitimacy in the eyes of established bureaucrats. Moreover, Hua had zero military background or bona fides with the PLA brass. Hua was also clearly a political beneficiary—rather than a casualty—of the Cultural Revolution, thus earning the enmity of all those who had suffered so greatly during the movement. Hua was also not viewed as terribly bright or politically astute.

But perhaps Hua's greatest vulnerability was his own total embrace of Mao and Maoism. Rather than trying to distance himself from Mao and the excesses of the Cultural Revolution, thus earning support from all those who had been casualties of the movement—and beginning to stake out his own policy agenda—Hua went all out to embrace Mao's mantle. Notwithstanding the Central Committee decision to entomb Mao in the middle of Tiananmen Square, the first thing Hua did was to authorize, only one month after Mao's death, the publication of Volume V of Mao's *Selected Works*—with himself as chairman of the editorial committee. He also permitted a widespread propaganda campaign repetitively publicizing Mao's (supposed) endorsement: "With you in charge, I am at ease." It seems that Hua initially questioned the idea of arresting the Gang of Four, before being convinced by Ye Jianying and Li Xiannian that it had to be done, because the Gang was intent on usurping his power too.[4] On October 26, 1976, Hua first mentioned his infamous "two whatevers" (两个方式) directive: "Whatever policy Chairman Mao decided upon, we shall resolutely defend; whatever directives Chairman Mao issued, we shall steadfastly obey." (This was reiterated more formally in a February 7, 1977 *People's Daily* editorial). Among all the other factors, this proved to be a real death knell for Hua, as well as for those other senior leaders who publicly endorsed it (thus becoming known as the "whatever faction" or the "wind faction": designating those who bent with the wind, without principle). Hua also began to establish his own cult of personality, emulating and embracing Mao: he let his crew-cut grow out, so that his hair was combed back like the Chairman, and he posed for a photo in a Mao tunic. The photos were framed and put up side-by-side in offices and schools nationwide. Hua also continued to refer to key radical Maoist concepts, as when he spoke of "continuing to grasp class struggle as the key link" in his speech inaugurating Mao's Memorial Hall in the center of Tiananmen Square on September 9, 1977. Finally, Hua gave a series of Great Leap Forward–style policy speeches in which he laid out dramatically overly ambitious economic targets. Perhaps the most elaborate of these came at the Fifth National People's Congress in March 1978, in which he said the Ten Year Plan (1976–1986) should nearly double grain output to 400 million metric tons per annum, triple steel output, quadruple oil production, and build 120 large-scale projects: ten iron and steel complexes, eight new coal mines, ten natural gas fields, nine non-ferrous metal complexes, thirty hydropower projects, six new long-distance rail lines, and five new harbors. Overall, the Ten Year Plan called for annual GDP growth of 8 percent and continued adherence to the Maoist policies of "Learn from Dazhai in Agriculture, Learn from Daqing in Industry." Hua's targets were considered grandiose, naïve, and an example of a continuing commitment to Maoist-style mobilization economics.

These were among Hua Guofeng's main self-inflicted mistakes and vulnerabilities—and Deng Xiaoping simply left Hua to self-isolate: by wrapping himself so tightly in Mao's mantle, making these tactical mistakes, and embracing the overly ambitious economic policy agenda. Thus, part of Deng's assault on Hua's position was simply to passively sit back and let Hua go further and further out on the limb of the dead Maoist tree, thus further and further exposing his unsuitability for the job, and thereby attracting internal criticisms, before ultimately self-destructing.

The other part of Deng's power play against Hua, however, was much more assertive. These actions included a series of calibrated steps during 1977. First, two of Deng's key supporters in the military, the commanders of the Nanjing and Guangzhou military regions (Xu Shiyou and Wei Guoqing, respectively), sent an unsolicited letter to "Chairman Hua Guofeng and the Party Center" on February 1, 1977, which was tantamount to insubordination. It criticized three things: the tendency to cover up the shortcomings of Chairman Mao; Hua's legitimacy as leader being based solely on Mao's deathbed anointment (which they argued only expressed Chairman Mao's personal opinion and not "the will of the Party, army, and whole people"); and the fact that incorrect verdicts on some cadres—notably Peng Dehuai and Deng Xiaoping—remained uncorrected. A month later an emergency work conference of central leaders was convened in Beijing, at which senior leaders Chen Yun, Li Xiannian, and Wang Zhen (in addition to the aforementioned generals) openly called for Deng's rehabilitation while denouncing Hua's "two whatevers."

These steps opened the door to Deng himself. Knowing that he had senior support and momentum on his side, and being the principled and stubborn individual that he was, Deng refused to kowtow to Hua. On April 10, 1977, Deng sent a letter to "Chairman Hua and the Party Center" in which he specifically criticized the "two whatevers" and went further to state: "We must guide the entire Party, army, and people with Mao Zedong Thought, which should be understood accurately and as an integral whole."[5] The Central Committee accepted Deng's letter and released it for circulation throughout the Party, thus laying the groundwork for his rehabilitation and reinstatement. This came in July 1977 at the Third Plenum of the Tenth Central Committee, which reinstated Deng to his former

Figure 3.3 Mao Zedong and Deng Xiaoping, 1959
Source: World History Archive / Alamy

positions, which had been stripped from him in April 1976: Vice-Premier of the State Council, CCP Vice-Chairman and Politburo Standing Committee member, and PLA Chief-of-Staff. Deng gave a short speech at the end of the session again calling for a "comprehensive view of Mao Zedong Thought" as well as resurrecting the 1930s Mao phrase to "seek truth from facts" (实事求是). This phrase subsequently became closely associated with Deng's pragmatism, even if it was originally Mao's idiom. Deng in fact had a close relationship with Mao dating from the 1930s, although Mao did purge him three times.

Deng was 72 when he returned to power—but he was a man in a hurry to change China. The job before him was both to undo the Maoist era while simultaneously launching the nation into a new era of "reform and opening" (改革与开放).

Following the 1977 Party Plenum Deng made his first public appearance: on July 30 the loudspeaker announced his presence, walking into the

Worker's Stadium for a China–Hong Kong soccer match, upon which he received a lengthy impromptu standing ovation from the crowd.[6] Two weeks later, Deng assumed center stage again, but in an understated manner, when the CCP convened its 11th Party Congress. Hua Guofeng, as Party leader, appropriately gave the main speech—which was filled with more Maoist platitudes and propaganda (including the "two whatevers") and included no fewer than 178 references to Mao! Altogether, Hua's oratory lasted seven hours. By contrast, Deng gave the closing address, which lasted a brief ten minutes, in which he pithily concluded: "We need more hard work and less empty talk." Touché! The contradictions between Hua and Deng were plain for all to see. Moreover, two days before the conclusion of the Congress, Deng met with visiting US Secretary of State Cyrus Vance—thus unmistakably signaling that relations with the United States, and foreign policy more generally, would now be run by Deng. Deng then met the Western press (another first) and criticized Vance's visit and proposals (essentially for a "two state solution" to the Taiwan issue) as a "step backwards." Deng may have been a pragmatist, but he also was a nationalist—who would not compromise on the "One China Principle."

The 11th Congress shifted the balance of power at the top of the system decisively against Hua Guofeng: a new Central Committee was elected (with a 30 percent decline in military representation from the previous one), as well as a new Politburo and its Standing Committee. In addition to Deng, veterans Ye Jianying and Li Xiannian were added to the PBSC, along with Deng protégé Hu Yaobang. The only Politburo members Hua Guofeng could count in his camp were former Mao bodyguard and Director of the CCP General Office General Wang Dongxing, Beijing Mayor Wu De, Beijing Military Region commander General Chen Xilian, and Minister of Agriculture Ji Denggui (who would all be removed from their positions by 1980 and were informally dubbed the "small gang of four").

Thus, Deng had quickly seized control of the very top decision-making body: the Politburo and its Standing Committee. He followed this up ten weeks later, on December 10, by maneuvering his loyal protégé Hu Yaobang into the important position of Director of the Central Committee Organization Department—*the* institution responsible for Party personnel assignments nationwide. In the CCP, control over personnel and the *nomenklatura* system is absolutely fundamental to its Leninist rule (as described in Chapter 1). If you control the cadres, you control the Party. Hu's appointment was presaged by a *People's Daily* editorial on October 7 calling for the widespread "reversal of false verdicts imposed upon cadres by the Gang of Four" (the editorial was written by theoreticians at the recently reestablished Central Party School, where Hu Yaobang was serving as Executive Vice-President). This set the stage for widespread sweeping "rehabilitations" of Cultural Revolution purge victims as well as "rightists" who had been suffering persecution ever since 1957. Hu's actions resulted in the rehabilitations of several million purged cadres, intellectuals, professionals, and alleged "rightists." Of course, many had perished in the intervening years, and all had endured psychological persecution, manual labor, and incarceration. There could not have been a single more important gesture for Deng to signal to the nation that the long, tormenting Maoist era was over and that the country would again be administered by experienced cadres rather than leftist ideologues and Cultural Revolution beneficiaries.

Having returned to power at the age of 72, Deng still had to tread carefully in managing relations with Hua Guofeng (Fig. 3.4).[7] He did this in two

Figure 3.4 Deng Xiaoping and Hua Guofeng, 1979
Source: Keystone Press / Alamy

ways. First, he did not publicly criticize Hua, and continued to allow him to retain certain (essentially ceremonial) roles.

The other way Deng maneuvered was to begin to push a policy agenda that was an alternative to Hua's neo-Maoism. For example, he gave a very important speech to the National Science Conference in March 1978, in which he spoke of science as a key "productive force" recognized by Marx (thus circumventing Mao and reaching back to Marx himself). He made an impassioned plea for the national development of science and technology as the "basis" of the "Four Modernizations." Perhaps most important, Deng said that all intellectuals were members of the working class: "Everyone who works, whether with his hands or with his brain, is part of the working people in a socialist society. Mental workers who serve socialism are part of the working people. . . . We must eradicate for good the pernicious influence of the Gang of Four and take up the major task of producing—as quickly as possible—experts in science and technology who are up to the highest international standards."[8] This was an extremely significant and lengthy (for Deng) speech—which clearly signaled a brand new approach to intellectuals, different from that which had been practiced by the CCP for the previous 23 years since the Hundred Flowers movement and the subsequent Anti-Rightist Campaign (which, ironically, Deng directed at Mao's behest). Deng did not explicitly apologize to the intelligentsia, but he did "salute" them in his landmark speech. He then reiterated many of the same themes to the National Education Conference the following month—making abundantly clear that in the "new China" knowledge and expertise were to be valued.

This was followed up by the publication of an article in multiple newspapers on May 10, 1978 entitled "Practice Is the Sole Criterion of Truth." The article was again written under the supervision of Deng protégé Hu Yaobang. This phrase was an oblique but fundamental statement that, henceforth, policy would not be deductively determined by ideology or by one man (Mao), but rather inductively through experimentation and actual practice. The publication kicked off a nationwide study campaign, which was promoted alongside Deng's other pragmatic aphorism to "seek truth from facts" (which he actually borrowed from Mao). But these were all tactical moves prior to Deng's real strategic strike.

This came in December 1978 with a pair of high-level leadership conferences: the Central Party Work Conference, which ran from November 10 through December 15, followed immediately by the Third Plenum of the Eleventh Central Committee (December 18–22). Together the meetings were a one–two punch. The first reframed the overall agenda of the CCP, while the second adopted and enacted a variety of key policy decisions. In CCP lore, but also in reality, the Third Plenum has the deserved reputation as the single most important meeting of the Chinese leadership in the post-Mao era.

The Central Party Work Conference fundamentally and officially shifted the overall focus of Party work from an amalgam of Maoist slogans and priorities to a singular mission of achieving "socialist modernization." The months preceding the meetings had seen a real shift in opinion, both within the leadership and among the citizens of Beijing. Throughout the year Hua Guofeng had been subject to considerable grumbling and increasing criticism among senior leaders for his stubborn clinging to the "two whatevers," delaying rehabilitations of purged cadres, and failing to reevaluate the 1976 Tiananmen incident.

Of even greater significance, beginning on October 1, wall posters began to spontaneously appear along Xidan Street in central-western Beijing (a popular commercial shopping district). Wall posters have a long and storied tradition in the modern political life of China. They accompanied the May Fourth Movement of 1919, the Hundred Flowers Movement of 1956, and the Cultural Revolution of 1966–1967. For the month of October there were not many posters, and they generally called for "liberating thought," "practice as the sole criterion of truth," and unshackling art and literature. Some people simply posted poems. Then in November the poster campaign experienced a sharp surge in quantity and became more pointed in their criticisms. Wu De, the Mayor of Beijing, came under personal attack for his role in the April 1976 Tiananmen incident—with others quickly calling for overturning the characterization of that event as "counterrevolutionary." Next came attacks on the "two whatevers"—a not-so-oblique criticism of Hua Guofeng. This then broadened into fuller critiques of the Mao era and Mao himself. On December 5, 1978, however, one wall poster was put up that distinguished itself from all the others. Written by an electrician at the

Beijing Zoo, Wei Jingsheng, this poster advocated a "fifth modernization": *democracy*. Wei's bold action stimulated many others—hence giving the movement the name "Democracy Wall."[9]

The critiques continued right through the two December leadership meetings and lasted until March 1979, when Deng finally ordered it closed down. Why? Why were the dissident posters not removed and the movement shut down earlier? Because the criticisms voiced directly served Deng's political purposes (criticism of Mao, the Cultural Revolution, and demands for greater freedoms) and they revealed that Hua alone did not have the power to put a stop to it. The spontaneous openness also gave Beijingers the first opportunity to vent their frustrations after years of trauma and persecution. This too served Deng's political purposes, as he was signaling that a new, more open era of expression had dawned. The posters also attracted the attention of the handful of Western journalists then resident in Beijing (mainly Australian, British, Canadian, and west European, as the United States and China did not yet enjoy diplomatic relations and hence no exchange of journalists) who reported on it worldwide. These were very heady days in Beijing, and there was a synergy between what was occurring on the streets (walls) and the leadership meetings taking place behind closed doors.

The Central Work Conference not only shifted the strategic focus of the CCP like a laser to economic transformation, and away from the primacy of politics that typified the Mao era; the 210 high-level participants also undertook a wide-ranging discussion of the very issues being critiqued in the wall posters outside. The political tide was definitely shifting against Hua Guofeng and in favor of Deng Xiaoping.

The Third Plenum was the pivot point which signaled that China was under new management and pursuing a new agenda. Hua Guofeng was not immediately deposed, but he was badly wounded politically and would continue to have his powers progressively stripped away over the next three years. A new leadership emerged from the Third Plenum: economic czar Chen Yun was added to the Politburo Standing Committee, while other Deng supporters—Hu Yaobang, Wang Zhen, and Deng Yingchao (Zhou Enlai's widow)—joined the Politburo. An obscure provincial official from Sichuan named Zhao Ziyang remained as an alternate member of the Politburo. Thus the leadership balance continued to tilt in Deng's direction.

In terms of policy decisions, the Third Plenum was nothing short of momentous.[10] In addition to reorienting the strategic program of the Party to "socialist modernization," it also opened the door to reexamining the past by explicitly critiquing the "two whatevers" and saying that "left mistakes" must be "comprehensively reviewed and corrected." It fundamentally shifted the approach in agriculture to the "household responsibility system," adopted performance-based incentives in industry, and recommended that economic administration and management be broadly "decentralized, rationalized, and reformed." Other priorities were made clear: it was advised that "advanced technologies and equipment from abroad should be introduced to China," and "great efforts to improve work in science and education should be made." The "rule of law" was to be followed, as well as the principles of "collective leadership," "democratic centralism," and "socialist democracy." In line with this, it was declared that there should be no "personality cults" (which Hua Guofeng was attempting to build, following Mao's) and that henceforth all leaders should simply be addressed as "comrade." Mao's "class struggle" was no longer to be the "key link" (to be replaced by the four modernizations), and the theory of "continuing the revolution under the dictatorship of the proletariat" was to be abandoned.[11] Unprecedentedly, Mao's "faults and mistakes" were to be further investigated and evaluated. The plenum nullified the "erroneous documents" concerning the 1976 Tiananmen incident, now declaring it a "revolutionary event." The plenum also approved the normalization of relations with the United States. These were among the main decisions taken (the Plenum communiqué indicates numerous other policy initiatives).[12]

While the Third Plenum was certainly a major turning point, Deng still had to contend with Hua Guofeng for another four years. He continued his piecemeal approach to undercutting Hua. Several steps were involved. Among the most important was the progressive stripping from Hua of his official positions. This process culminated when Deng appointed himself Chairman of the Central Military Commission in June 1981, thereby removing Hua Guofeng from his last remaining position. Prior to that, Deng maneuvered his protégés Hu Yaobang and Zhao Ziyang into the positions of General Secretary / Chairman of the CCP and Premier of the State Council, respectively.

Hu Yaobang

On December 25, 1978, three days after the conclusion of the Third Plenum, the institution of the CCP Secretariat and the position of General Secretary of the Party were recreated (both had been abolished during the Cultural Revolution). Deng himself had held this position in the mid-1950s, and later reflected in 1980 on its importance.[13] This was a job that made the gears of the Party apparatus turn on a daily basis. Deng's protégé Hu Yaobang was appointed to both positions. This directly infringed on Hua Guofeng's position as Party Chairman, and was Deng's first move to undermine—and then strip—Hua of his official positions.

As an uneducated peasant youth of Hakka descent (like Deng) born in Hunan, Hu left home to join the Communist Party at age 14. Like Deng, Hu was short in stature (5'1", while Deng was 4'11"). Both were veterans of the Long March (during which Hu was wounded) and years of fighting in the Red Army. Once the Long Marchers reached their sanctuary base in the rugged mountains and caves of Yanan in northern Shaanxi province, Deng became a young lecturer and Hu a student in the so-called Resistance University (抗大). Hu and Deng served together as political commissars in the Second Field Army that conquered Sichuan province in the closing days of the civil war. In fact, Hu was personally responsible for northern Sichuan and oversaw the conquest of Deng's native village of Guang'an.

After 1949 Hu served under Deng in Sichuan until both were promoted to Beijing at the same time in 1952. Thereafter, Hu's career was intertwined with Deng's. Hu served as head of the Communist Youth League from 1952 to 1966. Like Deng, he was attacked and purged during the Cultural Revolution—not once, but twice. In January 1967 Hu was denounced and purged for the first time and sent first to a "cow shed" to do manual labor and then to a May 7th Cadre School in Henan for more than four years.[14] Having fallen ill in 1971, Hu was moved back to Beijing for treatment. For three years he stayed at home convalescing, contemplating, but attending "reading classes." Beginning in 1973 he made a brief appearance at a memorial service, around the same time that Deng Xiaoping was rehabilitated from the tractor factory in Jiangxi. It is not clear, but quite likely, that Deng and Hu came in contact again during this period. Then, in mid-1975, Hu was rehabilitated and sent to work at the Chinese Academy of Sciences (CAS), which Deng was trying to resurrect, and he served there as Party secretary and Vice-President. In September 1975 Hu was responsible for the rehabilitation of thousands of researchers purged during previous campaigns. But when Deng himself was purged again in 1976, Hu and the CAS came under political attack by the Gang of Four and Hu lost his position and was hospitalized with depression, until Hua Guofeng appointed him as "Executive Vice President" of the Central Party School in March 1977.[15] Once Deng returned to power that summer, Hu became instrumental in fashioning Deng's "practice is the sole criterion of truth" campaign and other attempts to overturn Maoist dogma in CCP theoretical circles.

Hu was a very progressive and liberally minded individual, much revered by intellectuals. In December of that year, as noted above, Deng

Figure 3.5 Hu Yaobang (1915–1989)
Source: Associated Press

had Hu appointed as head of the CCP Organization Department. Thus it was not surprising that Deng should now similarly have him head up the newly resurrected CCP Secretariat as Secretary-General. In November 1980 Hu was put in charge of the routine work of the Politburo. Then in June 1981 Hu Yaobang was promoted to replace Hua Guofeng as CCP Chairman, taking away one of Hua's three positions. In September 1982 the position of Party Chairman was abolished altogether, making the General Secretary the top position in the CCP. Hu served in this position until he came under intense fire from conservative elder leaders following a series of pro-democracy demonstrations in December 1986, and was dismissed in January 1987 (although retaining his seat on the Politburo). It was Hu's sudden heart attack in a Politburo meeting and death on April 15, 1989 that triggered the unprecedented pro-democracy demonstrations in Beijing and many other cities across China, which culminated in the events on the night of June 3–4 when the PLA moved in and undertook the "Tiananmen massacre."

Zhao Ziyang

Deng's other protégé was a relatively obscure provincial official named Zhao Ziyang. In 1980 Zhao was the first Party secretary in charge of Sichuan province (a province with a population at the time of 97 million people). Deng had Zhao transferred there in 1975 from Guangdong province, where he was also Party secretary. A native of Henan province near Kaifeng, Zhao joined the anti-Japanese armed resistance in the Henan-Hebei-Shandong border region and became a CCP member at the age of 19 in 1938. From then on he had a wide range of experiences at the sub-provincial and provincial levels. My own first published book was a biography of Zhao's provincial career until the time he was promoted to Beijing and appointed as Premier of the State Council in 1980, succeeding Hua Guofeng.[16] I began the research while studying at Nankai University in Tianjin in 1980, where I had learned of the bold new economic reforms Zhao had been instituting in Sichuan, notably in the rural sector. They had been so successful that the peasants coined the pun/aphorism: "If you want to eat grain, look for Ziyang" (你要吃粮找紫阳). In fact, what Zhao had been implementing were

Figure 3.6 Zhao Ziyang (1919–2005)
Source: BNA Photographic / Alamy

the same agricultural reforms that Deng had introduced back in the early 1960s after the collapse of the Great Leap Forward.

While there is some circumstantial evidence that Deng and Zhao crossed paths during the later stages of the civil war against the Nationalists,[17] it is certain that Zhao and Deng interacted during the early 1960s, as Zhao was a zealous implementer of Deng's post-Great Leap rural reforms in Guangdong province. Prior to his assignment to Sichuan in 1975, Zhao had experienced a solid career in the Guangdong Party apparatus, becoming the youngest provincial Party secretary in China (at the age of 42) in 1961. Zhao served in this position before being toppled by the Cultural Revolution Red Guards in January 1967. On February 25 and again on October 16 of that year, together with several other overthrown provincial officials wearing dunce caps on their heads and placards around their necks, Zhao was paraded before 80,000 people for mass criticism sessions in the main city square in Guangzhou. Thereafter, he disappeared for three and a half years, until he resurfaced at the opposite end of the country last on a name list of Inner Mongolian provincial officials! Zhao had spent the intervening four-year period in Inner Mongolia working in a factory (although no specifics are known).

Having been one of the first wave of rehabilitated officials, on the order of Premier Zhou Enlai, Zhao was transferred back to Guangdong in March 1972. There he resumed his position as provincial first Party secretary, successfully navigating the interference of the Gang of Four, until Deng had him transferred to Sichuan in November 1975. Thereafter, Zhao began to gain national fame for the "Sichuan experience"—a collective term for a variety of material incentive-based reforms for both farmers and factory workers alike. In agriculture, Zhao introduced the so-called household responsibility system—which combined together the "three freedoms" (freedom to have private plots, freedom to grow "cash crops" and engage in private "sideline industries," establishing free rural markets) and "one contract" (each household contracted a specific amount of grain to deliver to the state, with any leftover surplus to be kept or sold by farmers). In industrial factories, Zhao introduced the wage bonus system and began to change the output criteria for state-owned enterprises to concentrate on meeting market demand and prioritizing quality over quantity of goods produced. In 1977 Zhao made a tour of Hungary, Romania, and Yugoslavia, where he learned about these methods.

Throughout his career agriculture had been Zhao's specialty—as it had been Hua Guofeng's—but Zhao practiced the complete opposite approach to Hua's emphasis on collectivized agriculture. Thus, when Zhao was selected to replace Hua as Premier in September 1980 (itself the second step in Deng's moves to strip Hua of his official positions) it was a clear signal to China's 800 million peasants that the era of socialist collective agriculture was ending. Also, in contrast to Hua, by the time Zhao replaced him he had developed a much broader policy portfolio—having worked on science policy, education, industrial management, foreign policy, Party rectification and recruitment, personnel management, trade unions, political-military relations, water conservancy, forestry, women's issues, youth, and ethnic groups.[18] Zhao Ziyang was very well suited to run the State Council and all of its multiple functional national responsibilities. Zhao became a national leader with his appointment as an alternate member of the Politburo in 1977, a full member in 1979, a vice-premier and then Premier in 1980, and a member of the powerful Politburo Standing Committee on 1982. In 1987, after Hu Yaobang's dismissal as CCP General Secretary, Zhao succeeded him in this top post until his own purge on the eve of the Tiananmen massacre in 1989 (after which he lived out his life under house arrest).

What Did Deng Inherit?

By 1979 the tide had turned. Deng was setting China on a new course. Over the next decade China would adopt "reform and opening" and experiment with a wide range of economic policies. In fact, the vast majority of these policies were *not new*—they had been presaged during the 1961–1965 post–Great Leap recovery period (see Chapter 2) when Deng, Chen Yun, Li Xiannian, Peng Zhen, and Liu Shaoqi were in charge. In some ways it was like reopening the file cabinet drawer, blowing off the dust, and saying "Now, where were we—before we were so rudely interrupted by the Cultural Revolution?" These reform policies in the 1960s, and again in the 1980s, were comprehensive in nature and very similar in content. They affected all policy areas: agriculture, industry, consumer production, science and technology, education, national defense, literature and the arts, the intelligentsia, finance, foreign trade, ethnic minorities, and many other reforms that had been short-circuited by the Cultural Revolution. But there were also many other new initiatives, like the creation of Special Economic Zones (SEZs), bonus systems, price reforms, and *political reform*. Deng did believe that some degree of political reform was necessary, but as an auxiliary facilitator of economic reform rather than an end in itself.[19] To put the significance of Deng's reforms in better context, consider several dimensions of the China that he inherited when he finally fully grabbed the reins of power in 1982.

Chinese society was thoroughly traumatized by the Cultural Revolution, but also by the wrenching impact of thirty years of Maoist social engineering. Unrelenting political campaigns had buffeted the nation one after another, producing a risk-averse citizenry who learned how to keep their heads down and feign compliance with the propaganda and campaign du jour. Moreover, people literally were not permitted to move around the country because of the draconian *hukou* household registration system, which only permitted people to live and work in the locality in which they were registered at birth. Such sequestration broke family lineages apart, even during the traditional New Year holiday when it is traditional practice to travel en masse by train to visit relatives at one's ancestral home. But in those days people were not permitted to even buy train tickets without specific letters of authorization from their work unit, and the *hukou* system was an added layer of control that made people prisoners of where they lived and worked. All urban citizens had been organized into *danwei* (work units), which were their only source of income, housing, schooling, primary healthcare, ration coupons for foodstuffs and cotton goods (clothing), and other staples of daily life. No one had private telephones, as they only existed in the *danwei* or in neighborhood "residence committees." Mao's idea behind the *danwei* was to give people an institutional rather than an individual identity, replacing the person with the collective.

In terms of consumption, all meat and grains were rationed, and there were few vegetables and little dietary diversity. Housing was extremely cramped, with families living on top of or with one another. The countryside was especially impoverished, with peasants living in truly primitive conditions. In 1978 average per capita consumption of grain was 196 kilos, 7.7 kilos of pork, 172 kilos of vegetables, and 19.1 feet of cotton. Out of 100 households only 34.5 possessed bicycles, 3.5 had sewing machines, 4.8 had wristwatches, 3 had radios, and none had televisions.[20] Possession of these consumer durables were considerably less in the countryside than in cities. Virtually all citizens had to use open-air latrines, and few cities had centralized sewer systems or sewage treatment facilities. Water was not potable. Household access to electricity was spotty and "brownouts" were common. Wages, already paltry, had been frozen since the outbreak of the Cultural Revolution in 1966, and there were no bonuses. China was, simply put, a very poor developing country. Given its size, China's GDP in 1978 still ranked tenth in the world ($147 billion), but its per capita income ranked 177th at only $156.[21] Even India's GDP scores were higher. China had the world's largest population but accounted only for 2 percent of global GDP and 1 percent of global trade. Even tiny Hong Kong accounted for a greater share of global trade than mainland China,[22] while Taiwan also had larger trade volume than the mainland.

For their part, China's intellectuals were profoundly traumatized from decades of brainwashing, professional persecution, personal torture, and one political campaign after another targeting them. Mao's wife Jiang Qing had labeled them the "stinking ninth category" of counterrevolutionaries (there were different categories in Mao's classification scheme).

Concerning the Communist Party itself, Deng inherited another traumatized institution and cohort of people. Those, like him, who had survived the attacks and persecution of the Cultural Revolution still bore emotional, psychological, and physical scars. The vast majority remained marooned in May 7th Cadre Schools, prisons, or under house arrest. Those who had joined the Party and benefitted from the Cultural Revolution still populated the majority of positions at the provincial and sub-provincial levels. At the national level, many ministerial positions were either vacant or occupied by "worker-peasant-soldier" individuals promoted between 1969 and 1976. The dilemma for Deng was how to get rid of these millions of Cultural Revolution beneficiaries who populated the Party and state apparatus. Even once the wholesale rehabilitation of purged cadres began after 1980, those who returned to work were very elderly and were not well educated in the first place. Here the question presented itself: how to retire the Old Guard, while still maintaining their loyalty and drawing on their experience and expertise? The twin pincers of low educational training and an aging cadre workforce presented a real dilemma for Deng. His answer: reopen and ramp-up domestic universities as rapidly as possible while dispatching millions of students for overseas study and training.

There were other problems in the Party that went beyond personnel. One concern was ideology—a fundamental element for all Marxist-Leninist parties. The problems were that the CCP's ideology had become dominated by "Mao Zedong Thought" and, relatedly, it had become excessively dogmatic. Deng believed in the pragmatic flexibility of ideology as much as he did in the flexibility of policies—in fact, without a flexible ideology China could not adopt flexible policies (and vice versa). One preceded the other. In short, without a wholesale jettisoning of the Marxist-Leninist-Maoist canon, what Deng did was to essentially reverse the relationship between ideology and policy—instead of deductively determining policy from ideology (as had been the case under Mao), now policy decisions were to be made on their own empirical and pragmatic merits inductively ("seek truth from facts" and "practice is the sole criterion of truth") but then *rationalized* in a *post-hoc* manner ideologically. Ideology thus became an after-the-fact justification rather than determining policy in the first place. It was a nifty move by Deng. And just to leave no doubt in people's minds that ideology was still important to Deng and the Party, in 1979 he proclaimed the "Four Cardinal Principles," which were not to be questioned or challenged:

1. The principle of upholding the socialist path.
2. The principle of upholding the people's democratic dictatorship.
3. The principle of upholding the leadership of the Chinese Communist Party.
4. The principle of upholding Marxism-Leninism-Mao Zedong Thought.

These four principles are so broad and generic that they can be applied very selectively. That was the point.

Deng also inherited problems concerning the normative procedures and decision-making bodies of how the Party and government operated. There were several interrelated aspects here, which Deng outlined in his August 1980 speech "On the Reform of the System of Party and State Leadership."[23] The first was to replace a single-leader dominant system, based on a cult of personality, with a collective leadership that made decisions in a consensual fashion (even voting when necessary). Second, policy decisions that had previously been based deductively on ideology were replaced by evidence and merit-based decision-making. Third, the top policy-making institutions had ceased to function normally. The Politburo and its Standing Committee met irregularly at best. The Leading Small Groups (领导小组), which oversaw a variety of functional policy arenas, had similarly been dissolved or had ceased to operate. Organs like the Central Secretariat had been dissolved during the Cultural Revolution. So, Deng quite naturally wanted to rebuild the Party apparatus—but more broadly he had in mind a Party that was *not all-pervasive*. Deng resented the totalitarian nature of Mao's China, which he blamed for the nation's backwardness, and instead he admired the "softer" types of authoritarianism then prevalent in East Asia (he particularly admired Singapore). This required "withdrawing" the CCP from its previous all-intrusive role in Chinese society, separating the Party's penetration and monopoly of government (党政分开), and reducing or eliminating the Party committee's decision-making monopoly within commercial enterprises.

Deng also inherited a bloated (a term he frequently used), inefficient, and technologically backward military. All of these tendencies were on full display during "Deng's War." In February 1979, on Deng's direct orders, an estimated 200,000 Chinese People's Liberation Army (PLA) forces crossed the border and attacked Vietnam from the north, proclaiming that China intended to "teach Vietnam a lesson." Deng deemed the "lesson" necessary for several reasons: Vietnam's (December 1978) incursion into Cambodia and Laos, Hanoi's apparent lack of gratitude for all of China's support during the war with America, Vietnam's treaty with Moscow and the deployment of Soviet naval forces to China's south, the persecution of ethnic Chinese in Vietnam, a disputed Sino-Vietnamese border, and armed border clashes that Beijing claimed were incursions into Chinese territory. For all of these supposed reasons, Deng unleashed his ire by attacking Vietnam (hypocritically dubbed a "self-defense counterattack" by China). After three weeks of fighting, in which Chinese forces bogged down and were beaten back by 70,000 battle-hardened Vietnamese troops before they finally seized the border village of Long San, Deng proclaimed "victory" and withdrew. The brief border war was a military humiliation for China. If anyone was "taught a lesson" it was the PLA—which demonstrated general incompetence, lack of coordination, no air cover, disrupted logistics supply lines, and no interoperability. Chinese forces endured heavy losses (perhaps as many as 25,000 killed in action and 40,000 casualties).[24] While the campaign was a military failure, China maintained a large contingent of troops on the Vietnamese border for the next decade, attempting to "bleed" Vietnam's occupation of Cambodia by forcing the Vietnamese to maintain its own large deployment of troops there.

As importantly, for Deng and the PLA it kicked off a four-decade-long military modernization program that is now coming to fruition. Cynics argue that Deng sent his troops into harm's way knowing full well their incompetence, and thereby making a vivid example of the PLA as "lazy and bloated," bearing out his previous criticism. In fact, in the wake of the Vietnam fiasco, Deng came as close to indicting the PLA for its failures as possible in a speech on March 12, 1980, pointedly entitled "Streamline the Military and Raise its Effectiveness."[25] In it Deng called for four things: reducing "bloatedness"; reforming structure; improving training; and strengthening political and ideological work. These were the lessons learned by Deng from the PLA's attempt to teach Vietnam a lesson. This catalyzed the lengthy process of modernizing China's military.[26]

In terms of the Chinese economy, Deng inherited a series of problems. In agriculture, how to increase grain output and how to achieve sustained improvements in land productivity? How to diversify diets and increase the production of vegetables, fruits, and meat? How to overcome disguised unemployment? In industry, how to improve the *quality* of heavy industrial output? How to increase the production of consumer durables and light industry in general (given the years of low and stagnant living standards)? In both heavy and light industry, how to improve the quality of labor, automation, and hence output? What role should material incentives play? What was the appropriate role to give to enterprise managers in determining production goals? How to stimulate industrial growth in the interior of the country, and thus rectify the coastal–inland imbalance? How to overcome bottlenecks in the transportation system? How to diversify energy supplies away from coal and ensure delivery to factories and cities? How to broaden foreign trade, and how to decide whether or not to accept foreign investment and aid?

Finally, in terms of foreign policy, Deng faced several dilemmas. How to deter the Soviet Union from attacking China (still a distinct conventional possibility, although the nuclear threat had receded after 1969), how to constrain Moscow's overseas adventurism in Africa, its new alliance with Vietnam, and support for client states elsewhere? Concerning relations with the United States, when Deng returned to power in 1977, normalization of diplomatic ties still needed to be finalized—which Deng personally saw through to completion on January 1, 1979, and consummated with a personal visit to the United States (when I had the opportunity to meet him). Although the PRC had regained China's seat in the United Nations in 1971, it

Figure 3.7 Deng Xiaoping Addresses United Nations, 1974
Source: UN Photo / Yutaka Nagata

still remained outside of most multilateral international institutions (including the World Bank and International Monetary Fund). Deng had addressed the UN in 1974 (Fig. 3.7) and had a positive view of what these multilateral organizations could contribute to China's modernization.

China also still lacked diplomatic ties with a number of nations, and Beijing had to overcome the reputation it earned under Mao for being a disruptive revolutionary power. Without ties to the advanced economies of the world, one of the key planks of Deng's modernization strategy would be hamstrung—he needed the investment from, trade with, exports to, and scientific and educational exchanges among these countries. Hong Kong, Macao, and Taiwan all also remained outside of Beijing's control. Thus, the array of foreign policy and national security challenges that Deng faced were significant.

Taken together, this is what Deng Xiaoping inherited and faced when he returned to power in 1977 and after he had finally displaced Hua Guofeng by 1982. By this time Deng was 80 years old. He did not have the luxury of time and felt in a hurry to set China on its new course before, as he put it, he had to "go and meet Marx." But before Deng could turn to implementing his reforms he still had one other major barrier to overcome: how to handle the legacy of Mao Zedong?

Deconstructing Maoism in Order to Reconstruct It

Deng's whole reform agenda first necessitated deconstructing Maoism and its more deleterious aspects. Not only did he have to initially contend with Hua Guofeng and the other perpetrators of dogmatic Maoism, but Deng himself was not prepared to jettison all of the Chairman's legacy. His goal was to strike a balance between preserving a positive legacy for Mao prior to 1957 and a negative one thereafter, without denouncing the Great Helmsman altogether. As he pointedly told the Italian journalist Oriana Fallaci in a 1980 interview: "We will not do to Chairman Mao what Khrushchev did to Stalin."[27]

The Trial of the Gang of Four. One principal way of selectively tearing down Mao was to put the Gang of Four on trial from November 1980 to January 1981.

At the show trial, before a panel of 35 judges, the defendants (but particularly Mao's reviled wife Jiang Qing) built their "defense" around the claim that they were simply carrying out Mao's directives. Shackled behind bars in the prisoner's dock, Jiang Qing frequently flew into rages and had to be restrained and forcibly removed from the courtroom. At one point she claimed, "I was the Chairman's dog—I bit whoever he asked me to bite" (我是主席的一条狗,主席要我咬谁就咬谁). The Gang was officially accused of "persecuting to death" 34,800 people and having "framed and persecuted" 729,511 others during the Cultural Revolution.[28] The trial's outcomes were of course predetermined. Wang Hongwen and Yao Wenyuan each received lengthy prison terms, while Jiang Qing and Zhang Chunqiao were both sentenced to death, with their sentences subsequently commuted to life in prison. In prison Jiang Qing was diagnosed with throat cancer and removed to a hospital in 1991. There, on May 14, she committed suicide by hanging herself in a bathroom. Much of the trial was broadcast live to the public,

Figure 3.8 Trial of the "Gang of Four," 1981
Source: Associated Press

drawing massive viewership. Its outcome did bring some degree of accountability and closure for all the destruction and misery the Gang had wrought on the country and the victims of the Cultural Revolution. For Deng, it was also due justice—but, for him, it was also a way to *disconnect* Mao from some of the excesses of the Cultural Revolution. This was finessed by distinguishing between "political errors" by Mao and "criminal offenses" by the Gang, a distinction Deng made in August 1980 in his interview with Oriana Fallaci. Although a very dubious distinction, at this juncture Deng tried to begin the process of trying to disentangle Mao the leader from the totality of his rule.

The Resolution on Certain Questions in Our Party's History. As important and definitive as it was, the trial of the Gang did not fully resolve the question of Mao's culpability and legacy. This was done by the CCP's specially commissioned *Resolution on Certain Questions in Our Party's History*, which was formally adopted at the Sixth Plenum of the 10th Party Congress in July 1981. Deng personally oversaw the writing of this document, which went through multiple drafts by a reported large team of some 4,000 leading Party cadres and theoreticians, and he frequently voiced his discontent with some of the early drafts (草案). On no fewer than nine separate occasions from March 1980 through June 1981, Deng provided his detailed input.[29] In his comments, for example he said: "First, affirmation of the historical role of Comrade Mao Zedong and [explanation of the necessity] to uphold and develop Mao Zedong Thought. This is the most essential point." At another point he noted: "Generally speaking, Comrade Mao Zedong's leadership was correct before 1957, but he made more and more mistakes after the Anti-Rightist struggle of that year." Concerning these mistakes, Deng included "excesses" of the Anti-Rightist Movement, the Great Leap Forward, the Lushan Plenum, and the Cultural Revolution, concluding that: "Comrade Mao Zedong bore chief responsibility for them." Yet elsewhere Deng noted: "Although Comrade Mao Zedong made mistakes, after all they are the mistakes of a great revolutionary, a great Marxist." Elsewhere in his comments on the drafts, Deng gave his case-by-case evaluation of many events, denouncing the erroneous judgments against Peng Dehuai and Liu Shaoqi. He also affirmed that previous judgments about intra-Party conspiracies by Gao Gang and Rao Shushi, Lin Biao, and the Gang of Four were correct. Deng himself took credit for exposing the Gao Gang escapade. Interestingly, he did not judge the 1957 Anti-Rightist Campaign to have been an error (probably because that would have involved his own role in running it). Deng argued: "There was indeed a force—a trend of thought—in the country that was bourgeois in nature and opposed socialism. It was imperative to counter this trend. . . . Our mistake lay in broadening the scope of the struggle." Who would have been responsible for that? Decidedly Deng himself. Curiously, Deng's comments on the *Resolution* drafts said not a word about the Hundred Flowers movement. Yet, overall, Deng concluded: "In a word, the 17 years following the founding of the People's Republic, our work was basically correct, although there were some setbacks and mistakes." So there was some ambiguity in Deng's views as he commented on various drafts. But Deng's personal investment of time and effort reflected the importance of the issues at stake for the CCP's credibility and legitimacy, how to treat Mao's overall legacy, and how to understand the events of the previous thirty years. As George Orwell aptly observed in his novel *1984*,

"Who controls the past controls the future, who controls the present controls the past." Deng clearly understood that authoring a definitive narrative of the past Maoist era was a key to shaping the future of the Party and the nation.

The *Resolution* was finally concluded and adopted at the Sixth Plenum of the Eleventh Central Committee on June 27, 1981.[30] The document covered the entire history of the CCP from its founding in 1921 through 1979. It was filled with predictable praise of struggle and heroism during the pre-1949 period. Concerning Mao's role, it summed up:

> Our Party and people would have had to grope in the dark much longer had it not been for Comrade Mao Zedong, who more than once rescued the Chinese revolution from grave danger, and for the Central Committee of the Party which was headed by him and which charted the firm, correct political course for the whole Party, the whole people and the people's army. Just as the Communist Party of China is recognized as the central force leading the entire people forward, so Comrade Mao Zedong is recognized as the great leader of the Chinese Communist Party and the whole Chinese people, and Mao Zedong Thought, which came into being through the collective struggle of the Party and the people, is recognized as the guiding ideology of the Party.

It then judged:

> Before the "cultural revolution" there were mistakes of enlarging the scope of class struggle and of impetuosity and rashness in economic construction. Later, there was the comprehensive, long-drawn-out and grave blunder of the "cultural revolution." All these errors prevented us from scoring the greater achievements of which we should have been capable. It is impermissible to overlook or whitewash mistakes, which in itself would be a mistake and would give rise to more and worse mistakes. But after all, our achievements in the past thirty-two years are the main thing.

Mao is then found to be "chiefly responsible" for errors during the 1957–1965 period, but blame was also to be shouldered by the collective Central

Committee. When it came to the Cultural Revolution (1966–1976) the *Resolution* was predictably lengthy, scathing, and laid the blame squarely on Mao: "History has shown that the 'cultural revolution' initiated by a leader laboring under a misapprehension and capitalized on by counterrevolutionary cliques, led to domestic turmoil and brought catastrophe to the Party, the state and the whole people. . . . Chief responsibility for the grave 'left' error of the 'cultural revolution,' an error comprehensive in magnitude and protracted in duration, does indeed lie with Comrade Mao Zedong. But after all it was the error of a great proletarian revolutionary."

The lengthy *Resolution* went into a great number of other subjects, running to over 30,000 characters in length. These included the need to redress the wrongs done to incorrectly purged and persecuted cadres (even if posthumously). At the end of the day, though, it sought to strike a delicate balance on Mao, arguing, "Comrade Mao Zedong was a great Marxist and a great proletarian revolutionary, strategist and theorist. It is true that he made gross mistakes during the 'cultural revolution,' but if we judge his activities as a whole, his contributions to the Chinese revolution far outweigh his mistakes. His merits are primary and his errors secondary." On this basis, the document applied a mathematical formula of Mao's place in CCP and PRC history: *70 percent correct, 30 percent wrong*. Despite his "serious leftist errors" (严重的左倾错误), Mao was deemed to have been a great revolutionary, nationalist, and modernizer. Many others (including this observer) would argue that the *Resolution* had the percentages backward.

With the twin events of the trial of the Gang of Four and the *Resolution* on Party history, Deng was able to tackle head-on the residual hangovers of the Cultural Revolution and the Maoist era. This permitted Deng and the Party leadership to look ahead and move ahead.

Implementing Reforms

Faced with such a plethora of complex challenges, Deng would probably have preferred to sequence his reforms. Trying to do everything at one time is usually a recipe for failure. Yet Deng really had no choice but to proceed on multiple reform fronts simultaneously. He also saw an interconnectedness among reforms—notably reform of the economic system and reform of the political system. "If we do not institute a reform of our political structure, it will be difficult to carry out the reform of our economic structure," Deng noted in 1986.[31] As early as 1980 he observed: "Some of our current systems and institutions in the Party and state are plagued by problems which seriously impede the full realization of the superiority of socialism. Unless they are conscientiously reformed, we can hardly expect to meet the urgent needs of modernization and we are liable to become seriously alienated from the masses."[32] Another interconnection Deng found to be fundamental was the development of science and technology talent, the higher educational system, the elimination of ideological dogma, and long-term modernization. Reading through his speeches during the 1978–1982 period in particular, Deng repeatedly emphasizes the importance and imperative of these themes. Reflecting its priority, only two weeks after his rehabilitation in July 1977 Deng convened a forum of scientists and educators, to which he said: "I have volunteered to take charge of the work in science and education, and this has been approved by the Central Committee. China must catch up with the most advanced countries in the world. But how shall we go about it? I believe we have to begin by tackling science and education."[33]

As we will see, the simultaneous nature of Deng's reforms gave them a certain start–stop quality during the 1980s—as bold experiments were launched, both positive and negative results became apparent, and then recalibration was called for. This propensity became known in Chinese as the "*fang-shou* cycle" (放手周期), a recurring pattern of oscillation between reform and retrenchment. As described in Chapter 1 (Table 1.2), China experienced no fewer than six separate *fang-shou* cycles during the 1980s alone.[34] The way the term is used in China generally refers to *political and ideological orientation* and the tug-and-pull between the liberals and the conservatives in the Party leadership. But there was a second distinct *fang-shou* dynamic at work in the *economy*, whereby a cycle of experimentalism and expansion resulted in unanticipated errors, inflation, and overheating—which in turn resulted in a period of retrenchment and reevaluation before recalibrated reforms were renewed. This pattern was experienced with periods of excessively fast growth and overheating in 1982–1983, 1985–1986, and 1988—followed by brief periods of retrenchment and consolidation in 1984,

1987, and 1989–1991. Thus, the political and economic *fang-shou* cycles were not exactly the same, but they were similar. The conservatives in the leadership (notably Chen Yun, Wang Zhen, Yao Yilin, Yang Shangkun, Song Ping, Deng Liqun, Hu Qiaomu, and Li Peng) tended to hold similarly suspicious (if not hostile) views of political liberalization and pseudo-capitalist economic methods—and they constantly attempted to put the brakes on the attempts by liberal reformers (Zhao Ziyang, Hu Yaobang, Wan Li, Li Ruihuan, Xi Zhongxun, Hu Qili, Tian Jiyun, and Qiao Shi) to loosen controls over both politics and economics. Li Xiannian tended to straddle the two camps. For Deng Xiaoping's part, he too had to straddle both, although it seems clear that his personal inclinations tended to align with the liberals. However, since Deng was the paramount leader he had to restrain both of these two factions (especially the conservatives, who were his personal peers), and thus it is appropriate to think of Deng's leadership style as one of maintaining a *coalition* of contending factions. On various occasions, usually when tensions between the two became heated and a deadlock needed to be broken, Deng would tilt toward and weigh in on behalf of one or the other side, but then within a year or two he would throw his support back behind the opposite group. While his inclination was to support the liberal reformers, one of the most difficult parts of his rule was to restrain his own conservative contemporaries.

Another reality was that Deng could not orchestrate it all alone. Even if he had wanted to go it alone, knowing how to delegate was one of Deng's key leadership attributes. Zhao Ziyang (until mid-1989) and Hu Yaobang (until late-1986) were his right-hand men. Deng's leadership style was to orchestrate and oversee broad policy initiatives, but to delegate authority for turning broad directives into specific policies to others (notably Hu and Zhao), and then allow the institutional machinery of the Party and government to actually implement the policies. Thus, Deng belongs to that category of world leaders who are *macro* managers, not *micro* managers. This decision-making style was shaped during Deng's time in charge of the Central Secretariat in the mid-1950s. To head the Secretariat was an extraordinarily sensitive and powerful position. Information is an important source of power in a bureaucratic environment—and as the Secretariat was the bureaucratic nerve center of the Party, Deng had a monopoly on it. He had ultimate control over a number of functional departments of the Central Committee, including propaganda, organization, rural work, foreign trade, investigation (intelligence), and international liaison. This was a very powerful cluster of institutions for which Deng had overall responsibility, assisted by other members of the Secretariat and head of the staff office (Yang Shangkun). These were powerful individuals in their own right and each was assigned to oversee one of these functional bureaucratic systems (系统). Each thus served as the main bureaucratic decision point for that issue area (what the Chinese refer to as a bureaucratic "opening" or "mouth," 口). So this was Deng's model of effective administration, as he reflected in a speech to the Fifth Plenum of the Eleventh Central Committee in 1980 (which resurrected the Secretariat): "I think it is fair to say that the former Secretariat was quite efficient, partly because once the relevant decisions were made, specific tasks were assigned to particular persons, who were given broad powers and allowed to handle matters independently."[35]

This system suited Deng's own personal work style. He mainly worked from home, on Kuang Street nestled next to Beihai Lake. As described by the revered Harvard scholar Ezra Vogel in his definitive biography of Deng:[36]

> Deng kept a regular schedule. He ate breakfast at home at 8:00 a.m. and at 9:00 went into his office. Deng's wife, Zhou Lin, and [his executive secretary since 1952] Wang Ruilin prepared materials for him to read, including some fifteen daily newspapers, reference materials with translations from the foreign press, a large stack of reports from the ministries and from provincial Party secretaries, internal memoranda collected from the New China News Agency (Xinhua) and drafts of documents sent for his approval. For understanding the latest developments, Deng relied most on summaries prepared by the Party Secretariat or General Office. Deng took no notes when he read. Documents were to be delivered to his home office before 10:00 a.m., and he returned them the same day. . . . Deng's circle of approval and his comments on such documents constituted his way of guiding the overall work of the Party. On some documents, he simply gave final approval; other documents he sent back for more work, clarification, or with suggestions for new directions to explore. Deng rarely met visitors during his three hours of morning

> reading. . . . After lunch at home, he generally continued to read materials but sometimes would ask various officials to meet him in his home office. When important foreign visitors came, he would meet them in one of the rooms of the Great Hall of the People and sometimes dine with them.

Deng only infrequently met with others. He preferred to meet one-on-one or in small groups, although he would attend Party meetings when necessary (for which he was said to extensively prepare). Part of the reason for his relative reclusiveness was his deafness. Deng had a degenerative nerve disease known as *tinnitus*, which was inoperable and caused distracting ringing in the ears and led to complete deafness in his right ear (by the late 1980s his family and interpreters had to shout into his left ear).[37] Neither his responsibilities of running a country nor his age or deafness kept Deng from the two things he loved most: his family and playing bridge. Deng took great pleasure in his time at home with his wife, children, and grandchildren. On some evenings in his living room he would convene bridge games, for which he had a ferocious reputation. After retiring from all official duties in 1989, Deng's only remaining title was chairman of China's Bridge Association.

So how did Deng's reforms unfold during the 1980s? As most progressed simultaneously, even if experiencing the oscillating *"fang-shou"* quality noted above, the best way to understand them is to view them by category: economic reforms, social reforms, political reforms, and foreign policy reforms. Each had their sub-elements, and I will organize the discussion around these.

Economic Reforms

Deng's approach to economic reform and development, at its heart, involved two core elements: increasing efficiency and productivity and being flexible in forging a hybrid economic structure. As he said in a meeting with an American delegation in 1985: "There is no fundamental contradiction between socialism and a market economy. The problem is how to develop the productive forces more effectively. . . . If we combine a planned economy with a market economy, we shall be in a better position to liberate the productive forces and speed up economic growth."[38] This eclectic flexibility led to the creation of a hybrid economy that had several elements. For all of his impact on China's economy, Deng was by no means an economist and did not have a deep micro understanding of economics. His approach was more macro and instinctive, leaving the details to others.[39]

Coastal Development and Opening to the World. Deng's twin policies of "reform and opening" were intimately interrelated. Unlike Mao, who believed in economic autarky and self-reliance, Deng was an economic internationalist who believed that China's domestic economic development had to be tied to the country's opening to foreign trade, investment, and interaction. This extended to his thinking about sending massive numbers of students, scholars, and scientific researchers abroad for training, while also opening China's universities more broadly to foreign students, researchers, and teachers. Deng believed that borders should not be boundaries that sealed China off from the advantages of interaction with the outside world. This had a number of dimensions—specifically the creation of Special Economic Zones (SEZs), accepting foreign investment, accepting foreign aid, and dramatically expanding trade based on export-driven industries.

The novel creation of SEZs was the first initiative. They were to be enclaves to attract foreign investment, offering foreign companies a variety of special incentives, but they were also to be export-processing platforms. The first four zones were formally initiated on July 15, 1979 (Central Document No. 50) and included three in Guangdong province (Shenzhen, Shantou, Zhuhai) and Xiamen in Fujian province.

One of the key advocates of the zones was newly appointed Guangdong Party secretary Xi Zhongxun (the father of China's current leader Xi Jinping). Xi was Deng's contemporary and they had served together during the revolutionary war and during the 1950s and 1960s in Beijing. Like Deng, Xi had fallen afoul of Chairman Mao and had been purged in 1962, not regaining his freedom until early 1978 (he was incarcerated for much of this time, half of which was in solitary confinement). Xi was then immediately assigned to Guangdong. Having been cooped up for so long, Xi was said to be brimming with energy and resolve. He pondered why it was that Hong Kong, adjacent to Guangdong, was so modern but his province so backward? Xi immediately grasped Hong Kong's economic attributes as an *entrepôt*. Xi, together with Yang Shangkun, became an ardent advocate of creating SEZs, and found a very willing ally in Deng. From then on, Guangdong became the pacesetter of China's economic opening to the world. Subsequently, Hainan Island was designated a separate province and an additional SEZ, along with fourteen other coastal cities in 1984, and then beginning in 1985 five more provinces (Shandong, Liaoning, Fujian, Hebei, and Guangxi) and two mega-regions (the Pearl River delta and Yangzi River delta surrounding Shanghai) were given similar special status. Thus, coastal development which concentrated inbound foreign investment and outbound exports became a centerpiece of Deng's economic reform program. In February 1984 Deng toured the four southern SEZs and gave a glowing report of his approval upon his return to Beijing.[40]

Relatedly, Deng was also not averse to receiving aid and advice from abroad. His attitude was simple: if foreign countries and international institutions wished to provide assistance, then there was much for China to benefit from. Many individual nations—notably Australia, Canada, Britain, Japan, and west European states—all established bilateral aid programs, either in the form of free grants or long-term low-interest loans. These countries also invested enormous amounts (billions of dollars) into so-called "capacity training" to train Chinese professionals in a wide range of fields (the legal system, media, and civil society were particular priorities). The Asian Development Bank, International Monetary Fund, and especially the World Bank also became deeply involved. China quickly became the World Bank's largest recipient, and its co-sponsored projects extended into a wide range of areas. Higher education, poverty alleviation, agricultural upgrading, environmental protection, and management training were priority areas—and much of China's progress in these areas was catalyzed by World Bank projects. Deng also specifically drew on the expertise of foreign economists, as Julian Gewirtz's superb study details.[41]

Rural Reforms. Overhauling agriculture, transforming the laggard countryside, and tapping the potential of China's 800 million farmers was also a key reform priority. This area of reform was actually more straightforward. That is, while Deng and his colleagues had no real prior experience with opening China's economy internationally, they did have ample experience with rural reform (dating to the post–Great Leap reforms of 1961–1965). Zhao Ziyang and Wan Li in particular had been successfully decollectivizing and experimenting in Sichuan and Anhui provinces respectively, beginning in 1975. Their reforms, as noted above, were anchored on the "household responsibility system," which—as the name suggests—placed responsibility on each rural household rather than on the collective. During 1982–1983 the collectives were dismantled, and every household gained long-term leases on their land (from the state), which could now be passed down from generation to generation. Since land was still collectively owned it was not private ownership per se; it may be more accurate to consider these land plots as privately *managed,* as the term in Chinese suggests (自留地). But in other respects farmers were given unprecedented freedom of decision-making.[42] Farmers (peasants) themselves were now freed to grow whatever crops they wanted, including many non-grain "cash crops" (mainly fruits and vegetables) that could be sold on free markets for whatever price they could bring.

Just as important, farmers were permitted to engage in "sideline production" (副业生产)—a euphemism for producing handicrafts and other light industrial goods. Subsequently, the former commune and brigade enterprises—which had produced inputs for agriculture (such as chemical fertilizers, cement, implements)—would morph into township and village enterprises (乡镇企业 or TVEs) which transitioned to producing goods for domestic consumers and later foreign export. The growth of TVE employment was really remarkable (as shown in Fig. 3.9) and became a major contributing factor to the rapid growth in rural incomes and living conditions during these years—which shot up 2.5 times between 1978 and 1985 (from 133.6 RMB to 397.6 RMB per capita),[43] while gross value of TVE output skyrocketed from 49.31 bn RMB to 354.09 bn between 1978 and 1986.[44]

The combination of household sideline and TVE income, together with the leaseholds on land, contributed much to the boom in the building of new homes that I saw increasingly dot the countryside during the 1980s. It is worth contemplating what a dramatic transition it was for the majority of rural residents to go from living in mud structures, sleeping on cement *kangs*, not having indoor plumbing or sanitation, even electricity—to moving into

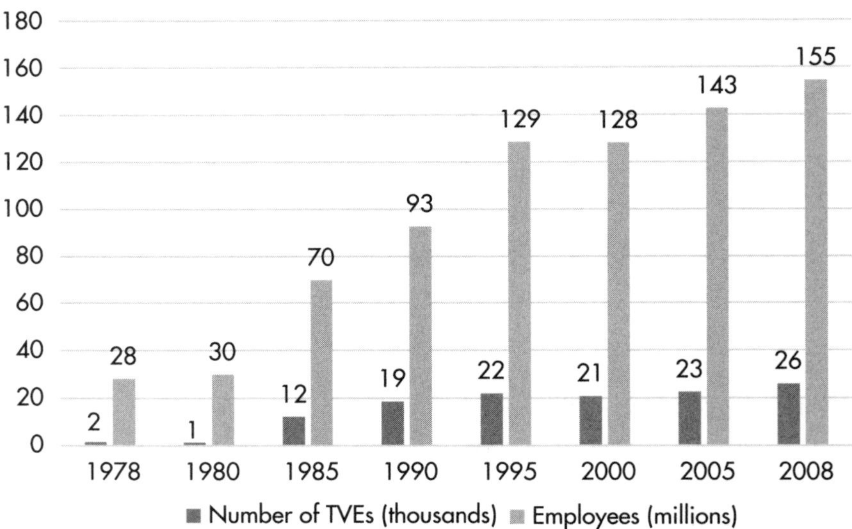

Figure 3.9 Growth of Township and Village Enterprises (TVEs), 1978–2008
Source: China, Ministry of Agriculture, *Xin Zhongguo Nongye Liushi Nian Tongji Ziliao* [New China's Agriculture – Sixty Years of Statistical Materials] (Beijing: Nongye chubanshe, 2009), pp. 47, 49.

new two- or three-level homes with running water, bathrooms, and multiple rooms.

All the rural households had to do in return for these "three freedoms" was to sign "one contract" with the state to grow and sell specified amounts of grains to the state; for which they were compensated by the state. In short order, Deng's rural reforms completely transformed the system of collective agriculture, land tenancy, rural markets, and produce prices. The result was an extraordinary explosion in rural production. The gross value of rural agricultural output doubled between 1978 and 1986 (from 139.7 bn to 401.3 bn RMB), with village industrial output growing sixfold during the same period (from 21.3 bn to 127.9 bn RMB).[45] Other measures show increased possession of consumer durables, although this did not rise as rapidly as in the cities.

Light Industry. Another emphasis of economic reform was to stimulate light industrial production to begin producing a variety of consumer durables.[46] Prior to Deng's reforms, very little was available to urban residents, and much less to rural ones. I recall visiting the main department stores in Beijing, Shanghai, Nanjing, Xian, and Guangzhou in 1979 and 1980; relatively little was available to customers and what was available was of low quality. There were *no* imported goods available for sale (except at the "Friendship Stores," with access only permitted to foreigners). I also vividly remember in 1980 seeing an enormous crowd in front of the No. 1 Department Store (第一百货公司) on Wangfujing Street in Beijing (the city's equivalent of Oxford Street in London or Fifth Avenue in New York)—when I got close enough to investigate I found that the crowd was attracted by a window display of imported washing machines (a first)! In those days all urban residents craved the "four rounds" (things that went around: a wristwatch, a bicycle, a sewing machine, and washing machine) and the "three electrics" (telephone, refrigerator, and television). By 1985, though, 48 percent of urban households owned a washing machine, 66.8 percent a black-and-white TV (18.8 percent had color sets), while 6.8 percent had refrigerators.[47] The acquisition of such items in the countryside did not really occur until the 1990s. Deng understood well how the country needed basic consumer durables, and how far behind advanced countries China had fallen in the area of light industrial production. The lag was largely a lingering consequence of the Soviet economic system that China imported during the 1950s, which emphasized heavy industry, but there had also been an ideological bias against producing such goods, as it reflected individualism and ostentatiousness in a socialist society. The Deng regime jettisoned this prejudice and began retooling factories to crank out consumer goods.

Heavy Industry and State Enterprise Reform. During these early reform years heavy industrial production declined relative to the newly prioritized light industry (Fig. 3.9):

Contributing to this was the low priority placed on military modernization, which was distinctly ranked as the lowest priority among the four modernizations. Deng specifically told the PLA and defense community that they came last and that a broad base of science and technology had to be laid first. In 1984, for example, Deng gave a pointed speech entitled

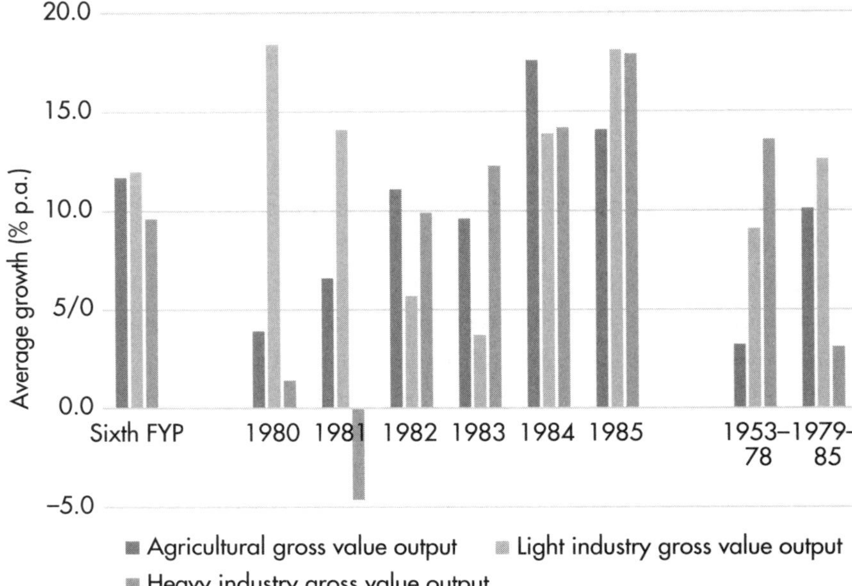

Figure 3.10 Average Annual Growth by Sector, 1980–1985
Source: National Bureau of Statistics, *Zhongguo Tongji Nianjian, 1980–1985*.

"The Army Should Subordinate Itself to the General Interest, Which Is to Develop the Country."[48] China's defense industries at that time were, in fact, a mess. The "third front" initiative launched by Mao in the mid-1960s (see discussion in Chapter 2) had overly dispersed military factories and, because they were located in isolated mountainous regions in Sichuan and western interior provinces (on the assumption they would be less vulnerable to attack by the US or USSR), it made the delivery of inputs logistically very difficult. Moreover, China had been cut off from any form of external military aid since 1960. The whole defense industrial system was very backward (with the notable exception of nuclear weapons and ballistic missiles, which had benefitted from scientists trained in the United States, Soviet assistance, priority funding, and political protection during the Cultural Revolution).[49]

But the problems with China's heavy industrial structure went well beyond the military-industrial complex. On the civilian industrial side, the Soviet Union's withdrawal in 1960 also contributed to laggard development and diversification of production. The *quality* of output was a more serious problem than the quantity. Owing to the command economic planning system inherited from the Soviets, industrial output was totally plan-driven (see discussion in Chapter 2). All that mattered was meeting the annual plan quotas. Thus, the real challenge was—in the well-chosen words of China economist Barry Naughton—to "grow out of the plan."[50]

To do so required *enterprise reform*: replacing the plan-driven system with one that responded to market signals (which, in turn, required markets to send signals), where supply reflected demand, where loss-producing enterprises were not subsidized by the state (at least less so), where profits were sought and retained by enterprises, where management decisions were made by managers rather than Party secretaries and were based on economic rationales, and where workers were incentivized by a piece-rate wage system and bonuses that were linked to enterprise and individual performance.[51] These capitalist reforms were all introduced to the industrial system throughout the 1980s. Deng approved these initiatives, but Premier Zhao Ziyang was the one who was bold enough to flesh them out and experiment with them. Zhao's flexible and hybrid view of economic development was captured well in a February 1981 speech: "Socialism means two things: public ownership of the means of production and paying each according to his work. As long as these two principles are safeguarded, we should feel free to adopt all those structures, systems, policies, and measures which can promote the development of production and not bind ourselves as silkworms do in cocoons."[52]

State-owned enterprises (SOEs), which dominated the economy prior to the reform era, also required a thorough overhaul. Yet, because they were the backbone of a socialist economy there was deep ideological opposition among Deng's conservative peers, such as Chen Yun and Deng Liqun. The other reason for protecting the 83,700 SOEs (1978) was because they employed over 74.5 million workers (constituting 78 percent of urban employment), whose families were completely dependent on them for wages, housing, healthcare, and their entire livelihoods. If they were laid off, it would catalyze hardships and possibly create significant urban unrest. Marxists do not need to be told of the revolutionary potential of a disenfranchised proletariat. The SOEs thus could not be done away with, but they

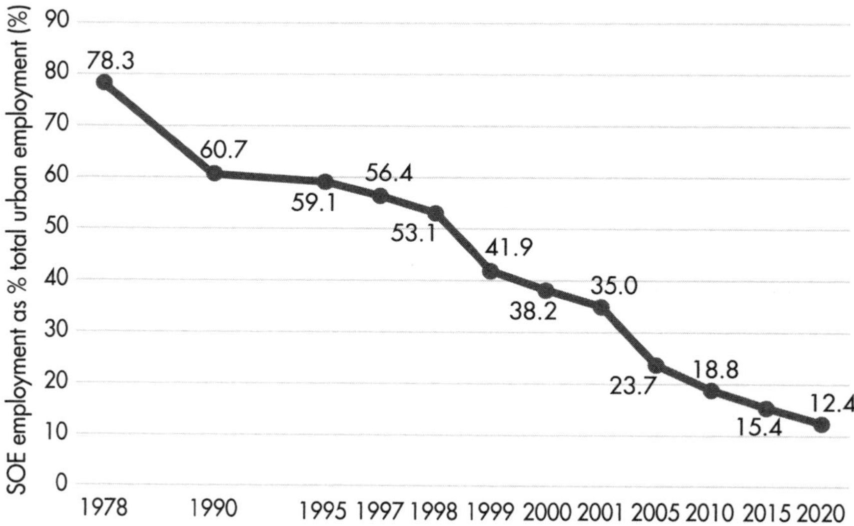

Figure 3.11 Restructuring of SOEs and Their Employment Impact
Source: China National Bureau of Statistics Annual Yearbooks, 1978–2019.

had to somehow be reformed. By 1995 they had come to employ 112 million workers (the peak) before declining steadily thereafter (Fig. 3.11). They were mired in "triangular debt"[53] and required approximately $50 billion in annual subsidies.

The decline began during the 1990s with a variety of experiments (mainly initiated under Premier Zhu Rongji) to make the SOEs less of a drag on the economy and more efficient. A modest number were permitted to go bankrupt. Another reform method was to retrain workers to enter the service sector. But the main method was one of mergers (合并) whereby the large SOEs would absorb smaller ones, thus attempting to achieve greater economies of scale and efficiencies (see Fig. 3.11). This absorption process was known as the "big fish eating small fish" (大鱼吃小鱼). Chinese economic planners also had long admired the South Korean *chaebol* and Japanese *zaibatsu* systems of large horizontally integrated industries. This model led (under Premier Zhu Rongji during the subsequent Jiang Zemin era, as discussed in the next chapter) to the creation of many large *jituan* (conglomerates) across many sectors. While SOE reform has been a long-standing challenge for China's industrial economy, as we will see in Chapter

6, China's current leader Xi Jinping has reembraced SOEs and enhanced their role in the national economy.

Another core problem confronting Deng, Zhao, and the economic planners was price reform. Prior to the 1980s all prices were set by the state. There were simply no market signals involved in price setting. This resulted in severe price distortions. Zhao Ziyang in particular was committed to reforming the pricing system. In rural areas, commensurate with the "three freedoms" agricultural policy that Zhao pioneered in Sichuan and then took nationwide beginning in 1980, prices for agricultural produce began to free-float in rural markets. By 1985 the state's monopoly procurement system for rural produce (which had existed since 1953) was dismantled altogether. The significance of this policy shift was immense, signaling the end of thirty years of mandatory planning in agriculture. This proved to be a major boost to rural incomes.

Cities, though, were another story. When controls over prices for foodstuffs and meat (mainly pork) were allowed to float in 1985 it resulted in dramatic price increases and inflation. For citizens who had long been accustomed to paying state-subsidized prices for food, this came as quite a shock. The price of foodstuffs increased by double digits in 1985—with the price of eggs and meat rising 22 percent, fish 34 percent, and vegetables 33 percent.[54] A student at Beijing University then, I vividly recall the rush on markets and hoarding of foodstuffs. Overall retail inflation for the year was 9 percent. But Zhao was undeterred and went forward with further lifting of fixed price ceilings in 1986. This caused further inflation in 1987. Although there was considerable urban discontent, Zhao's initiative was supported by Deng, who gave a pair of speeches on May 19 and 25, 1988, advocating a continuation of price reform and overall acceleration of reform.[55] The unfortunate result was a further 18.5 percent increase in retail prices for the year, renewed panic buying, depletion of food stocks, hoarding and stockpiling of goods, runs on banks, and widespread urban discontent. This put Zhao seriously on the political defensive and under attack from the conservative Old Guard. Over the summer of 1988 a comprehensive plan to control inflation and stabilize the overheated economy was worked out by senior leaders Yao Yilin and Li Peng, as well as State Council think tank economists—which was presented to the Third Plenum of the Thirteenth

Central Committee in September. As a result, prices were frozen, foreign trade was recentralized, a very tight fiscal policy forced on state banks, investment controls were put in place, and capital construction halted. Zhao himself came in for six-and-a-half hours of harsh criticism and was forced to make a self-criticism. This was the all-important backdrop to the dramatic demonstrations of the spring of 1989 (which were triggered by economic discontent as much as by political demands).

Among the many other economic reforms stimulated during Deng's tenure, two others deserve brief mention. The first concerned changes in the ownership structure, and the second concerned efforts to establish a regulatory structure (as distinct from an administrative structure) for qualitative oversight of economic activity.

With regard to the first, a key part of creating the hybrid state-collective-private economy that Deng and his colleagues envisioned necessitated the creation of truly private enterprises and private ownership.[56] Citizens in both rural and urban areas were permitted to purchase long-term leaseholds on property (often their homes) and to pass it from generation to generation. Another example of diversified ownership affected the corporate sector. Stock markets were experimented with (in Shenyang, Shanghai, and Shenzhen) and citizens were allowed to buy stocks in companies that had listed.

With the control of production shifted to collective and private enterprises, quite naturally supervision of—and quality control over—the production of a wide variety of products was lacking. This resulted in a series of consumer scandals related to lead toys, tainted drugs, poisoned baby formula, and other unregulated products. Intellectual property theft was rampant, with false brands and fake products saturating markets. China's counterfeiting culture led to multiple abuses, including the issuance of bogus securities on stock exchanges. Then came a series of environmental disasters as a result of unmonitored factories dumping toxic chemicals into the ground, the water table, rivers and lakes. Unregulated air pollution darkened the skies and made it unhealthy to be outdoors. By the 1990s China had become a dystopian environmental nightmare. All of this led the state—again with Zhao Ziyang as a driving force—to adopt a series of regulations and laws aimed at quality control of consumer goods and improvement of the environment.[57]

Overall, during the 1980s and Deng's time in charge, the miraculous transformation of the Chinese economy began to take shape. It was all uncharted territory—which required a lot of experimentation, occasional retrenchment, recalibration, and uncertainty. As Deng himself said, it was like "feeling the stones while crossing the river" (摸着石头过河), illustrating the incremental and experimental nature of the whole reform process. But by the end of the decade China had enjoyed its strongest sustained growth in PRC history and the structural and qualitative reforms of the economy were well advanced.

Social Reforms

Deng did not necessarily think or speak about social reforms per se, but his policies in other areas had direct impacts on society. Let us briefly consider several key examples.

First and foremost, Deng's rolling back of the totalitarian state built by Mao, which exerted *total control* over people's livelihoods (as described above under "Deng's Inheritance"), was fundamental. He authorized and catalyzed the withdrawal of the party-state from the daily life of the society. In the rural areas, he dismantled collective agricultural structures, so that family households—which had knitted together Chinese society for centuries—could again be masters of their own lives, farm the land as they wished, and tap their inherent entrepreneurial instincts. Villages literally came alive again with markets, fairs, community activities, and the revitalization of religious practices. A powerful Promethean impulse was unleashed for 800 million citizens.

Similarly, in cities Deng's reforms relaxed the total dominance of the *danwei* structure.[58] People were allowed to increasingly change and look for jobs on their own. The previous job assignment system (分配制度) for high school and university graduates began to be relaxed in 1983, and by the end of the decade there was almost total freedom for university graduates to apply for and choose from multiple jobs (the exceptions were those who were conscripted into the military or other occupations deemed critical by the government). Job fairs and headhunters appeared on the scene, and a real labor market began to take shape. With the construction boom in apartment blocks, for the first time urbanites were allowed to purchase their own flats (those few who could afford it), rather than being forced into *danwei* housing. Throughout the 1980s urban neighborhoods sprang to life, with *getihu* (petty business entrepreneurs) selling all kinds of products on the streets, while those who could raise the capital opened small private shops. Commercial advertisements began to replace propaganda slogans on city walls. As I biked through the streets, neighborhoods, and back alleys (胡同) of Beijing in those years, one could just feel the commercial energy bursting forth at the neighborhood level. Urbanites also quickly shed their drab blue uniform dress (which was predominant when I first visited in 1979) for a variety of colored clothing. Women and girls began to wear dresses, something unheard of during the previous thirty years. Some began to have their hair permed, wear makeup, and sport fake jewelry. Beauty contests even began, and cosmetic surgery became a craze among the more affluent. Men commonly began to wear Western suits and ties. Hotels and discotheques opened (mainly for foreigners). Imported goods became more widely available beyond the ubiquitous Friendship Stores (some smuggled in) and local Chinese took pride in displaying foreign brands. With the ideological relaxation (which waxed and waned throughout the decade) salons of intellectuals and pseudo-intellectuals popped up, and local newspapers began to carry news other than from the party-state. All in all, it was a very heady time in the coastal Chinese cities.

Deng also relaxed the strict *hukou* registration policy (at least by not enforcing it), thus allowing people to travel and work in other localities. In particular, this contributed to the development of the southeastern provinces and SEZs, where cheap labor from the interior migrated and found construction work.

With Deng's emphasis on "cultivating talent" (人才),[59] all kinds of professions blossomed. "Think tanks" were created (although they all remained connected to the party-state), universities had reopened after the Cultural Revolution hiatus, and a wide variety of professional associations (指会) were formed and created national networks of experts in various fields. Deng's appreciation of expertise and intellectuals had a profound effect on a whole class of people who had known nothing but persecution for three decades.

In sum, what Deng offered Chinese society was *diversity* and the freedom to pursue private desires. This was Deng's genius. He knew the entrepreneurship and vitality that was in the DNA of every Chinese. After thirty years of conformity and control, the society responded instinctively to rapidly grasp their newfound opportunities.

Political Reforms

Deng's reforms were not simply about unleashing new social and economic forces—as he very much believed that changes in the political system went in tandem with and underlaid socioeconomic reforms. On several occasions he spoke of this interconnection. While Deng was no democrat, or even a liberal, he was very much a pragmatist who was deeply opposed to dogmatism and constraining orthodoxies. He also had learned a number of key lessons from the disastrous Mao era, which he was determined to eliminate from Chinese politics.

Deng laid out his proposals for political reform in a pair of important speeches—his August 1980 speech "On Reform of the System of Party and State Leadership" and his September–November 1986 speeches collectively titled "On Reform of the Political Structure." The former was considerably longer than the latter, and six years of experimentation and initiatives had passed between then. In his 1980 speech Deng identified four specific problems:[60]

- "It is not good to have an overconcentration of power."
- "It is not good to have too many people holding two or more posts concurrently or to have too many deputy posts."
- "It is time for us to distinguish between the responsibilities of the Party and those of the government and to stop substituting the former for the latter."
- "We must take the long-term interest into account and solve the problem of the succession in leadership."

In his 1986 speech (actually a combination of four separate talks he gave), Deng said, "We feel the need to reform our political structure is growing more and more urgent, and we haven't sorted everything out yet."[61] He then specifically noted three objectives:

- "The first objective is to ensure the continuing vitality of the Party and the state."
- "The second objective of political structural reform is to eliminate bureaucratism and increase efficiency."
- "The third objective of political reform is to stimulate the initiative of grassroots units of workers, peasants, and intellectuals."

Deng's concern with overconcentrated leadership derived directly from the errors he attributed to Mao's dominance and excessive exercise of power, combined with his own experiences of how the Party leadership operated in a more collective manner during the periods 1949–1957 and 1961–1965. So, as noted above, he resurrected the CCP Secretariat as the operational nerve center for operations of the Politburo and its Standing Committee (both of which were again to meet regularly). The leading small group (领导小组) system was also resurrected to oversee and coordinate policy across a wide variety of functional sectors. Policy decisions were now to be deliberated *collectively* and *collegially*, instead of by fiat. Deng himself became *primus inter pares*. Deng was authoritarian but not autocratic. Policy decisions were also to be made on the basis of empirical research provided by a number of newly created research institutes and centers (including the new Chinese Academy of Social Sciences, the National Development Research Council, and others). Policy decisions were also usually based on the performance of experimental "test points" that had been carried out and monitored over a period of several months, and even after adoption there was to be built-in flexibility and adjustments for constant recalibration.

This collective collegiality at the top was to be paralleled by Deng's initiative to restore so-called intra-Party democracy (党内民主). Deng believed that Mao's dictatorship had rendered the Party itself (and Party committees down to the local level) dysfunctional totalitarian tools. The traditions of "democratic centralism" and the "mass line" had been lost. Deng began to speak about the need to restore "Party life" (党的生活) to Party organizations from top to bottom of the system. A dead dysfunctional Party apparatus, in his view, was a recipe for inefficiency and institutional lethargy (Deng thus anticipated key causes of the coming collapse of the Soviet Communist Party and its rule).

Closely related to this malady was the question of Party membership. Deng deemed the CCP membership to be too old and too incompetent. Deng spoke of these twin problems many times. The former problem Deng dealt with by creating the Central Advisory Commission (CAC) in 1982, which in theory was to be equal in authority to the Central Committee. In fact, it was a ruse for getting sixty-five Central Committee members and alternates to retire, relinquish their positions, and move to the CAC.[62] This move at the top of the system was paralleled by the institution of formal retirement ages throughout the Party, state, and other professional institutions (age requirements varied).[63] Having served its purpose to move the "first generation" Old Guard out of active policy-making, Deng then dissolved it ten years later in 1992. In terms of incompetent Party members, at the Second Plenum of the Twelfth Central Committee in October 1983 Deng launched a purge of Party members he called the "three types of people" (三种人): those who rose to power during the Cultural Revolution; those who engaged in factionalism and other forms of subversive behavior; and those guilty of "beating, smashing, and looting" during the "ten years of chaos."[64]

A related move to tighten up the Party apparat was the creation in February 1980 of the Central Discipline Inspection Commission (中央记录检查委员会), which was put under the joint supervision of Chen Yun and Hu Yaobang. The CDIC was given a broad brief to investigate Party members (and later non-Party members) for a wide range of breaches of "discipline" and illicit activities. The establishment of the CDIC did not anticipate the rise of rampant corruption that appeared beginning around 1983 as a result of Party members cashing in (literally) on their privileged status and connections, and subsequently policing corruption became a major preoccupation for the commission.

The other major political reforms launched by Deng (but carried out by Zhao Ziyang and later Zhu Rongji) concerned the government. There were two interconnected aspects here. First was Deng's desire to decouple and "separate" the Party and the government (党政分开), based on his belief that the CCP was overly empowered and too intrusive into matters in which it had no particular expertise. Decisions needed to be made on pragmatic grounds by state officials and enterprise managers, he felt, rather than by political cadres on political grounds. This decoupling worked well throughout the 1980s and was one reason for the success of economic and enterprise reform, but the policy was terminated after the Tiananmen events of 1989 and the collapse of the Soviet Union in 1991 (the CCP argued that one of the reasons for the collapse of the USSR was Gorbachev's decoupling of the Soviet Communist Party from both the government and the armed forces). Of course, the Party–government separation policy was never intended to be total, as both Party committees and the *nomenklatura* system continued in place, but Deng's and Zhao's idea was to withdraw the Party from its former total interventionist ways so as to stimulate economic growth and empower government ministries and officials to do their jobs.

The other element concerning the government bureaucracy was Deng's persistent critique that it was "bloated," inefficient, and needed a thorough restructuring, streamlining, and downsizing. Deng repeatedly railed about this problem. As a result, during the 1980s Zhao Ziyang oversaw two rounds of streamlining (further rounds were carried out in 1993, 1998, and 2018). In 1982, prior to the first round of restructuring, China's government (State Council) had no fewer than 50 ministries—counting its additional committees, commissions, and agencies, the State Council had ballooned to 98 organs! At the March 1982 National People's Congress Zhao proposed reduction of the number of State Council vice-premiers from thirteen to two. Ministers and vice-ministers were reduced from 505 down to 167, and the overall number of cadres in central government organs was reduced from 49,000 to 32,000.[65] He further announced the proposed slashing of the 98 organs by almost half, to 52. As announced, this was indeed an impressive undertaking. But what in fact occurred was more a series of mergers and amalgamations rather than the wholesale elimination of bureaucratic organs. For example, the Ministry of Water Conservancy and the Ministry of Electric Power became the Ministry of Water Conservancy *and* Electric Power. Merged ministries did not physically move nor shed many staff. In Chinese this phenomenon is known as "two signs, one organ" (两块牌子,一个机构), a reference to the signs that hang outside all organizations in China.

Despite the subterfuge, the first and second rounds of consolidation did nevertheless improve efficiencies and policy implementation.

Zhao also had the novel idea of instituting an autonomous civil service (公务员制度) that would act independently of the CCP. Apparently, Zhao was influenced by the examples of British Hong Kong and Singapore, and he began dispatching study teams to understand how these systems operated.[66] Once it was (quickly) determined that they were worthy of emulation, both the Hong Kong and Singapore governments established training programs for Chinese civil servant administrators. More broadly, the Singaporean political system held a fascination for both Deng and Zhao. Deng visited the Lion City as early as 1978, meeting and holding long talks with Prime Minister Lee Kuan Yew. Zhao and his advisors (notably Yan Jiaqi) were enamored with Singapore's style of "neo-authoritarianism" (新权威主义), and had Zhao not been overthrown in 1989 it is quite likely that this was the political model that he sought to emulate with the PRC.[67]

Foreign Policy Reforms

Deng's legacy in foreign policy can be seen in four principal initiatives: normalization of diplomatic relations with the United States; *rapprochement* with the Soviet Union; establishing ties with China's neighbors in Asia; and the "one country, two systems" formula for Hong Kong.[68]

Throughout 1978 Deng took personal charge of the final negotiations with the Carter administration to achieve the establishment of formal diplomatic relations between China and the United States, which were consummated on January 1, 1979. Thereafter he personally visited the US for a triumphal tour. Thus opened a new era of Sino-American relations (Fig. 3.12). Normalization with the US brought increased strategic pressure on Moscow, which by 1979 was at the apex of its "hegemonic" and assertive policies abroad. By 1982, though, Moscow was clearly on the defensive and Deng sensed that the tide was turning. As a result, the 12th Party Congress that year proclaimed an "independent foreign policy," a euphemism for greater equidistance between the two superpowers, and Deng initiated a thaw with Moscow by initiating some cultural and student exchanges. In 1985 Mikhail Gorbachev came to power and took several unilateral

Figure 3.12 Deng Xiaoping Dons Ten-Gallon Cowboy Hat During State Visit to the United States in Recognition of Normalization of Diplomatic Relations, January 1979
Source: Associated Press

actions to ease tensions. By May 1989, when Gorbachev visited Beijing in the midst of the Tiananmen demonstrations, the step-by-step reciprocal process had succeeded in renormalizing relations following the twenty-nine-year hiatus after the Sino-Soviet Split of 1960 (diplomatic relations were never severed).

The third initiative Deng undertook was to normalize diplomatic relations with several Southeast Asian states and South Korea. Deng personally toured Southeast Asia to symbolize the shift. Previous to that time, China had largely been viewed by its neighbors as an untrustworthy, subversive, and disruptive power.[69] But Deng saw these countries as important models for China's own modernization, and he understood the importance of having a peaceful regional environment in order for China to concentrate on its own development.

Finally, having notified the British government that China would not renew its 99-year lease on Hong Kong, Deng came up with the novel concept of "one country, two systems" (一国两制).[70] This provided for a range of freedoms and semi-autonomy (except in defense and foreign affairs) for the territory, designating it as a "Special Administrative Region," and promising fifty years of a "high degree of autonomy." The concept was to initially apply to Hong Kong and Macao, but also eventually to Taiwan (where even greater elements of autonomy were promised, such as maintaining its own armed forces).

China's foreign policy certainly included other dimensions during the 1980s, but I would identify these four key Dengist initiatives as the most important.

Taken together, these Dengist reforms to the Party and state were instrumental in reconceptualizing the roles and reconfiguring the operations of the political system.[71] However, while flexible and willing to loosen up (and to some extent liberalize) the system, Deng never wavered in his conviction that the Chinese Communist Party had to remain in control (to wit, his Four Cardinal Principles) and would not tolerate any threats to its hegemony. This was, of course, fundamentally challenged by the dramatic and traumatic events of the spring of 1989.

Deng Xiaoping's Stain: Tiananmen

Despite the zigs and zags and the *fang-shou* oscillation of economics and politics in China during the Deng decade of the 1980s, the country was on a very positive overall path of development. The first revolution of 1949 had given way to the second revolution of the 1980s reforms. But by the end of the decade a third revolution loomed: the *revolution of rising expectations*. After three decades of stultification under Mao, Deng had unleashed powerful forces of change in his country. Once the genie had been let out of the bottle, the Chinese people confronted a phenomenon common to all upwardly mobile developing countries: new aspirations. This is not at all uncommon in the process of development and modernization. People inevitably want more. And one thing that has been repeatedly demonstrated across a wide

Figure 3.13 Tanks in Tiananmen Square, June 5, 1989
Source: Associated Press

range of countries since the 1950s is that economic development begets demands for expanded political freedoms and improved "public goods."

It was these forces that congealed in the spring of 1989 with the mass demonstrations in Beijing and in dozens of other cities across China that ended in bloodshed and loss of life when People's Liberation Army soldiers shot their way into Tiananmen Square in central Beijing on the night of June 3–4, 1989 (Fig. 3.13).

Much has been written about these events, and it is not my intention to recount them here.[72] What is important to note, though, is that the demonstrations were sparked by four different catalysts: popular discontent with corruption; popular discontent with the overheated economy, inflation, and escalating prices of staple goods; popular demands for greater government accountability; and popular demands for democracy and a range of greater freedoms. The demonstrations were kicked off by the sudden death of deposed liberal leader Hu Yaobang (who died of a heart attack in a Politburo meeting on April 15) and they mushroomed in size and scope over the ensuing six weeks. It was real-time high drama, and it was carried on live television worldwide. The entire world was riveted by the events unfolding in Beijing and across China. Coming in the wake of the "people's power" uprising in the Philippines and other popular assaults on authoritarian rule during the "third wave" of democracy around the globe, the remarkable confrontation between ordinary citizens and the powerful communist state was breathtaking to behold (even more so as it was occurring simultaneously with similar popular uprisings against communist states across Central and Eastern Europe). In fact, the very day that tanks rolled into Tiananmen (June 4) the Polish people went to the polls in their first democratic election, following years of protests by the Solidarity workers' movement.

The decision to enforce martial law was presaged by the Politburo decision to remove Zhao Ziyang from power, as he had opposed the imposition of martial law, favored negotiating with the students, and was blamed by the conservative elders as responsible for the "bourgeois liberalism" that gave rise to the demonstrations (just as they had blamed Hu Yaobang for the December 1986 student demonstrations in Hefei, Nanjing, and Shanghai). Now the conservative Old Guard had succeeded in toppling *both* of Deng's key protégés and the most senior leaders of the Communist Party. Immediately following the Politburo decision to dismiss Zhao in the early morning hours of May 19, he went directly to Tiananmen Square where he grabbed a megaphone and, with tears in his eyes, emotionally apologized to the students, saying, "We have come too late." This was Zhao's last public appearance. As we will see in the next chapter, he was put under house arrest and investigation for "splitting the Party," "grave errors and mistakes," and other "crimes." Zhao was never jailed, but he lived out the rest of his life in seclusion under house arrest before passing away on January 17, 2005—but not before he secretly tape-recorded his memoirs and version of the events that led to his downfall (which were smuggled out of China and published in Hong Kong and the US).[73]

With Zhao out of the way, the decision to use armed force to end the demonstrations in Tiananmen and the six-week standoff between the government and the public was taken by a group of Chinese leaders, many of them long retired. The key ones were Deng Xiaoping, Yang Shangkun (then state President), Li Peng (Premier), Wang Zhen, Qiao Shi, Yao Yilin, Bo Yibo, and Li Xiannian. These men were aged 77 on average at the time. While it was a collective decision to use lethal force, it was Deng—and only Deng—who approved the April 26 *People's Daily* editorial that defined the demonstrations as "a planned conspiracy and turmoil." This decision by Deng defined the Party and government's understanding of the events. To them, the demonstrators were not patriotic—rather, they were participating in an organized conspiracy (in cahoots with the United States) to overthrow the Chinese Communist Party and to bring to an end the People's Republic of China after forty years in power. The movement was judged to be more than subversion—it was seen as an existential threat to Party rule and the nation-state itself. Following the crackdown, in which between 1,500 and 2,000 citizens perished, the official judgment was that it had been a "counterrevolutionary rebellion"(反革命暴乱).

Speaking to an assembly of martial law troops five days later, on June 9, Deng went on record with his own judgments.[74] He began with the understatement, "Comrades, you have been having a hard time!" He then called for silence to honor the fallen "martyrs." Then Deng explained his understanding of the events:

> This disturbance would have occurred sooner or later. It was determined by both the international environment and the domestic environment. It was bound to occur, whether one wished it or not; the only question was the time and the scale. . . . The nature of the incident should have been obvious from the very beginning. The handful of bad people had two basic slogans: overthrow the Communist Party and demolish the socialist system. Their goal was to establish a bourgeois republic, an out-and-out vassal of the West.

The PRC and CCP, according to Deng, had just had an existential near-death experience. The Party elders who made the decision to use force never looked back. They remained convinced that had they not used force, the CCP and the PRC would have been overthrown. Maybe, maybe not. Deng's comments about the inevitability of a liberal uprising of this nature reveals that he was keenly aware of the potential political forces that his tolerant reforms had unleashed in society. Perhaps he was also aware of the depth of discontent over Party rule and the deep crisis of credibility that the Party still faced after four decades in power. One thing is not in question, though: Tiananmen will forever be the darkest stain on Deng Xiaoping's otherwise accomplished legacy.

Deng's Last Stand

Having overseen the most consequential decision in his life and career, Deng began to withdraw from an active role in national and state affairs. On September 4, 1989, in a letter addressed to the Politburo, he resigned his one remaining official position as Chairman of the Central Military Commission,[75] ceding it to the newly appointed Jiang Zemin (who had been elevated from Shanghai in late May and formally replaced Zhao as CCP General Secretary at the Fourth Plenum in late June).[76] On the same day he called a group of top leaders to his home and informed them of his intention to fully retire. Deng was now 85 years old, was totally deaf in one ear and barely able to hear out of the other, although he did tell a visiting foreigner in September 1989 that "I am still in good health and have a clear mind and a good memory. Recently I began to swim for an hour every day. . . . I am trying to get used to complete retirement."[77] Deng enjoyed nothing more than his time at home with his family.

Over the next three years Deng stopped attending regular high-level meetings and did not often appear in public. But his *Selected Works* do indicate that he met occasionally with "leading members of the Central Committee" and several visiting foreigners (including former American President Richard Nixon, US National Security Advisor Brent Scowcroft, Thai Prime Minister Chatichai, former Tanzanian President Julius Nyerere, a Japanese trade delegation, a Thai businessman, Canadian Prime Minister Elliott Trudeau, and a Malaysian businessman). In these conversations Deng continually emphasized several themes: China should continue on the road of reform and opening up; the Tiananmen "disturbance" was the result of Western (especially American) interference; China should not compromise its independence and principles by groveling for re-acceptance by the international community in the wake of the post-June 4 ostracism and sanctions.

Despite his revered and venerable reputation, Deng had to learn something new in his career: he was not being listened to. The post-June 4 leadership was composed of ultra-hardline conservatives, who unleashed a rigid security crackdown, arresting and jailing thousands, while systematically interrogating Beijing's citizens. The military declared and occupied nine institutional "major disaster zones" (重灾区) in Beijing which had been active in the protests. The city of Beijing itself continued to remain under martial law with roadblocks and checkpoints, a sweeping security presence, and a heavy pall hanging over daily life. I know, as I lived there at the time and my institution (the Chinese Academy of Social Sciences) was itself one of the "major disaster zones" and was occupied by military troops. Economically, under the direction of Premier Li Peng (known abroad as the "butcher of Beijing" for his instrumental role in the June 4 massacre), the regime instituted a stiff austerity program intended to cool down the economy and eliminate inflation. The government choked off the money supply, bringing domestic investment and capital construction to a standstill. The harsh politics of the period contributed to depressed consumer demand and factory output. GDP growth plummeted from 11.2 percent in 1988 to 4.2 percent in 1989 and 3.9 percent in 1990.

Realizing that the draconian policies were not intended to be temporary, Deng became increasingly uneasy and agitated. He was particularly concerned that his entire "reform and opening" program, on which his legacy rested, was being abandoned by a group of retrograde Leninists. By early 1991 he allegedly complained, "No one is listening to me now. If such a state of affairs continues, I will have no choice but to go to Shanghai and issue some articles there."[78] And in February 1991, over Chinese New Year holiday, that is exactly what he did. But even then, Deng's commentaries were not immediately published. He was not only experiencing the consequences of retirement, but also the power of the propaganda system under the control of ideologue Wang Renzhi, which continued to echo the Li Peng line of tight economic and political controls. Finally, Deng's daughter Deng Rong (who acted as her father's gatekeeper, executive assistant, and translator), in collaboration with liberal Shanghai Party secretary Zhu Rongji, arranged for Deng's commentaries to be published under a pseudonym in the Shanghai *Liberation Daily*. In them Deng criticized "ossified thinking" and called for a renewed "emancipation of the mind."[79] But that was it. Still no change in rhetoric or policy from the conservative leadership in Beijing throughout the remainder of 1991.

As a result, Deng grew even more distraught and agitated. Now 87, almost totally deaf and unsteady on his feet, Deng knew he had one last chance to change the course of China and plant it soundly on a renewed road to reform and opening. On January 17, 1992, he embarked in secret from the Beijing railway station on what became known as his "southern tour" (南巡), an imperial euphemism used by China's emperors. Two days later his special train reached Guangzhou, where it stopped briefly before proceeding to the Special Economic Zones of Shenzhen and Zhuhai. It had been almost eight years to the day since Deng had first visited to inspect and praise the zones that Xi Zhongxun had initiated. The choice of destination could not have been more pointed. Local Party officials received and escorted Deng during his tour, although it is not clear if they knew in advance of his visit. During his few unscripted public appearances he was mobbed by genuinely enthusiastic well-wishers who couldn't believe their eyes.

Deng took with him a very small group of family members and handpicked aides. One was Zheng Bijian, a semi-liberal CCP theoretician and former head of the Propaganda Department. Zheng's presence was no accident. He had been tasked with turning Deng's cryptic remarks (which he made at various stops during his "inspection" of enterprises) into full-fledged "speeches" and article-length exposés. In them Deng echoed his previous year's comments about "ossified thinking" and the need to be bold in reigniting reform. "Do not act like women with bound feet," Deng declared. But he went further by repeatedly criticizing the trend of "leftism," as he perceived it.

Then a strange thing happened: Deng's observations were again blocked from publication in the media. How could this be? China's paramount leader unable to get his views published? Having been blocked by the propaganda system again, as he had the previous year in Shanghai, Deng's team did what Chinese politicians sometimes did in order to affect the policy agenda: leak to the more free Hong Kong media. Quickly, reports of Deng's visit and commentaries appeared in Hong Kong papers—prompting the *Shenzhen Ribao* (across the border in the mainland) to publish a series of eight articles about the southern tour, which included lengthy passages, as drafted by Zheng Bijian. Deng himself had only offered brief remarks at each stop, but Zheng and his speechwriting team had turned them into lengthy documents. Still, there was no immediate reprint in the national media in Beijing. Yet, Deng had succeeded in his purpose—his trip and words had boxed in the leadership; the message was impossible to ignore. Jiang Zemin was forced to convene a Politburo meeting, which authorized a compressed version of Deng's supposed speeches to be circulated within the Party as Central Document No. 2. This was followed by the full publication of Deng's views.[80] There were numerous themes included in the speeches, but two stood out: criticize "leftism," and full-speed-ahead with economic reform.

At nearly 88 years old, Deng had succeeded, once again, in shifting the national agenda. His gravitas mattered after all. But Deng was not quite done yet. Having successfully shifted the national narrative, with the 14th Party Congress approaching in September 1992 he now sought to shape the composition of the leadership one last time. Deng succeeded in removing his old ally Yang Shangkun, along with his half-brother General Yang Baibing, who together were accused of building a family clique in the military after 1989. He also succeeded in forcing senior leaders (also his contemporaries) Yao Yilin and Song Ping into retirement. In their place he threw his full support behind CCP General Secretary Jiang Zemin and Premier Zhu Rongji. The Congress also enshrined "Deng Xiaoping Theory" in the Party constitution.

This was Deng's final political act. His actions triggered a dramatic uptick in economic growth. In 1992 GDP growth leapt 14.2 percent, its second highest mark ever. In 1993 it grew a further 13.9 percent, 13 percent in 1994, and 11 percent in 1995. As for politics, Deng had also succeeded in beating back the conservative tide (described euphemistically as "leftism"). While by no means returning to the Zhao Ziyang–Hu Yaobang political reforms of the 1980s, as we will see in the next chapter, Jiang Zemin did indeed embrace some neo-liberal political reforms.

In a little more than a decade Deng Xiaoping had truly moved the nation. He picked up the pieces of a broken China that Mao had bequeathed to him, he cleaned out the inherited impediments, and moved boldly ahead with reorienting the country in many dimensions. It was Deng who really established China on the path to modernization. While that effort is still a work in progress, Deng deserves the credit for turning the country around after the multiple traumas of the Maoist era, and setting it on the road to becoming a great power. To be certain, the Tiananmen massacre is a stain that will forever tarnish Deng's legacy, but his accomplishments were many and profound. In Chapter 7 we will also reflect on other characteristics of Deng, and weigh his place in history.

CHAPTER 4

JIANG ZEMIN (江泽民)

Bureaucratic Politician

"The end of the Cold War and the demise of the Soviet Union gave us a lot of insight. We did not lower the banner of Marxism; rather, we more firmly resolved to uphold Marxism-Leninism and the leadership of the Communist Party and adhere to the path of socialism with Chinese characteristics suitable for China's conditions."

—Jiang Zemin, discussion with Fidel Castro, November 21, 1993[1]

JIANG ZEMIN WAS AN UNEXPECTED AND UNLIKELY NATIONAL LEADER when he was abruptly summoned and promoted from the position of Shanghai Party secretary to become CCP General Secretary in Beijing in June 1989. Many foreign China watchers assumed he would be a relatively brief transitional caretaker leader, like Hua Guofeng. Hua turned out to rule longer than expected and so did Jiang Zemin (thirteen years altogether, even longer than Deng Xiaoping).

A relatively unknown figure at the time of his elevation, despite being in charge of China's largest city and already a member of the Politburo for two years, Jiang was quite an obscure figure—even within China. But after the decision was made at an expanded Politburo meeting on May 19, 1989 to remove Zhao Ziyang from his position as General Secretary—a decision confirmed by the Fourth Plenum on June 24—Jiang was personally selected by Deng (on the recommendation of Li Xiannian with the acquiescence of other Party elders) to replace Zhao. Jiang was a good compromise candidate

Figure 4.1 Jiang Zemin (1926–)
Source: Richard Ellis / Alamy

(the other option was apparently Tianjin Party secretary Li Ruihuan) as he was not beholden to the liberal-conservative factional cleavage that characterized leadership politics in the pre-Tiananmen period. As we will see in this chapter, Jiang was not saddled with any particular political baggage, having had a very mainstream bureaucratic career up to that point. He had, however, helped to defuse the spring 1989 demonstrations that had spread to Shanghai, and he personally took the decision to shut down the liberal and popular Shanghai newspaper *World Economic Herald* (世界经济导报); both actions had impressed Deng and the elders in Beijing. Jiang was also supportive of economic reform, although he had a distinctly non-liberal orientation on ideological matters. All of this appealed to Party elders, who made the decision to elevate Jiang to replace Zhao Ziyang. It also seems that Jiang did not come to the capital until the immediate aftermath of the Tiananmen crackdown (as he appears in no photos of leader meetings during this period). He did not appear in public until just before the Fourth

Plenum, when he was photographed attending a Politburo meeting on June 19–21, 1989. He was then confirmed as CCP General Secretary at the plenum two days later.

Once in power it took Jiang some time to find his feet and establish himself as an independent leader. For one thing, he served in the shadow of Deng Xiaoping—who, although retired, still cast a strong shadow and influence, and occasionally inserted himself into the policy process. Being an outsider and being thrust into the post-Tiananmen maelstrom was an extraordinary challenge for Jiang. While his outsider credentials worked in his favor for his elevation, they were also a significant weakness, as he had no ties to any of the main civilian or military constituencies. In other words, he had no institutional or factional power base to draw upon. He did have the imprimatur of Deng Xiaoping's anointment, the support of other elder leaders and the longtime patronage of Wang Daohan (the former Mayor of Shanghai and a senior Party elder), as well as having been a loyal career functionary in the Party and the industrial planning apparatus—but Jiang still lacked an insider's connections to the Beijing Party and military elite. Moreover, he was taking the reins of power at an exceptionally sensitive time, in the wake of Tiananmen and the ensuing international condemnation.

Jiang thus instinctively and intelligently adopted a low-key approach at first, earning him the dismissive nickname of "the flowerpot"—for being ornamental but serving little practical function. Indeed, the initial foreign impressions of Jiang were that he was a dull, classic bureaucrat-apparatchik, lacking in intelligence and persona—which all turned out to be very misinformed and wrong. As time passed and Jiang emerged on the world stage, it became quickly apparent that he was the very *opposite* of these descriptors. He possessed a buoyant and lively personality, was gregarious and even egotistical, was highly intelligent, was a true cosmopolitan and cultured intellectual with broad knowledge in many fields, who had his own ideas and was by no means a bureaucratic robot, who understood many of the intricacies of the modernization process, who knew how to forge political coalitions without alienating others, and had a refined sense of the balance between control and toleration in politics, the economy, and society.

Indeed, as we will see in this chapter, after the first few years of consolidating his rule, Jiang's time in office was distinctly characterized by *liberalization* in these three realms. This is an important point. When compared with Xi Jinping's hardline repression today, or Hu Jintao's relatively limited impact, we look back wistfully on Jiang Zemin's rule as relatively liberal and tolerant politically, socially, and economically. *Real* political reform and institutionalization *occurred* on his watch, Chinese society blossomed in a number of ways following the post-Tiananmen funk, and the economy absolutely boomed after 1992, with real structural reforms being undertaken, and the military embarked on true modernization. China's foreign relations also improved dramatically—not just climbing out from under the Tiananmen shadow and sanctions, but more generally as the PRC broadened and deepened its ties with a wide variety of countries and played an increased role in international institutions. Jiang effectively asserted his control over the People's Liberation Army brass by dismissing the entrenched fiefdom of the Yang brothers (Yang Shangkun and Yang Baibing) and constrained the military's vast business dealings. He cracked down on corrupt princelings and provincial officials and he forced retirements from the Politburo, repacking it with his own associates (many from Shanghai). He undertook several important institutional reform initiatives within the Party, revitalizing it following the trauma of Tiananmen (known among Western scholars of the CCP as the "authoritarian resilience" paradigm).[2] On balance and in retrospect, Jiang Zemin's record is quite impressive on a number of levels and looks very positive.[3]

Yet none of this was evident during Jiang's first few years in power. While observers at the time were preoccupied with the question of how long Jiang would last at the top, and what would come after the expected transitional period, Jiang assiduously went about building his power base and carefully studying the environment he faced. He spent much of his first two years in power visiting various provinces, military regions, and government bureaucracies to get a sense of the lay of the land and who was who in each place. In my interpretation, Jiang proceeded to build a power base and stabilize his rule by drawing on the one thing he knew well—bureaucracy. China invented bureaucracy and so much of contemporary Chinese politics is really about bureaucracy, and not so much about individuals and ideas (yes, the latter matter, but bureaucracies are the machinery that really makes the Party and state systems run). Jiang had been a career industrial bureaucrat, and he had a first-hand understanding of how bureaucratic constituencies and coalitions were forged, how policies were implemented (or blocked), and the importance of institutions in politics. This background knowledge and experience would serve him well, as Jiang treated various Party, state, and military bureaucracies as *constituencies* to be won over. Such functional bureaucratic systems (系统) are far more durable than factions formed around individual loyalties. Jiang was also intellectually broad and erudite enough to understand many of the specific issues of concern to multiple bureaucracies. This chapter will demonstrate how Jiang went about this process of bureaucratic cultivation—which proved to be a solid anchor sustaining his rule.

Jiang Zemin's Past as Prologue to the Future

Jiang Zemin's background was typical of his generation, and it was also well-suited to the situation he confronted when elevated to the top of the system at this tenuous time.[4] Jiang was a well-educated, true intellectual. Born into an intellectual family in Yangzhou, a charming city near the Grand Canal in Jiangsu Province with a rich cultural and commercial heritage in imperial China, in secondary school Jiang was exposed to a wide variety of literatures, philosophies, histories, foreign languages, sciences, and music. He was accomplished in playing the *erhu*, was proficient on the piano, dabbled with the violin, and loved to sing. His repertoire ranged from Elvis Presley love songs to Italian opera (when Luciano Pavarotti visited Beijing in 2001 Jiang joined him on stage in singing *O Sole Mio*). Jiang's Yangzhou Middle School education was deeply influenced by Western-style (mainly American) curricula. It was here that he began to learn English, mainly by repetition of speeches such as Abraham Lincoln's Gettysburg address (which he loved to recite for visiting Americans once he became China's leader). Jiang later referred to this as the "bourgeois" stage of his education: "I received a lot of education in capitalism and Western culture," he also later reflected.[5] Like many intellectuals of the Nationalist period, Jiang believed that only "science could save China." Jiang's generation were deeply influenced by the liberal scientific outlook of the May Fourth generation, who touted the slogan "Mr. Science, Mr. Democracy" as the prescription for modernizing the country. Jiang pursued electrical engineering studies at the prestigious National Central University in Nanjing, which was merged with Jiaotong (Communications) University in Shanghai following the defeat of Japan and end of World War II (he graduated in 1947). All of his classes, textbooks, and assignments at Jiao Da were reportedly taught in English—thus further grounding Jiang in the language. He supplemented this by reading a lot of English literature and watching American films. His English was by no means fluent but was sufficient to carry on rudimentary conversations throughout his life. It is indeed unusual that this American educational background did not cost Jiang politically during Mao's many anti-American and anti-intellectual campaigns (this is likely because he was the adopted son of a communist martyr and was an early member of the CCP, becoming a pro-communist student activist before joining the CCP and Shanghai Party underground in 1946).

It was not so much Jiang's formal education as it was his post-1949 career that gave him the tools to navigate Beijing's treacherous politics. That is, Jiang was both a technocrat and a bureaucrat. By the 1990s China's modernization and reforms had reached the point at which a revolutionary pedigree and background were no longer sufficient to guide the country's increasingly complex development; possessing actual systematic knowledge and university degrees in economics, the sciences or engineering, law, and social sciences became more sought-after attributes for the "third generation" of leaders. Beyond training in these fields, practical experience in administering China's sprawling bureaucracies was also valuable. Jiang was the perfect combination of the two. His post-1949 career path had taken him through a series of appointments in the state industrial system—primarily in the automotive, machine-building, and electronics industries.

Following a stint as a power engineer in two large Shanghai factories, Jiang was transferred in 1952 to the Shanghai No. 2 Design Bureau, the main local industrial planning body affiliated with the State Planning Commission and new Ministry of Machine Building in Beijing. This gave Jiang brief experience with the new Soviet-style economic system then being implanted in China. This in turn catapulted him to his first job in and exposure to Beijing. In 1954 he was summoned to help draw up the First Ministry of Machine Building's five-year plan (the transfer was arranged by the vice-minister,

Wang Daohan, who would become Jiang's lifelong professional patron and family friend). His stay in Beijing was brief, however, as he was then assigned to northeastern China and the main vehicle production facility in Changchun, capital of Jilin province. This massive plant, which fell under the purview of the First Ministry of Machine Building (the bureaucratic system in which Jiang would spend most of his career),[6] was a priority project of the 156 Soviet-aided factories then being built across China's urban landscape. In 1955 Jiang was sent off to Moscow, as one of 700 Chinese technicians, for two years of training in the Stalin Autoworks. This was another important step in Jiang's education, being his first trip out of China. While in Moscow he broadened his foreign-language repertoire by becoming quite proficient in Russian (more so than his English); he read classic Russian literature, learned Russian songs, and became very comfortable with his Russian counterparts. He apparently developed a taste for vodka and singing Soviet revolutionary songs in after-work get-togethers. After this apprenticeship he returned to Changchun for six years of work in the First Automotive Works and continued to interact regularly with Russian technical experts assigned to the facility. All of this exposure to the Soviet Union and Russians would prove useful once he was China's leader.

Following Changchun, Jiang returned to Shanghai to work in the electrical power industry (still in the First Ministry of Machine Building system) during 1962–1965 before being assigned to a similar position in the interior industrial city of Wuhan between 1965 and 1968. After three years there and a two-year stint of physical labor (1968–1970) at a May 7th Cadre School in Henan province during the Cultural Revolution, Jiang was again summoned to return to work in the capital. With a brief interruption in 1976–1977, when he was sent back to Shanghai to help weed out the local influence of the deposed Gang of Four (not an easy task), Jiang spent a decade working in the Foreign Affairs Bureau of the First Ministry of Machine Building (in the middle of this assignment he was sent to Romania in 1971–1972 to administer an aid project). In 1980 Jiang received a lateral assignment (but involving promotion to vice-ministerial status) to work in the Ministry of Foreign Economic Relations and Trade. This was an important time and opportunity for Jiang, as it brought him in direct contact with Deng Xiaoping's "opening to the world" policy and gave him exposure to a foreign trade and investment portfolio that was brand new to him. He was involved in attracting foreign companies and investors to the first Special Economic Zones in the south of the country. It also brought him into direct contact not only with Deng himself but also with other senior leaders such as Zhao Ziyang and Li Xiannian. From 1982 to 1985 he was reassigned again—being successively appointed vice-minister, then minister, and Party secretary of the newly formed Ministry of Electronics. After serving successfully in these roles, the CCP Organization Department determined that Jiang was ready for a less bureaucratic and more overtly political role. Thus, in 1985 he was assigned back to Shanghai as Mayor and then from 1987–1989 as municipal Party secretary.

All of this background about Jiang's career trajectory is very important in understanding who he was and his orientation when he was rapidly propelled back to Beijing to become the CCP's General Secretary in 1989. He was the type of Party official who certainly "climbed the ladder"—but he did so within the *state* apparatus. Not until late in his career, when he was named Party secretary in the Ministry of Electronics (mid-1980s) and then Party secretary of Shanghai (late-1980s), did he serve in explicitly *Party* positions. This is unusual as a career path to the top. As we will see in the next chapter, it was completely distinct from Hu Jintao, who served almost exclusively in Party positions. Hu and Xi Jinping also both spent decades serving in the provinces, whereas Jiang had no such provincial appointments until he was assigned to Shanghai in the late 1980s—and managing Shanghai is much different from managing a whole province. The career paths of the fourth and fifth generation of leaders—represented by Hu and Xi respectively—were distinctive for having logged years in the provinces. Not Jiang Zemin. His career ladder and professional milieu were entirely in the state sector, and the industrial component of it. He can thus be considered a *ministerial bureaucrat*.

While his limited exposure to other policy spheres was a comparative weakness at the time of his appointment, Jiang astutely adopted a strategic approach of "learning and co-opting." That is, he systematically visited a variety of institutions and geographic regions, listening, and learning what their concerns and aspirations were, and then *adopting these as his own*. This allowed Jiang to co-opt these varied constituencies while simultaneously giving them a sense of being empowered stakeholders. This is a wise strategy for politicians in any political system. Rather than trying to force change from above on institutions and constituencies, as Mao and to a lesser extent Deng had done, Jiang thus adopted a "bottom-up" style of rule that gave these constituencies a stake in his policies. A careful study of his speeches reveals that he physically visited relevant bureaucracies and adopted their language and aspirations.[7] Jiang also smartly performed what all politicians know to be a winning formula: he showered constituents with financial resources. This was facilitated by China's booming economy following Deng Xiaoping's 1992 Southern Tour. China was flush with cash. And, under Premier Zhu Rongji's strong hand, the tax system was overhauled so as to centralize revenue streams from the provinces to Beijing with a system of reallocating funds thereafter. A rigorous auditing system was also implemented, making units accountable for their substantial off-budget revenues (预算外) earned from off-the-books and often corrupt dealings. The budget system was reorganized by Zhu to adopt the practice of "zero based budgeting"—a system whereby units could no longer roll over unspent funds to the next fiscal year and were forced to remit them to the central government (end-of-year audits ensured that this was done). This new budgeting system also instituted a "bidding" type of system, whereby units across the country and central bureaucracies (including the military) would put in their requests for next year's budget based on actual expenditures and anticipated costs for the coming fiscal year. The Ministry of Finance was empowered and put in charge of evaluating these bids and then authorizing what it thought was an appropriate level of allocation. All of these initiatives helped to rein in the overly decentralized and unaccountable practices that had developed during the Deng era. In this way Jiang both strengthened the role of the central state and put it (and him) in a better position to parcel out resources. To some extent this resulted in a kind of patronage system—but one that was based on meritocratic performance rather than on cronyism.

Thus, once in power, rather than trying to reinvent himself, Jiang drew on his past experiences. And they served him well. His bureaucratic background was actually very well suited to the times. This is why I describe him as a *bureaucratic politician*.

Rather than assessing his time in office chronologically, Jiang's record is best illuminated by evaluating it through four different policy arenas: the Party, the military, the economy, and foreign affairs.

Reforming the Party

Jiang Zemin inherited a traumatized Communist Party and leadership, which had just gone through the near-death experience of the Tiananmen uprising of 1989. Jiang's immediate tasks were severalfold:

- Restoring at least the appearance—if not the reality—of unity in the leadership.
- Ensuring the loyalty of the military (about three dozen officers had balked at enforcing the crackdown and were subsequently court-martialed).
- Reestablishing social order across the country (the demonstrations had reached nearly 40 cities).
- Continuing to enforce martial law in Beijing and carrying out systematic interrogations and prosecutions of those involved in the demonstrations.
- Refining the propaganda narrative, domestically and to the world, about the events of June 4.
- Continuing the cooling off of the overheated economy (a process begun in late 1988).
- Dealing with the multiple sanctions and cancelled exchanges levied by Western countries (the worst international isolation China had experienced since the 1960s).

As if these pressing problems were not enough, to make matters worse, during that summer and fall of 1989 a number of East European communist regimes were overthrown like dominoes: Poland, East Germany, Czechoslovakia, Hungary, Bulgaria, and Romania.[8] On top of the fallout on China from its own June 4 actions, these cascading events further fueled the paranoia gripping the CCP leadership.

Having arrived in Beijing, Jiang himself made no apparent independent impact on the ultra-conservative leadership that had ordered the massacre. Premier Li Peng, Politburo Standing Committee member and internal security/intelligence czar Qiao Shi, President Yang Shangkun, and the retired elders (who all had blood on their hands) doubled down by maintaining martial law and instituting a draconian security presence over the capital. Thousands of citizens were detained and arrested, subjected to torture and rough justice, and were incarcerated. Curfews and military checkpoints were maintained throughout the city. The military physically occupied numerous university campuses and institutions that had been deeply involved in the demonstrations. Nearly all citizens were made to account for their actions during April through June in front of special interrogation teams or Party committees; many were forced to write confessions and self-criticisms; and many lost their jobs as a result. Many leading intellectuals and student leaders of the demonstrations had arrest warrants issued for them, but most were successful in fleeing the country through an underground network. No government accounting of those killed was made. It was a dreadful draconian period that stretched well into 1991. I know, as I lived there as a visiting scholar during 1990–1991—when the stark contrast between the exuberance and optimism of the spring of 1989 and the dour repressive period that followed could not have been more extreme.

Jiang Zemin went along with all of these repressive measures. If there is one aspect in which he distinguished himself from others in the leadership, it concerned the need for intensified ideological indoctrination of China's youth. He personally launched a new "patriotic education" campaign and a "moral values" campaign, while fully endorsing a new round of a "counter bourgeois liberalization" campaign, as well as mandatory military training for entering university students. This is somewhat interesting, and a slightly different emphasis from the regime's otherwise dominant narrative: that the spring 1989 uprisings were the result of a combination of American subversion combined with indulgent and indecisive leadership on the part of Zhao Ziyang. In Jiang's inaugural speech before the Fourth Plenum of the Thirteenth Central Committee on June 24, 1989—just three weeks after the crackdown—Jiang emphasized the roles of the demonstrators themselves, particularly the youth:[9]

> We will definitely ferret out and expose all political conspiracies that gave rise to the disturbances and rebellion, and we will not stop halfway. . . . We must crack down firmly and show no leniency. As for those who merely

> became drawn into the disturbances and rebellion in varying degrees, we need to do more to educate them and win them over [through education]. As for the young students and others who committed errors in word and deed because they failed to comprehend the true situation, we need to help them review the lessons from this experience and thereby improve their understanding. . . . Most young people support reform and opening up, but many of them do not understand China's past and present. Consequently, they cannot understand how protracted, formidable, and complex reform is, and they dream of bringing the West's material civilization to China overnight. These people are susceptible to propaganda promoting the capitalist system.

In September 1989, presaging his Patriotic Education Campaign, Jiang gave a strong speech about patriotism and the need to better inculcate it among youth.[10] In another speech a month later he also dwelled on youth and their "false understanding" of democracy.[11] In a major speech on "Party building" at the end of the year, he emphasized the importance of giving "top priority to ideological matters."[12] Thus, in the immediate aftermath of Tiananmen, Jiang did not disagree with or challenge his colleagues' emphasis on beefing up internal security or blaming the United States as the behind-the-scenes conspirator—but, rather, he did somewhat differently emphasize the factors of ideology, patriotism, and youth. Perhaps that reflected his own personal intellectual background, but it did subtly distinguish him from the other hardline leaders at the time. After these initial emphases, beginning in 1994 Jiang began to concentrate considerably on "Party building" (党建),[13] a subject that would preoccupy him throughout his tenure.

The Key Impact of the Fall of Other Communist Party-States

Following on the heels of the East European revolutions and two years of intensified repression in China, as if the leadership's siege mentality was not already severe enough, in August 1991 the unthinkable occurred for the CCP: the Communist Party of the Soviet Union (CPSU) and the USSR itself were overthrown (it is often said that they "collapsed," but in fact they were overthrown). This seminal event produced what China scholar Richard Baum described as "post-Soviet traumatic stress syndrome" for the CCP leadership and Party.[14] However, following the initial shock, the CCP under Jiang Zemin's leadership (and directed by his right-hand man Zeng Qinghong) undertook probably one of the most important acts in its history: a systematic and thorough post-mortem analysis of the causes of the fall of the USSR and other East European communist party-states. Many—if not all—of the political actions and reforms undertaken on Jiang Zemin's watch derived *directly*, I would argue, from the CCP's diagnoses of the causes of collapse of these other communist regimes. It is thus extremely important to understand these analyses. In my previous book *China's Communist Party: Atrophy & Adaptation* I offered a thorough reconstruction of the CCP's internal deliberations.[15]

Following the initial overly simplified conclusion that Mikhail Gorbachev was responsible for the East European overthrows (because he let each of these regimes know that they were on their own and Moscow would not intervene) and also for the dissolution of the Soviet Union (because of his liberalizing reforms of *glasnost* and *perestroika*), by mid-1990 CCP analysts began a more painstaking and systematic investigation into the underlying causes and individual complexities of each case. One authoritative analysis conducted by the Institute of Soviet and East European Studies of the Chinese Academy of Social Sciences (CASS) attributed the East European regime overthrows to seven factors: the deterioration of the economy; high levels of debt; a low standard of living; dictatorships (转正); ruling parties divorced from the populace; a lack of local-level Party building (基层党建); unions that were not a "bridge" (桥) between the Party and the working class; and "peaceful evolution" (和平演变) by Western countries.[16] As time passed the post-mortems became much more variegated and sophisticated. Specific country-by-country analyses appeared. The Polish case was judged to be the result primarily of a variety of economic factors. The Hungarian case, however, was seen as political in nature—owing to problems in the regime itself. East Germany's failures were deemed to have been a combination of economic and political factors. Czechoslovakia was said to have experienced "reform from below," stimulated by intellectuals and nascent civil society (and Václav Havel's "coffeeshop dissent"). In Romania, the party leadership (Ceaușescu) had lost control of the military and internal security services. Bulgaria, according to CASS analysts, simply experienced a "domino effect." Thus, as time went by, a more variegated and detailed set of analyses emerged from Chinese researchers concerning the causes of the demise of East European communist party-states. It may be no accident that these more diversified and daring analyses began to emerge after Deng Xiaoping's fabled Southern Tour in February 1992 and his pointed criticisms of "leftist thinking."

The post-mortems on the Soviet collapse followed a similar pattern. At first, everything was attributed to Gorbachev's reforms (errant ways in the CCP's view). This was certainly a factor, but they were more a convenient excuse for the Chinese than a more analytically rigorous explanation. Over the next few years Chinese analysts undertook a systematic dissection of the Soviet case in much more detail and identified a wide range of contributing factors (see Table 4.1).[17] The analytical effort involved a number of key Party-affiliated research institutions: the Central Party School, the International [Liaison] Department, the Institute of World Socialism, the Central Editing and Translation Bureau, the Policy Research Office of the Central Committee, the Academy of Social Sciences, and others. The research and analysis effort actually lasted an entire *decade*—finally culminating at the Fourth Plenum of the Sixteenth Central Committee in September 2004.

While this extraordinary effort stretched into Hu Jintao's period of rule, the bulk of it came on Jiang Zemin's watch. But it is vitally important to note that the effort during both Jiang's and Hu's reigns had one key commonality: a man named *Zeng Qinghong*. Jiang brought Zeng from Shanghai to Beijing with him in 1989 and he thereafter became Jiang's most trusted senior official and troubleshooter. Zeng had already distinguished himself as early as 1984 in the Shanghai municipal Party committee's Organization Department, where he had experimented with administrative and political reforms that had attracted the attention of Hu Yaobang.[18] Jiang oversaw Zeng's successive appointments as deputy director of the General Office of the Central Committee (the day-to-day organizational nerve center of the Party), head of the Central Committee Secretariat (the central unit for policy coordination), director of the CCP Organization Department (responsible for Party personnel nationwide), president of the Central Party School, member of the Politburo Standing Committee, and PRC vice-president. Zeng Qinghong's rapid ascent through the upper ranks of the CCP was by any standards remarkable and, in my view, his elevation was singularly important in formulating CCP political reforms during Jiang's and Hu Jintao's rule. They effectively ended when Zeng was forced to retire, for mandatory age reasons, in 2008 (I describe these reforms below and in the next chapter).

Another acolyte Jiang elevated from Shanghai named Wang Huning (a former Fudan university political science professor and at that time a colleague of mine) was also extremely important in these reforms. One of Wang's fortes has been in the "branding" of policy initiatives and campaigns. Many of the slogans (口号) attached to Jiang's and Hu's (and now Xi Jinping's) policy initiatives are widely believed to have been generated by Wang Huning. Among many others they include Jiang's "Three Represents" and Hu's "Harmonious Society." In terms of sheer political survival Wang is indeed unique, as he has now been at the very upper reaches of the CCP under three consecutive leaders for over *thirty years*. Today he is a Politburo Standing Committee member and in charge of all intra-Party affairs. No other Party official has had such a lengthy tenure during the post-Mao era (he is discussed further in Chapter 6).

Zeng and Wang together had an outsized impact on Party reform during the 1995–2008 period—drawing key lessons from the Soviet and East European experiences. This was what I consider to be a "liberal" period of Party reform—in contrast to the years after 2009 when Party reforms took a distinctly more "conservative" direction during Hu Jintao's last three years in office and throughout Xi Jinping's subsequent tenure. This shows that Wang Huning is something of an ideological chameleon—first liberal from 1995 through 2007, and then distinctly conservative after 2008. His own shift is representative, however, of two different contending schools of interpretation among Chinese analysts concerning the *lessons* of the Soviet and East European regime overthrows. The two contending schools did not so much differ over the analytical *causes* of the regime changes—but they did definitely differ over the *lessons* to be drawn for China and the CCP.

Let us digress to consider first the generally agreed-upon causes and then the two divergent schools that emerged in the CCP concerning the lessons and the actions that the CCP would need to take in order to sustain itself in power and avoid a Soviet-style meltdown. I emphasize that this is my own personal interpretation—the CCP itself has never identified two such contending schools and other foreign specialists in Chinese politics may not agree with what follows. But after years of careful analysis and reflection, this is the way I see it. Readers are further reminded that the whole reason why understanding this intra-Party analysis and discourse matters is because it is absolutely central to the political, social, and economic policies adopted by the Jiang, Hu, and Xi regimes. It is about *more* than simply political intra-Party reforms—as the CCP also drew clear lessons about the Soviet and East European regimes' economic and social policies that affected the political durability of the party-state. So much of what China and the CCP have done over the past three decades can, I believe, be traced *directly* to the collapse/overthrow of the Soviet Union and East European states (plus the lessons drawn from their own Tiananmen crisis of 1989). This is indicative of the CCP's ability to *reflect, learn*, and *adapt*. I am of the view that in some policy areas—notably foreign policy—the CCP is rather rigid and inflexible. But in economic policy, and in this instance of Party reform, it must be said that the CCP has been remarkably adaptable. Adaptation does not necessarily have to be liberal in nature—retrenchment and repression are also forms of adaptation. We have seen these two alternating features during the Jiang, Hu, and Xi regimes: 1995–2008 was generally liberal, with a shift to extreme conservativism thereafter. Readers will immediately wonder: why the shift after 2008? The answer, in my view, had to do with a number of factors: the retirement of Zeng Qinghong left no powerful advocate at the top of the system, and Hu Jintao himself was a weakened "lame duck" leader by that time; the "color revolutions" that had occurred around that time in former Soviet republics (Georgia in 2003, Ukraine in 2005, Kyrgyzstan in 2005, and Moldova in 2009); the "saffron revolution" in Myanmar in 2007; the 2010 "jasmine revolutions" across North Africa and the Middle East; riots in Lhasa and Urumqi in 2009; the strengthening of the internal security apparatus under Zhou Yongkang; the 2008 Olympics had ended and the global financial crisis was occurring; and, finally, conservative Xi Jinping was the heir apparent. For these multiple reasons, Chinese leadership dynamics definitely shifted in 2009.

Returning to the conclusions drawn about the *causes* of the Soviet collapse (*not* including the East European regimes), these can be clustered into four categories (economic factors, political and coercive factors, social and cultural factors, and international factors) and they are captured in Table 4.1.

Table 4.1: Chinese Assessments of Factors Contributing to the Collapse of the Soviet Union

Economic Factors	Political and Coercive Factors	Social and Cultural Factors	International Factors
Economic stagnation	All features of "totalitarianism" (*jiquanzhuyi*)	Intimidated population due to totalitarian terror	"Peaceful Evolution" campaign of the West
Overly centralized economy and retarded market mechanisms	Overconcentration of political power in top leader; personal dictatorship	Low standard of living	Economic stresses caused by Cold War containment policies
Collectivized and large-scale state agriculture	Failure to replace political leaders systematically	Society cut off from outside world in all respects	Military stresses caused by the Cold War
Nonintegration into international economic systems and international financial institutions	No intra-Party democracy	Alienation from workplace and party-state	Expansionist and hegemonic policies, especially under Brezhnev
Party dominance of government economic apparatus	Ideological rigidity and distorted Marxism	Low levels of worker efficiency, poor incentives, shoddy production	Soviet chauvinism within international communist movement
Low tax base	Party dominance of the state	Production slowdown and workplace unrest	Domination of Eastern Europe and other client states (Cuba, Vietnam)
Severe price distortions, owing to heavy subsidies	Prolonged "leftist" tendencies from Stalin until Gorbachev ("rightist")	Pervasive alcoholism	
Overdevlopment of heavy industry to detriment of tertiary industries	Party enjoys special privileges and becomes "ruling class"	Repression of, and chauvinism toward, non-Russian ethnic groups—including ethnic cleansing, forced labor, and forced relocation of ethnic minorities	

Table 4.1: *continued*

Overemphasis on defense industries and military sector of economy	Bureaucratic inefficiency	Rising autonomous nationalist identities separate from USSR
State monopoly of property rights	Overconcentration of power in *nomenklatura*; overly large bureaucracy	Moral vacuum, public cynicism, and public "crisis in faith" in the system
Little revenue sharing between center and localities	Poorly developed mechanisms to police party members for breach of discipline	Persecution of intellectuals
Inefficiencies of scale of production	"Crisis of trust" in party leaders → "crisis of faith" in socialist system	Dogmatism among intellectuals
Dogmatic ideological bias against capitalism	Began political reforms (*glasnost*) before economic foundation was ready	"Pluralization" of the media under Gorbachev
Perestroika too little, too late, and too fast	Emasculation in role of Supreme Soviet and local Soviets → checks and balances of state on part became meaningless. Falsehood of federalism—dominance of other republics and communist parties Success of Western "Peaceful Evolution" campaign to usurp Soviet power Gorbachev tried to democratize Communist Party of the Soviet Union (too much, too late), and remake it as a social-democratic party	Breakdown in the relations of Communist Party of the Soviet Union with various social sectors Disillusion of youth

From this general consensus concerning the causes of collapse of the Soviet Union, two main—and contending—schools emerged within the CCP concerning the lessons to be drawn for China and the CCP in order to avoid a similar fate.[19] The first group were the Conservatives: those who believed that the proto-liberal reforms of Gorbachev worked in tandem with the subversive "peaceful evolution" tactics of the West to directly precipitate the collapse of the Soviet Union and sow the seeds of "counter-revolution" elsewhere. They similarly concluded that the compromises made by the ruling regimes with protestors in East Germany, Poland, and Czechoslovakia contributed directly to their downfalls—arguing that if force had been used instead, as in Beijing in 1989, they would likely have survived. When the Ceaușescu regime in Romania decided to use force in Timişoara in December 1989 the military and state security services split and abandoned the regime, with the result that Ceaușescu and his wife were overthrown and executed on Christmas Eve. We now know the same occurred in Leipzig on October 9, 1989. The East German (GDR) leadership had decided to opt for the "Chinese solution" (the term used by GDR leadership) on that evening: Stasi forces were armed and instructed to use lethal force, but they demurred when confronted by massive demonstrations far larger than they anticipated.[20] Unlike Beijing, where regular army units were called in, the dozens of paramilitary Stasi was not equipped or prepared to undertake a large-scale lethal suppression.

From these events, the CCP Conservatives drew three principal conclusions:

- Do not engage in proto-liberal reforms within the Party or government, and maintain absolute dominance of and resolute control over the party-state apparatus.
- Anticipate unrelenting efforts from the West (particularly the United States) to undermine and subvert the regime from within—the so-called policy of "peaceful evolution" (和平演变), to peacefully evolve communist systems into democratic systems. In particular, be on high alert against the development of civil society and religious actors—which are subversive in their own right, but will receive support from Western governments, intelligence agencies, and NGOs.

- Strengthen and maintain absolute control by the Communist Party over the internal security services and military and resist dangerous attempts to "nationalize" them.

These were—and still are—the central lessons learned by the Conservatives in the Chinese Communist Party. In addition, they concluded that growing the economy and being integrated into the international system were further guarantors necessary for survival (both of which the Soviet and East European regimes lacked). The Conservatives implemented these consensus measures between 1989 and 1995.

However, over time, a second line of analysis, and second group, emerged within the CCP—advocates of *proactive and managed political reform*. I call them the "Reformists." They agreed with the Conservatives that splits in the security apparatus at critical moments precipitated the ultimate unraveling of those regimes. They also agreed that economic growth and integration into the world order were essential elements that would likely have helped sustain the regimes' grip on power. And the Reformists were aware of the "peaceful evolution" efforts of the West. But the political reformers broke with the Conservatives over the issue of Gorbachev's *glasnost* and *perestroika*. They did not necessarily agree with all of his policies, but they concluded that the Soviet party-state was in dire need of reformation. The essence of their critique of the causes of Soviet collapse had to do with the decades-long atrophy of the Party apparatus itself. In their revisionist but reformist view, the Soviet Union actually began to decline under Stalin in the 1930s! With the exception of Nikita Khrushchev's reforms from 1956 to 1964 (when he was ousted from power), this line of Chinese analysis concluded that the USSR had experienced an inexorable six-decade-long decline during which the party-state became sclerotic, ossified, top-heavy, elitist, overly bureaucratic, and corrupt, while the country's economy had become militarized during the Cold War, and Moscow's foreign policy had become adventurist, revisionist, chauvinistic, hegemonic, and "social imperialist."

The upshot of the Reformists' analysis was that by the time Gorbachev came to power and launched his reforms, the economic and political systems were already too badly broken and thus unable to withstand his shock therapy. In their view Gorbachev's reforms were *not* intrinsically wrong—they just came too late and too fast. To be sure, they did not agree with all of Gorbachev's reforms, but they drew the principal conclusion that for a ruling communist party to stay alive it was imperative to be proactive and dynamic. Stasis was a recipe for sclerosis, atrophy, decline, and ultimate collapse. These Chinese reformist analysts perceived many of the same processes to have precipitated the institutional crises that gripped the East European party-states (in addition to the important fact that they had not experienced their own indigenous revolutions, but were regimes imposed by the Soviet Union).

Thus, in the decade after 1989 the CCP's internal assessments evolved and two distinct factions emerged—those who favored managed political opening from above, and those who resisted it. The latter cohort believed and argued that it was not only inadvisable to liberalize, but that the ability to manage the process was a chimera, as such incremental liberalization would quickly mushroom out of control. The Conservatives prevailed until around 1995–1997, especially when the leadership balance shifted at the 15th Party Congress.[21] Thereafter, Li Peng, the reviled Premier and public face of the Tiananmen massacre, was finally shunted aside to a ceremonial position at the National People's Congress. He was replaced by the dynamic, decisive, get-things-done Zhu Rongji. Zhu took immediate charge and oversaw five years of systematic overhaul of the nation's economic structure. Hu Jintao was also elevated to the Politburo Standing Committee. The remaining Tiananmen hardliners went into retirement, and other senior leaders were reshuffled. It was in this changed leadership context that Jiang Zemin devoted a whole section of his speech to the Congress to political reforms, explicitly declaring that "we should press ahead with the reform of the political structure."[22] It subtly signaled that the political reformers had reasserted themselves—thus kicking off a ten-year period of efforts to manage political change from above.

During this period, which began during the last four years of Jiang Zemin's tenure (1998–2002) and continued through the first six of Hu Jintao's term (2002–2008), the political reformers stealthily but steadily experimented with loosening a variety of political controls in several spheres. During this decade the CCP:[23]

- strengthened local Party committees;
- experimented with voting for multi-candidate Party secretaries, while expanding nationwide multi-candidate elections for local government officials;
- recruited more businesspeople and intellectuals into the Party (Jiang Zemin's theory of the "Three Represents");
- expanded Party consultation with non-Party groups—so-called "consultative democracy" (协商民主) and "multi-party cooperation" (多党合作);
- increased the transparency of the Politburo's proceedings;
- improved discussion and feedback mechanisms within the Party—so-called "intra-Party democracy" (党内民主);
- regularized consultations between the CCP and Chinese People's Political Consultative Congress (政协);
- implemented more meritocratic criteria for evaluation and promotions for all cadres (by the CCP Organization Department and State Council Ministry of Personnel);
- instituted a system of mandatory mid-career training for all 45 million state and Party cadres (three months every three years);
- enforced term limits and retirement requirements;
- rotated officials and military officers between job assignments every couple of years;
- loosened controls on the state and private media;
- gave intellectuals greater scope and license to create and voice more pluralistic opinions;
- allowed the dramatic growth of civil society, including domestic and foreign NGOs;
- introduced more foreign ideas in the higher educational system.

Through these reforms the Party leadership was clearly trying to *strengthen* the Party and political system by incrementally liberalizing and loosening it (from above) without losing control of the process. This led to greater regularization and institutionalization of the Party and the policy process—captured by Western scholars' description of "resilient authoritarianism." This managed approach grew directly out of the political reformers' alternative interpretation of the causes of collapse of the former communist party-states. The goal was not at all to institute truly liberal policies in the Western sense—which were rejected outright by Jiang Zemin in his 2001 speech "The Objective of Political Restructuring Is to Improve the Socialist Political System."[24] Yet, Jiang, Zeng Qinghong, Wang Huning, and the political reformers believed that *proactive change* was the only way to avoid the trap of stagnancy that afflicted all of those former regimes. The Conservatives were more *reactive* in trying to *prevent* the emergence of civil society, a more independent media, a more autonomous military, a more liberal intelligentsia, and a more open society. The Conservatives were present within the CCP throughout the Jiang Zemin and Hu Jintao periods, but they were effectively neutered by Jiang Zemin and Zeng Qinghong. Jiang was, after all, the Party and state leader—and it very much matters what the paramount leader supports in that system. With Jiang and Zeng removed from power, and Hu being weakened, by 2009 the Conservatives were able to reassert themselves.

While this was the overall dynamic guiding Party reform during Jiang's reign, he also undertook several individual political campaigns that were part of the overall Party reform agenda. These included:

- The "spiritual civilization" (精神文明) campaign of 1996. This was an amalgam of traditional Chinese values, frugal communist values, Asian values (epitomized by the example of Singapore), public virtues of morality and politeness, and a cultured society.[25]
- The "talk about politics" (讲政治) campaign of 1996. This was a campaign to improve Party cadres' "spirit," discipline, and organizational rectitude.[26]
- The "three stresses" (三讲) campaign of 1996. This was an ideological rectification campaign for cadres to "stress study, stress politics, stress integrity."[27]
- The "Three Represents" (三个代表) campaign of 2000–2001 (see discussion below).[28]
- The "well-off society" (小康社会) campaign of 2002, to make China a "moderately well-off society" by 2020.[29]

Thus, Jiang Zemin did indeed leave his imprint on several dimensions of Chinese politics, ideology, and Party rectification during his tenure. These

Figure 4.2 Jiang Zemin Delivers Deng Xiaoping's Eulogy, February 26, 1997
Source: Associated Press

initiatives would continue through the end of his term in 2002 and well into Hu Jintao's term. This was particularly the case after the death of Deng Xiaoping in February 1997. Jiang presided over the memorial service and presented the eulogy while weeping (Figure 4.2).[30] Thereafter, no longer in Deng's shadow, Jiang clearly was seen to be the paramount leader of China.

With the help of Zeng Qinghong, Jiang also managed to maneuver out of the senior leadership two potential rivals: Beijing Mayor Chen Xitong and internal security czar Qiao Shi. Taken together with the replacement of Li Peng by Zhu Rongji as Premier, by 1997 Jiang was able to clear out potential rivals from the Politburo. This permitted him to promote a number of others (many from Shanghai) that included Huang Ju, Wu Bangguo, Li Changchun, Han Zheng, and Jia Qinglin. These individuals formed a nucleus of support around Jiang in the Politburo.

The "Three Represents".[31] Jiang Zemin's "important thought" (重要思想) of the "Three Represents" (三个代表) was first enunciated by him in a series of speeches between February 2000 and a high-profile speech at the Central Party School commemorating the 80th anniversary of the establishment of the CCP on July 1, 2001.[32] The originators of the concept were apparently Liu Ji, a theoretician whom Jiang brought with him from Shanghai to Beijing,[33] and Wang Huning, another key aide Jiang also brought from Shanghai and appointed as head of the Central Committee Policy Research Office. The Three Represents were:

1. The Party should represent the advanced productive forces in society.
2. The Party should represent advanced modern culture.
3. The Party should represent the interests of the vast majority of the people.

Jiang's odd-sounding theory was quickly dismissed by most Western analysts (and ordinary Chinese alike) as yet another propagandistic cliché in the long liturgical litany of much-ballyhooed but quickly forgotten Party mantras. Yet, upon closer examination, the Three Represents indicated an important, even radical, shift in Party philosophy, Party composition, and Party orientation. At the 16th Party Congress in 2002 the Three Represents were added to the CCP Constitution.

The main policy significance of the new ideological initiative at the time lay in the "first represent." This reflected an opening to recruit the so-called advanced productive forces into the Party—for example, entrepreneurs and intellectuals from the private sector. Jiang first signaled this initiative in a speech during a May 2000 inspection tour of the lower Yangzi River region. Cloaked in oblique Marxist language, Jiang's remarks put the Party on notice that a major change in recruitment policy was forthcoming: "We must correctly understand and handle the relationship between emancipating and developing the social productive forces on the one hand and readjusting and perfecting the production relations on the other under new historical conditions, and *consciously reform and readjust those parts of the superstructure* that do not match the development of the economic foundation."[34]

This initiative was a demonstrable break with the eighty-year Marxist/Maoist emphasis on recruiting workers, farmers, and others of a traditionally proletarian background into the Party. But, Jiang argued, the class composition of Chinese society and the proletariat had changed as a result of two decades of economic reform, and if the Party was to remain the vanguard of the proletariat, it needed to become more inclusive of the newly emergent elements of the working class, particularly in the private sector. In so doing Jiang echoed Deng Xiaoping's reclassification (at the 1978 National Science Conference) of intellectuals as members of the working class. But this was a very controversial move within the Party, given its proletarian origins, identity, and ideology. Viewed more broadly, Jiang was also signaling that the CCP intended to go the way of many other ruling political parties in East Asia—to become a party of elites, including commercial elites.

Although the emphasis of the campaign was initially placed on this aspect of Party recruitment, Jiang's speeches and exposition of the Three Represents also discussed other aspects of Party reform: reforming the Communist Youth League; intensifying propaganda work; experimenting with new economic reforms; combatting corruption; strengthening Party cells and committees nationwide, but particularly at the local level; building a "political civilization" (政治文明); and building a party of an "advanced nature" (先进性). These other facets of the Three Represents became clearer and were emphasized over the period 2002–2005 following the 16th Party Congress.

According to Zheng Bijian, then the Executive Vice-President of the Central Party School and a key Jiang adviser, the Three Represents theory was actually a comprehensive program for Party reform that grew directly out of the CCP's assessment of the reasons for the failure and collapse of the Soviet Communist Party, as well as a three-year internal assessment of the CCP's own weaknesses.[35] In another interview with the Xinhua News Agency, Zheng emphasized that the Three Represents was also a theoretical attempt to come to grips with four phenomena that were affecting China and the CCP: globalization and the advance of science and technology; the diversification of Chinese society, social organizations, and lifestyles; lax Party organizations; and the need to improve the CCP rank and file.[36]

Jiang developed a number of these themes in his July 2001 Central Party School speech. In the wake of his speech, a major national propaganda campaign was launched to publicize and propagate it. Special classes were taught at the Central Party School (中央党校) for Central Committee members, study sessions were convened for Party cadres across the country, the media was filled with entreaties for the public to assiduously study the concept, and countless study guides were published to explain the concept to Party members and the public alike.

Like other ideological campaigns of the post-Mao era, however, Jiang's new theory was a codification of experimental policies already under way. As my George Washington University colleague Bruce Dickson's research demonstrates, the Party had experimented with recruiting greater numbers of intellectuals and entrepreneurs over the previous decade.[37] University of Glasgow scholar Jane Duckett's research also demonstrates the cozy partnership between Party committees, local government, and private business at the local urban level dating to the late 1980s.[38]

Having put the official stamp of approval on the new policy, CCP efforts to recruit from these sectors—but particularly from the private-sector entrepreneurial class—accelerated. Yet, interestingly, following Jiang's announcement of the new policy initiative, the recruitment of entrepreneurs into the Party lagged substantially behind what the CCP envisioned. This was probably due to the fact that in China's market economy, where the Party no longer controls various goods and services, the incentives for joining it are substantially fewer. If anything, the Party represents a de facto "political protection racket" for those in private business. The CCP seeks to co-opt the entrepreneurial elites, while some in this newly emerging class seek the political "cover" of the Party to more safely pursue their business interests. Official figures, however, indicate that the Party's attempts to recruit entrepreneurs and establish Party cells in private-sector enterprises were slow. By the end of 2003, 30 percent of private-sector entrepreneurs were Party members—but, as Dickson points out, this number largely represented the widespread privatization of state firms and factories rather than the recruitment of *new* businesspeople into the CCP.[39] With this wave of privatizations, former firm managers and Party secretaries could be counted officially as members of the "private sector."

Thus, Jiang Zemin's Three Represents was an attempt to bring the newly emergent business elites within the CCP's orbit and thereby to co-opt and control them. This was another lesson that the Party learned from examining the East European cases—where entrepreneurial elites in Hungary, Czechoslovakia, and Poland all joined the anti-regime forces.

Jiang Zemin and the Military

Another sphere in which Jiang had a pronounced impact was on the People's Liberation Army. This is ironic insofar as he previously had zero experience in, or relationship with, the PLA or its brass when he came to office in 1989. Jiang had never served in the military himself and his only tie was through his uncle Jiang Shanqing. His lack of military connections was a distinct vulnerability, as all Chinese leaders need military support politically. But by 1995 Jiang had completely reversed this vulnerability and had built a strong power base in the military. How he did so is an interesting story and a prime example of the "bureaucratic politician" approach to his rule.[40]

Jiang succeeded Deng as Chairman of the Central Military Commission (CMC) in November 1989, thus becoming the fifth CMC chairman in 40 years. On this occasion Jiang reportedly admitted to the CMC members:[41]

> At the Fourth Plenum I said that I was not worthy of being elevated to the position of General Secretary; I did not have the ideological preparation. This decision to promote me to the position of Central Military Commission Chairman has also left me without proper ideological preparation. I have not undertaken work in military affairs and have no experience in this regard. I deeply feel the responsibility, but my ability is insufficient. The Party has placed a big responsibility on me. I shall certainly assiduously study military affairs, strive to become quickly familiar with the situation in the military, and diligently and quickly carry out the duties of the position.

Despite his understandable uncertainty and no false modesty, over the course of his tenure as China's leader Jiang Zemin did a remarkable job of cultivating a strong base of support in the armed forces. He certainly did a better job of this than either Hu Yaobang or Zhao Ziyang, neither of whom had a great deal of PLA support. Jiang weathered the 1995–1996 Taiwan Straits crises and the 2001 EP-3 spy plane crisis with the United States; he oversaw the highly sensitive removal of the Yang brothers (Yang Shangkun and Yang Baibing) at the 14th Party Congress in 1992, and carried out a subsequent thorough purge of their supporters throughout the PLA (replacing them with a new cohort of generals loyal to him); and he undertook the difficult task of divesting the PLA from its vast business empire in 1998.

In cultivating a base of support in the PLA, Jiang was careful, persistent, and above all methodical in his strategy and tactics. From the very beginning of his tenure in office he frequently visited military bases and units, cultivated relationships with various high-ranking officers, staked out supportive positions on policy issues that mattered to the military, and then followed through with unprecedented financial resources. China's official military budget grew at an average of 14.6 percent per annum from 1989, when Jiang took over, to 2002 when he left office—tripling in volume from $11.4 to $32.14 billion.[42] In his speeches Jiang echoed all of the right themes that mattered to the PLA: professionalization; modernization of equipment, doctrine, and research and development; protection of state sovereignty and core national security interests; internal stability; and "absolute loyalty to the Party" (党的绝对领导).[43] Importantly, he also cultivated support among institutional sub-constituencies within the armed forces—each of the four central departments, the regional commands, the Second Artillery missile forces, the military-industrial complex (given his industrial engineering background Jiang took particular interest in upgrading the defense industries), and the People's Armed Police. Jiang adopted a deliberate and methodical building-block approach of being all things to all quarters of the PLA, showering each with resources (what might be described as "pork barrel politics with Chinese characteristics"), thereby adopting and thereby co-opting each institutional constituency. It paid off. This is the same tactic that he pursued with the civilian party and government apparatus as well. It was very astute, and it played to his own background as a bureaucratic technocrat.

Soon after his appointment Jiang made sure to pay courtesy calls on, and cultivate, the retired military elders: Admirals Liu Huaqing and Chen Zaidao, and Generals Xiao Ke, Zhang Aiping, Zhang Zhen, You Taizhong, Yang Dezhi, Ye Fei, Wang Zhen, among others. Before he acquiesced in the removal of the Yang brothers in 1992, he was also solicitous of them. Having done so, though, Jiang tacked hard toward the "professional" wing of the

PLA and away from the political commissars (thoroughly purging Yang Baibing's entrenched network inside the General Political Department). Jiang also made a point early on of visiting military units around the country. Within the first year of his tenure Jiang had "inspected" (调查) *all* seven military regions and met with their commanders (the first CMC chairman to ever do so). By 1993, the *Liberation Army Daily* itself estimated that Jiang had visited on average one military unit per month.[44] During these visits Jiang not only met with regional commanders, but also made a point of inspecting rank-and-file troops. He questioned them about their living conditions—following up by raising their wages three times in his first five years as commander-in-chief.[45] Interestingly, and not by coincidence, several of the regional military (MR) commanders with whom Jiang came into contact during these initial inspection tours were later promoted by him to key central-level positions in military hierarchy in Beijing. Lanzhou MR commander Fu Quanyou became Jiang's choice to take over the General Logistics Department in 1992; Guangzhou MR commander Zhu Dunfa would be promoted to commandant of the National Defense University; and a visit to the Jinan MR in July 1992 brought Jiang into contact with General Zhang Wannian, whom Jiang promoted to be Chief of General Staff (the most senior ranking PLA officer) and vice-chairman of the CMC.

Following the promotions and reshuffles in the wake of the Yang brothers' purge in 1992, Jiang next rescinded the proposed promotions of forty senior officers that General Yang Baibing had put forward on the eve of the 14th Party Congress. Then the real housecleaning began. Within two months, by the end of 1992, an estimated 300 generals—about half of those in the entire PLA—were replaced. After the quick strike on the upper echelons of the PLA, in which the commanders and political commissars of all seven military regions were outed, the personnel shake-up then reached down into the Military Districts and Group Army levels. These changes were said to be "presided over personally by Jiang Zemin."[46] In December 1993, May 1994, and August 1995 Jiang again ordered additional shake-ups of the upper echelons of the senior brass, involving approximately 1,000 officers altogether.[47] These rounds of personnel change-outs were more extensive than the 1992 overhaul. Jiang's next move in his personal network building came with much-publicized promotions and the conferment of the rank of full general on eighteen lieutenant and major generals. This included Deng Xiaoping's trusted military aide de camp General Wang Ruilin, who had played an instrumental role in dismantling the Yang network. He also tightened his personal control over the Central Guards Unit of the Beijing Garrison, which is responsible for the personal protection of all CCP leaders and security of the capital. By 1996 Jiang had his own network of loyal PLA officers in place.[48]

One of Jiang's riskiest, but most important, moves came in 1998 when he issued the divestiture order to remove the PLA, People's Armed Police (PAP), and all military units from their lucrative business dealings (which had resulted in rampant corruption).[49] This was necessary to reduce off-budget secondary monies, to control corruption, and to focus the armed forces single-mindedly on military modernization. Time spent in business was net time lost in military training. The PLA's plunge into business had caused serious negative effects on force readiness, morale, and discipline in the ranks. The military owned and operated an estimated 15,000 commercial enterprises at the time. Smuggling was facilitated by PLA units, military airfields and ports were being used for illicit purposes, lavish hotels were being built across the country, brothels were operated, multiple mansions were maintained for indulgent lifestyles, promotions were bought and sold, and many generals grew rich—very rich. As the divestiture order was implemented, large caches of cash and gold were discovered at the residences of corrupt generals. Jiang's moves to crack down on the armed forces' commercial involvement, to tighten up command and control, and to place loyal lieutenants in key positions addressed the broader need for military loyalty and discipline, but also redounded to Jiang personally.

In sum, although Jiang Zemin came to power in 1989 with no ties to the PLA, within just a few years he had managed to build substantial support and respect from the military brass. This took work and did not occur by osmosis. But it paid off for Jiang. It may even have been a crucial reason, in fact, why he became more than a temporary transitional leader and was able to stay in power for thirteen years (in fact, he tenaciously clung to his position as CMC chair into 2004, even after he had stepped down from his Party and state positions). In some ways Jiang struck a marriage of mutual benefit with the PLA whereby he supported the military's professional goals and budgets in exchange for their political loyalty. It was during these years that the military moved decisively forward with its modernization and professionalization, leaving behind its longstanding symbiotic politicized relationship with the Party and its often interventionist role in national politics. It was during Jiang's tenure that I have argued elsewhere that the military and the Party became "bifurcated"[50]—with a de facto *quid pro quo:* the armed forces were to solely focus on their professional mission (following the 1998 commercial divestiture order) with the Party supporting this and providing the resources to do so. This constituted, in effect, a "depoliticization" of the PLA—although the military was constantly reminded of the requirement to be "absolutely loyal" to the Party. These were Jiang Zemin's legacies with the military.

Jiang Zemin and the Economy

Unlike the Party and the military, Jiang Zemin did not invest himself and his time very much in economic affairs. Other than his speech to the 15th Party Congress in 1997, in which he laid out an ambitious program of economic reform focused on overhauling the state sector, Jiang had relatively little to say and launched relatively few initiatives concerning the economy during his tenure.

This was due in large part to the appointment of his Shanghai colleague Zhu Rongji, who served as Vice-Premier from 1991 to 1998 and then as Premier through 2003. Zhu had succeeded Jiang as Mayor and Party Secretary of Shanghai, following the latter's elevation to the Center. The two were close, and Jiang could trust Zhu with the economy. Zhu was known as a shrewd and decisive administrator who knocked heads and got things done. The other reason is that prior to Zhu's appointment as Premier, Li Peng served in that position and there was a de facto division of labor between him and Jiang (the so-called "Jiang-Li system"), with Li Peng having overall charge of the State Council and the economy. As we have seen, Jiang ran the Party and the military while Li ran the economy. During Jiang's first few years in office, the economy had been in the doldrums following Tiananmen and the severe austerity program Li Peng had instituted in its aftermath. There was no positive political value for Jiang to get involved. His *Selected Works* reveals not a single speech given on the economy during his first three years in power until one in which he coined the term "socialist market economy" in June 1992 (which was subsequently formally adopted by the CCP at the Third Plenum in 1993).[51] He did give another speech that month concerning development in the lower Yangzi River delta.[52] If anything, during his tenure Jiang did emphasize the development of his native Shanghai and he showed real favoritism toward the metropolis. Toward the end of 1992 he also gave an extensive speech on the rural economy.[53] But, otherwise, Jiang did not have much to say about economic affairs in his first few years in office.

Perhaps the other reason that Jiang underinvested himself in economic affairs is because after 1992 and Deng's Southern Tour, the economy boomed. Why mess with success? So, whether things were going badly or going well, Jiang had no strong incentive to meddle with it. And he had bigger concerns with the Party, military, foreign affairs, and building his own power base. To be sure, problems of overheating initially accompanied the boom years—with inflation surging to 20 percent during 1993–1995 (owing to unrestrained fixed asset investment and a banking system that doled out cash like a open water spigot). Jiang did express his concern about this in a speech in March 1993 when he spoke of the need to maintain fiscal discipline.[54] But then Vice-Premier Zhu Rongji instituted a sixteen-point plan that was successful in engineering a "soft landing" by 1996. Thereafter the major problems remained overhauling the state-owned enterprises (SOEs) and the banking sector (which Zhu oversaw and rectified).[55] While Jiang had spent his entire career prior to the 1980s in the state industrial sector, he did not seem particularly involved or invested in this reform, leaving it to Zhu.[56]

What Jiang did take interest in was innovation. He gave several speeches on the subject,[57] and he made a habit of visiting research institutes, laboratories, and universities. During the 1990s he spearheaded the "Sparks Program"—an effort to create high-tech industrial parks and encourage the development of new innovative domestic companies—and in 2008 he launched the "Thousand Talent Program" (千人计划) to attract overseas scientific talent to China (and Chinese studying and working overseas to return to China). Jiang's emphasis on innovation fit well with his own career background in engineering.

A second initiative that is associated with Jiang was the "develop the west" (西部大开发) policy, which he launched in 2000.[58] It was a massive plan of development essentially for the vast and arid western regions of Gansu, Qinghai, Tibet, and Xinjiang, including a wide range of infrastructure, communications, new rail lines, public utilities, education, mineral extraction and energy development (including oil pipelines to Kazakhstan and Russia), reforestation, irrigation, and large-scale water diversion projects, harnessing of hydropower by building multiple dams on the Tibetan plateau (much to the consternation of downriver India, Bangladesh, Myanmar, Vietnam, Laos, and Thailand), and urban redevelopment. By promoting accelerated growth in the region, it also sought to narrow development and welfare gaps between the western provinces and other parts of China. The funding for this extremely ambitious plan was to come from four sources: the central government, transfer payments from coastal provinces, the World Bank, and foreign businesses.

A third economic initiative that is directly associated with Jiang was the "go out" (走出去) policy aimed at China's corporations, directing them to invest overseas and develop a global corporate presence. The earliest indication of the policy came in some internal speeches Jiang gave in mid-1992 in the lead-up to the 14th Party Congress that autumn.[59] In one indicative sentence in his report to the Party congress, Jiang said: "We should grant to enterprises and to science and technology research institutes the power to engage in foreign trade, and we should encourage enterprises to expand their investments abroad and their transnational operations."[60] From 1993 to 1996 Jiang continued to give internal speeches encouraging overseas investments, particularly in developing countries. On July 26, 1996, after returning from a state visit to Africa, Jiang gave an important speech in the city of Tangshan that for the first time explicitly encouraged Chinese firms to "go out." At the end of 1997, he again touted the idea when receiving participants at the National Foreign Investment Work Conference. Also that autumn, in his speech to the 15th Party Congress, Jiang again touted the initiative—but this time he coupled it with a call to "bring [investment] in and go out" (引进来, 走出去) and "take advantage of both markets" (domestic and foreign). He also signaled that "We should form internationally competitive companies and enterprise groups through market forces and policy guidance."[61]

In 1998 he stressed the new policy again on several other occasions. Finally, Jiang convened a Politburo meeting on the subject on January 20, 2000.[62] Thus, the "go out" policy is definitely associated with Jiang Zemin (I traced this in my previous book *China Goes Global*).[63]

Yet, other than these three areas (innovation, develop the west, and going out to invest abroad), there is little indication of Jiang's direct role in economic affairs. He did not invest much time in it, and when he did become involved it was usually on occasions of mandatory speeches to Party plenums or the National People's Congress (in these cases the speeches were certainly written for him). To be fair, the CCP leader is not mandated to become involved in economic affairs—that is the primary job of the Premier of the State Council, and Jiang had two very strong premiers to count on to oversee the economy.

This said, the Chinese economy did very well on Jiang Zemin's watch. National GDP (not adjusted for purchasing power parity) averaged 6 percent growth, tripling in value from $347.7 billion in 1989 when he took over to $1.47 trillion when he stepped down in 2002.[64] Progress was made on the gnawing problem of restructuring state-owned enterprises, but this was due entirely to Zhu Rongji's efforts. A banking crisis was averted in the mid-1990s, also due to Zhu's adroit management. Zhu also navigated China virtually unfazed through the Asian Financial Crisis of 1997.

However, on the negative side of the ledger, the coastal–inland development and income gap widened considerably during Jiang's time. This is illustrated in Figure 4.3, which shows changes in contributions to GDP by coastal, central, and western regions in 1989 when Jiang came to power and 2002 when he stepped down.

Jiang was definitely identified with favoring investment into coastal provincial development, notably his native Shanghai and the lower Yangzi delta. The widening coastal–inland gap was one principal reason to launch the "develop the west" program. Social inequalities also increased during his tenure. China's Gini Coefficient (a widely recognized measure of income inequality) increased dramatically from .35 in 1989 when Jiang took over to .45 in 2002 when he left office.[65] Corruption also deepened markedly.

On balance, Jiang certainly did no harm to the economy, and by discharging management of it to the Premier he could benefit from any

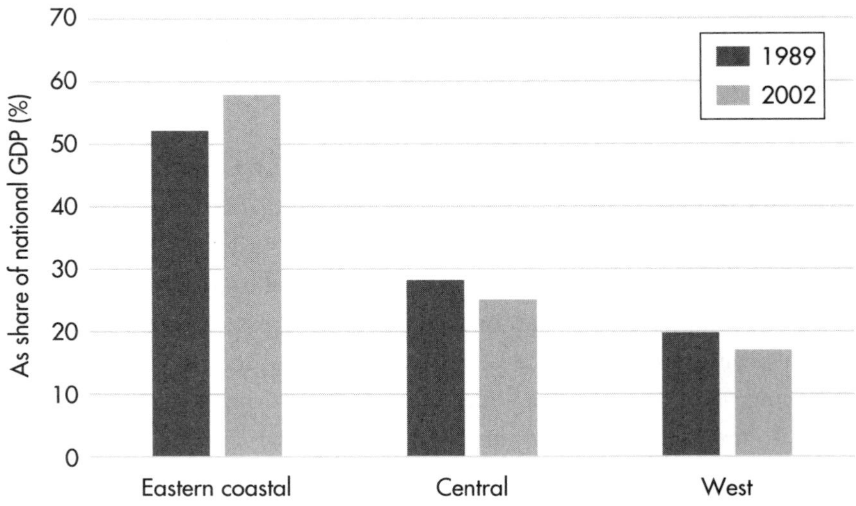

Figure 4.3 Regional Shares of National GDP, 1989 and 2002
Source: 1989 data from *Zhongguo Tongji Nianjian, 1990*, pp. 38 and 91; 2002 data from *Zhongguo Tongji Nianjian, 2003*, pp. 55 and 98.

accomplishments without being tarred with any fallout if things went wrong. This luxury of not being burdened with overseeing the economy freed up Jiang to concentrate on the three areas he cared much more about: political and Party affairs, the military, and foreign policy. Let us now turn to the latter.

Jiang Zemin and China's Foreign Policy

Jiang clearly enjoyed foreign policy and he did invest his time and energy in it. He particularly enjoyed bilateral exchanges with visiting foreign leaders, during which his extroverted persona was frequently on display before the cameras. He also reveled in hobnobbing together with other world leaders at multilateral forums. Jiang was often unscripted on such occasions, ignoring the "talking points" that had been prepared for him by aides, and speaking extemporaneously. After such occasions his aides would often slip a version of the prepared talking points to their foreign interlocutors, so as to "set the record straight" and convey what President Jiang had intended to convey. Jiang's behavior was highly unusual for a

Chinese leader, who are normally tightly scripted. This was a reflection of his extroverted personality, but it also reflected his comfort level as China's paramount leader.

While it is not easy to disentangle Jiang's personal roles from the PRC's collective actions and initiatives, it does seem to this observer that his actions with respect to the United States and Russia did have an impact beyond events simply occurring on his watch. Jiang also presided over the symbolic return of Hong Kong to China's sovereignty in 1997. Jiang also made an important speech in Geneva, Switzerland (in March 1999), where he laid out China's "New Security Concept"—which explicitly rejected alliances and collective security while promoting "cooperative comprehensive security"—an initiative that subsequently found its way into a variety of official PRC foreign policy and national security statements.[66] In 2000 Jiang kick-started what would become the Forum on China–Africa Cooperation (FOCAC), an unprecedented initiative that continues to this day. In a negative sense, Jiang's unsuccessful state visit to Japan in 1998—notably his speeches and actions while there—actually set back Sino-Japanese relations (squandering an opportunity to advance them). But, overwhelmingly, it must be said that Jiang Zemin's contributions to stabilizing—and then growing—China's ties with the world in the aftermath of the calamitous impact of the 1989 Tiananmen events were one of his signature accomplishments as leader. Let us consider two illustrative examples—relations with the United States and post-Soviet Russia.

Jiang Zemin and Relations with the United States

Managing strained relations with the United States, and trying to stabilize them, was a constant feature during Jiang's tenure. He inherited severely strained ties with the US following the Tiananmen massacre. For the next few years there was not much Jiang could personally do about that, and he still had to defer to Deng Xiaoping's continued management of foreign relations through the end of 1989. His inaugural speech to the Fourth Plenum on June 24, 1989 echoed the standard line on the legitimate need to quell the "counterrevolutionary rebellion," but—unlike Deng—he stopped short of blaming the uprising on the "hidden black hand" of the United States.[67]

On December 10, 1989, Jiang did meet with visiting American emissary (National Security Advisor) Brent Scowcroft and offered quite conciliatory remarks.[68]

The relationship remained in the deep freeze until November 19, 1993, when President Clinton invited Jiang to the inaugural APEC (Asia-Pacific Economic Cooperation) summit on Blake Island near Seattle. This was the first encounter between the American and Chinese heads of state following Tiananmen. As Clinton's chief China aide, Robert Suettinger of the National Security Council later observed about the stakes for Jiang going into the meeting: "For Jiang, the meeting with Clinton was a critical appearance. Still untested and considered a Deng puppet and a consensus seeker without strong views of his own, Jiang had a complex and nearly impossible agenda for the scheduled one-hour meeting. He had to show himself as a tough and determined leader . . . but at the same time encourage the American leader to take a more balanced, long-term approach to China and establish some personal rapport with him."[69] Jiang apparently didn't get the memo about the casual dress code—which was a harbinger of how the leaders interacted. Jiang showed up in a suit while Clinton donned a leather bomber jacket, lumberjack shirt, blue jeans, and cowboy boots.[70] Their one-on-one bilateral meeting (with aides and interpreters) did not go well. Jiang was very stiff and, uncharacteristically, stuck closely to his talking points.[71] Suettinger recalls that, "Jiang appeared nervous and seemed to address most of his remarks to the Chinese officials who accompanied him rather than at his American interlocutors."[72]

The next tests for Jiang were the 1995–1996 twin Taiwan Straits crises (during which China's military launched short-range missiles near Taiwan in 1995 in protest of a visit by its President Lee Teng-hui to the United States, and again in 1996 in an attempt to intimidate Taiwan voters after their election of Lee as president). These events interrupted feelers sent by both sides to find a new accommodation and roadmap to advance the relationship. As Chairman of the Central Military Commission, Jiang had to approve the missile firings. They backfired (figuratively) and the aggressive actions set back relations further—even causing President Clinton to deploy two aircraft carrier battle groups to the vicinity of Taiwan for some saber-rattling in return.

More acrimonious encounters over human rights, trade, and nonproliferation followed. Then, in an attempt to get the relationship back on track, President Clinton's and Jiang's top national security aides (Tony Lake and Liu Huaqiu) met in Beijing in June 1996. The discussions went better and, at their conclusion, Jiang expressed pleasure during a bizarre free-ranging dialogue with Lake (mixing Chinese with idiomatic English) covering Chinese history, philosophy, poetry, computer chips, and other subjects.[73] As a result, the two governments agreed to reciprocal official visits. In October 1997 Jiang Zemin paid an official state visit to the United States (the first by a Chinese president in almost a decade). Behind closed doors at the White House, President Clinton pressed Jiang on improving human rights, and at a subsequent live press conference he took Jiang and China to task for being "on the wrong side of history" with regard to Tiananmen.[74] Otherwise, though, the two governments tried to turn the corner from their post-Tiananmen acrimony and put in place a new framework to "build toward a constructive strategic partnership for the 21st century."[75] Jiang's journey to the US also included visits to Honolulu, Williamsburg, Washington, Philadelphia, New York, Boston, and Los Angeles. Although shadowed by protesters at every stop, he was generally well received. This set the stage for a reciprocal visit by President Clinton to China the following year (June 1998). The eleven-day state visit included a highly symbolic review of an honor guard in Tiananmen Square, the site nine years earlier of the mass protests and massacre. The visit also went generally well, and the relationship seemed to be back on track.

But then, on May 7, 1999, a US Air Force strategic bomber flying a NATO mission during the Serbian/Kosovo conflict mistakenly bombed the Chinese embassy in Belgrade, destroying part of it and killing three Chinese embassy staff members. The Chinese public was understandably outraged and refused to accept the American claim that it was mistakenly hit as a target. Crowds in Beijing surrounded the US Embassy and pelted it with rocks, breaking windows and trapping Ambassador James Sasser and staff inside. For his part, Jiang Zemin refused to take phone calls of explanation and condolences from President Clinton for a week. Subsequently, an agreement was reached whereby the US Government undertook to pay $4.5 million in compensation to the families of those killed, while the Chinese side shelled out $2.7 million to compensate for damage to the embassy. To this day, however, the Chinese government and public have never accepted the American explanation that the bombing was an accident.

Jiang also presided over a second tense incident in Sino-American relations in April 2001, when an American surveillance plane (EP-3) on routine patrol along China's coastline (but well outside of China's sovereign airspace) was intercepted by a Chinese J-8 fighter, which buzzed the US plane a number of times at dangerously close proximity—the last time flying underneath and then suddenly arching upward in front, severing the nosecone of the EP-3. Both planes went into immediate downward dives. The Chinese J-8 crashed into the sea, killing the pilot. The EP-3 was headed for a similar fate, losing 8,000 feet in altitude, before pilot Lieutenant Shane Osborn used his sheer physical strength to arrest the nosedive and stabilize the plane's trajectory just 200 feet above the water. The damaged plane had to land at the nearest airfield—which turned out to be a Chinese military base on Hainan Island. The twenty-four crew members were taken into custody and interrogated over the course of ten days, before a diplomatic deal was arranged for their release. Jiang was stuck between strong nationalistic sentiment and the loss of life of the Chinese pilot, on the one hand, and the need to defuse the crisis with Washington and the new George W. Bush administration on the other. He adroitly managed both. He also agreed to a compromise whereby the American ambassador (Joseph Preuher, himself a former naval aviator and Commander of the Pacific Fleet) wrote a letter acknowledging the "two sorries": the US side was "sorry" for entering Chinese airspace and landing on Chinese soil without permission and was "sorry" about the loss of life of the Chinese pilot. This defused the crisis and allowed for the crew to return to the United States. No doubt, for Jiang, managing relations with the senior (and hawkish) PLA brass was a tricky element of the incident as well—but, as described above, by this time (2001) Jiang had built very strong ties with the military leadership (which paid off). He still had to assuage public sentiment, though, which was indignant about the surveillance flights and death of the Chinese pilot, and he received considerable domestic criticism for "capitulating" to the Americans.[76] But his somber demeanor in receiving the deceased pilot Wang Wei's widow and young son in the Great Hall of the People, proclaiming him a "people's martyr," helped to soothe public opinion.

Having navigated the tricky EP-3 incident, just over four months later came another challenge in US–China relations: the September 11 terror attacks on New York and Washington, DC. Jiang was reported to have coincidentally been watching CNN when the two planes struck the World Trade Center, thus witnessing the calamity live in real time. According to Chinese officials with whom I later spoke,[77] Jiang sought to immediately put through a call to President Bush at the White House. Of course, President Bush and the White House were in no position to take such a call—but within a week the two had talked, with Jiang offering China's condolences and full cooperation and assistance against al-Qaeda and the new "war on terror." This was a strategic stroke of genius on Beijing's and Jiang's part, and it fundamentally reoriented the Sino-American relationship—which had been extremely tense in the wake of the EP-3 incident, but also because of the hawkish views of China held by many senior Bush administration officials. In the immediate aftermath of 9/11, President Bush decided to take his first foreign trip in mid-October to China for the APEC summit in Shanghai, where he and Jiang were noticeably friendly before the cameras. Then just two weeks later, Bush hosted Jiang and his wife Wang Yeping at his family ranch in Texas. Thus, the US–China relationship, which had been marked by deep suspicions and high tensions at the outset of the Bush administration, enjoyed more than seven years of sound and steady improvement thereafter (they have never been as good since).

Jiang Zemin and Relations with Russia

Jiang also adroitly managed relations with Moscow in the aftermath of the momentous collapse of the Soviet Union.[78] After a hiatus and brief unease in Sino-Russian relations during 1991–1992, as the dust was settling and the new Russian Federation government was taking shape, Moscow and Beijing pragmatically decided to resume relations.[79] The Chinese invitation for new Russian President Boris Yeltsin's state visit to Beijing in December 1992 was a key step (ostensibly reciprocating Jiang Zemin's Moscow visit in May 1991 prior to the Soviet *dénouement*). Yeltsin's visit was reciprocated by another Jiang Zemin presidential visit to Moscow in September 1994, which triggered subsequent annual summits between either premiers or presidents.

Throughout these 1990s exchanges, the two sides signed a series of important bilateral agreements.[80] The more important ones included a military cooperation pact (1993, renewed in 1998 and 2003); a "constructive partnership" agreement (1994) which morphed into China's first "comprehensive strategic partnership" (1996); an Agreement on Mutual Non-Aggression (1994); an agreement on mutual nuclear de-targeting and "no first use" (1994); agreements on a "zone of stability" together with three Central Asian states (this became the basis of the "Shanghai Five" which later morphed into the Shanghai Cooperation Organization or SCO); and a series of agreements on trade, energy development, culture, and scientific cooperation (1997). All of these agreements did much to institutionalize the new Sino-Russian relationship. The capstone of this process came in 2001 with the signing of a Treaty of Neighborliness and Friendly Cooperation. The 25-article treaty covered a wide range of political, societal, scientific, regional, border, and other elements.

If there had been doubt about whether post-communist Russia and still-communist China could work together, the treaty and more than fifty other bilateral agreements signed after 1991 put these doubts to rest. Over this period Beijing and Moscow built a sound and strong relationship on many levels.[81] Jiang Zemin oversaw all of this and personally invested himself in the relationship. The fact that Jiang spoke fairly fluent Russian, owing to his time in the Soviet Union during the 1950s, and his apparent comfort with Russians (he and Yeltsin would greet each other with effusive bear hugs when they met), were not unimportant factors. Jiang also oversaw the establishment and development of the Shanghai Cooperation Organization (formerly the Shanghai Five), which opened a whole new chapter in China's relations with post-Soviet states in the Central Asian region. All in all, Jiang must be credited with overseeing the transformation of ties with the former Soviet Union in the aftermath of the collapse of the USSR.

The End of Jiang Zemin's Rule and Transition to Hu Jintao

Jiang Zemin certainly far exceeded all skeptical expectations that accompanied his elevation to the pinnacle of power in 1989. Thirteen years in office was the longest reign of any Chinese leader since Mao. Few anticipated this, and Jiang defied the political obituaries. Beyond his staying power, though, we have noted in this chapter the very real impact Jiang had on a variety of policy spheres. He proved to be no "flowerpot" as first thought. Jiang selected several policy areas in which he had personal interest and thought he could make an impact—notably reform of the CCP, military affairs, foreign policy, and several specific elements of economic policy. He was actually quite progressive in these realms, moving the country forward in each—"changing with the times" (与时俱进), as Jiang was fond of saying.

While his progressivism does seem distinctive, particularly in retrospect and in contrast to the retrogressive repression of Xi Jinping, Jiang also had his repressive side. This was particularly apparent in a series of "Strike Hard" campaigns carried out against a range of crimes throughout the 1990s. Although the numbers were disputed by the Chinese government, Amnesty International documented almost 20,000 executions during the decade.[82] Jiang is even more closely associated with the crackdown on Falun Gong practitioners—a quasi-religious spiritual movement that emphasizes meditation and breathing exercises. By 1999 the popular (but largely underground) movement had as many as 70 million adherents throughout China. On April 25 of that year, on a sleepy Sunday morning in Beijing, all of a sudden the Chinese leadership compound of Zhongnanhai was surrounded by 10,000 Falun Gong followers. They came to protest the police detention of 45 practitioners in the nearby city of Tianjin. In a city known for its extremely tight security, especially in central Beijing around government and Party offices, it was nothing short of astounding that such a large-scale protest could have occurred with no forewarning. Jiang Zemin was irate. He took Politburo member Luo Gan (who oversaw domestic security) to task, put the Ministries of Public and State Security on high alert, and initiated a sweeping nationwide crackdown on the movement (which continues to this day). For some reason, Jiang took the challenge very personally and was dedicated to its suppression. So, while Jiang was primarily a progressive leader, he had his hard edge too.

As the year 2002 and the planned 16th Party Congress drew near, eyes increasingly focused on Jiang's anticipated retirement and the transition to the Hu Jintao era. Jiang was constitutionally mandated to step down from the state presidency, and the CCP wanted to revert to the same norm of

Figure 4.4 Jiang Zemin with His Successor Hu Jintao at 16th Party Congress, November 2002
Source: Associated Press

two five-year terms for its General Secretary. Moreover, it was none other than Deng Xiaoping who had pre-designated Hu Jintao (then an obscure provincial official) to be the center of the "fourth generaton" leadership at the 14th Party Congress in 1992. Thus, Jiang Zemin had to live with this eventuality and Hu's shadow for most of his time in power (even if he was uncomfortable with it).

Jiang thus could not handpick his own successor—if he could have, there is considerable evidence that it very likely would have been Zeng Qinghong.[83] More to the point, though, Jiang was not ready to depart the stage. He was enjoying his jobs. In 2001 he floated the idea of resurrecting the position of CCP "Chairman," on the premise that he could slide into that exalted position while Hu Jintao became General Secretary (the exact same model that Hua Guofeng and Hu Yaobang had followed briefly back in 1980). But this idea was nixed by other senior leaders. Unlike Xi Jinping, who eighteen years later maneuvered to abolish the term limits on the presidency, Jiang did not try to resist having to give up this post (no matter how much he enjoyed the international limelight). What he was successful in doing was to bend the rules and stay on in his capacity as Chairman of the Central Military Commission until September 2004, when Hu took the title. Jiang also succeeded in "packing the Politburo" with his associates at the 16th Party Congress in 2002.[84] Only three of the fifteen Politburo members had ties to Hu Jintao—all the others were closely associated with Jiang. This included, all-importantly, the elevation of Zeng Qinghong to the Politburo Standing Committee. The Central Military Commission remained under Jiang's control and all the senior PLA brass owed their loyalties directly to him. Jiang's signature "Theory of the Three Represents" was also written into the Party constitution. Thus, from the get-go, Hu Jintao's tenure was powerfully circumscribed by Jiang Zemin and his close associates. For his part, Jiang Zemin did not go quietly into the night—but rather remained very active behind the scenes.

CHAPTER 5

HU JINTAO

(胡锦涛)

Technocratic Apparatchik

"We will promote fairness and justice; long-term, steady and rapid economic development; and social harmony and stability."
—Hu Jintao, Speech on the 90th Founding Anniversary of the CPC, 2011[1]

IF JIANG ZEMIN HAD NO TIME TO PREPARE FOR ASSUMING HIS POSITION AS China's leader, but wound up building a strong, broad, power base and making the most of his time in office, Hu Jintao may have been just the opposite. Having been anointed in 1992 at the 14th Party Congress as the youngest member of the Central Committee of the "fourth generation" of leaders, Hu had *ten full years* to prepare for the top job. However, I would argue that he largely squandered this time and opportunity by failing to build a diversified institutional power base that he could draw upon once he succeeded Jiang in 2002. This is just the opposite of what Jiang Zemin did after being catapulted to the top. Hu had time—lots of it—to cultivate diverse constituencies and master the intricacies of multiple policy portfolios. While Hu's *Selected Works* do indicate his giving a number of speeches on diverse topics during his decade-in-waiting—including concerning ethnic groups, agriculture, youth, military enterprises, intellectuals, social stability, and foreign affairs—the vast majority of his speeches and activities during this period concentrated on Party affairs.[2] This was to be expected given his portfolio, his career-long ties in the Communist Youth League (共青团), serving as president of the Central Party School, and being the successor-

Figure 5.1 Hu Jintao (1942–)
Source: Pete Souza / Public Domain

in-waiting as CCP General Secretary. Moreover, these speeches were little noticed or reported on in the national media—the majority of them taking place at meetings of the Politburo or other intra-Party organizations.

While Hu did "play to the Party" during his decade of apprenticeship, he really did little to cultivate other bureaucratic constituencies and build up a diversified institutional power base for himself. Perhaps this was no accident, as Jiang Zemin and his close advisors had not selected Hu for promotion in the first place (Deng Xiaoping, Song Ping, Yao Yilin, and other elders had, back in 1992), and thus "keeping Hu in his place" may have been intentional. Hu was, after all, second in command, leaving Jiang Zemin to grab the spotlight during this time. So, perhaps we should not expect Hu to have distinguished himself while he was the successor-in-waiting. To have done so would have been viewed as overstepping his bounds. It also no doubt reflects Hu's modest demeanor and persona. Nonetheless, Hu probably could have done more to develop a broader portfolio of expertise, institutional ties (particularly with the military), and a public profile—all of which would have better prepared him to run the country when he inherited the leadership mantle from Jiang.

Hu's failure to build a broad base of institutional support revealed itself once he gained the reins of power. One way of putting it is that Hu held office but did not wield power. That is, he was primarily a role-player, appearing when and where he was supposed to, delivering speeches when instructed to, and carrying out his official duties. But this is *different* from building up a diversified institutional power base and network of political allies, making policy decisions, and *leading*. Another way of putting it is that Hu had ex-officio *respect* for the offices he held, without exercising real *power* and *influence*. Despite appearing detached and aloof, Hu seemed a nice enough man—but he did not have the appetite or background for the rough and tumble world of power politics in Beijing.

Once he became the leader on his own, I argue in this chapter that Hu started off well during his first term in office (2002–2007) by launching several policy initiatives, but that these failed to gain traction and mostly fizzled out during his second term (2007–2012). I would argue that this reflects several factors. First, it reflects the fact that Hu did not have a diversified and strong backing among a variety of central-level bureaucracies and non-Party institutions. Second, it reflects the fact that Jiang Zemin's power and influence behind the scenes were still quite strong. Third, Hu's own personality was too dull and did not inspire followership. Leaders need to motivate and inspire followers, but Hu's persona was not up to it. Fourth, by his second term he had become a "lame duck," as the clock was counting down to his expected retirement in 2012, and everyone knew it. Relatedly, as I explain later in the chapter, during 2009–2010 in the wake of the global financial crisis and a shifting power balance in the Politburo following Zeng Qinghong's retirement in 2008, the "arch conservatives" (led by leader-in-waiting Xi Jinping, propaganda chief Li Changchun, and security czar Zhou Yongkang) became much more forceful and pressed a much more internally repressive and externally assertive policy agenda. By this time, Hu was truly a lame duck and could do little to thwart the rising conservative tide.

After Hu and Premier Wen Jiabao stepped down together at the National People's Congress in March 2013, many Chinese lamented the country's "ten lost years" (失去的十年). Yet this description may in fact be unfair. Some important policy initiatives *were launched,* and some things certainly *were accomplished* on their watch—notably in social policy, Party reform, and foreign policy—but the perception of a relatively few achievements remains prevalent both inside and outside of China. If anything, Hu's tenure was marked by an attempted shift in policy emphasis away from the growth-at-all-costs economic calculus and bias toward coastal China associated with the Jiang Zemin era—toward a new emphasis on the geographic prioritization of the inland provinces of China and on issues of social equality, social justice, improving basic living standards and social services, environmental protection, poverty alleviation, reducing burdens on farmers, public safety and anti-corruption, job retraining, and other "public goods." This was, in essence, Hu Jintao's agenda. It was a very commendable and progressive agenda, which was suitable to the time but stood in quite sharp contrast to Jiang Zemin's emphases. While it was publicly popular and well received during Hu's early years in power, it simply faltered in its implementation.

Perhaps with the passage of time Hu's reign will get better marks and be more highly regarded (as Jiang Zemin's has been). Once he gained the full reins of power in 2012, and during the ensuing decade, Hu became a "transactional" rather than "transformational" leader (as distinguished in Chapter 1). His rule was more notable for "muddling through" a series of complex challenges rather than having a transformative impact on the country. He didn't change things. His tenure was noteworthy for its stability, predictability, and incremental improvements in domestic and foreign policy. To be sure, these are *not* bad things—indeed they are highly desirable for most countries, and are so particularly in China, where they are considered sacrosanct. Hu Jintao could credibly claim at the end of his decade in power that he had maintained social and political stability, had overseen considerable economic growth, paid attention to the less fortunate sectors of society, protected national security and continued military modernization, enhanced China's position and reputation in the world. These accomplishments should certainly count as *success*! Hu kept China's development train on the tracks, the CCP in power, the country out of a war, and enhanced the nation's standing in the world—all critically important metrics by Chinese standards. So, his tenure should perhaps not be undersold—even if it was understated. Perhaps in retrospect and with the passage of time, Hu Jintao's historical reputation will be burnished for the better.

Much of the critique of Hu and his time in power may superficially derive from his own stilted personality. Hu's personal blandness was widely ridiculed inside and outside of China. Foreign caricatures frequently used the adjectives "wooden" and "stiff" in describing him. One notable biographical study of Hu's rule was even titled *China's Silent Ruler*.[3] Hu was seemingly invisible to many people inside and outside of China, triggering the overused question "Who's Hu?" He never seemed to evince any emotion, hardly ever smiled, never joked, and was rarely spontaneous. He appeared to be a programmed robot. While his policy program was definitely populist in its orientation, and Hu had genuine experience with and compassion for the downtrodden citizens of China's interior provinces and countryside, his own personality was definitely not that of a populist leader who aroused the emotions of those left behind by China's reforms. He did not give voice to their grievances.

Hu's leadership style was ultra-cautious, low-key, and very tightly scripted—never saying anything he was not supposed to (no need for aides to "clean up" after meetings with foreigners, as was the case with Jiang Zemin). He read all of his speeches verbatim with no improvisation or even eye contact with his audience. Foreign officials who met with Hu have commented to me that they were quite impressed by his photographic memory and retention—Hu never had any briefing notes with him but was able to recall and recite with great precision as he expounded at length on the topic du jour. While Hu memorized his briefing points well, he and his handlers were extremely reluctant to put him in any kind of spontaneous situation. For example, I spoke with one senior British government official who was deeply involved in organizing the July 2005 G-8 Summit at Gleneagles resort in Scotland. Although not a formal member of the G-8, China (and President Hu) was invited along with Brazil, India, Mexico, and South Africa by Prime Minister Tony Blair to attend as observer-participants. The British side sought an intimate one-on-one "informal fireside chat" between Prime Minister Blair and Hu Jintao at the end of one afternoon prior to the official dinner. The response that came back from the Chinese side was "President Hu doesn't do informal fireside chats."[4] American officials I have spoken with and who interacted with Hu had similar observations.

Hu's personality and leadership style were very much that of a disciplined Party man—schooled in the intra-Party norms of depersonalized selflessness, collective rule, consensus seeking, rigid adherence to rules, and disciplined policy implementation. He was a self-effacing low-profile *apparatchik* who prized the collective. Hu Jintao was a model Leninist cadre. But model cadres do not make for impactful transformational leaders. Hu was a perfect product of the institutional political system in which he was trained. He was also a leader whose policy agenda was centered on average citizens, and particularly the downtrodden in rural areas and the central-western interior of the country. The policy program that he and Premier Wen Jiabao forged was notable for its emphasis on these sectors of society. Despite this populist agenda, neither Hu nor Wen personally aroused the masses. I would also describe Hu as a technocrat. He was educated in engineering, although he worked much of his career as an intra-Party cadre. Hu adopted a very conservative approach to policy, not at all that of risk-taker or bold initiator. His most pressing preoccupation, it seemed, was to simply keep the machine running—not to change anything. To the extent he did seek change, it was very much in the technocratic tradition of gradualism and incrementalism. Technocrats are not change-agents, they are tinkerers—who approach problems incrementally based on their constituent parts, rather than on the whole.

Hu Jintao's Life and Career Path

Hu Jintao was born on December 21, 1942, in Taizhou city in northern Jiangsu province, which is not far from Yangzhou (Jiang Zemin's home).[5] The family had moved there from their Jixi County ancestral home in Anhui province. Hu's father opened a store there selling teas and other products. Tea merchandising had been the family business since Hu's great-grandfather had established franchises in Shanghai (where Jintao's father had worked) and Zhejiang province. So, Hu's family and class background can be described as bourgeois merchant class. Hu grew up in Taizhou, together with his two sisters. However, unfortunately, their mother died when Hu was seven, and the three children were raised by an aunt. Nothing else is known (at least to me) about his childhood. Hu performed very well in high school, which earned him a place at the prestigious Tsinghua University in Beijing—known as "China's MIT" and the cradle of China's "red engineers." Indeed, being selected for Tsinghua was an extremely difficult feat. Hu entered the university in 1959, majoring in hydroelectric engineering, with a specialization in multipurpose power stations. Tsinghua's president at the time was the well-known educator-politician Jiang Nanxiang, who served as a member of the Central Committee and led Tsinghua from 1952 to 1966.[6] Jiang was very well connected in senior Party circles and served as a "talent spotter" for prospective Party members at Tsinghua and was known for looking for "double-sided" students who were both "red and expert" (又红又转). Hu Jintao was one whom Jiang spotted. He became active in campus CCP activities beginning in his sophomore year and became a full Party member in 1964, a year before his graduation in 1965. It was at Tsinghua during this time that Hu met his future wife Liu Yongqing.

Upon graduation, rather than being immediately assigned by the state (分配) to an engineering job, Hu was asked to stay on at Tsinghua as a "political instructor" (政治指导员), teaching CCP political study classes for students from various departments across the university. In the spring of 1966, of course, the Cultural Revolution broke out; Tsinghua was one of the first campuses to experience the movement, and it was the first campus where the Red Guards became violent (under student leader Kuai Dafu).[7] It is, however, unclear how this affected Hu Jintao, whether he witnessed the Red Guard demonstrations and violence (highly likely) or whether he participated in them. Try as I have to ascertain what happened to Hu during this time, querying both knowledgeable Chinese and international scholars, no one seems to know. This is a distinct gap in his biography. All that is known is that he remained in Beijing during this tumultuous period, and that sometime toward the end of 1968 he was dispatched to remote Gansu province to work on the construction of the Liujiaxia hydroelectric power station (part of a massive dam first begun during the Great Leap Forward) in a distant part of the desolate inland province.

Thus began Hu's lengthy exposure to the impoverished parts of China's deep interior. At first he worked building dormitories, but quickly progressed to become a technician on the power plant, then worked as an office assistant, and subsequently as a deputy Party secretary of the facility. This combination epitomized his *technocratic apparatchik* background. During 1969–1974 he worked in the same dual-hatted position in a different power project (the Fourth Power Project of the Ministry of Hydroelectric Power). In 1974 he was transferred to the provincial capital of Lanzhou to become the deputy head and Party secretary of the provincial Construction Committee. This was a big break and a major promotion for Hu at age 32.

There Hu had a career-changing encounter, meeting the Gansu provincial Party secretary Song Ping. Song immediately took a shine to Hu, promoted him, and became his lifelong political patron. Song Ping was also a Tsinghua graduate whose wife Chen Shunyao had served as deputy secretary of the university Party committee under Jiang Nanxiang. While Hu had come to her attention during his time as a student and was known for his "good grades and political zeal,"[8] he did not meet Song Ping until their paths crossed in Gansu. Song Ping would later prove instrumental in promoting and guiding Hu through the upper ranks of the Party—including facilitating his appointments to the Central Committee, Politburo, and ultimately as CCP General Secretary. Still in Gansu, in 1982 Song arranged for Hu to be transferred from the provincial Construction Committee to serve as secretary of the provincial branch of the Communist Youth League (thus beginning a long affiliation for Hu with CYL affairs).

After fourteen years of climbing the provincial ladder in Gansu, in 1981 Song arranged for Hu to be sent on a special training course for cadres at the Central Party School in Beijing. This was a distinct honor for a provincial Party cadre and a clear indication that his career path was on a strongly upward trajectory. The Central Party School (中央党校) has long been a key breeding ground and launchpad for rising Party cadres, as well as being the principal "think tank" for the CCP.[9] One of Hu's Central Party School classmates was Hu Deping, son of the recently appointed CCP General Secretary Hu Yaobang. Hu Deping apparently introduced Hu Jintao to his father (no relation) on the eve of the 12th Party Congress in 1982. Hu Yaobang was in the midst of overhauling the central Party apparatus and he was looking for fresh blood to head up the Youth League.[10] Upon completion of the Central

Party School course and on the eve of the 12th Congress, Hu Jintao was quickly catapulted into a position on the Secretariat of the national CYL and became a member of the CCP Central Committee. Song Ping likely had a hand in this appointment too, as he was then serving as Director of the CCP Organization Department and thus was in charge of *all* senior Party personnel appointments. At age 40, Hu Jintao was clearly seen to be one of the Party's rising stars. Two years later (1984) Hu became first secretary of the entire CYL. During his three years with the Youth League Hu came into direct contact for the first time with senior Party leaders, including Deng Xiaoping, Zhao Ziyang, and others.

In July 1985, though, Hu was reassigned and returned to the provinces. This time he was appointed as Party secretary for an entire province (Guizhou), becoming the youngest provincial secretary in CCP history. A beautiful but landlocked and extremely poor province in southwestern China, famous for its *maotai* liquor, Guizhou offered Hu the opportunity to engage in poverty alleviation, agriculture, water conservancy, and ethnic nationalities work. During his three years there, Hu visited all 86 counties and districts, inspecting many poor areas and expressing his concern for the residents.

In January 1989 it was time to move again—this time to yet another poor, landlocked, and disenfranchised part of China: Tibet. While the Tibetan Autonomous Region had many things in common with Gansu and Guizhou (where Hu had already spent a total of seventeen years), it had two unique features: the high altitude and the existence of ethnic unrest. The altitude apparently bothered Hu throughout his tenure there, causing persistent headaches and nausea. He occasionally had to fly to Chengdu to rest before returning to Lhasa. Finally, the strain and pain become so severe that Hu had to leave Lhasa altogether and move to Beijing, in June 1990. He continued to serve as Party secretary *in absentia* for two more years.

A greater test for Hu than the altitude came soon after his arrival. March 1989 was the thirtieth anniversary of the 1959 uprising in which the Dalai Lama and his followers fled to northern India, where they established their government-in-exile in Dharamsala. As the anniversary approached there were fears that unrest would flair again, as Tibetans had remained resentful of the Beijing regime's heavy hand of repression and religious-cultural persecution (I visited Tibet in October 1984 and can attest to the simmering discontent). Sure enough, violence broke out on the eve of the anniversary, with armed security forces shooting and killing a dozen and injuring more than one hundred Tibetan monks and protesters on March 5 and 6. Several police were also killed. After three days of violence and brutal police repression in Lhasa (which was captured on film and is now available on You-Tube),[11] martial law was declared and all foreigners were expelled from the region. Hu Jintao personally ordered it (although undoubtedly in concert with the authorities in Beijing). On March 8 Hu appeared in a Xinhua photograph wearing a military helmet and riot gear.[12] On March 9 he gave a radio address in which he invoked the security forces: "You must maintain vigilance against the separatists now that martial law has been declared, and you must take even sterner measures against those who stubbornly resist."[13] A week later Hu told Xinhua News Agency, "The imposition of martial law, subduing the riots, stopping sabotage, opposing separatism, and safeguarding national unification, is a major measure to stabilize the situation in Tibet."[14] Martial law continued to be forcefully imposed through April 1990 and foreigners remained barred from the region.

This period, of course, also coincided with the June 4, 1989 armed suppression of demonstrators in Beijing's Tiananmen Square. Tibet and Beijing were both under lockdown, while the security blanket extended across the country. In the eyes of the leadership in Beijing, Hu Jintao had proven his mettle by adopting a hardline stand against the Lhasa uprising. Given that they had just done the same thing in Beijing, Hu now had bona fides among the post-1989 hardline CCP leadership. When he returned to live in Beijing in June 1990, because of his altitude sickness, he was welcomed as a true comrade-in-arms.

Prior to his departure, Hu gave two important speeches. The first came just a matter of weeks after the crackdown in Lhasa, ostensibly on the occasion of the thirtieth anniversary of Tibet's "reform, construction, and ethnic unity."[15] Besides rattling off a series of statistics illustrating Tibet's development, in it Hu also had tough words for the domestic and international forces seeking "separatism" (分裂主义) for Tibet: "In the unremitting struggle against the domestic and foreign separatist forces, we must be clear that this is neither an ethnic problem nor is it a religious problem. Moreover, it is not a 'human rights' problem. We have to recognize it plainly as a power struggle, one which has implications for the unification of the motherland and has implications for the important interests of the Tibetan people and every single person in the country."[16] In the second speech, Hu doubled down on his tough line and tough warnings against Tibetan "separatist forces."[17] This is one of the toughest speeches or documents I have ever come across concerning China's internal security generally or Tibet specifically. It is a chilling outline of the harshly repressive measures taken against the Tibetans, but it is also illustrative of the siege mentality that characterized the Chinese leadership at the time, in the wake of martial law in Tibet and the June 4 massacre in Beijing.

Through the actions he took in putting down the March 1989 uprising in Lhasa and ruthlessly implementing martial law thereafter, and then delivering these two tough speeches, Hu clearly proved his hardline credentials to the other reactionary leaders in Beijing. Hu was very much in step with the *zeitgeist* of the time. In retrospect, it would seem that these undertakings greatly contributed to the perception among conservative Party elders that he was a good candidate to succeed Jiang Zemin, even if the latter was only at the start of his own tenure. Although now based in Beijing, Hu continued to serve as Party secretary for Tibet until the 14th Party Congress in October 1992, when he was elevated to the CCP Politburo, Politburo Standing Committee, and Secretariat.

Hu Jintao's Decade in Waiting

With this elevation to the inner circle of the CCP leadership, Hu's place at the center of the "fourth generation" of leaders was cemented (although he was never given the moniker "core"). It was again his old patron Song Ping who put Hu forward to Deng Xiaoping and other leaders, securing their agreement that this 49-year-old should assume important responsibilities. Hu was put in charge of the Secretariat, which oversaw policy coordination and daily operations for the Politburo and Central Committee. He was simultaneously appointed president of the Central Party School and would play a central role in formulating and overseeing Party propaganda and personnel policies.

Judging from his *Selected Works*, Hu Jintao took these responsibilities seriously. Shortly after the Fourteenth Congress, his first speech—to a conference of Organization Department cadres—emphasized the imperative of strengthening leadership teams (领导班子) at all levels of the Party. This initiative reflected one of the key lessons the CCP was learning about the causes of the collapse of the Soviet Communist Party (CPSU)—namely, that the Party had badly atrophied and "ceased to function" at the local level. In 1992 the CCP was only beginning its long post-mortem analysis of the causes of the overthrow and collapse of the CPSU and Soviet Union, but preliminary analysis had already revealed deterioration of the Soviet Communist Party from the bottom up. The CCP Organization Department was directed to undertake a nationwide survey of local level Party organs (基层党组织),[18] which revealed that the exact same phenomenon was transpiring in the CCP (multiple other maladies were also found to exist).[19] Thus, a major initiative was launched to rebuild and strengthen the CCP at the grassroots level. During that decade Hu gave further speeches on the subject of Party organization work.[20] He also gave several speeches focusing on relations between the Party and the masses,[21] which had also been identified by the CCP as another failure of the CPSU. In other speeches he focused on Party theory, ideology, and propaganda work,[22] as well as championing the work of the CCP International Department.[23] He also gave two speeches on youth, two on agriculture, two on the role of Party committees in economic enterprises, one on retired cadres, two on social organizations, one on the importance of social stability, one on counterterrorism, and two on foreign policy.[24]

Thus, Hu's focus during his ten years as leader-in-waiting was somewhat diverse, but primarily concentrated on Party affairs. Notably missing from this list is anything concerning the military or national security, science and technology, economic reform, anti-corruption, education, the environment, public health, Taiwan or Hong Kong, or relations with specific foreign countries (although after his appointment as Vice-President in 1998 Hu began to receive foreign dignitaries and travel abroad with increased frequency). One crisis that Hu was thrust into was the aftermath of the U.S. bombing of the Chinese embassy in Belgrade, Yugoslavia in 1999. On May 9 it was Hu who appeared on national television condemning the bombing.[25]

This bolstered his nationalist credentials with the public and was the first time that many Chinese citizens had ever heard him speak.[26]

By the time of the 16th Party Congress in 2002, when he formally succeeded Jiang Zemin as CCP General Secretary (he would do so as state president in March 2003), Hu had thus demonstrated the bona fides of a Party leader, having worked at the nexus of central-level Party affairs (especially propaganda and organization). His institutional credentials, reputation, and ties within these central Party organs were strong. Yet, I would note again that they were virtually nonexistent with the military and the governmental ministries and organs of the State Council. These included the internal security services (Ministry of Public Security, Ministry of State Security, People's Armed Police). Nor did he demonstrate any interest in—or grasp of—economic affairs. Moreover, while Hu did have ties to those provinces in which he had served (Gansu, Guizhou, and Tibet), these were not very consequential provinces and he did not come into contact with any other key figures from more important provinces. For all of these reasons, I judge that Hu's power base was quite narrow and therefore weak. He had strong ties in the Party apparatus, but that was about it.

Hu's Inheritance

Although it may not have been expected, Jiang Zemin was a hard act to follow for Hu Jintao.[27] In fact, the deck was stacked against him—as Jiang Zemin had not only left a deep policy imprint but also packed the Politburo and senior party, government, and military leadership positions with his allies and cronies. Fully 21 of 24 Politburo members elected at the 16th Party Congress could be said to have been handpicked by and loyal to Jiang, with only three tied to Hu. Nonetheless, the Congress did represent a very significant generational turnover of personnel—from the "third" to the "fourth" generation of Chinese leaders. Strict retirement norms were enforced—over 61 percent of the Central Committee were sent into retirement, with 13 of 21 Politburo members also retiring. A new 198-member 16th Central Committee (plus 158 alternates) was elected in their place, headed by Hu Jintao as the new General Secretary of the CCP. As a result of the personnel changes, 16 of the Politburo's 25 members were new to the body; six of the nine members of the Politburo Standing Committee were new; seven of the eight members of the Party Secretariat were new; the directors of all five main Central Committee departments (Organization, United Front, Discipline Inspection, International, and Propaganda) were new; four of the five State Council vice-premiers and all five of the State Councilors were new; 18 of 28 State Council ministers were new; three of eight Central Military Commission members were new; and 11 of 31 provincial Party secretaries and 15 of 31 provincial governors were newly appointed. In sum, this was the largest and most thoroughgoing turnover of the Party elite since the CCP came to power in 1949. The fact that it occurred peacefully and according to institutional procedures, absent a purge, was also a noteworthy symbolic demonstration of the institutionalization and regularization of intra-Party norms.

Although this "fourth generation" also exhibited the third generation's predominant characteristic of coming from "technocratic" (i.e., engineering and industrial management) backgrounds, seven other attributes characterized the new Party leadership. First, this was the post-Sino-Soviet Split generation, who came of age (actuarially and politically) in the aftermath of the 1960 rupture between Moscow and Beijing—thus their affinity for the Soviet Union was weaker than that of their predecessors. Second, the vast majority had backgrounds of Party work in the provinces. Many, like Hu Jintao and Premier Wen Jiabao, had held office in very impoverished interior parts of the country (Hu had spent fourteen years in Gansu, three in Guizhou, and four years in Tibet, while Wen had also spent fourteen years in Gansu). Third, though the majority came from engineering, industrial, and Party work backgrounds, a growing cohort who possessed backgrounds in finance, economics, and law was evident for the first time. Fourth, they were substantially younger than the previous Central Committee (55.4 years old). Fifth, they were the best-educated leadership in CCP history: fully 99 percent of the 16th Central Committee had attended university (as compared with a much lower 23 percent for the entire CCP membership). Sixth, the "fourth generation" leadership was the "Cultural Revolution generation"—although not all of them had experienced the Cultural Revolution in the same ways. Some, like Hu Jintao, graduated from university on the eve of the event (1965), whereas others had had their educations interrupted by the movement. Many participated in the Cultural Revolution as Red Guards or "sent-down youth" (to the countryside). Seventh, because of their backgrounds, when they assumed office this generation of CCP leaders was quite inexperienced in international affairs, was very insular in their backgrounds, had not been educated overseas and had not traveled much abroad, and therefore did not possess any strong foreign leanings (like the Soviet Union for the third generation and the West for the successor fifth generation). These were the essential features of the 16th Party Congress and its new leadership.[28]

For Hu Jintao's part, the first thing to note is that by the time he reached the top of the system he had *not* cultivated a web of patron–client ties and did not seem eager to supplant Jiang's network. Even if he had, he was substantially outnumbered. Over the next few years, it was interesting to watch how Hu set about trying to co-opt, rather than undermine or supplant, Jiang's lieutenants. Hu's style was much more one of consensus and coalition building. He was also smart not to try and directly challenge a dominant leadership faction, but rather to bide his time and work progressively to increase his own influence and insert his own people into positions of power, progressively modifying the Party's national policy agenda.

Following the 16th Party Congress, those few individuals promoted to positions in the central Party apparatus who did have ties to Hu came from diverse backgrounds. Some had careers that had *intersected* with Hu's—but it cannot be said that they were affiliated with Hu in faction-like relationships over time. Former Premier Wen Jiabao must be considered in this group, as he and Hu worked in Gansu at the same time (although it does not seem that they had known each other). Secretariat member and former head of the CCP Propaganda Department Liu Yunshan also had ties to Hu dating to their tenures as provincial Party secretaries (from 1987 to 1991 Liu was the secretary of the Inner Mongolia Autonomous Region CCP Committee while Hu served in Tibet). The two apparently interacted fairly regularly in provincial Party forums and meetings concerning ethnic minority work, and both had ties to former CCP General Secretary and Youth League chief Hu Yaobang. Hu similarly had ties to General Liao Xilong dating to these years, when Liao was deputy commander of the Chengdu Military Region (and responsible in part for the 1989 Lhasa suppression). Liao was promoted to the CMC and simultaneously became director of the People's Liberation Army General Logistics Department. Other than these three, however, Hu Jintao was notable for his *lack* of factional or patronage ties in the Central Party apparatus.

However, analysis of *provincial-level* officials reveals that a greater number of these individuals shared ties with Hu through the CYL. The then Liaoning Party secretary, Li Keqiang (today's Premier), and the Jiangsu Party secretary Li Yuanchao (later Vice-President) both served under Hu when he was secretary of the CYL from 1982 to 1984. The CCP's former United Front Work Department head Liu Yandong, the Minister of Civil Affairs Li Xueju, and the Minister of Supervision Li Zhilun also overlapped with Hu in the CYL. The well-respected scholar of Chinese elite politics Li Cheng of the Brookings Institution has written a great deal about the "youth league faction" (团派) in Chinese politics, personified by Hu Yaobang and Hu Jintao, but I remain unconvinced that this group of individuals really constituted a "faction." Perhaps "relationship network" (关系网) would be a more apt description. Simply because they all served in the one institution that is the principal incubator for *all* CCP members—through which all Party members must pass—does not in my view constitute a faction per se. Thus, while Hu had some high-level associates in the leadership, he mainly had to deal with the hand dealt to him by Jiang Zemin.

Hu Jintao's Partner: Wen Jiabao

Among the leadership Hu's closest associate was Wen Jiabao. Wen and Hu had very similar backgrounds and career paths. They were born in the same year, attended university and joined the Communist Party at the same time, and their career paths paralleled each other.

Wen was born and raised in Tianjin, a pleasant industrial port city with colonial architecture near the Bohai Gulf 175 kilometers southeast of Beijing. He attended the same middle and high school affiliated with Nankai University as did former Premier Zhou Enlai (when I was a student at Nankai in 1980 I visited this middle school). Wen subsequently attended the Beijing Institute of Geology (now China University of Geosciences) where he earned his undergraduate and graduate degrees. There, like Hu

Figure 5.2 President and CCP General Secretary Hu Jintao with Premier Wen Jiabao, March 2009
Source: Associated Press

at Tsinghua, Wen also served as a political instructor and joined the CCP in his senior year. Also like Hu, it is unclear what happened to Wen when the Cultural Revolution broke out in 1966–1967—but (again like Hu) he was assigned to work in Gansu province in 1968. There Wen began working on the Gansu Geomechanics Survey Team (Gansu is rich in minerals and energy and many prospecting surveys were being undertaken at this time). He participated in such earth surveys but also served as a CCP political representative on the team.

After thirteen years of this work, Wen was promoted to the provincial Geology Bureau. While their careers in Gansu exactly paralleled each other, it is not clear if Hu Jintao and Wen Jiabao actually met each other. It is also unclear if Wen came to the attention of provincial Party chief Song Ping during this time.

Wen's big break came in 1982 when the Minister of Geology (Sun

Deguang) paid an inspection tour of Gansu and Wen was assigned as one of the cadres to escort and brief him. So impressed was Sun by Wen's breadth of knowledge, that upon his return to Beijing he requested that Wen be transferred to the capital. This was immediately done, and Wen moved up through a succession of posts, becoming a vice-premier in the Ministry of Geology and Mineral Resources from 1982 to 1985.

At this point Wen had another big break and promotion in his career—being reassigned to be the Deputy Director and then Director of the General Office of the Central Committee (中办). It is unclear who was responsible for this sudden upward elevation, but it is quite likely to have been the doing of then CCP General Secretary Hu Yaobang. This is an extremely important position in the CCP, as the General Office is the executive office for arranging all high-level Party affairs: arranging meetings; transmitting and archiving confidential paperwork; providing security, housing, healthcare, and other perquisites for the senior leadership; scheduling travel for the senior leaders; and carrying out other specialized tasks as assigned. There are few more important positions in the CCP than working in the General Office, and it gave Wen Jiabao first-hand contact with all of China's leaders. It was in this capacity that Wen accompanied Zhao Ziyang to Tiananmen Square at 05:00 a.m. on May 19, 1989, just after an expanded Politburo meeting had dismissed Zhao from his position as General Secretary and China's leader. This was Zhao's final public appearance, in which he shed tears and apologized to the students: "We have come too late." Much was made of Wen appearing at Zhao's side on such a sensitive occasion, suggesting that Wen had similar sympathies for the student demonstrators, but it did not seem to tarnish Wen's career. He continued to serve as Director of the General Office until 1993, when he was promoted to become a full member of the CCP Secretariat. In 1997 he was promoted to be a full member of the Politburo and one of the State Council's four vice-premiers.

In 2003 Wen succeeded Zhu Rongji as Premier, thus beginning to work alongside Hu Jintao for the next decade. This period became known in China as the "Hu–Wen leadership" as the two men became a truly tandem team. The two had very similar backgrounds and both were trained as technocrats. As discussed further in Chapter 7, technocrats approach policy problems very methodically, incrementally, and rationally. They also practice collective decision-making. As China scholar Willy Wo-Lap Lam observed in his book on the Hu Jintao–Wen Jiabao era, the two leaders had a "penchant for 'throwing a committee at a problem'."[29] That is, they were very "process-oriented" leaders who instinctively were predisposed to creating leading groups, special policy committees, and crisis management and rapid reaction teams to deal with a wide range of policy challenges. This was indicative of the "institutionalization" of CCP politics that was observed by several Western scholars at the time (e.g., Andrew Nathan, Cheng Li, Alice Miller, Bruce Dickson, Kjeld-Erik Brodsgaard, and myself). Under Hu and Wen it was "the system that mattered"—policies were largely the result of collective institutional (bureaucratic) deliberation rather than being arbitrarily decided by Hu or Wen. This is what was meant by the term *scientific* in Hu's "scientific development concept"—to approach issues and decide on them on an empirical basis.

While Hu was aloof, Wen was known to be a "people's leader." Unlike Hu, Wen often directly engaged with the public and had a warm personal touch. He was involved on the scene during the 2003 SARS crisis, the 2004 AIDS crisis, the 2008 Sichuan earthquake, and the 2009 paralyzing snowstorm. He spent the 2005 New Year holiday in a mine with coal miners in Shanxi. These benevolent acts earned Wen the affectionate nickname "Grandpa Wen" and he was very popular with the public—in contrast with, but perhaps offsetting, Hu Jintao's general aloofness.

Hu Jintao's Major Policy Initiatives

During his first few years in office Hu Jintao (and Wen Jiabao) launched three main policy initiatives: the "Scientific Development Concept," the "Socialist Harmonious Society," and several interrelated Party reforms. Hu also floated a parallel idea of a "Harmonious World" in foreign policy, but it was short-lived. All of these policy initiatives were launched during his first few years in power and suggested that he was his own man, starting afresh after Jiang Zemin. While all three sets of initiatives were well intended, timely, and addressed pressing problems, unfortunately they were neither well implemented nor sustained. They all were launched during Hu's first five-year term (2002–2007) but were not prioritized during the second term

(2007–2012). The second term was largely a washout—which probably has a lot to do with why the "ten lost years" judgment of the Hu–Wen period was so harsh.

The "Scientific Development Concept"

A central feature of Hu Jintao's policy agenda, and the most lasting, was his "Scientific Development Concept" (科学发展观). Early in his tenure as Party and state leader he began to discuss "scientific development" in the context of Jiang Zemin's "Three Represents," but it became quickly clear that it was not science per se that he had in mind. An inspection trip to Jiangxi Province in September 2003 was apparently the first time that Hu used the terminology "Scientific Development Concept." Over the next month, during another inspection trip to Hunan, he began to elaborate his thinking. Two elements emerged as the core of the concept: "taking people as the basis" (以人为本) and "comprehensive development" (综合发展). Both seemed to be deft but substantial modifications of Jiang's previous policy priorities. The former phrase contrasted with Jiang's "first represent," which had emphasized commercial and social elites, and was closer to his "third represent" which had made more explicit mention of the broad masses. The latter phrase was an implicit criticism of the unbalanced growth that had favored the coastal provinces, neglected the interior and agriculture, and damaged the environment. As noted above, Hu's use of the term "scientific" signaled an empirical and rational approach to policy issues, laying the basis on which many of the social inequality, social justice, and environmental problems that had arisen during the Jiang Zemin era could be addressed.

Hu was thus subtly—but substantively—shifting the Party's reform agenda, and at the same time giving evidence of his own attentiveness and concern for the downtrodden and those left behind by the reforms of previous years. The concept was discussed at the November 2003 Central Committee Third Plenum, although it was not referred to in the resulting communiqué. But the following month, at a November Politburo economic work conference, it was referenced. Thereafter it achieved what is known in Chinese as *tifa* (提法, or official narrative) status. After the Politburo formally endorsed Hu's Scientific Development Concept at its November 24, 2003 meeting,[30] the Central Party School was given the research task of fleshing out the concept and developing it theoretically.[31] The media and propaganda system then began to widely use the term, and Wen Jiabao explicitly used it in his March 2004 report to the National People's Congress. During the remainder of 2004 and into 2005, the Central Party School, the CCP's propaganda organs, and Hu himself began to further develop and elaborate the concept. In so doing they turned it into an umbrella theory—under which numerous policies were included.

By the end of 2005 Hu published a lengthy article in *Qiushi* (the CCP's theoretical journal) which lumped all the following topics (and more) under the rubric of the Scientific Development Concept: improving the rural situation; accelerating economic growth; overcoming energy bottlenecks; efficiently using resources; fostering competitiveness and a culture of innovation; reforming the administrative system; improving government transparency and introducing e-government; continuing the transformation of state-owned enterprises without allowing state asset stripping; breaking up pricing and production monopolies; controlling pollution and environmental degradation; further opening up to the global economy; developing high-quality talent (人才); addressing social justice (公益); improving public health and safety; increasing employment, job retraining, and reemployment; opening up the labor market; solving the internal migration problem; constructing new social security systems for basic services and pensions; improving tertiary and secondary education, particularly in rural areas; deepening poverty relief programs; improving workplace safety standards; dealing more effectively with social unrest; improving relations with ethnic minorities; and undertaking a series of measures to strengthen the Party apparatus from top to bottom—all in the name of the "Scientific Development Concept"![32] The elasticity of the concept was perhaps its beauty—many diverse elements could be folded into it. Yet, the essence of it was to rectify the unbalanced growth-at-all-costs approach of the Jiang Zemin era—and to shift national socioeconomic policies to a more humane and environmentally friendly agenda.

By 2007 concerns were accumulating about the overall trajectory of the economy. The national debt load was approaching 280 percent of GDP, fiscal stimulus was triggering inflationary pressures, the investment share of GDP was in excess of 40 percent, exports were booming, but the consumption share of GDP was repressed. China was entering the "middle income trap" and there was a pressing need to transition the macro economy away from a growth model based on domestic fixed-asset investment plus exports to one driven primarily by innovation and value-added technologies, an expansion of the service sector, and domestic consumption.[33]

The "Socialist Harmonious Society"

The second significant (and closely related) policy initiative of the Hu Jintao era was his idea of building a "socialist harmonious society" (社会主义的和谐社会). Toward the end of his tenure in office, Jiang Zemin began to promote the overarching goal of building a "moderately well-off society" (小康社会). After succeeding Jiang, Hu Jintao began to modify and replace Jiang's vision with his own.

Hu's first major exposition of his concept came in a speech at the Central Party School in February 2005.[34] In his speech Hu defined his idea thus: "The socialist harmonious society we want to build should be a society featuring democracy, the rule of law, fairness, justice, sincerity, trustworthiness, amity, full vitality, stability, orderliness, and harmony between mankind and nature." Hu then elaborated on these components of his vision:

> Democracy and the rule of law mean that the socialist democracy should be fully developed, the general plan for running the country according to law should be earnestly implemented and the positive factors of all social sectors should be extensively mobilized; fairness and justice mean that the relationship of interests between various social sectors should be properly coordinated, the contradictions among the people and other social contradictions should be correctly handled and social fairness and justice should be earnestly safeguarded and realized; sincerity, trustworthiness, and amity mean that members of society should help each other, be honest and keep their word, and all people should be equal and amiable and get along with each other harmoniously; full vitality means that all wishes for creation that are conducive to social progress should be respected, creative activities

> should be supported, creative ability should be brought into play and creative achievements should be affirmed; stability and orderliness mean that social organization mechanisms should be sound, social management should be perfected, social order should be good, the people should be able to live and work in peace and contentment, and the society should be able to maintain stability and unity; harmony between mankind and nature means that production should be developed, people should be able to live a prosperous life, and the ecology should be good.[35]

This was Hu Jintao's manifesto and vision for the nation and society. It was a very positive vision, one rooted both in traditional Confucian concepts like *Datong* (Great Harmony) and in more contemporary socialist precepts.

However, Hu's vision also reflected and illustrated many of the social problems that had developed in China during the Jiang Zemin era—in particular social stratification and inequality. Later in his speech, Hu stressed that "we must pay attention to social justice."[36] When Hu took power in 2002, China had among the world's highest and fastest-growing Gini Coefficient ratings (a measure of the pace of income disparity and social stratification) at 0.45, as large numbers of the populace had been left behind while others had enriched themselves from the reforms. This disadvantaged and disenfranchised sector, known as *ruoshi tuanti* (若是团体), had mushroomed over the previous decade. During the Jiang era, economic policies had disproportionately benefitted the coastal areas to the neglect of the interior. The rural sector in particular experienced relative deprivation. According to Wang Weiguang, then Vice-President of the Central Party School, in 2004 there were 49.77 million people with an annual net income of between 669 and 924 *renminbi* (about $82 to $113), with an additional 26.1 million earning less than 668 *renminbi* ($81).[37]

Hu's society-oriented policy program reflected his awareness of what Western scholars term the "Tocqueville Paradox," the phenomenon in authoritarian societies where demands arise for a more responsive and transparent government, combined with demands for increased political representation and "public goods." This normally occurs when societies have their basic human needs met and begin to demand improved "quality of life" provisions (which includes greater political voice). This is usually associated with having achieved middle-income status: about $11,000 per capita. As my colleague Bruce Dickson has demonstrated in his excellent book *The Dictator's Dilemma*, Chinese leaders are quite aware of the Tocqueville Paradox.[38] As I showed in my book *China's Future* and Minxin Pei did in his *China's Trapped Transition*, the pressures of the "middle income trap" and demands for better public goods began to hit China during the late Hu Jintao era.[39]

Rising social inequities—particularly in the countryside—had also led to rapidly rising incidents of social unrest. The Ministry of Public Security reported that there were 87,000 "public order disturbances" (i.e., demonstrations and riots) in China in 2005, a sizable increase over the 74,000 reported in 2004 and 58,000 in 2003.[40] As Figure 5.3 indicates, these protests mushroomed to over 140,000 in 2008, declined to approximately 90,000 in 2009, before *doubling* to 180,000 in 2010 (thereafter the ministry ceased reporting the figures).

Clearly, there was large-scale discontent in China's countryside and cities. These protests were not only about income disparities—the vast majority were in response to the abuse of power by local cadres; ad hoc fees, taxes, and levies on peasants; arbitrary land seizures by local governments and

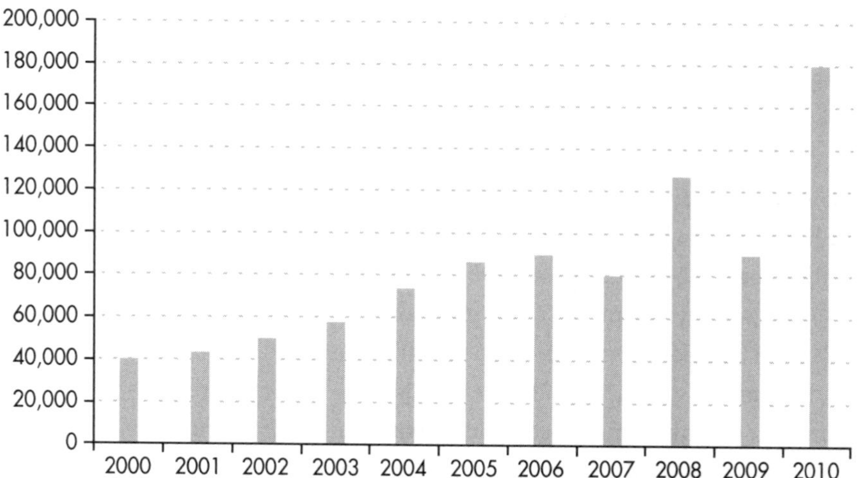

Figure 5.3 China's Reported Incidents of Mass Unrest, 2000–2010
Source: Financial Times and China Labor Bulletin

companies; wage arrears; environmental pollution; factory working conditions; and systemic corruption. Most such protests were resolved peacefully, usually through cash payment to the protesters—but sometimes force was used by the police or People's Armed Police. The size of protests varied widely—ranging from several dozen people to the 60,000 farmers in Huaxi, Zhejiang, who turned out against government indifference over the pollution caused by two chemical plants. In October 2004, a clash in Urumqi between ethnic Han Chinese and Uighurs left 100 people dead (including 15 police officers) and over 400 injured. The tensions in Urumqi exploded again in the summer of 2009, lasting for weeks and involving hundreds of Han-Uighur killings and counter-killings, before they were forcefully put down. In December 2005 in Dongzhou, Guangdong, the security forces opened fire, killing 20 villagers protesting the construction of a local power plant.

In addition to continually rising unrest in both the countryside and cities, Hu's regime also had to cope with a surprising spike in political dissent during these years. In 2008 a stealthy protest movement sprung up and quickly spread. It came in the form of an organized petition called Charter '08. The document was so named to parallel Charter '77 (written in that year by a group of Czech dissidents, including Václav Havel). It was intentionally published on December 10, 2008 on the 60th anniversary of the United Nations Universal Declaration of Human Rights. Initially, it had about 300 individuals who endorsed it, but once it was put online more than 10,000 people associated their names with the Charter.[41] Charter '08 was a broad-gauged and inspiring manifesto which called for nineteen specific changes in China—including the separation of powers, an independent judiciary, legislative democracy, freedom of association and expression, freedom of religion, establishment of a federal republic, direct election of public officials, and other elements associated with Western democratic systems. One of the principal drafters of the document was veteran dissident Liu Xiaobo. For his efforts Liu was arrested, tried, and sentenced to an eleven-year prison sentence in Jinzhou, Liaoning Province for "subversion of state power." Liu was subsequently awarded the 2010 Nobel Peace Prize—an act that enraged the Chinese government—which was given *in absentia* in Oslo, Norway. Liu was only the third person awarded the Nobel Peace Prize while incarcerated. Liu's wife, Liu Xia, who herself was under a form of house arrest, was (not surprisingly) prevented from leaving China to accept the award on her husband's behalf. In 2017, after eight years in solitary confinement, Liu contracted cancer. By the time prison authorities allowed him to be transferred to a hospital it was too late. He died shortly thereafter on July 13, 2018: A true tragedy.

The priority that Hu Jintao, Wen Jiabao, and the government attached to addressing the problems of income distribution, social stratification, social justice, public unrest, and to building a "new socialist countryside" subsequently became hallmarks of the 11th Five-Year Program, adopted by the Fifth Plenum of the 16th Central Committee of October 2005 and 2006 National People's Congress. The State Council also enacted a series of policies aimed at improving the income distribution system and narrowing disparities. The main objectives of the 11th Five-Year Program, as submitted to the Fifth Plenum and subsequently adopted by the March 2006 National People's Congress, included:[42]

- doubling the 2000 gross domestic product per capita of 7,086 RMB by 2010;
- markedly improving efficiency in utilizing resources, including energy consumption per unit of gross domestic product by 20 percent by 2010;
- developing a number of major enterprises into internationally competitive companies with well-known brands;
- improving the market economic system and achieving a basic equilibrium in the balance of international payments;
- universalizing and consolidating nine-year compulsory education and developing a sound social security system;
- improving the income levels and the quality of life for urban and rural residents and keeping the overall price level stable;
- significantly improving living, transportation, educational, cultural, health, and environmental conditions for the population;
- making progress in building socialist democracy, legal institutions, and spiritual civilization; and
- further advancing social order and production safety and making progress in building a socialist harmonious society.

In addition to the above, the final program document also stressed a number of specific social and environmental goals: for example, stabilizing the low birthrate, enhancing services for the elderly, safeguarding the interests of women and children, protecting orphans, improving services for the handicapped and disabled, comprehensively raising living standards and ameliorating income gaps, introducing a proactive and coordinated national employment policy, enlarging basic pension insurance coverage in urban areas, increasing poverty relief, improving nutrition, providing economical and low-rent housing, raising health standards and providing comprehensive universal health provision and coverage, controlling the spread of infectious diseases, strengthening workplace safety, ensuring food and drug standards, and controlling crime.[43]

These and other policy priorities associated with the "Socialist Harmonious Society" were further officially approved by the Central Committee at the Sixth Plenum in October 2006. The Plenum communiqué noted:[44]

> There are quite a lot of contradictions and issues that impair social harmony in China today. We must place more attention on developing social services and push forward economic and social development in a coordinated way. Social equity and justice are a basic condition of social harmony, while a sound system provides the fundamental guarantee to social equity and justice. We must accelerate construction of the system that ensures social equity and justice to guarantee people's rights and interests in political, economic, cultural, and social fields and guide our citizens to exercise their rights and fulfill their obligations according to the law.

These were all admirable goals, and they represented a dramatic shift away from the growth-at-all-costs agenda of the Jiang Zemin era. The Hu–Wen administration were to be commended for identifying and enunciating such a humanist policy agenda. This was the right agenda on which to focus, and it certainly resonated among the populace. In many cases, they were also attainable goals. But, after launching them during the first term of Hu and Wen, the initiative was lost and they failed to carry through and implement most of the well-intended reforms. One exception concerned

China's farmers, who were chafing under the burden of what was known as the "three rural problems" (三农问题): agriculture (农业), farmers (农民), and rural villages (农村). Preeminent among these challenges were stagnant or declining incomes (due to low market prices and government purchase prices for crops); heavy taxes and arbitrary fees fixed on farming households; and predatory practices by local cadres (particularly expropriation of land). Premier Wen Jiabao was able to address these concerns in 2006 with a series of new initiatives that abolished rural taxes, provided for free tuition for rural youth to attend post-secondary schools, and new rural price support subsidies. These welcome rural initiatives were embodied in Central Committee Document No. 1 of 2006 on creating a "new socialist countryside."[45]

For all their efforts to address these issues during their first term in office, the Hu–Wen regime struggled to make real progress in policy priorities, other than the rural sector. This caused Premier Wen Jiabao to dramatically declare in 2007 that the economy was "unstable, unbalanced, uncoordinated, and unsustainable" (which became known as the "four 'uns'").[46] Three years later at the Fifth Plenum of the 17th Central Committee in November 2010 the resulting communiqué still lamented: "In contemporary China the adherence to development as a task of overriding importance means sticking to scientific development, laying more stress on the 'people first' principle, paying more attention to comprehensive, sustainable development and overall planning and coordination, and putting more emphasis on security and improving people's livelihood to promote social equity and justice."[47] To be certain, the range and complexity of these nagging social issues could not be solved overnight. Indeed, many of the problems had *intensified*. For example, China's Gini Coefficient had actually *increased* from 0.45 to 0.47 from the time Hu and Wen entered office to the time they departed in 2013. Environmental degradation had also worsened substantially. China had five of the top ten most air-polluted cities in the world in 2010. Beijing (where I lived during 2009–2010) frequently had excessively unhealthy air quality readings. Corruption had also become more widespread, as had social unrest.

As these nagging issues all intensified, a palpable sense of malaise began to set in during Hu and Wen's second term (it was also apparent during

2009–2010 in my many conversations in Beijing and around the country). The totality of policy challenges outpaced the regime's responses to them. "Lame duckism" also contributed to this sense at the time, as the state constitution mandated that both Hu and Wen would have to step down from their government positions (President and Premier) in 2013. The leadership balance was also beginning to shift—with Xi Jinping only a couple of years away from taking the reins of power; Politburo strongman Zeng Qinghong having to retire in 2008; internal security czar Zhou Yongkang becoming increasingly powerful; Propaganda Department Director Liu Yunshan also becoming increasingly powerful and having commandeered the ideology portfolio from Hu; and Chongqing Party secretary Bo Xilai attracting increased national attention. The 2008 global financial crisis was also a major economic policy challenge (one that Wen Jiabao handled effectively with a massive fiscal stimulus package).

For all of these reasons, Hu Jintao's star had begun to substantially fade by 2009, and only continued to wane in the final three years of his term before he handed over power to Xi Jinping in 2012–2013. This transitional period is discussed further in the next section.

Hu Jintao's Party Campaigns and Stealth Political Reforms

The third principal set of initiatives launched under Hu Jintao came in the political sphere. These came mainly in the context of the twin Party campaigns on "governing capacity" (执政能力) and the "advanced nature" (sometimes translated as "progressivism," 先进性) of the CCP. However, because the term *political reform* (政治改革) had become forbidden following 1989, any reforms in this realm had to be couched in terms of "Party building" (党建).[48]

Hu moved on several fronts somewhat simultaneously. First, and most important, he simply allowed the Party reforms launched during the Jiang Zemin period under the aegis of Zeng Qinghong to continue (see Chapter 4). It was a "through train" that Hu had no incentive to derail. But several new elements were added after Hu became the supreme leader.

One initiative that many knowledgeable Chinese associated with Hu personally was his effort to improve the transparency of the CCP. He mandated that all central Party departments designate spokespersons (government organs had been slowly doing so since the late 1990s), who should give periodic briefings to the media to discuss new policies and make their departments more accessible to the public. A related transparency initiative, also linked directly to Hu, was to report regularly and publicly on Politburo meetings.[49] While Party plenums and major meetings had previously been reported in the press, routine meetings of the Politburo or its Standing Committee had never been regularly reported publicly. These news items usually now contained the names of participants (including non-Politburo members who had also attended), the agenda of each meeting, the policy decisions taken, and other relevant information. Under Hu the Politburo also began to convene regular "study sessions" on various topics—leadership seminars at which outside scholars and experts would be invited to brief a specific topic, followed by discussion, and then ending with a "summing up" by Hu himself. Many of these seminars debated and incubated policy ideas prior to adoption.

Another important contribution of Hu's was to significantly broaden "democratic consultation" throughout the Party system. This was done in three principal ways, which I call the "three democracies." The first was to invigorate "intra-Party democracy" (党内民主). This concept had long been a normative feature of the CCP dating back to the Yanan period in the 1930s. The idea was that "inner Party life" (党内生活) should be "democratic" and not dictatorial. Vertical feedback mechanisms (from the bottom upwards) should be routinized and respected, so that the lower-level organs and all Party members should feel free to provide their honest viewpoints to high-level authorities without fear of retribution. Intra-Party democracy was to be something of a parallel to the "mass line"—another Yanan-era initiative designed to facilitate consultations between the Party and the mass public prior to adopting a policy. Although a longstanding norm, it atrophied badly after the late 1950s and disappeared altogether until Deng Xiaoping, Hu Yaobang, and Zhao Ziyang attempted to resurrect it during the 1980s. Jiang Zemin paid some heed to the idea, but Hu Jintao paid it much greater attention by arguing that Party organs at all levels—from village committees up to the Politburo—as well as individual Party members should feel free to speak their minds.

Parallel to this vertical initiative within the CCP, Hu also set in train a related horizontal reform for "consultative democracy" (协商民主). Again, this idea had earlier origins—notably in the concept of CCP "united front" outreach to various sectors of society and China's eight noncommunist parties (so-called "multi-party cooperation," 多党合作). Although Deng Xiaoping also mentioned the need to boost this type of consultation toward the end of his life, it had long been a ruse. Hu Jintao took personal efforts to revive it and make it much more genuine. In February 2005 the Central Committee issued the important document *Opinions of the CCP Central Committee on Further Strengthening the Building of the System of Multi-Party Cooperation and Consultation Under the Leadership of the CCP*. Under this initiative, the CCP was to consult more closely with these noncommunist parties, to submit major policy programs to the CPPCC for feedback before adoption, and to better respect their views.

The third type of "democracy" advocated by Hu was "electoral democracy" (选注民主). While the CCP had experimented with multi-candidate village government elections beginning in the 1980s, it had never done so with elections for Party committees. But during 2005–2007 these too were experimented with. I witnessed one such experiment in a medium-sized town in Zhejiang (its population was approximately 10,000) where five different local Party members all took turns standing before constituents for about ten minutes, each stating why they were the best candidate and what they would do for the township (the election took place two weeks later and I never learned the outcome).

Hu's next important steps in Party reform were to launch the Party's twin "ruling capacity" (执政能力) and "advance nature" (先进性) initiatives at the Fourth Plenum of the 16th Central Committee in September 2004.[50] Two years later in another speech commemorating the 85th anniversary of the CCP in 2006, Hu declared: "Building up the Party's governing ability and construction of the Party's advanced nature are two closely related things that supplement and enhance each other. They should run through the Party's ideological construction, organizational construction, improvement of work style, and institutional construction."[51] A year later in his address to the 17th Party Congress Hu devoted an entire section to the twin initiatives—focusing his remarks on six aspects in particular: adapting Marxism to Chinese conditions; building a corps of high-quality leading

Party bodies and committees; expanding intra-Party democracy; reforming the cadre and personnel system; educating Party members about their "vanguard" roles and strengthening base-level Party organizations; and combatting corruption and enforcing Party discipline.[52]

These twin Party reform initiatives grew directly out of the Fourth Plenum of September 2004, presided over by Hu and Zeng Qinghong. The CCP Plenum adopted the important *Decision on the Enhancement of the Party's Governing Capacity* (中共中央关于加强党的执政能力建设的决定).[53] This was probably the most important CCP meeting and document to be published since the critical Third Plenum of 1978. Although the *Decision* itself had been drafted over the course of the previous year by a group of CCP theoreticians at the Central Party School led by Executive Vice-President Yu Yunyao (under close supervision by Zeng Qinghong),[54] the contents of the document reflect many previous years of self-reflection by the CCP and were the culmination of the intensive intra-Party discourse on the causes of the collapse of the former Soviet Union and other communist party-states (discussed in Chapter 4). As the *Decision* noted: "We must develop a stronger sense of crisis, draw experience and lessons from the success and failure of other ruling parties in the world, and enhance our governance capability in a more earnest and conscientious manner."[55]

Not only was the *Decision* a reflective and cumulative statement of policy, which had been gestating for over a decade, but it was also a surprisingly candid and objective one. It explicitly identified, rather than glossing over, problems faced by the Party. It was also quite straightforward about the stakes and consequences of the challenges facing the CCP. As it notes at the outset, "Vigorously enhancing the Party's governing capabilities is a major strategic subject with a bearing on the future and destiny of the Chinese nation, the life and death of the Party, as well as the lasting stability and prosperity of the country."[56] Elsewhere, it referred with remarkable candor to weaknesses that characterized Party work, as the following quotations suggest:[57]

- "The problem of corruption remains quite serious in some areas, department and units. The fight against corruption is a life and death issue for the Party."

- "Some leading Party members do not have a strong sense of responsibility, personal integrity, a down-to-earth style of work or a close connection with the general public."
- "Some Party organizations at the grassroots level are weak and slack, while some Party members have failed to play an exemplary role."
- "Weak, slack, and impotent Party committees must be frequently reshuffled and unqualified Party members must be severely dealt with."

If one compares the conclusions and the "lessons" of the CCP's post-mortem on the Soviet collapse (discussed in the previous chapter) with the organization and content of the *Decision on the Enhancement of the Party's Governing Capacity,* they are remarkably similar. Virtually all the major "lessons" are incorporated into this document:

- Place priority on economic, material, and social development.
- Pay attention to ideology and make it flexible and adaptable to national conditions.
- Combat corruption and strengthen Party discipline.
- Rotate, retire, and change leading personnel.
- Promote intra-Party democracy and extra-Party consultation.
- Reform and reinvigorate local Party branches.
- Improve cadre competence and recruitment into the Party.
- Combat Western attempts at subversion and "peaceful evolution."
- Pay attention to a range of social development problems.
- Pursue a foreign policy of openness and integration into the international community.

Following the September 2004 Fourth Plenum and the adoption of the *Decision,* a major national campaign was launched to propagate and implement the document's recommendations. Zeng Qinghong—by then Vice-President, a Politburo Standing Committee member, Chairman of the Central Committee Secretariat, and President of the Central Party School—led the way with a lengthy and widely publicized speech on October 8, 2004.[58] Hu had put Zeng in charge of the drafting committee for the *Decision* (an astute move to test and co-opt Zeng's political allegiance). In his speech,

Zeng went much further than simply reiterating (often verbatim) the content of the document (which is normally the case during the implementation phase of such campaigns). For example, Zeng provided a candid connection between the lessons learned from the collapse of the Soviet Union and the *Decision*:[59]

> We can gain profound enlightenment from the painful lesson of the loss of power by the communist parties of the Soviet Union and Eastern Europe. A number of old and big parties throughout the world lost power one after the other in the late 1980s and early 1990s. The Soviet Union used to be the world's leading socialist country, but overnight the country broke up and political power collapsed. The Communist Party of the Soviet Union was a big party with an 88-year history and 15 million members, yet it was disbanded. Communist parties in the Soviet Union and Eastern Europe lost their status as parties in power. Although many factors were involved, one important reason was that in their long time in power their system of governing became rigid, their ability to govern declined, people were dissatisfied with what the officials accomplished while in charge, and they became seriously alienated from the broad masses of the people. It is not easy for a proletarian political party to gain power, and even harder to exercise political power well, especially when it is held for a long time, and the Party's status as a party in power does not necessarily last as long as the Party does, nor is it something once achieved never lost.

These incisive judgments in the *Decision* drew directly on the CCP's lengthy analysis of the collapse of communist parties in the Soviet Union and Eastern Europe. As Zeng put it: "The intent [of the *Decision*] is to get all the Party's comrades, and especially leading cadres at all levels of the Party, to wake up, think of danger in times of peace, heighten their sense of hardship and their sense of governing, and earnestly strengthen the Party's ability to govern."[60] Zeng then proceeded to elaborate, embellish, and interpret the content of the *Decision*, often going beyond—in tone and content—the original document. He soberly concluded, "If our Party does not undertake to correct our ways and implement the *Decision*, our Party might even lose its governing status!"[61]

Following Zeng's hard-hitting speech, a vigorous national campaign unfolded to promote and implement the *Decision*. This involved the publication of multiple study volumes, the dispatch of central-level teams to provincial and local levels to explain the *Decision*, and the convening of countless study sessions from the top to the bottom of the national party apparatus.[62] Thus, the Fourth Plenum of 2004 and resulting *Decision on the Enhancement of the Party's Governing Capacity* was a true watershed in the post-Deng era concerning *political reform* in China (even if it was technically limited to the Party). It represented the culmination and summation of years of research, reflection, and retrospection on the erosion, overthrow, and collapse of other communist parties—and it turned these retrospective conclusions into prospective future-oriented decisions and actual policies for governing China's political sphere. Zeng Qinghong's personal stamp,

Figure 5.4 China's Vice-President Zeng Qinghong, 2008
Source: Associated Press

thinking, and hands were all over the document—reflecting Zeng's role as the mastermind who oversaw the entire process of political and Party reform that carried over from the second half of Jiang Zemin's reign through the first six years of Hu Jintao's, until 2009.

Then everything changed.[63] The fact that Zeng had to step down and officially retire after the National People's Congress in 2008 (Fig. 5.4) meant that the political reform program now lacked its principal mastermind and top-level benefactor. With Zeng's retirement the only remaining senior leader in favor of political reform was Premier Wen Jiabao. Wen's thinking seemed to go even further than Zeng's, as he was less concerned with intra-Party reform and more welcoming of some type of enfranchised democratic reform. During Wen's final years in office (he retired in March 2013), he gave several speeches and interviews calling for enhanced political reform and openness. In one interview with CNN in 2010 (which was not circulated inside China) Wen said: "I and all the Chinese people have such conviction that China will make continuous progress and the people's wishes and need for democracy and freedom are irresistible. I hope you will be able to gradually see the continuous progress of China. In spite of some resistance, I will advance within the realm of my capabilities political restructuring."[64] Two years later Wen described political reform as an "urgent task."[65] In his swan song at his 2012 National People's Congress, Wen opined again that political reform was direly needed lest "China experience another historical tragedy like the Cultural Revolution."[66] Wen's brave voice was the lone one in the senior leadership during 2009–2012.

While Wen spoke out, and quite surprisingly so, Hu did not do the same. Hu remained his conservative self and said little about politics or even Party reform during this final three years in office. His last speech discussing "intra-Party democracy" came in June 2009,[67] and thereafter he essentially went silent on these Party reform initiatives. However, just prior to stepping down as Party leader in 2012, Hu gave the address in 2011 commemorating the 90th anniversary of the CCP, in which he pointedly said:[68]

> In enhancing the building of Party institutions we should exercise democratic centralism, adhere to and improve the Party's leadership system, reform and improve its leadership and governance. We should develop intra-Party democracy, promote transparency in Party affairs in an active yet prudent manner, ensure the principal status and democratic rights of Party members, improve the system of Party congresses and the intra-Party electoral system, and improve the mechanism for democratic decision-making in the Party.

Such a statement by Hu (although undoubtedly written for him) does seem to reflect the essence of his views on Party building and political reform.

Retrenchment

It is difficult to put an exact date on it, but throughout the years of 2009–2010 the CCP leadership retrenched and reverted to the conservatives, completely abandoning the political reformers' agenda described above (with the exception of term limits, retirement regulations, and mid-career cadre training). No formal announcement was made, but the atmosphere unmistakably shifted during the second half of 2009 (I was living in Beijing on sabbatical at the time and witnessed the changes first-hand). Although the CCP endorsed another very progressive *Decision* at its Fourth Plenum in September 2009, it was a stillborn document. The contents had already been overtaken by events and had died a quiet death before this *Decision* was published. The document reiterated many of the political reforms of the previous decade and suggested that Zeng's political reforms would outlast him. It was not to be. Discussions I had with Party members at the time indicated that the Fourth Plenum document had been one year in preparation, had passed through multiple drafts, and was seen as a kind of culmination statement of the reforms in the political arena over the previous decade (official Chinese documents are frequently this way, summarizing policies that have already been undertaken rather than announcing new initiatives). But this *Decision* went nowhere after its publication.

Readers will naturally therefore wonder: *why the abrupt shift in 2009*? It is a very good and valid question; I can only speculate on the causes.

A series of events during 2008–2009 contributed to the Party's increased nervousness and political about-face. In March 2008 Lhasa, Tibet, erupted in riots. This was repeated in Urumqi, Xinjiang, during the summer of 2009. The Arab Spring and so-called "jasmine revolutions" coming on the heels of the "color revolutions" across Eurasia also contributed significantly to the regime's cautionary mindset.[69] The 2008 Olympics and the preparations for the massive military parade in Beijing to commemorate the 60th anniversary of the People's Republic of China on October 1, 2009 also offered the regime a golden opportunity to test its security procedures and erect a tight security dragnet over the capital city. The rising number of incidents of mass unrest across the country had also catalyzed a growing sub-provincial security apparatus.

Personnel and bureaucratic considerations were also important, I believe. Very importantly, Zeng Qinghong had retired, and there was no senior patron of the political reform program. Hu Jintao was not viewed as a strong leader and by that time (his ninth year in office) he did not command a great deal of authority within the Party or military; his authority derived mainly from his official position. Hu was, I would argue, easily manipulated, and overrun by more powerful figures and institutional interests. Around that time four bureaucracies that had a strong stake in tightening state control coalesced into a powerful coalition: the Party propaganda apparatus, internal security organs (Ministries of State and Public Security), the state-owned enterprise sector, and military and paramilitary (People's Liberation Army and People's Armed Police) forces. These four powerful bureaucracies and the Politburo members that headed them (including now disgraced and imprisoned Zhou Yongkang) were in a position to persuade the pliable Hu Jintao (who was no longer subject to Zeng Qinghong's active role in the Politburo) that political liberalization from above would cascade out of control and endanger Party rule. Instead, they likely made the case for abandoning the political reform program, reversing the main elements of it, and instituting tight security and Party controls in its place.[70] These bureaucracies also stood to financially benefit from a political tightening-up, as there is big money in repression. The internal security budget topped the military budget for the first time in 2011 ($83.5 billion versus $81.2 billion) and did so for the three subsequent fiscal years. Finally, the 2008–2009 global financial crisis imbued the Chinese leadership with a sense of hubris over the decline of the Washington Consensus and seeming vindication of the Beijing Consensus models of development. Taken together, I believe these factors all contributed to Beijing's political pivot in 2009.

Reflections on Hu Jintao's Rule

Hu Jintao's decade in office may not have resulted in major noteworthy and newsworthy accomplishments, for which he and Wen Jiabao were criticized, but they were not a complete washout either. History may even judge them positively over time. As indicated at the outset of this chapter, Hu kept the "train on the tracks" and there were no real failures on his watch. The economy continued to grow astoundingly—with GDP expanding from $2.63 trillion in 2002 to $7.19 trillion in 2012, with a stunning average annual growth rate of 10.5 percent.[71] The Party did not suffer any significant challenges to its rule, despite pockets of unrest. Indeed, during their first six years in power, under Zeng Qinghong's aegis the CCP undertook broad-gauged reforms intended to strengthen the Party through opening it up and making it more accountable. This included Hu's own innovation to publicize the detailed results of Politburo meetings and make the Central Committee departments more open to the public. While only limited success was achieved in addressing the wide range of challenging social and environmental problems, the Hu–Wen regime *did* succeed in shifting the national policy agenda away from a growth-obsessed one to a much more balanced and socially conscious one (even if they were unsuccessful in implementing all of their policies). This was popular with the people and was a much-needed corrective to the Jiang Zemin era, which had prioritized the coastal regions and business elites. Hu also presided over three major events for the nation: the 2008 summer Olympic Games, the parade on October 1, 2009 celebrating the 60th anniversary of the founding of the PRC, and the 2010 Shanghai World Expo (all of which I had the pleasure of attending).

Hu Jintao also spent a considerable amount of time on foreign affairs. During the period of his rule, a relative shift in China's foreign relations occurred when compared to the Jiang Zemin era: a shift from prioritization on relations with the main powers (United States, Russia, EU) to more variegated and omnidirectional diplomacy, with a new emphasis on the Global South. This was evident on regional, bilateral, and multilateral levels. It was during this decade that China established a wide range of regional multilateral institutions and dialogue groupings with every continent.[72]

Hu did not, however, make a large impact on China's military. After he became Chairman of the Central Military Commission in 2004 through the end of his term Hu did perform all of the perfunctory roles that came with the office, including presiding over the 2009 military parade commemorating the 60th anniversary of the PRC. But his relationship with the PLA brass was always much more a function of his ex-officio positions than of real respect or personal ties. Indeed, on his watch, corruption in the PLA burgeoned (something he left to Xi Jinping to clean up). If Hu did have an impact, it came in 2004 with his "New Historic Missions" speech—which is widely seen as the doctrinal transition in the PLA's primary mission, from preparing for Taiwan contingencies to becoming a broader global "expeditionary" force.[73]

During Hu Jintao's reign we also witnessed the Chinese recognition and embrace of "soft power." It was in Hu's speech to the 17th Party Congress in 2007 that the term *soft power* (软实力) was first officially used. Thus began a major effort by Beijing to go on the offensive in the international information domain, in attempts to improve China's global image and influence international narratives about China. This has become a huge, multifaceted, and extremely well-resourced effort, which began under Hu Jintao.[74] Hu also unveiled his concept of a "harmonious world" in 2005 as a kind of external parallel to his domestically focused "harmonious society" concept.[75] This came in tandem with his re-embrace of the Dengist concept of "peaceful development." The significance of this was mainly because the term signaled a shift from "peaceful rise" (和平崛起), which had been coined and advanced in late 2003 by senior Party theoretician Zheng Bijian (a close advisor of Deng Xiaoping who was responsible for writing his 1992 "Southern Tour" speeches).[76] Zheng's idea and phrase was meant as a direct rebuttal of what Chinese referred to as the Western "China threat theory" (中国威胁论). But after a couple of years of this concept circulating in China and abroad, it was decided by the CCP authorities that the term "rise" raised more fears abroad than it extinguished. Thus, Hu and the government reverted to the more traditional and innocuous mantra of "peaceful development."

Despite the relative shift, from focusing on the Global North to the Global South in China's foreign relations, Hu did a good job of managing relations with the United States. In fact, it is no exaggeration to say that in the 30 years since 1989, Sino-American relations enjoyed their greatest stability and longest period of positive ties precisely during Hu's tenure. This long run in generally constructive and cooperative ties was capped by

Figure 5.5 President Hu Jintao Meeting the Author, Washington, DC, January 2011
Source: Author's photo

his January 2011 visit to Washington and the United States, during which I had the opportunity to meet him (Fig. 5.5).

While the 2000s under Hu's rule were on balance quite positive for China's foreign relations, toward the end of the decade a new—and more ominous—shift in China's external relations became evident. The year 2009–2010 thus became known as China's "year of assertiveness."[77] While some scholars dispute that there was any appreciable change in China's behavior,[78] many observers noted a more caustic and confrontational approach in Beijing's external posture. In rapid succession Beijing confronted many of its neighbors over seemingly innocuous events. It threatened Tokyo with diplomatic and economic retaliation over the arrest of a drunken Chinese fisherman who had strayed into Japanese waters near the disputed Senkaku/Diaoyu islands. It did the same against the Philippines over conflicting claims in the South China Sea. It irritated South Korea by blocking a resolution in the UN Security Council condemning the North Korean sinking of the ROK Navy submarine *Cheonan*, taking 46 sailors to their deaths. It escalated

China's claims to disputed territory with India and deployed more military units in these contested zones. It arrested and imprisoned Australian businessmen, allegedly in response to Canberra's blocking of a mega-merger between Chinese and Australian energy giants Chinalco and Rio Tinto. It put Denmark in the diplomatic deep freeze for a year in retaliation for hosting of the Dalai Lama in Copenhagen. It did the same to Norway for seven years after imprisoned Chinese intellectual and dissident Liu Xiaobo was awarded the Nobel Peace Prize. Multilaterally, China's diplomats undermined the Copenhagen Climate Change Conference by blocking a final agreement and communiqué. Beijing became very testy with the EU over several issues and gave the cold shoulder to new American President Barack Obama when he paid a state visit to Beijing in November 2009.

All of these "assertive" moves transpired over the course of an eighteen-month period from mid-2009 through the end of 2010. Thus, what was quite a successful decade in China's ties with the world ended on a series of bad notes. While the previous decade had given the world a sense of China as an increasingly productive partner—particularly in Asia and Europe—Beijing's behavior during 2009–2010 resurrected bad memories from the past and caused many countries to be more wary of China. This trend carried over into the next decade, although by 2011–2012 (before Hu handed power over to Xi Jinping) Beijing tried to recalibrate and sought to ameliorate strains with a number of the aforementioned countries. Still, on balance, Hu Jintao must be given very good marks for foreign policy on his watch.

The other area in which Hu deserves high praise concerns relations with Taiwan. It was quite simply the best period in cross-strait relations since 1949. Beginning in 2008 and through 2012, when Hu completed his term, he partnered together with Taiwan President Ma Ying-cheou to substantially ease tensions between the mainland and Taiwan (which had heightened under the Democratic Progressive Party administration of President Chen Shuibian), restoring the semi-official channel of direct communications and brokering various agreements focused on cross-straits trade and investment, communications links, direct air flights and shipping, tourism, cultural and educational exchanges, and other practical areas. These unprecedented steps carried over from the Hu regime to that of Xi Jinping. So positive had they become toward the end of Ma Ying-cheou's own eight years in office, that Ma and Xi met in a highly publicized event in Singapore on November 7, 2015. Thereafter, following the election of Tsai Ying-wen as Ma's successor, relations have deteriorated. But it was under Hu Jintao that the key decisions and key steps were taken to ameliorate the decades of estrangement between the two sides.

All in all, Hu Jintao may have had more impact than he is usually given credit for. Actually, in the policy areas noted above, he did have a substantive impact. But, as noted at the outset of this chapter, his sterile personality and public persona seemingly gave the impression of an under-achieving leader. Such is certainly not the case with his successor Xi Jinping.

CHAPTER 6

XI JINPING (习近平)

Modern Emperor

"The Chinese nation, which since modern times began had endured so much for so long, has achieved a tremendous transformation: it has stood up, grown rich, and is becoming strong; it has come to embrace the brilliant prospects of rejuvenation."

—Xi Jinping, Speech to 19th Party Congress, October 18, 2017[1]

When Xi Jinping introduced himself and the new Politburo Standing Committee to the international media in the Great Hall of the People following the 18th Party Congress on November 15, 2012 (Fig. 6.2), everyone wondered what kind of leader he would be and in which direction he would lead China. As usual, Western China watchers speculated as to whether the new leader would be "China's Gorbachev"—finally opening and reforming the political system. Others, myself included, were more skeptical.[2] After ten years of perceived malaise and drift under his predecessor Hu Jintao, Chinese and foreigners alike wondered if Xi would provide new vigor to the leadership and exercise a strong impact on the policy agenda.

Xi's initial statements to the assembled media offered a few clues to his priorities:[3]

Our responsibility is to unite and lead people of the entire Party and of all ethnic groups around the country while accepting the baton of history and continuing to work for realizing the *great revival of the Chinese nation in order to*

Figure 6.1 Xi Jinping (1953–)
Source: Voice of America / Public Domain

> *let the Chinese nation stand more firmly and powerfully among all nations* around the world and make a greater contribution to mankind.

This is fairly boilerplate language, but in the italicized words (emphasis added) Xi did cast his, the Party's, and the nation's mission in both historical and international terms. This would be a central theme of Xi's tenure and would contribute to a renewed emphasis on patriotic studies in Chinese schools and society.[4] For him, China was not merely continuing "reform and opening" or moving to the next stage of its development. Rather, Xi very much couched the country's position in terms of reclaiming China's position as a major world power. He also served notice of his intention to prioritize combatting corruption (the *only* specific policy issue he mentioned that day):[5]

> In the new situation, our Party faces many severe challenges, and there are many pressing problems within the Party that need to be resolved, especially

Figure 6.2 Xi Jinping Introduces CCP Politburo Standing Committee, November 15, 2012
Source: UPI / Alamy

> problems such as corruption and bribe-taking by some Party members and cadres, being out of touch with the people, placing undue emphasis on formality and bureaucracy must be addressed with great effort. The whole Party must be vigilant. The metal itself must be hard to be turned into iron. Our responsibility is to work with all comrades in the Party to be resolute in ensuring that the Party supervises its own conduct; enforces strict discipline; effectively deals with the prominent issues within the Party; earnestly improves the Party's work style and maintains close ties with the people.

Xi soon unleashed the most thoroughgoing and harsh crackdown on corruption in the Party's history. By 2018 Chinese authorities had investigated more than 2.7 million officials and punished more than 1.5 million.[6] Xi's purge incarcerated a former member of the Politburo Standing Committee, two Politburo members, 42 members of the Central Committee, 71 PLA generals (including two members of the Central Military Commission), and over 4,000 military officers.[7] Thus, in his initial appearance as China's new leader, Xi staked out two prominent themes that would characterize his leadership: China as a world power, and combatting corruption.

Shortly thereafter Xi added a third prominent theme: the Chinese Communist Party (CCP) as national savior. Xi did so by leading the entire Politburo to the National Museum on the east side of Tiananmen Square to view the permanent exhibition on China's "Road to Rejuvenation" (复兴之路展览会).The majority of this exhibition and the section to which Xi and his colleagues paid particular attention pertained to the pre-1949 period of modern Chinese history. This section emphasizes China's national dismemberment, deprivation, and humiliation at the hands of Western imperialist powers and Japan. As they toured the exhibition, dressed in matching windbreakers and dark jackets, as if out of communist central casting, the group lingered in front of photos and artifacts from the Opium Wars (1840–1842), the time from which the CCP dates the beginning of the "century of shame and humiliation" (百年国耻). There Xi paused and gave a brief "keynote speech" in which he said, "The Chinese nation has suffered unusual hardship and sacrifice in the world's modern history. But the Chinese people have never given in, have struggled ceaselessly, and have finally taken hold of their own destiny and started the great process of building our nation." In touring the exhibition and making these comments Xi was clearly linking China's accomplishments to the CCP's narrative about the country's past hardships. Actually, this is not a new or novel theme. Since the 1950s the Party's propaganda apparatus has claimed "no CCP, no New China" (没有中国共产党,没有新中国). Nowadays, Chinese often say, "Under Mao the Chinese people stood up (站起来), under Deng Xiaoping the Chinese people became rich (富起来), under Xi Jinping the Chinese people have become strong (强起来)."

A few weeks later Xi added a fourth key theme that would highlight his priorities as China's leader: the need to learn from the downfall of the Soviet Union. Of course, this was nothing new either—the post-1991 Jiang Zemin and Hu Jintao leaderships had both been similarly obsessed with this issue. But Xi drew *very different* lessons from the collapse of the USSR than did Zeng Qinghong (who led the post-mortem assessment under Jiang and Hu, as discussed in Chapters 4 and 5).

Recall from Chapter 4 that two very different schools of analysis emerged in CCP circles concerning the lessons of the Soviet overthrow/collapse. The first, advocated and implemented by Zeng while he was in power, was that without *proactive reforms* and *managed but careful political reforms* in particular, the CCP would fall prey to the same features of atrophy that had afflicted the Soviet Communist Party. Without "adaptation," "atrophy" would corrode the Party from within like a cancer.[8] Proactive management was the key to survival from this perspective. Moreover, Zeng and his cohort concluded that *relative opening* of civil society, media, and intellectual life were intrinsic elements that ran parallel to the intra-Party reforms they were undertaking (increased transparency, the "three democracies," merit-based promotion, mid-career training, and other CCP reforms described in Chapters 4 and 5). These reforms were premised on the conclusion that Mikhail Gorbachev's reforms in the Soviet Union were *not incorrect* (on the whole)—they just came *too late* and by that time the Soviet system was already so broken that it could not absorb the "shock therapy." According to this viewpoint, advocated by Zeng Qinghong and many CCP analysts (and *accepted* by leaders Jiang Zemin and Hu Jintao), it was not so much Gorbachev's reforms that were the real problem and the systemic cause of collapse, even if they had been the precipitating catalysts. They believed it was a combination of policies—begun under Stalin and continued through Brezhnev, Andropov, and Chernenko—which had progressively corroded the Soviet system so severely that, by the time Gorbachev came along and launched his reforms, the system could not absorb them. Ironically, this line of analysis also held that had Khrushchev's liberal reforms (1956–1964) been permitted to continue, the USSR could have avoided its long period of bureaucratic decay.[9]

However, there was an alternative line of analysis and second school of thought that existed within the CCP.[10] According to this perspective, it was *precisely* Gorbachev's reforms that brought the Soviet system down. This school believed that they were not just a catalyst that collapsed an already broken system—they were the problem and cause in themselves. By this line of reasoning, it was precisely the combined attempt to simultaneously open the system politically (*glasnost*) and implement economic and institutional reforms (*perestroika*) that opened the floodgates to the opposition. Once the popular protests began, the Party system and the security services could not withstand the pressure and the whole edifice cracked and came crashing down. The lessons to be learned, according to this second school of analysis: *do not open the political system at all and maintain absolute control over the military and security services*. Political reform, they concluded, is a slippery slope that cannot be "managed"; it will inevitably cascade out of control and bring great pressures on the ruling party, likely leading to its fall from power. This second cohort of analysts in the CCP had their own conservative supporters in the leadership—and one of them was Xi Jinping.

Xi made his position concerning the Soviet collapse known on a visit to Guangdong province and Shenzhen just one month after taking power. Ostensibly the trip was to signal Xi's support for the "reform and opening" launched by Deng Xiaoping and his father (recall from Chapter 3 that Xi's father had been instrumental in launching the first three Special Economic Zones in Guangdong during 1978–1980). After the obligatory pilgrimage to Shenzhen, Xi gave an unpublicized speech to Party cadres in Guangzhou. In it he focused on the collapse of the Soviet Union and its lessons for the CCP.[11] He explicitly blamed the collapse on Gorbachev's reforms—which included "nationalizing" the armed forces so that they were loyal to the state and not the Party—but Xi went further by blaming other Soviet leaders for not resisting Gorbachev and his reforms. While an authorized version of the speech has never been released, in a leaked and apparently accurate version Xi said:[12]

> Why must we stand firm on the Party's leadership over the military? Because that is the lesson from the collapse of the Soviet Union. In the Soviet Union, where the military was depoliticized, separated from the Party and nationalized, the Party was disarmed. A few people tried to save the Soviet Union; they seized Gorbachev, but within days it was turned around again, because they didn't have the instruments to exert power. Yeltsin gave a speech standing on a tank, but the military made no response, keeping so-called "neutrality." Finally, Gorbachev announced the disbandment of the Soviet Communist Party in a blithe statement. A big party was gone—just like that. Proportionately, the Soviet Communist Party had more members than we do, but *nobody was man enough to stand up and resist*.

So, for Xi, it was not only Gorbachev and his reforms that were to blame—it was also that no other leaders *resisted* him during the *dénouement*. In Xi's eyes the Soviet Politburo and Party elite buckled when they should have found their backbone and resisted. That was the lesson for Xi Jinping: don't go there (political reform) in the first place, if someone tries to do so it must be resisted, and complete control must be maintained over the military at all costs.

Thus, within his first month in office, Xi Jinping had signaled these four themes—China as a great power, anti-corruption, the CCP as national savior, and no political reforms in order to avoid a Soviet-style collapse of the Party. These early themes would mark his first five-year term in office (2012–2017). Xi would, of course, add many more signature initiatives during his first few years in power. These included the "Chinese Dream"; the "two centenary goals" (achieving a "moderately well-off society" by the Party's 100th anniversary in 2021 and becoming a "strong, democratic, civilized, harmonious, and modern socialist country" by the 100th anniversary of the PRC in 2049); the Belt and Road Initiative, and his "Community of Common Destiny of Mankind."

In very short order Xi Jinping signaled that he would be a bold and transformative leader who would break from many practices that had been in place from Deng Xiaoping through Hu Jintao, and that he would embark in many new directions. This was, however, not at all clear when Xi was elevated to the upper CCP elite in 2007 or when he took the reins of power in 2012. This is often the case with transformative leaders—that is, they do not reveal themselves as such until they are ensconced at the top. In retrospect, were there earlier indicators that may have indicated Xi's policy priorities and modalities of rule? What can be gleaned from his biography and background? What did his past possibly indicate about the orientation of the man who has now led China since 2012?

Xi Jinping's Rise to Power

Xi Jinping had a very different upbringing and career path from the previous Chinese leaders we have examined in this book. As the late senior Singaporean statesman Lee Kuan Yew observed about Xi when he ascended the throne of power in the Forbidden City: "He has iron in his soul, more than Hu Jintao, who ascended the ranks without experiencing the trials and tribulations that Xi endured."[13]

Xi Jinping was born on June 1, 1953 in Beijing. He was the first son, but third child, of Xi Zhongxun and Qi Xin. His father was one of the senior Party leaders, director of the CCP Propaganda Department at the time; he was a veteran of the Long March and the Yanan revolutionary period, and the Sino-Japanese and civil wars. When Xi was five years old his father was promoted to vice-premier and simultaneously worked as a chief secretary (秘书) to Premier Zhou Enlai.

As the child of senior Party elites, Xi and his siblings enjoyed a very pampered existence. He grew up with military guards, nurses, cooks, and other accoutrements of "red privilege" inside the Zhongnanhai leadership compound adjacent to the Forbidden City in central Beijing. Xi Jinping is the quintessential "high cadre princeling" (高干子弟), also known as the "second red generation" (红二代). During summers his family would decamp, along with other leadership families, to the seaside resort at Beidaihe. His schooling was also privileged. He attended the Beihai kindergarten and elementary school, a short walk from the Zhongnanhai. Here his classmates included the children of Liu Shaoqi, Chen Yun, and Bo Yibo.

Box 6.1 Xi Jinping and Bo Xilai

Xi's childhood contemporaries included Bo Xilai, who was four years older, was a neighbor, and an elder classmate. Their careers paralleled each other, as did their fathers. Although Xi had been selected to be Hu Jintao's successor in 2007, Bo Xilai was also a contender for the Politburo Standing Committee. Bo—a handsome, suave, and charismatic personality—had a great deal of stature and national following in his own right, and had become famous as Party secretary of Chongqing municipality in Sichuan province (2007–2012). There he fostered an eclectic series of popular policies collectively known as the "Chongqing model": neo-leftist ideological policies that venerated the Cultural Revolution; a tough-on-organized-crime campaign; robust economic growth policies; and egalitarian social policies that played to the downtrodden. It was an odd mixture, but Bo Xilai rode this wave to national and international fame (and personal fortune). Then, the roof fell in on his career in 2012, when his wife Gu Kailai (also an attractive personality known for her expensive tastes and jet-setting lifestyle) was found to have poisoned to death a British national named Neil Heywood, who had been a family "fixer" and manager of their overseas assets. The exact circumstances behind this bizarre story remain opaque, but the police also implicated Bo Xilai in the cover-up. In February 2012 Chongqing's police chief Wang Lijun, who knew of the murder, confronted Bo Xilai about his wife's role and his complicity. Bo erupted in rage and Wang, feeling that his life was in danger, fled to the U.S. Consulate in Chengdu. The Americans first admitted him to the premises, but then turned him over to the Ministry of State Security. This whole sordid story is a tangent from Xi Jinping's upbringing—but it is relevant because Xi's childhood classmate had become something of a political rival to Xi on the eve of his enthronement at the 18th Party Congress in October 2012. Bo was arrested along with his wife, tried and convicted of bribery, abuse of power, and embezzlement (although being an accomplice of murder was not a charge), stripped of his Party membership, and sentenced to life in prison.

Figure 6.3 Bo Xilai Sentenced to Life in Prison, September 23, 2012
Source: Associated Press

While Bo's actions were his own undoing, having him out of the way certainly benefitted Xi Jinping by removing the one individual who could potentially be a serious challenger to his rule.

At some point during middle school (at an unknown age) Xi transferred to the August First School (八一学校) in the Haidian district of northwestern Beijing. This meant, according to one biography of Xi, that he was a boarding student there—returning home to the Zhongnanhai only on occasional weekends.[15] The school was situated in a sprawling and lovely Qing dynasty pavilion (大观园) in the Western Hills of Beijing, not far from the Summer Palace. The school was replete with gardens, orchards, swimming pools, medical clinics, shops, laundries, gymnasiums, and other accoutrements of pampered elite life.[16] The school not only accepted children of the CCP elite, but also those from other communist parties in Asia. When Xi visited Laos in June 2010 he had a reunion with several former classmates whose parents had been leaders in the Pathet Lao communist guerrilla movement.[17]

Being separated from his parents and siblings at such a tender age must have had an emotional impact on young Xi. A psychologist colleague of mine suggests that it would not only have created a sense of emotional separation, but also an early sense of autonomy for Xi, making him an unemotional individual who did not easily develop personal attachments. This in turn, my colleague suggests, can lead to a callousness and detachment from interpersonal relations—to the relinquishing of any sense of responsibility or guilt when someone else suffers (Mao is similarly diagnosed). Even without being sent to boarding school, Xi's early sense of independence was likely the result of his parents being frequently absent from home. His mother worked and lived at the Central Party School in the northwest suburbs (actually close to Xi's boarding school) and his father was working all the time in the Zhongnanhai leadership compound in the city center or traveling around the country, although he was said to have been a doting father toward his children when they were together. At the Ba Yi school (which was named for the date that the PLA was founded), Xi's classmates included many military offspring—including Marshal Nie Rongzhen's daughter, and the sons of Marshals He Long, Su Yu, Liu Bocheng, and Xu Xiangqian. Given the insular world of the PLA, this early exposure to military families was important, and was likely instrumental in Xi's comfort level and familiarity among the PLA in later years. It also provided Xi with a "PLA pedigree" that would help him throughout his career, including when he became the national leader. As we will see below, Xi has fawned on the PLA and paid extraordinary attention to its modernization.

Xi Jinping's life was traumatically upended when he was only nine years old, when his father was abruptly purged in 1962. Chairman Mao approved of the purge on the recommendation of internal security czar Kang Sheng. Xi Zhongxun's alleged "crime" had occurred six years earlier when he was head of the Propaganda Department and the department had approved the publication of a novel about Liu Zhidan, a revolutionary martyr.[18] It is highly unlikely that, as department director, Xi himself would have been involved in such a routine decision—but he was nonetheless blamed for it. The novel had been written by the wife of Liu's younger brother, Li Jiantong. Problematically, the novel had mentioned Gao Gang—Politburo member and strongman of northeastern China, whom Mao had purged in 1954 for an alleged power grab (see discussion in Chapter 2). Kang Sheng further accused Xi Zhongxun of actually trying to posthumously "rehabilitate" Gao Gang (who had committed suicide in 1954) through authorizing publication of the novel. Xi Zhongxun was, absurdly, charged with leading an "anti-Party clique," was denounced, stripped of his positions, and abruptly purged. But he was not imprisoned—instead being held at home under house arrest. It cannot have failed to come as an extreme shock to young Xi and his siblings. In a memory from when he was nine years old, Xi Jinping recalls seeing his father "sitting in the darkness in the hallway without talking," while his younger brother Xi Yuanping allegedly asked, "Daddy, why aren't you going to work in the Zhongnanhai?"[19] This must have been emotionally traumatic for young Xi, although it probably provided a useful lesson about the capriciousness of Chinese communist elite politics. One biographer of Xi argues that witnessing his father's and others' purges during the Cultural Revolution gave him a "hero-martyr complex."[20]

In 1965 Xi Zhongxun was removed from Beijing and sent to Luoyang to do manual labor in a factory that manufactured mining machinery. In 1967, when Xi was a mere 14 years old, and the Cultural Revolution was raging, his father was again denounced and dragged before hordes of raging Red Guards in the city of Xian (but apparently he was not beaten or tortured) and sent to a nearby labor camp. A year later, in 1968, he was returned to Beijing (perhaps at the behest of Zhou Enlai, who did his best to protect purged senior officials) and incarcerated. He was only released and rehabilitated following Mao's death and Deng Xiaoping's return to power in 1978. As noted in Chapter 3, the elder Xi was then appointed Party secretary of Guangdong Province, where he was instrumental in starting the Special Economic Zones. When he was finally released after sixteen years of detention, his wife Qi Xin understatedly observed, "I admire his unfailing perseverance."[21]

Meanwhile, as Xi the father languished in confinement, Xi the son felt the stigma of his father's purge, commenting later that his classmates had ostracized him.[22] This too likely contributed to his sense of emotional and psychological detachment and his autonomy at a very young age.

Four years later, when the Cultural Revolution erupted, Xi found himself caught up in Mao's machinations. He was thirteen when the Red Guards began to form on university campuses in the capital, and he wanted to join the group of Little Red Guards (小红卫兵) that had begun to form in middle schools, but his father's "reactionary" status prevented him from being accepted at first. It was probably a good thing too, as the initial groups to form in the Ba Yi School were egged on by violent university Red Guards and reportedly were quite brutal (even toward their parents). On January 25, 1967, a throng of several thousand Red Guards (including Bo Xilai) surrounded the campus demanding that teachers and other "reactionaries" be "dragged out" for criticism.[23] Some teachers were persecuted, and the school was formally disbanded. Some reports claim that Xi himself was briefly detained by the Red Guards and forced to denounce his father.[24] Subsequent to the siege at Ba Yi, Xi Jinping was sent to another middle school, the No. 25 Middle School near the Beijing Zoo. He did not last long there, as that school also was dissolved in the unfolding chaos gripping the capital. Xi had only one option: to move in with his mother on the campus of the Central Party School (which he did). But Qi Xin was also enduring her own struggles; as the wife of Xi Zhongxun she was subjected to numerous criticism sessions before being banished to a May Seventh Cadre School (五七干校) in Henan in late 1968, where she remained for seven years.

Still an adolescent, just shy of sixteen, Xi was once again on his own. This time the state intervened in Xi's life. In January 1969 Xi was dispatched along with 5,000 Beijing youth to the loess plateaus and mountains of northern

Shaanxi Province—ironically to Yanan, the revolutionary wartime capital where his own father had lived thirty years earlier. Xi's being sent to Shaanxi was part of Mao's "down to the countryside youth" (下乡青年) program, aimed at "rusticating" urban youth, exposing them to the hardships of rural life, and inculcating them with the revolutionary spirit of the peasants. For a child who had known nothing but the considerable privilege of an elite revolutionary upbringing in the capital city, the transition to the dry and dusty steppes of Shaanxi came as quite a physical and psychological shock, even if the young urbanites were brimming with propagandized fervor to "exchange experiences" with the peasantry.

After arriving in Yanan, Xi was selected to go to a village in nearby Yanchuan County called Liangjiahe (梁家河). This county, about 80 kilometers northeast of Yanan, is extremely dry and windy with poor conditions for agriculture, although it does hold deposits of coal, gas, and oil. Xi was assigned to a production brigade in the Weinanyi commune. The 200

Figure 6.4 Xi Jinping as Teenager in Rural Liangjiahe Village, Shaanxi Province, 1969
Source: Xinhua / Alamy

villagers all lived in caves for warmth and protection from the harsh natural elements of the high plateau. Food consisted mainly of millet, noodles, and maize dumplings (包子). Life was tough, and Xi apparently did not easily adapt himself to his harsh new conditions. "The intensity of the labor shocked me. The hard labor afforded no breaks at all and made me feel uncomfortable," he later recalled.[25] Food was scarce and on one occasion he was criticized for feeding dumplings to stray dogs. But Xi slowly adapted and began to gain acceptance among the villagers. He ferried pails of water for irrigation, dug wells, did a lot of hoeing and planting, herded sheep, and learned some rudimentary healthcare from visiting "barefoot doctors." Xi's hardship experience deep in the countryside made him a member of what Chinese refer to as the "eat bitterness generation" (吃苦代), those who were "sent down" (下方) to the countryside. After three years Xi had acclimated and had ingratiated himself with the villagers to the point where, in 1972, he joined the local branch of the Communist Youth League. This facilitated his applying to become a Party member—which he reportedly tried to do eight times before finally succeeding in 1974 at the age of 21 (his repeated failures apparently had to do with his father's stigmatized political status). Xi quickly became the secretary of his production brigade.

In the midst of this, in the winter of 1972, Xi was summoned back to Beijing, as his maternal grandmother was dying. His mother, two sisters (Qiaoqiao and Anan), brother (Yuanping), and aunt were allowed to travel there from their internal exiles as well. While in the capital for a few weeks, Xi's mother put in a request to Premier Zhou Enlai seeking permission to visit Xi Zhongxun in a nearby prison, where he was incarcerated. The request was promptly granted and the family had an emotional reunion.[26] When Xi Zhongxun met them and first saw his family he apparently could not distinguish between his two daughters and had difficulty recognizing his sons after eight years of separation.[27] Following the family reunion, Xi returned to Liangjiahe, where he stayed and worked in the local Party committee until 1975.[28]

At the age of 22 Xi was selected as the *only* youth from the entire province to be admitted to prestigious Tsinghua University, ironically as a "worker-peasant-soldier" (工农兵) student, which was a new admittance program to send children from the countryside and proletarian class backgrounds (which Xi certainly did not possess) to universities once they had begun to reopen following the worst of the Cultural Revolution disruption. Xi bid an emotional farewell to his village compatriots, where he had lived and with whom he had bonded for six years, and returned by train to Beijing. In August 2018 he paid his own emotional return to Liangjiahe, which of course became fodder for the propaganda apparatus. The entire experience, while trying at first, had left a powerful and positive impression on Xi. If nothing else, it provided him with a first-hand real exposure to rural life and hardship, he did manual labor, and had developed a genuine appreciation of the countryside and peasant life. Xi has carried this experience with him to this day—thus providing authenticity to his subsequent "man of the people" reputation.

At Tsinghua Xi enrolled in the Chemical Engineering Department in the autumn of 1975, majoring in basic organic chemistry and synthesis. Having been in the countryside for seven years, with a truncated middle school education, Xi apparently struggled with basic math and the foundational sciences (including physics), showing more interest in literature, history, and sports. Being tall and thin, he was fast and competed on the track as a runner.

Following Mao's death and Hua Guofeng's ascension to power in 1976, various purged senior cadres began appealing directly to Hua and the Politburo for their releases and rehabilitations. Xi Zhongxun was one. Xi's wife Qi Xin had been released from her cadre school in Henan and had returned to Beijing by this time, and she too directly appealed to Marshal Ye Jianying, Wang Zhen, and Hu Yaobang to overturn her husband's case and have him released from detention. The appeal succeeded, and the elder Xi was released in February 1978. The family was reunited at long last—following sixteen years of political purgatory, incarceration, and separation.

The reunion would not, however, last long. Within weeks of his return Marshal Ye Jianying (who was de facto running the government, Party, and military while Hua Guofeng was the titular head of each) proposed that Xi Zhongxun be immediately reassigned to active work in the Party and that, moreover, he be sent to Guangdong as deputy Party secretary (where Ye had previously served and where he had a continuing interest). On April 5, 1978, he departed by plane from Beijing to Guangdong. Younger

Xi Jinping, now 26, was photographed among family members seeing him off at the airport. Xi's older sister Qiaoqiao and his mother accompanied Xi Zhongxun to their new assignment and life in southern Guangzhou. By December of 1978 Xi had replaced Wei Guoqing as Party secretary and was in charge of the province. During the next two years he was instrumental in conceptualizing and implementing new policies to welcome foreign investment and turn the southern province into a major export processing zone. He remained in Guangdong until December 1980, when he returned to Beijing to take up a position on the Standing Committee of the National People's Congress, subsequently joining the Politburo and Secretariat in September 1982 at the 11th Party Congress. He held these positions until retiring in April 1988.

Meanwhile, as the elder Xi was running Guangdong and opening it to the world, younger Xi was completing his studies at Tsinghua. He graduated in 1978 and was immediately assigned to be a secretary (秘书) to Central Military Commission (CMC) secretary-general and Defense Minister Geng Biao. It appears that Xi was enlisted in the army in order to do this job, because he wore a green khaki uniform with PLA red tabs on the collar (although his official biography does not list him as having been in the active duty military). Geng Biao was also a veteran revolutionary who was close to Deng Xiaoping as well as to Xi's father, and had previously served abroad as ambassador to several European and Asian countries. In his new job Xi traveled abroad for the first time in his life, visiting Eastern Europe, Scandinavia, and the United States. Xi was a member of Geng Biao's entourage when it visited the Pentagon on May 28, 1980, thus giving the 26-year-old a first-hand view of the heart of American military power.[29] The delegation subsequently visited a number of important US military bases—from Fort Bragg to Pearl Harbor.

Xi's family background and connections certainly helped him get the position working for Geng Biao in the CMC and Ministry of Defense, but it is also illustrative of his personal ties to the military and senior military families. These would prove extremely useful when Xi became a candidate to be national leader and commander-in-chief of the PLA. It also helps to explain the ease with which Xi interacts with the military brass and his own exceptionally strong commitment to modernizing and transforming the military into a world-class force by mid-century (see discussion below). Xi's position as Geng Biao's personal assistant allowed him to witness first-hand, for the first time in his life, how the most senior Chinese Party leaders really interacted. As one exposé about Xi described this time in his life: "It gave him a three-year crash course in elite politics, international relations, and military affairs."[30] He also was exposed to the mechanics of policy and personnel management at that level—learning about the secret document transmission system, about planning high-level meetings, about organizing bodyguards and security details, and the other day-to-day mechanics of leadership life. It was far more than an ordinary graduate in organic chemistry could have expected. Xi subsequently re-enrolled at Tsinghua from 1998–2002 (although not in residence, as he was working in Fujian during this time) to undertake a PhD degree in law. He completed and submitted a dissertation entitled "A Tentative Study on China's Rural Marketization," for which he was awarded the degree. Unfortunately, there have been multiple accusations that Xi plagiarized parts of his thesis.[31]

Despite this rare opportunity, when Geng Biao entered the Politburo and Standing Committee of the National People's Congress in 1982 and began to assume other civilian duties, Xi decided it was also time for a personal change. Already a Party member for eight years by this point, he apparently took the individual initiative to request an assignment at the local level. The CCP Organization Department, then headed by Song Renqiong (father of one of Xi's classmates in middle school) assigned him to be deputy Party secretary of Zhengding County in Hebei province. A former Neolithic village about 260 kilometers south of Beijing and only 20 kilometers from the provincial capital Shijiazhuang on the North China Plain, Zhengding was famous as a cultural site during the Three Kingdoms period (AD 220–280) and home to many historical Buddhist pagodas and monuments. A year later he was promoted to be Party secretary of the county. Although Xi's career record has been embellished to emphasize certain proletarian and leadership characteristics, he did apparently leave an impression for selflessness, hard work, and connecting with the masses during his time in Zhengding. The hagiographic narrative has it that he slept in his office on a bed propped up by two benches next to a coal-heated stove for cooking and warmth in the winter, and rode his Phoenix (凤凰) bicycle all around the county. He established a reputation for opening up the rural market economy, improving the lives of retired military veterans, and establishing a tourist attraction with an old mansion (*Rongguo Dasha*) which would be used for the re-filming of a popular made-for-television series, *The Dream of the Red Mansion*.

After three years in Zhengding, where Xi got very favorable reviews for his modest lifestyle and earnest cadre work, he was transferred in June 1985 to Xiamen (where he arrived on his 32nd birthday), a beautiful coastal city in Fujian province. Xi himself has fond memories of his time in Zhengding and he has returned to visit the county seat four times (in 1991, 1993, 1997, and 2005).

Upon arriving in Xiamen he was first assigned to be deputy mayor of the city. Xi would wind up serving there for 17.5 years altogether, a very lengthy stint, and would subsequently refer to the province as his "second home."[32] During these years (1985–2002) Xi served in a variety of provincial Party and government positions. This was, of course, a period in which Fujian was also at the forefront of China's coastal development strategy—and being directly across from Taiwan was a natural locale to open up to Taiwanese investment on the mainland. His work in promoting the foreign investment and export industries was another important résumé builder for Xi. He also devoted his energies to poverty alleviation and building road and rail linkages to the interior mountainous regions in the province. Being directly opposite the offshore islands of Jinmen and Matsu (both visible two miles offshore from Xiamen), which are still occupied by Nationalist military forces, put Xi in direct communication with the frontline PLA garrison in Fujian.

It was during this time that Xi met and married Peng Liyuan on September 1, 1987. They were introduced through mutual military friends, as Peng was a soldier and singer in the PLA Song and Dance troupe (she would go on to great national fame as one of the performers in the annual televised New Year's gala, as well as being promoted to the rank of Major General). Xi's first marriage to Ke Lingling only lasted from 1979 to 1982, when she was posted as a diplomat to London (where her father Ke Hua was China's ambassador).[33] By that point the marriage had broken down, but Xi's own career was taking off.

Xi Jinping was in eastern Fujian throughout the 1989 Tiananmen crisis, serving as head of Ningde Prefecture (where he had been reassigned in late 1988). Although his father was among the Party elders who collectively made the decision to send in the troops and clear Tiananmen Square on June 4, 1989, younger Xi remained silent in Fujian. His wife Peng Liyuan, however, was among those PLA performers who, following the massacre, entertained the martial-law troops, commemorating the military "martyrs."

During Xi's tenure in Fujian the province was also hit by a series of high-profile corruption cases. One notable instance was the unmasking of a deeply corrupt set of officials in Zhouning, one of the nine counties under Xi's jurisdiction. Several county leaders had taken huge bribes and facilitated operations for a multifaceted organized crime network. It was exposed; a thorough housecleaning of Ningde officialdom in 2005 ensued, which included the provincial Party secretary whom Xi had replaced. Xi oversaw the takedown of the corrupt group of local leaders, arguing that "a new broom sweeps clean."[34] The other notable case was the Yuanhua smuggling case that was exposed in 2000. Masterminded by the farmer-turned-businessman Lai Changxing, the operation was involved in smuggling an array of products valued at $6.38 billion—oil, foodstuffs, cigarettes, appliances, and luxury cars stolen in Hong Kong—into the province from 1996 to 1999. When the group was busted in 2000, 84 involved individuals were put on trial, of whom eleven were sentenced to death.[35] A second round of prosecutions in 2002 resulted in seven more death sentences.[36] The ringleader, though, fled to Canada. Following twelve years on the lam as China's most wanted fugitive, Lai Changxin was extradited by the Canadian government to China in 2011, where he was sentenced to life in prison (part of the extradition agreement with Canada, which opposes capital punishment, was that Lai would not be sentenced to death upon return).

For Xi—now newly appointed governor of the whole province—this high-profile case could not be avoided. He surely must have known about it while it was going on, but he took the high road by embracing the crackdown on the smuggling ring in his report to the provincial People's Congress on January 20, 2000: "We should resolutely follow the arrangements of the Central Committee and the CCP Fujian Committee to make great efforts to investigate and punish the activities violating the law and discipline, especially when major and serious criminal cases occur. We will be resolute in clearing away corrupt elements, regardless of who they are and what positions they hold. We will work through to the end to deal with the problem seriously."[37]

Thus, with his role in cracking down on the Ningde and Yuanhua corruption cases, Xi Jinping had staked his claim as an anti-corruption politician. Given how serious the problem had become within the country, the Party, the government, and the military, this was another key résumé builder for Xi Jinping's climb to the top. Xi would make anti-corruption one of his signature policies once he became China's paramount leader.

Toward the end of Xi's assignment to Fujian, on May 24, 2002, his father Xi Zhongxun passed away. In his upper eighties, his health had been deteriorating for some months. Three years earlier, on the occasion of the 50th anniversary of the founding of the People's Republic on October 1, 1999, Zeng Qinghong arranged to fly the elder Xi from Guangdong to Beijing to join other national leaders and stand atop Tiananmen Gate to review the National Day parade. He was warmly received by Hu Jintao, Wen Jiabao, Jiang Zemin, and other senior and retired leaders. Xi Zhongxun stayed in the capital for twelve days before returning to Shenzhen. Thereafter, however, at his advanced age his health began to deteriorate. Xi Jinping would frequently travel from Fujian to visit his father during this period. By April 2002 Xi Zhongxun had become critically ill and was flown by special plane to Beijing and hospitalized in the 304 PLA Hospital.[38] In mid-May Xi Jinping also flew to stay by his father's bedside until he passed away in the early morning hours of May 24 at the age of 89. Xi Zhongxun was given a state funeral and interred in the Babaoshan Revolutionary Cemetery on the outskirts of Beijing, although Xi Jinping, accompanied by his mother, returned some of his cremated ashes to the ancestral home in Taoyi village, Fuping County, Shaanxi Province.

Xi's experiences in Fujian—notably in foreign trade and investment, tourism promotion, infrastructure building, and anti-corruption work—would all serve him well in his next onward assignment in Zhejiang Province. About a month before the opening of the 16th Party Congress in 2002, Xi received orders to move to Hangzhou and assume the position of deputy secretary of the Zhejiang CCP committee and acting governor of the province. Within six weeks he was elevated to provincial Party secretary and appointed as a member of the Central Committee at the 16th Party Congress. He was only 49 years old, making him one of the two youngest provincial Party secretaries in the country (Li Keqiang in Henan being the other). Xi later claimed that his transfer to Zhejiang came as a surprise—but to have served the previous sixteen years in one province (Fujian) was highly unusual, and it was beyond time for him to be rotated elsewhere by the CCP Organization Department. The 16th Party Congress was also an action-forcing event, as Jiang Zemin and Zeng Qinghong were maneuvering to "pack the Politburo" and Central Committee with their political acolytes. While Xi was not close to Jiang during his time in Fujian, following Jiang's retirement in 2002 he and his wife paid several visits every year to rest in scenic Hangzhou—during which Xi personally accompanied them and made sure their needs were met.[39] While it cannot be said that Xi was one of Jiang's protégés, he had been on Zeng Qinghong's radar screen for some time. Recall from Chapter 5 that Hu Jintao was *not* Jiang Zemin's choice to succeed him, and thus it is entirely possible that Zeng (and Jiang) had identified Xi at this juncture as the successor-in-waiting to Hu Jintao. A few months after Xi's arrival, Zeng Qinghong paid an inspection visit to Zhejiang. Xi accompanied him everywhere. One can only speculate whether they discussed Xi's political future, but having such a powerful connection at the very top of the system would prove to be important during the remainder of Zeng's tenure prior to his retirement in March 2008 (and likely afterwards).

Zhejiang is located adjacent and just to the north of Fujian, and the two provinces have much in common. Both are coastal, with temperate climates, covered with hills and mountains in the interior, and rich in cultural history. Fujian and Zhejiang have both had long histories of seafaring and foreign trade, particularly throughout the South China Sea (南海).[40] Zhejiang benefitted at least as much from China's open-door policies as had Fujian, becoming a powerhouse of export industries—everything from toys and textiles to chemicals and appliances to personal computers and Christmas decorations. Zhejiang was also one of the pioneering provinces to encourage private enterprises. When Xi took over in 2002, 70 percent of the provincial GDP was created in the private sector, where there were more than 1.9 million registered private enterprises and about 1.5 million self-employed individuals.[41] The Zhejiang city of Wenzhou became famous throughout China and abroad for its freewheeling capitalism. Xi went on record numerous times praising Zhejiang's private-sector dynamism, and even invited the prestigious Chinese Academy of Social Sciences (CASS) in Beijing to establish a research project on the "Zhejiang experience."[42] This project heralded Xi's province as a national model, beginning in 2007. Today Zhejiang is China's fourth wealthiest province, with annual per capita income of 107,624 RMB ($16,611) in 2020.[43] It is a large and populous province, with over 90 counties, cities, and districts. Within his first nine months Xi visited 69 of them,[44] exhibiting again his penchant to get to the grassroots rather than being confined to the provincial capital and interminable meetings.

After nearly five years in charge of Zhejiang (for which he received high marks and national attention), Xi was suddenly shifted to neighboring Shanghai. The precipitating event was the arrest and prosecution of Shanghai Party secretary Chen Liangyu—a key member of Jiang Zemin's "Shanghai Gang" (上海帮) of leaders—on charges of corruption for embezzling Shanghai's pension fund and living a lifestyle of debauchery. Chen's fall from grace and power had come swiftly when he was arrested on September 24, 2006, but the central leadership did not have an immediate successor to tap. At first Hu Jintao's Communist Youth League ally Liu Yandong's name was floated—but she had no experience running a locality or province, much less a metropolis the size of Shanghai (she was currently serving as Director of the United Front Work Department). Jiangxi provincial Party secretary Meng Jianzhu's name was also in the mix. Next it seemed that Shanghai Mayor Han Zheng, who was locally popular, would be a natural appointment (in fact, Han was elevated as acting Party secretary immediately following Chen's arrest). But over the winter months of 2006–2007 another candidate emerged: Xi Jinping. It was reported that Zeng Qinghong had pushed Xi's candidacy, as stressed in Xi's biography.[45] CCP Organization Department chief He Guoqiang was also a key figure in making the appointment. Premier Wen Jiabao was also supportive, and CCP General Secretary Hu Jintao went along with the consensus. Xi was accordingly transferred to Shanghai in March 2007.

However, Xi did not stay long in Shanghai—just seven months—nor did he accomplish much of note. He did criticize the corruption that had brought Chen Liangyu down, he emphasized that Shanghai welcomed foreign commerce, he oversaw the initial building of the 2010 World Expo, and he made symbolic visits to places such as the site of the founding and first congress of the CCP. Shanghai was an intermediate stepping-stone in Xi's career advancement to the top.

That autumn, when the 17th Party Congress convened in Beijing—the midway point in Hu Jintao's term—Xi was suddenly elevated to the Center (中央) and appointed to a series of important national positions: member of the Politburo and its Standing Committee, President of the Central Party School, member of the Central Committee Secretariat, Chairman of the Central Leading Group for Party Building, and Vice-Chairman of the Central Leading Group for Taiwan affairs. The following March 2018, at the National People's Congress, he added a key government position: Vice-President of the PRC. Two years later in 2010 he added another title: Vice-Chairman of the Central Military Commission. It was thus unmistakably clear that Xi Jinping was now heir-apparent to Hu Jintao (even if Hu's favored candidate was his Youth League colleague Li Keqiang). Again, it is alleged that Zeng Qinghong was instrumental in Xi's elevation—one of his last acts as national leader before his own retirement in March 2018.

Xi's Rise in Retrospect

Thus, Xi Jinping had a highly unusual childhood and considerably different career path to national power from that of Hu Jintao or Jiang Zemin, to say nothing of Mao or Deng Xiaoping. He did have in common with Hu (as well as Zhao Ziyang and Hua Guofeng) significant grassroots local and provincial level experience in the Party apparatus. His "red princeling" parentage certainly set him apart, although his being "sent down to the countryside" was not dissimilar from the experiences of Hu Jintao and Wen Jiabao. Unlike Hu Jintao, who benefitted from the personal patronage of Song Ping and Hu Yaobang, and Jiang Zemin who benefitted from the career-long patronage of Wang Daohan, Xi Jinping does not seem to have had any single and strong central-level patron during his lengthy service in the provinces. By the time Zeng Qinghong began to praise him during his Zhejiang years, Xi was already launched on an upward trajectory. It does seem that, from this point on, Zeng did play an instrumental role in propelling Xi's rise to the top (despite this the two men also had very different understandings of the lessons to be learned from the collapse of the Soviet Union). Xi's rise to the top also seems to have benefitted from his family's military connections, his father's stature in the Party, and his own record over nearly three decades in the provinces away from Beijing.

While Xi had no consistently strong political patrons throughout these decades, neither did he have any clear clients who followed him from position to position. There are some whom he met during his time in the provinces, and others he encountered after reaching Beijing.

Two such key individuals are Li Zhanshu and Wang Huning. Li Zhanshu has had a career not dissimilar from Xi—serving in rural counties in Hebei province, then as Party secretary of Xian city, governor of Heilongjiang province, and Party secretary of Guizhou province, before being vaulted to Beijing in 2012 to serve as head of the Central Committee General Office. Li and Xi got to know each other first when they served as Party secretaries in neighboring Hebei counties during 1983–1985, but after that their respective career paths diverged. However, they both arrived in Beijing around the same time in 2012 and Li has been Xi's right-hand man ever since. Another key senior leader today is the ubiquitous Wang Huning—now a Standing Committee member in charge of intra-party and ideological affairs. As we have seen in the two previous chapters, Wang (a former Shanghai professor) had successively served as a close advisor to both Jiang Zemin and Hu Jintao, and now fulfills the same role for Xi Jinping. This is no small accomplishment—no other senior CCP official has served three different leaders at the pinnacle of power over three decades. As they had no previous career ties, Xi "adopted" Wang, keeping him on and promoting him to the Politburo Standing Committee. Wang's genius seems to be in political campaigns—both conceptualizing and "branding" them. Among others he was behind Jiang Zemin's "Three Represents," Hu Jintao's "Harmonious Society" and "Scientific Development Concept," and he is reported to have generated the "Chinese Dream" for Xi. Wang Huning has also been a key foreign policy advisor to Jiang, Hu, and Xi (often traveling abroad with them and sitting by their side in meetings with foreign counterparts). Xi also inherited and built a close relationship with Liu Yunshan, who was a rather hardline ideologue and Director of the CCP Propaganda Department. Upon gaining ultimate power in 2012, Xi selected Liu to succeed him as secretary-general of the Central Committee Secretariat, as well as President of the Central Party School. Another individual Xi seems to have promoted and drawn close to him is Zhao Leji, who hails from Shaanxi and was appointed to head the CCP Organization Department at the same time as Xi's appointment as General Secretary in 2012. In 2017, Xi then moved Zhao to replace Wang Qishan as head of the Central Discipline Inspection Commission (the CCP's anti-corruption organ).

One individual who *did* have longstanding ties to Xi is Wang Qishan, whom Xi met when they were both sent to the same county as part of the "down to the countryside" program during the Cultural Revolution. Wang wound up marrying Yao Yilin's daughter (Yao Mingshan), which gave him entry into the "red nobility." While their career paths varied after serving together in Shaanxi, with Wang mainly working in academia and finance, they reunited in 2012 in Beijing. Wang was five years older than Xi and was more experienced in the internecine elements of Zhongnanhai politics. Wang is a no-nonsense administrator and was the one to whom Xi turned to take charge of his hard-hitting anti-corruption campaign after 2012. Wang's foreign policy experience—particularly with the Americans—was also useful to Xi. If Xi has a mentor and alter ego, it would be Wang Qishan.

Another longtime associate of Xi is economist Liu He. They overlapped in middle school in Beijing in the 1960s, although their career paths varied thereafter. But in 2013 Xi had Liu appointed as his closest economic advisor, putting him in charge of drafting the Third Plenum (2013) economic plan, and making him the point man for trade negotiations with the Trump administration.

Other leaders whom Xi knew earlier in his career and promoted include Cai Qi and Huang Keming, both of whom worked under Xi in Fujian: Cai is now Party secretary of Beijing while Huang is director of the Central Propaganda Department. In Fujian Xi also got to know the local air force commander Xu Qiliang, whom Xi subsequently elevated to be first-ranking vice-chairman of the Central Military Commission. In Zhejiang Xi got to know Chen Min'er, who served in the provincial propaganda department, and whom Xi has now installed as the Party secretary of Chongqing municipality. Chen is sometimes mentioned as a possible successor to Xi. Another individual is Ding Xuexiang, who worked under Xi in Shanghai, and was subsequently elevated to be his chief-of-staff and head of the CCP General Office.[46]

People aside, what can be teased out of the above biographical career path that may have given hints about the kind of leader Xi would become once he reached the top? Actually, not that much. His time in the Shaanxi countryside certainly had a lasting impact on him—giving him a "feel" for the peasantry, agriculture, manual labor, the out-of-doors, very simple living, and village life. This experience stands in stark contrast with his familiarity with the life of the most senior Party and military elites in Beijing. These twin experiences certainly seem to have left a lasting imprint on him about the need for Party members to live a frugal lifestyle and remain close to average citizens. Relatedly, Xi has also been a "clean" Party member untainted by corruption scandals throughout his career. Indeed, from Fujian through Zhejiang to Shanghai he distinguished himself for criticizing and cracking down on corruption. But it actually remains unclear if Xi understands the *sources of corruption*—as distinct from its *manifestations*. That is, his statements on the subject all tend to attribute corrupt behavior to conscious hedonistic lifestyle choices that cadres make—rather than focusing on the systemic opportunities to make illicit money, engage in rent-seeking, or the lack of institutional checks and balances (independent media and judicial organs) that could expose and act as a check on corruption. During his rise through the ranks of the provincial Party apparatus, Xi also promoted the "reform and opening" policies—but there is little to indicate that he made any real *specific* impact in economic matters. *Any* leader of coastal provinces like Fujian and Zhejiang at the time would have been expected to promote outward-looking trade and investment.

It is equally curious that there are no real indicators from his past of three elements which would become hallmarks of Xi's rule once he gained ultimate power—the *sweeping political and ethnic repression, the assertive foreign policy, and the substantial military modernization*. Other than socializing with children of generals and marshals, and his brief stint as Defense Minister

Geng Biao's military aide-de-camp from 1978 to 1980, Xi had no apparent interactions with the PLA throughout his provincial career. Xi has also made a personal effort to reintroduce and promote orthodox Marxism-Leninism ideology in the Party and society. Where did that come from? Thus, like Gorbachev in reverse (Gorbachev's background as an ordinary Party apparatchik gave no indication that he would become a radical reformer once he gained national power), there is little in Xi's past to suggest the type of "strongman" dictator he would become once he reached the top.

Once Xi came to power in 2012, what have we seen from him as China's leader? There are many ways to explore this question. I will adopt two. The first is to describe how Xi has changed and rolled back so many of the political reforms first initiated during the Deng Xiaoping era, that continued under Jiang and Hu. The second is to examine a number of specific policy issue areas where Xi has had an impact.

Dismantling Dengism

Great leaders usually have grand visions. Xi has actually voiced his views on a wide variety of issues. In his 1,784-page three-volume tome, *The Governance of China*, Xi has had something to say on seemingly every subject. Yet, his core vision for China, which resonates deeply with the Chinese people, is actually not at all that new. Like all Chinese leaders dating back to the Qing Self-Strengthening Movement of the 1870s, Xi's prime objective is to achieve what he describes as "the great rejuvenation of the Chinese nation" (中国的大复兴). He has rebranded this longstanding national mission as the "Chinese Dream" (中国梦), but the quest is no different: for China to acquire the material attributes of a major international power and gain the commensurate respect from others. Xi has expressed optimism that the long journey is nearing conclusion. As he told the 19th Party Congress in 2017: "Today, we are closer, more confident, and more capable than ever before of making the goal of national rejuvenation a reality."[47]

The legacy of the country's former weakness and humiliation thus continues to deeply haunt Xi and his generation. So too does the collapse of Communist Party rule in the former Soviet Union. Now having ruled as long as their Soviet counterparts, Xi and his peers in the Chinese Communist

Party (CCP) live in constant trepidation of a similar meltdown. These two issues—augmenting China's strengths and making China a major global power while rectifying the Communist Party's weaknesses and preventing its institutional implosion—are intertwined in Xi's thinking and dominate his agenda. For him, these meta-challenges are complementary, not contradictory. In his view, to strengthen the Party is to strengthen China. Without a revitalized and invincible CCP, China will be unable to achieve its great rejuvenation. No strong Party, no strong China, goes the logic. As Xi proudly proclaimed in his 2017 speech to the 19th Party Congress:[48]

> Over the past five years, we have acted with courage to confront major risks and tests facing the Party and to address prominent problems within the Party itself. With firm resolve, we have tightened discipline and improved Party conduct, fought corruption and punished wrongdoing, and removed serious potential dangers in the Party and the country. As a result, both the intra-Party political atmosphere and the political ecosystem of the Party have improved markedly.

In a significant way, though, the question is more about the means than the end. In my view, Xi is trying to take China forward by moving it backward. In many policy spheres, but particularly with regard to the Party, Xi is *retrogressive* rather than *progressive*, *repressive* rather than *empowering*. His preferred leadership style and policy preferences are rooted in the Mao era and early years of the People's Republic. Indeed, there is an apparent element of neo-Stalinist style in his rule.[49] Xi clearly has nostalgia for the 1950s and early 1960s—a period of strong Soviet influence in China and a time when his own father was in the leadership—and he has resurrected many of the hallmarks of that period.

In so doing, Xi has been systematically rolling back many of Deng Xiaoping's core *political* reforms that have guided China and its leaders for the past four decades: no personality cult around the leader; collective leadership and consensual decision-making; bottom-up "intra-party democracy" rather than top-down *diktat*; active feedback mechanisms from society to the party-state; relative tolerance of intellectual and other freedoms with limited dissent; some de facto checks and balances on unconstrained Party power; fixed term limits and enforced retirement rules for leaders and cadres. Deng also sought a society and economy that was open to the world and he adopted a cautious foreign policy. Deng sought to remove Party committees in enterprises from day-to-day economic decision-making. These and other norms were central elements of Deng's post-1978 reform program, and they all continued under Jiang Zemin and Hu Jintao — but *all* are being dismantled by Xi.

Xi wants to move China forward as a major power in the 21st century, but his means of fulfilling this goal are deeply illiberal and harken back to a much earlier totalitarian era. Like other nationalist/populist autocratic leaders, Xi absolutely and unapologetically rejects the linkage of progress with liberalism. Quite the contrary. Xi is a hardcore Leninist and in some ways a throwback to the Stalinist era. He may preach Marx, but he practices Lenin and Stalin. Above all, he believes in the absolute hegemonic power of—and control by—the Communist Party. In his speech to the 19th Party Congress in 2017 Xi boldly proclaimed: "The Party exercises *overall leadership over all areas of endeavor in every part of the country*. . . . It doesn't matter whether it is the government, the military, the people, or the schools; east, west, north, south, or the center—*the Party rules everything*" (emphasis added).[50] Xi then elaborated on his priorities for the CCP: "The general requirements for Party building for the new era are: [51]

- Uphold and strengthen overall Party leadership and ensure that the Party exercises effective self-supervision and practices strict self-governance in every respect;
- take strengthening the Party's long-term governance capacity and its advanced nature and purity as the main thrust; take enhancing the Party's political building as the overarching principle; take holding dear the Party's ideals, convictions, and purpose as the underpinning; and take harnessing the whole Party's enthusiasm, initiative, and creativity as the focus of our efforts;
- make all-round efforts to see the Party's political building enhanced, its theory strengthened, its organizations consolidated, its conduct improved, and its discipline enforced, with institution building incorporated into every aspect of Party building;

- step up efforts to combat corruption and continue to improve the efficacy of Party building; and
- build the Party into a vibrant Marxist governing party that is always at the forefront of the times, enjoys the wholehearted support of the people, has the courage to reform itself, and is able to withstand all tests.

Accordingly, Xi has launched many initiatives to strengthen the Party. Xi believes deeply in ruling through Party-led institutions and regulations. This is the essence of Leninism: *total* penetration of all elements of state and society by Party cells and committees, like microbes that permeate the entire body politic. Following Mao's Cultural Revolution destruction, as Chapter 3 describes, Deng sought to rebuild Party institutions—but at the same time to *devolve* power within the Party, between the Party and the state, and from Beijing to localities. Deng fundamentally believed that *loosening* controls actually *strengthened* Party legitimacy and longevity.

Xi too is trying to rescue and rebuild the Party—as Deng did following the debacle of Maoism—but unlike Deng he is all about *recentralizing power* in the Party and at the national level, rather than devolving it to lower levels and empowering other actors in the system. This is apparent in multiple ways, including the sweeping reorganization/recentralization of the State Council and Central Committee organs at the March 2018 National People's Congress. These institutional reforms suggest a return to the Stalinist-style centralized bureaucratic controls that China inherited from the Soviet Union in the 1950s. Subsequently, Party controls over the government were reinvigorated at all levels. The reassertion of the central planning system and the reemphasized role of the state sector in the economy also suggest a return to neo-Stalinist economic approaches. Both Mao (after 1958) and Deng (after 1978) sought to *de*centralize the party-state's role in the economy—but not Xi. He wants to bring the party-state back into *all* aspects of national life.

The CCP under Xi has also reached back to the Maoist (if not Stalinist) era by constructing a massive personality cult around himself. Maoist rhetorical throwbacks such as *zhuxi* (chairman), *lingxiu* (leader), *hexin* (core), and even *da duoshou* (Great Helmsman) are again commonly used to refer to Xi. He has also added *shouxi zhihuiguan* (commander-in-chief) to his list of titles.

Moreover, the official ideological canon of "Xi Jinping Thought on Socialism with Chinese Characteristics for a New Era" has now been enshrined in both the Party and state constitutions. Xi kitsch is to be found in shops across the country; television programs celebrate his "wise leadership"; multimedia follow his every utterance and activity; and his exhortations bombard the public daily through a ramped-up propaganda apparatus. There is even a Xi Jinping app available for cell phones, where Party members and citizens can log in and gain social credit points. It is required viewing for all Party members, but everyone in society can benefit: one point for every Xi essay read, one point for every Xi speech watched, ten points for every thirty minutes of "Xi time," and extra points are earned if you log on during non-working hours between 06:00 and 08:30 in the morning or after 8:00 in the evening.[52]

Xi personally dominates policy-making by chairing all central Leading Groups and Party and military organs. He has also weakened the authority of Premier Li Keqiang. So dominant is Xi that no other leader has any real stature, and Chinese politics have become a sycophantic echo chamber. This personalization of political leadership in Xi combined with his institutional strengthening of the party-state creates a paradigm of what I call "Patriarchal Leninism." In these ways, Xi is very much a mid-twentieth-century Leninist leader ruling a huge country in a globalized era during the twenty-first century. He is ruling in a fashion not unlike a patriarchal Mafia godfather. Xi is trying to run the Party like a military organization by giving orders to be followed, rather than as a collective organization with collegiality, feedback mechanisms, and procedures to curtail dictatorial practices. *All* of the political reforms that we have witnessed during the Deng, Jiang Zemin, and Hu Jintao eras have been halted and rolled back.

To be sure, Xi has definitely succeeded in strengthening the Party institutionally since coming to power, but it is fair to wonder whether he will not have actually weakened it in the longer term. How long can these retrograde actions endure in an increasingly globalized, wealthy, and sophisticated society? Does Xi's strongman rule actually obscure much deeper insecurities and weaknesses rather than strengths? Could it be that the hard exterior of Xi's rule actually masks a much more fragile interior—as embodied in the Chinese aphorism 外硬内软 ("hard on the outside, soft on the inside")?

There already exist numerous anecdotal examples of discontent with the way Xi is leading the country in several sectors of society, including within the Party itself. Indeed, there appears to be an increase of simmering discontent. Xi is frequently lampooned as Winnie the Pooh, and acerbic Xi jokes circulate on the internet and social media (and are promptly taken down). Xi's signature anti-corruption campaign, which lasted from 2012 until 2016 and ensnared more than a million allegedly corrupt Party and state cadres plus more than 4,000 military officers, also had the side effect of paralyzing multiple bureaucracies. *Tingzhi* (停滞) the Chinese call it: to "freeze up." Bureaucrats and capable technocrats throughout the system have frozen up in their work out of the combined fear of being detained on corruption charges (real or trumped-up), being accused of not sufficiently supporting the Xi agenda, or by simply feigning compliance. Wealthy Chinese are emigrating abroad in record numbers.

There would thus seem to be a significant contradiction between Xi's tactics, the realities of the modern world, and China's developmental needs. Since coming to power in 2012, Xi has sought to relatively *close* China's doors rather than further opening them (all the while professing that China continues to follow the open-door policy). He has certainly cracked down on corruption in the Party (and government and military) and he has presided over the most draconian purges and political repression in China since the 1989–1992 post-Tiananmen period. There has been a significant *tightening* of the foreign investment and corporate operating environment, a recentralization of economic decision-making and strengthening of the role of SOEs, a sweeping suppression of civil society and foreign NGOs (most of which have abandoned China), stepped-up study of Marxism and an assertion of ideological controls over the entire educational sphere (especially universities), xenophobic campaigns against "hostile foreign forces," strict enforcement of party-state controls on all media, new technological practices of pervasive public security surveillance, continued tightening of control over Xinjiang and Tibet, persecution of Christians and other organized religions, and the chilling implementation of the National Security Law in Hong Kong.

These repressive and retrogressive policies have much more in common with Maoism than with Dengism.[53] They would all appear to be the actions of an *insecure* leader and ruling party, rather than secure and confident ones. Opening a system and a country shows confidence—closing up and cracking down reveals lack of it. There is thus a contradictory dichotomy between the personal confidence that Xi exudes and his domestic policies and actions, which suggest just the opposite.

With these general observations about Xi's illiberalism and rolling back of many of the norms and policies first instituted under Deng Xiaoping and carried out subsequently under Jiang Zemin and Hu Jintao, let us zero in more closely on Xi Jinping's agenda and record across multiple issue areas.

Navigating the Middle Income Trap

When one examines Xi's impact on the Chinese economy, his record is very mixed.[54] On the positive side, prior to the onset of COVID-19, GDP growth rates continued to hum along at 7 percent from 2012 through 2019 (nominal, not adjusted for prices, according to official PRC statistics), state investment continued to flow into fixed assets and building yet more hard infrastructure, and China had relatively low unemployment (8 to 10 percent) with general social stability. Xi also launched programs that eliminated "absolute poverty" in 2020 , increased urbanization, spurred innovation and high-tech manufacturing under the "Made in China 2025" program, and expanded coverage of social services. On the environmental front, he also initiated programs to build eco-cities, attack pollution and transition to a green economy while decreasing desertification and increasing reforestation. Xi has prioritized expanding domestic consumption and services as drivers of growth. While corporate and local debt is still alarmingly high (now over 300 percent of GDP), Xi has also prioritized its deleveraging. These are all commendable goals and initiatives.

Yet, on the other hand, when one reviews the regime's expansive and ambitious Third Plenum economic reform plan of November 2013—the benchmark economic blueprint personally unveiled by Xi—his administration has come up far short of the stated goals. By virtually all foreign evaluations, only a meager 15 to 20 percent of the Third Plenum package has been implemented (despite much official rhetoric about "supply-side structural reform").[55] The significance of this shortfall is that the Chinese economy is *not* making the multiple structural adjustments needed to move up the value-added chain to become a developed economy over time. To make these adjustments, however, runs counter to Xi's party/state-centric view of economic development and requires considerable decentralization and empowerment of non-state actors. It also contradicts his own words in 2017: "China's economy has been transitioning from a phase of rapid growth to a stage of high-quality development. This is a pivotal stage for transforming our growth model, improving our economic structure, and fostering new drivers of growth."[56]

At the heart of China's economic reform aspirations lies the stated desire to "rebalance" from the old (post-1978) growth model to the new (post-2013) one.[57] Both the old and new growth models are based on key components. The "old two" drivers of development were fixed asset investment (primarily into infrastructure) plus low-wage, low-end manufacturing primarily for exports (this sector benefitted from large inflows of foreign direct investment). This model was wildly successful beyond anyone's expectations over the past thirty years. But a new growth model is needed which requires a recalibration of macro-economic drivers. The "new three" envisioned catalysts for the next thirty years are domestic consumer spending plus domestic innovation plus expansion of the services sector.

The main reason for the need to rebalance has to do with the so-called middle income trap. This is a concept used by developmental economists to describe a newly industrializing economy that reaches a certain mean income threshold—usually about $11,000 (in 2019 China's per capita income was $10,261, according to the World Bank)[58]—which begins to compromise the economy's competitive advantages in low-wage manufacturing. A related concept is the Lewis Turning Point, named after the Nobel Prize–winning economist W. Arthur Lewis, who found that there is a point in the development process when cheap and excess rural labor is negated by wage increases as the supply of "surplus" labor is exhausted. At this point in the developmental process the comparative advantage of countries like China begins to erode—thus causing a fundamental shift in the structure of the labor market (especially for low-skilled workers)—and forces them into the middle income trap. Thus the trap (precisely what China faces now) is that the economy needs to transition up the productivity ladder by producing more knowledge-intensive, technology-intensive, and skill-intensive goods.

This requires investing in innovation and retraining workers from production to service and other value-added industries. In addition, to facilitate these transitions governments must have a more modern financial system, a more open political system, and make more efficient use of factor endowments (land, labor, and capital). There is nothing automatic about Newly Industrializing Economies (NIEs) successfully navigating their way through and out of the middle income trap. Some countries have successfully done so (including in East Asia Japan, South Korea, Singapore, and Taiwan).[59] In fact, *most do not* succeed—hence the term trap. Chinese governmental economists are well aware of the historical record. Reiterating World Bank findings, a comprehensive study of China's development possibilities undertaken by the State Council's Development Research Center itself observed:[60]

> Around the world 101 economies joined the ranks of middle-income countries after 1960. As of early 2008, only thirteen of them moved up to the higher-income club and achieved a soft landing successfully, including Japan, South Korea, Taiwan, Hong Kong, Puerto Rico, Mauritius, Singapore, and Israel. Most of the rest of the countries failed to finish this process and saw economic stagnation, even recession, half-way catching up but getting stuck in the middle income trap. Latin American nations and the countries of the former Soviet Union and Eastern Europe are typical examples of that.

A key part of China's and Xi's economic rebalancing strategy is thus to boost technological innovation.[61] This is no secret and was originally signaled when the government identified ten priority "strategic industries" as part of the "Made in China 2025" program: new information technologies, numerical control tools and robotics, aerospace equipment, ocean engineering equipment and high-tech ships, railway equipment, energy-saving and new-energy vehicles, power generation equipment, new materials, biological medicine and medical devices, and agricultural machinery. China has real ambitions to become *the* global leader in these high-end manufacturing sectors by 2025.[62] It is already the world's largest producer of 220 kinds of industrial goods, and overtook the United States in 2006 to be the largest exporter of high-tech products in the world (garnering 17 percent of global market share).[63] Chinese companies eye even greater global potential.

China will certainly innovate over time—that is not the question. The questions are *how much, in which fields, and what are the impediments/facilitators* of broad-gauged long-term innovation (and can they be overcome)? Here I am more skeptical. So are others.[64] The Chinese government seems to believe that all that is needed to spur innovation is to invest in it—like building high-speed rail or other infrastructure. China's government is indeed investing increasingly large sums into research and development (R&D), now 2.3 percent of GDP.[65] While rising, China's R&D spending still lags behind many OECD states: South Korea (4.3 percent); Japan, Sweden, Denmark, and Finland (all 3.1 percent); Germany and Switzerland (2.9 percent); and the United States (2.7 percent). Although not a member of the OECD, Taiwan registers the second highest percentage in the world at 3.3 percent. At the current rate of accelerating growth in its state R&D budget (from 1.6 to 2.3 percent since 2012), or even with a modest increase to 2.5 percent, China could overtake the United States around 2025, when it will spend more than $452.2 billion annually. At current GDP growth rates, if it were to spend on the level of the European countries noted above, an average of 3 percent, China's R&D expenditures would amount to $542.4 billion by 2025. If it were to increase spending to 3.5 percent to be in the league of South Korea, this would amount to a staggering $632.8 billion in 2025 and $1.3 *trillion* per annum by 2040! Needless to say, this level of investment into innovation would be unprecedented in world history and, even if at lower levels, will produce a techno-superpower on a significant scale.

Xi Jinping has made it very clear on multiple occasions that this is exactly China's aim. The country has a huge R&D network in terms of personnel and institutions.[66] Xi has also made a repeated point of emphasizing that China needs to increase its "self-reliance" (自力更生) in technology. This new emphasis was largely triggered by the Trump administration's "decoupling" policies in the tech realm—when it began to ban the export of sophisticated computer chips to China, worked to constrain Chinese acquisition of high-tech companies abroad, and stifled the plans of Huawei and ZTE to build 5G broadband around the world. The Fifth Plenum of the 19th Central Committee, convened in October 2020, put China's own technological decoupling at the center of the 14th Five-Year Plan (2021–2025).[67] The

Plenum communiqué stated that "big breakthroughs will be forthcoming in key core technologies" (which were not specified but likely include semiconductors, telecommunications, artificial intelligence, Big Data, robotics, and biotechnology). The plan was formally adopted at the 13th National People's Congress in March 2021.

Another huge challenge is undertaking state-owned-enterprise (SOE) reform.[68] Unlike the SOE problem twenty years ago, when the rust-belt factories in the northeast and eastern seaboard cities were bleeding the national economy by running deeply in the red while not turning profits or producing goods that were competitive in the marketplace, today's challenge is to make them more competitive and less monopolistic. At least that is the way Xi Jinping sees it (and Xi has been a major advocate of *strengthening*—not weakening—SOEs). A special directive from the General Office of the CCP Central Committee issued in August 2015 specifically rejected widespread privatization and explicitly stated, "The Party's leadership of state-owned enterprises must be upheld."[69] Xi himself has continued to speak positively about the state sector and the need to strengthen SOEs.[70] Reducing the monopolies that SOEs hold over various key sectors of the economy—energy and raw materials, power generation, transportation (air, rail, shipping), telecommunications, aerospace, defense industries—is not easy given the interlocking ties that these behemoths have to the party-state (their senior management is controlled by the CCP's Organization Department). China's SOEs are the epitome of deeply vested interests, with no small degree of cozy corruption deeply embedded within them.[71] The symbiotic relationship between SOEs and state banks is also a form of protectionism that will be very difficult to break, as SOEs absorb over 60 percent of corporate loans from the four big state banks and 90 percent of bonds issued.[72] They account for a significant percentage of China's total debt load (now nearing 320 percent of GDP). Indeed, despite Xi's rhetoric, it is clear that he personally, and the government, do *not* seek to break up the SOES. Rather, Xi's own speeches and various government documents indicate that they seek greater efficiency and profits from the SOEs. This could involve downsizing some, growing others, or maintaining the current size of many SOEs—the goal is to *maintain* them, protect them, make them more efficient and industry dominant, but *not* to get rid of them.

Indeed, the Third Plenum of 2013 specifically declared that "state ownership is a central pillar of the economy," while at the same time claiming that "markets should play a decisive role" (Xi reiterated this in his 19th Party Congress report). While there have been some experimental moves in the intervening years since the plenum to introduce more diversified "mixed ownership" (state–private), and to publicly list parts of the SOEs in some pilot stock market experiments, overall, not much reform has taken place in this sector under Xi Jinping.

As a result, under Xi's direction SOEs have been strengthened, not weakened.[73] In 2014, right after Xi took power, SOEs had combined assets of $10.5 trillion;[74] by 2016, under Xi's favoritism, net value of SOE assets had grown to 118 trillion RMB ($16.5 trillion), according to the Chinese Academy of Social Sciences.[75] Today, SOEs still account for at least a fifth of China's total industrial output, they employ one in seven urban workers, and receive 80 percent of net bank loans.[76] Chinese economic planners have long admired the South Korean *chaebol* and Japanese corporate models of large-scale horizontally integrated firms—under Xi the PRC is trying to create its own version of such conglomerates (集团).

Xi's signature Belt and Road Initiative (BRI) has also been a noteworthy economic hallmark of his rule. The BRI is a gargantuan $1.2 trillion mega-project that spans the globe; it connects Asia to Europe through an overland route across Eurasia (the "Silk Road Economic Belt"), and a second route, a sea route spanning the South China Sea through the Indian Ocean and Red Sea to the Mediterranean (the "21st Century Maritime Silk Road"). An infrastructure development initiative unparalleled in history, BRI will build rail lines, pipelines, telecommunications networks, electric grids, deep-water ports, highways, new cities, commercial and financial centers, residential housing, and other needed infrastructure from Asia to Europe. As of 2019, China claims that 123 countries and 29 international organizations have signed on in one way or another to the initiative (according to China's Foreign Minister Wang Yi).[77] While it remains several years premature to render an ultimate verdict on its relative successes or failures—and there will be both—BRI is another example of China's new international activism under Xi (see below). Indeed, BRI has already generated negative impressions and criticisms in some countries. These include accusations of "debt trap diplomacy" (where countries are forced to surrender sovereign assets to compensate for debt repayments that they cannot meet); the exclusive use of Chinese labor (to the neglect of local labor); environmental damage; implementation of some unnecessary projects (such as high-speed rail); occasional provision of low-quality infrastructure that deteriorates quickly; opening mineral mines and building rail lines from the interior of countries to ports (also built or refurbished by China) that extract raw materials to ship back to China; and ancillary corruption. As one detailed study of BRI put it: "BRI is a middleman's dream. Its megaprojects offer ample opportunities for bribery, kickbacks, and theft. . . . Corruption is a feature, not a bug, of the BRI's design."[78] The author, Jonathan Hillman of the Center for Strategic and International Studies (CSIS) in Washington, further argues in this in-depth study that, "Since leaving the station, China's BRI has become a gravy train without a conductor. Its fevered pace has already exceeded China's ability to accurately measure, let alone manage, these activities. Corruption and rent-seeking are thriving in the chaos."[79] I have encountered these criticisms in my own research across Southeast Asia, but they have also arisen in other regions of the world.[80]

Revamped Repression

Since coming to power Xi Jinping has unleashed a sustained reign of repression and comprehensive controls on China not seen since the Maoist era (the 1989–1991 post-Tiananmen massacre crackdown was intense but largely limited to Beijing and relatively short-lived). Xi has also reembraced Marxist ideology, while practicing Leninist dictatorship. No sector of society has escaped the reach of the Xi regime. The Ministries of Public and State Security have had their budgets and their briefs expanded to ferret out any and all dissent. Intellectuals and professors have been subjected to regular monitoring and the closest state scrutiny in many years, while teachers at all levels must strictly toe the Party line. The use of Western textbooks (in the original or in translation) has been formally banned by the Ministry of Education (although some teachers still surreptitiously use them, mainly in translation). Course syllabi now have to be vetted and approved by university Party committees, cameras and microphones have been installed in classrooms to monitor lectures, students sometimes report on professors who stray from the Party line, and some faculty have been relieved of their positions and punished for saying or publishing heretical things. Hundreds of defense lawyers (who try to defend accused citizens) have been detained and many charged with "subverting state power." Popular bloggers and individuals who transmit unacceptable social media posts are also subject to interrogation and punishment under China's 2016 Cybersecurity Law, which prohibits "fabricating or disseminating false information or rumors and disturbing public order"—all under the mandate of what Xi has termed the "struggle for public opinion" (he has also designated the internet as an "ideological battlefield").[81] Anyone who shares a "rumor" or other designated illicit social media posting faces up to three years in prison. For example, Shandong citizen Wang Jianfeng was sentenced to 22 months in prison for calling Xi a *baozi* (dumpling) and "Maoist thug" on his WeChat account.[82] The Chinese private media has sometimes pushed the envelope of investigative journalism in the past, but now it (together with all official state media) has been brought to heel by Xi. In February 2016 Xi made a highly publicized and carefully choreographed visit to the headquarters of Xinhua News Agency, CCTV, and *People's Daily* in Beijing.[83] Xi demanded "absolute loyalty" of the media to the Party. Xi did not mince his words: "All the work by the Party's media must reflect the Party's will, safeguard the Party's authority, and safeguard the Party's unity. They must love the Party, protect the Party, and closely align themselves with the Party leadership in thought, politics and action."[84]

In addition to the Cybersecurity Law, the government adopted several other sweeping draconian laws between 2014 and 2016—all aimed at severely restricting any kind of autonomous behavior in the public sphere: the National Security Law, NGO Law, Charity Law, and Counterterrorism Law. Among the many restrictions contained in these laws was a common thread to severely constrict and closely monitor any foreign connections. This grew out of the CCP's paranoia arising from the Eurasian "color revolutions" and alleged subversive roles played by foreign NGOs (particularly those linked to the United States). The 2020 Hong Kong National Security Law mirrored these others.

Another common linkage can be found in the 2013 Central Committee

General Office Document No. 9, *Communiqué on the Current State of the Ideological Sphere*. Although a definitive directive intended for "provinces, autonomous regions, municipalities, central ministries and state organs, People's Liberation Army headquarters, major Party committees, and Party leadership groups of civilian organizations," the secret document was definitely not intended to fall into the hands of foreigners. It did so because a brave 71-year-old veteran journalist and grandmother named Gao Yu leaked the text to a Chinese-language publication in the United States. For this act, Gao was detained, tried, and convicted for "leaking state secrets," and sentenced to seven years in prison by a Beijing court.[85] Document No. 9 is so important because it reveals seven elements of extreme concern to the CCP:[86]

Box 6.2 CCP Central Committee Document No. 9 (2013)

(Excerpts)

1. **Promoting Western constitutional democracy: An attempt to undermine the current leadership and the socialism with Chinese characteristics system of governance.**
   The point of publicly proclaiming Western constitutional democracy's key points is to oppose the Party's leadership and implementation of its constitution and laws. Their goal is to use Western constitutional democracy to undermine the Party's leadership, abolish the People's Democracy, negate our country's constitution as well as our established system and principles, and bring about a change of allegiance by bringing Western political systems to China.

2. **Promoting "universal values" in an attempt to weaken the theoretical foundations of the Party's leadership.**
   Given Western nations' long-term dominance in the realms of economics, military affairs, science, and technology, these arguments can be confusing and deceptive. The goal [of such slogans] is to obscure the essential differences between the West's value system and the value system we advocate, ultimately using the West's value systems to supplant the core values of socialism.

3. **Promoting civil society in an attempt to dismantle the ruling party's social foundation.**
   Civil society is a socio-political theory that originated in the West. It holds that in the social sphere, individual rights are paramount and ought to be immune to obstruction by the state. For the past few years, the idea of civil society has been adopted by Western anti-China forces and used as a political tool. Additionally, some people with ulterior motives within China have begun to promote these ideas. This is mainly expressed in the following ways: promoting civil society and Western-style theories of governance, they claim that building a civil society in China is a precondition for the protection of individual rights and forms the basis for the realization of constitutional democracy; viewing civil society as a magic bullet for advancing social management at the local level, they have launched all kinds of so-called citizen's movements; advocates of civil society want to squeeze the Party out of leadership of the masses at the local level, even setting the Party against the masses, to the point that their advocacy is becoming a serious form of political opposition.

4. **Promoting neo-liberalism, attempting to change China's basic economic system.**
   Neoliberalism advocates unrestrained economic liberalization, complete privatization, and total marketization and it opposes any kind of interference or regulation by the state. Western countries, led by the United States, carry out their Neoliberal agendas under the guise of "globalization," visiting catastrophic consequences upon Latin America, the Soviet Union, and Eastern Europe, and have also dragged themselves into the international financial crisis from they have yet to recover. This is mainly expressed in the following ways: [Neoliberalism's advocates] actively promote the "market omnipotence theory." They claim our country's macroeconomic control is strangling the market's efficiency and vitality and they oppose public ownership, arguing that China's state-owned enterprises are "national monopolies," inefficient, and disruptive of the market economy, and should undergo "comprehensive privatization." These arguments aim to change our country's basic economic infrastructure and weaken the government's control of the national economy.

5. **Promoting the West's idea of journalism, challenging China's principle that the media and publishing system should be subject to Party discipline.**
Some people, under the pretext of espousing "freedom of the press," promote the West's idea of journalism and undermine our country's principle that the media should be infused with the spirit of the Party. This is mainly expressed in the following ways: Defining the media as "society's public instrument" and as the "Fourth Estate;" attacking the Marxist view of news and promote the "free flow of information on the Internet;" slandering our country's efforts to improve Internet management by calling them a crackdown on the Internet; claiming that the media is not governed by the rule of law but by the arbitrary will of the leadership; and calling for China to promulgate a Media Law based on Western principles. [Some people] also claim that China restricts freedom of the press and advocate abolishing propaganda departments. The ultimate goal of advocating the West's view of the media is to promote the principle of abstract and absolute freedom of press, oppose the Party's leadership in the media, and gouge an opening through which to infiltrate our ideology.

6. **Promoting historical nihilism, trying to undermine the history of the CCP and of New China.**
The goal of historical nihilism, in the guise of "reassessing history," is to distort Party history and the history of New China. This is mainly expressed in the following ways: Rejecting the revolution; claiming that the revolution led by the Chinese Communist Party resulted only in destruction; denying the historical inevitability in China's choice of the Socialist road, calling it the wrong path, and the Party's and new China's history a "continuous series of mistakes"; rejecting the accepted conclusions on historical events and figures, disparaging our revolutionary precursors, and vilifying the Party's leaders . . . By rejecting CCP history and the history of New China, historical nihilism seeks to fundamentally undermine the CCP's historical purpose, which is tantamount to denying the legitimacy of the CCP's long-term political dominance.

7. **Questioning Reform and Opening and the socialist nature of Socialism with Chinese Characteristics.**
Western anti-China forces and internal "dissidents" are still actively trying to infiltrate China's ideological sphere and challenge our

> mainstream ideology. Some of their latest major efforts include: Some people have disseminated open letters and declarations and have organized petition-signings to vocalize requests for political reforms, improvement of human rights, release of "political prisoners," "reversing the verdict on '6/4' [the Tiananmen Massacre]," and other such political demands; they have made a fuss over asset disclosure by officials, fighting corruption with the Internet, media supervision of government, and other sensitive hot-button issues, all of which stoke dissatisfaction with the Party and government. Western embassies, consulates, media operations, and NGOs operating inside China under various covers are spreading Western ideas and values and are cultivating so-called "anti-government forces." They cook up anti-government publications overseas. Within China's borders, some private organizations are creating reactionary underground publications, and still others are filming documentaries on sensitive subject matter, disseminating political rumors, and defaming the party and the national leadership. Those manipulating and hyping the Tibetan self-immolations, manufacturing the violent terrorist attacks in Xinjiang, and using the ethnic and religious issues to divide and break up [the nation]. Accelerating infiltration of the Internet and illegal gatherings within our borders. "Dissidents" and people identified with "rights protection" are active. Some of them are working together with Western anti-China forces, echoing each other and relying on each other's support. This clearly indicates that the contest between infiltration and anti-infiltration efforts in the ideological sphere is as severe as ever, and so long as we persist in CCP leadership and socialism with Chinese characteristics, the position of Western anti-China forces to pressure for urgent reform won't change, and they'll continue to point the spearhead of Westernizing, splitting, and "Color Revolutions" at China. In the face of these threats, we must not let down our guard or decrease our vigilance.

Document No. 9 makes clear the overall targets of the Xi regime's political priorities for control and elimination of all forms of perceived political opposition. It clearly exposes the regime's extreme hostility to the West, Western systems, Western values, and Western practices. There may be no more revealing indicator of what the CCP under Xi Jinping is *against* and determined to combat.

Xi supplemented these seven dictates with five more "never allows" in a September 2020 speech:[87]

- The Chinese people will never allow any individual or any force to distort the history of the CCP or smear the Party's nature and mission.
- The Chinese people will never allow any individual or any force to distort and alter the path of socialism with Chinese characteristics or deny and vilify the great achievements the Chinese people have made in building socialism.
- The Chinese people will never allow any individual or any force to separate the CCP from the Chinese people or counterpose the Party to the Chinese people.
- The Chinese people will never allow any individual or any force to impose their will on China through bullying, change China's direction of progress, or obstruct the Chinese people's efforts to create a better life.
- The Chinese people will never allow any individual or any force to jeopardize their peaceful life and right to development, obstruct their exchanges and cooperation with other peoples, or undermine the noble cause of peace and development for humanity.

Taken together, these are clear indications of the Xi regime's rigidity and insecurity, and the resulting proactive posture against what it perceives to be politically existential threats to its continued rule.

Ethnic Repression

Xi also has taken an uncompromising position and has implemented unparalleled repressive policies toward ethnic minorities in China's border regions, telling the 19th Party Congress in 2017: "We must rigorously protect against and take resolute measures to combat all acts of infiltration, subversion, and sabotage, as well as violent and terrorist activities, ethnic separatist activities, and religious extremist activities."[88] Under Xi, across the vast regions of Tibet, Xinjiang, and Inner Mongolia, ethnic Tibetans, Uighurs, Kazakhs, Hui Muslims, and Mongols have all encountered increasingly harsh controls.

Tibet has effectively been under paramilitary occupation since 1989; the religious practice of Tibetan Buddhism is strictly surveilled and controlled; Tibetan temples have been destroyed; the Tibetan language has been eradicated from schoolrooms; and Tibetans are now outnumbered by Han Chinese in the population. Although Tibet has experienced draconian security, religious restrictions, and cultural decimation for many decades—but most notably since Hu Jintao led the province—the situation there has become even more dire under Xi. As Human Rights Watch noted in its 2019 annual report: [89]

> Authorities in Tibetan areas continue to severely restrict religious freedom, speech, movement, and assembly, and fail to redress popular concerns about mining and land grabs by local officials, which often involve intimidation and arbitrary violence by security forces. Authorities have intensified surveillance of online and phone communications. Intensified political education has been reported in monasteries and schools, and for the public at large. Tibetan authorities have used a nationwide anti-crime campaign to encourage people to denounce members of their communities on the slightest suspicion of sympathy for the exiled Dalai Lama or opposition to the government.

The Xi regime's systematic crackdown on Muslims in the northwestern region of Xinjiang (where Uighurs constitute 46 percent and Kazakhs 7 percent of the region's 22 million inhabitants) has drawn international attention and condemnation. Several nations, including the United States, have explored charging China with genocide and crimes against humanity under the 1948 Convention on the Prevention and Punishment of Genocide, which has been ratified by 149 countries including China.[90] The plight of Uighurs in particular has always been tense, and their violent attacks on Hans perpetrated in Xinjiang and elsewhere across China (in Beijing, Guangzhou, Kunming, Shijiazhuang) have definitely fueled tensions. Some Uighurs have also participated in the secessionist East Turkestan Independence Movement (ETIM). But the uprising and inter-ethnic killings between Uighurs and Hans in Urumqi (the capital of Xinjiang) in July 2009, which killed about 200 and injured 1,700, was a turning point.[91]

As a result of these acts, beginning around 2011, the Chinese security services began to considerably increase electronic surveillance by installing thousands of cameras throughout Xinjiang towns and cities.[92] This was followed by increased deployments of People's Armed Police paramilitary forces. In 2014 the crackdown was further intensified and (according to leaked documents) authorized by Xi Jinping himself, who gave orders to use "all organs of dictatorship" and to "show no mercy" against the Uighurs. This was revealed in more than 400 pages of internal CCP documents that were leaked to the *New York Times* and published in 2019.[93] In 2017 Xi further called for building a "Great Wall of Iron" around Xinjiang in order to "maintain stability."[94]

Xi's directives have spawned a range of unprecedented measures being taken. The whole region has become a highly surveilled police state—with the security forces quadrupling in size and spending on surveillance technology soaring to $3.5 billion.[95] Most alarming has been the mass incarceration of over a million Uighurs (and some ethnic Kazakhs) in walled prisons and labor camps sprawled across the vast Xinjiang desert. Inside, prisoners are subjected to extensive indoctrination, regimented routines, forced labor, religious and cultural deprivations, rape, and physical torture.[96] Forced labor in cotton harvesting has also been documented. The detention facilities (which China's government does not deny but describes as for "vocational training") mainly hold men, but some women and male children have also been incarcerated. Hundreds of thousands of men have been taken from their homes and forced into these prisons and camps with no trace, and no communication with family members. Some who have been released have managed to escape over the border to Kazakhstan and have found asylum in Turkey, Germany, the United Kingdom, and other countries. These individuals have provided vivid and terrifying first-hand evidence of the scale of these detention facilities and evidence of what life inside them is like.[97] They have also become targets of PRC monitoring and harassment abroad.

Outside of the prisons and camps, government controls on Xinjiang residents are pervasive and Orwellian. As Human Rights Watch describes it:[98]

> Outside these detention facilities, authorities subject Turkic Muslims in Xinjiang to extraordinary restrictions on personal life. Authorities have recalled passports throughout the region, and to travel from one town or

> another people have to apply for permission and go through checkpoints. They are subjected to persistent political indoctrination, including compulsory flag-raising ceremonies and political or denunciation meetings. With unprecedented levels of control over religious practices, authorities have effectively outlawed the practice of Islam in the region. They have also subjected people in Xinjiang to pervasive surveillance. Authorities employ high-tech mass surveillance systems that make use of QR codes, biometrics, artificial intelligence, phone spyware, and big data. And they have mobilized over a million officials to monitor people, including through intrusive programs in which officials regularly stay in people's homes.

The government is also literally trying to shrink the Uighur population through monitoring for pregnancies, forcing abortions, sterilizing women, and mandatory fitting of intrauterine devices.[99]

Another front in ethnic repression has been opened against China's Mongolian population. In Inner Mongolia, in August 2020, the Chinese authorities announced that all primary school classes would henceforth be taught totally in Mandarin Chinese (普通话) rather than partially in Mongolian. This triggered a protest by 300,000 ethnic Mongolian students who resisted the policy change and refused to attend fall semester classes. Boycotts of classes continued throughout the fall, with several hundred being arrested for civil disobedience. The authorities retaliated by drawing up lists of "untrustworthy persons," cutting off access to government services, and denying bank loans to families and businesses of protesters.[100] It is likely that future restrictions will be placed on other traditional Mongolian religious and cultural practices, as has been the case in Tibet and Xinjiang.

The Surveillance State

Across the country, under Xi Jinping, the security services have erected a modern surveillance state of unprecedented scale, and an intrusiveness unmatched anywhere in the world. As the respected international monitoring group Human Rights Watch describes it:

> Authorities increasingly deploy mass surveillance systems to tighten control over society. In 2018, the government continued to collect, on a mass scale, biometrics including DNA and voice samples; use such biometrics for automated surveillance purposes; develop a nationwide reward and punishment system known as the "social credit system"; and develop and apply "Big Data" policing programs aimed at preventing dissent. All of these systems are being deployed without effective privacy protections in law or in practice, and often people are unaware that their data is being gathered, or how it is used or stored.[101]

To be certain, surveillance is nothing new to China—but it has reached new heights with the advent of artificial intelligence (AI), Big Data, electronic and video monitoring, the internet Great Firewall, and social media censorship. China's new surveillance state is the subject of the well-researched and eye-opening book *We Have Been Harmonized: Life in China's Surveillance State*, authored by German journalist Kai Strittmatter. Based on seven years of in-country first-hand research, Strittmatter has compiled an extraordinary and chilling exposé of Orwellian China under Xi Jinping. The author catalogues all of the means and mechanisms that the PRC authorities use to monitor its population.

Closed-circuit cameras and facial recognition form the ubiquitous backbone of the network of monitoring technologies. He notes, for example, that eight Chinese cities are among the top ten in cameras per capita in the world (London ranks sixth and Atlanta tenth). There are 2.6 million CCTV cameras in the metropolis of Chongqing alone. Altogether it is estimated that China actively operates *22 million* closed-circuit surveillance cameras across the country.[102] In Chinese cities *every single face* is photographed, logged, and stored on interconnected national police "Skynet Cloud" databases. Jaywalkers in several large cities are photographed, loudspeakers bark out orders to stop while their faces appear in real time on street-side video screens, and soon they will soon be sent instantaneous text messages to halt in their tracks. Cameras catch drivers of cars to whom they are not registered. People checking into hotels are instantly checked against national databases (a disincentive to illicit activities). Soon secondary schools across China are to be outfitted with classroom cameras that will monitor children's behavior as well as teacher's instruction. Companies have also been quick to understand the commercial potential of such monitoring, as it amalgamates Big Data on consumer preferences (which can be sold to businesses for a fee). Surveillance can thus be commercially lucrative, as well as an instrument of control in the hands of the state. China has already become the most digitized society on earth. Barcodes and e-commerce platforms like WeChat and Alipay are used for all kinds of transactions—from buying groceries and consumer goods, to riding public transport, to getting in and out of parking lots, and monitoring public health. Even toilet paper in public toilets at Beijing's Temple of Heaven is now dispensed according to facial recognition: the machine releases 60 centimeters of tissue per face (one wonders what other body parts the camera catches); anyone requiring more must wait nine minutes before another 60 centimeters is doled out.[103]

Through this far-reaching network of cameras and other tracking and monitoring devices, the government is not only trying to control its population—it is trying to mold it as well. The goal is to build a "socialist spiritual civilization" in which people regularly obey laws, regulations, and norms. This is indeed the way in which "well-functioning" totalitarian systems operate—*individuals control themselves*. They do so for two reasons: first, because they know they are being monitored and such monitoring is a powerful deterrent to unauthorized activities; and second, because compliance is rewarded. The latter is the purpose of China's new Social Credit System—a nationwide system of recording and cataloguing people's every action, on the basis of which points (social credit) are awarded and deducted for individuals' political, economic, social, and moral behavior.[104] "In this vision," says Strittmatter, "omnipresent algorithms create economically productive, socially harmonized, and politically compliant subjects, who will ultimately censor and sanction themselves at every turn."[105]

Through all of these repressive actions, Xi and his regime evince deep insecurities and even paranoia concerning threats to CCP rule. They clearly feel embattled—or they have an insatiable control complex (or both). In internal speeches Xi also regularly invokes the Cultural Revolution term *struggle* (斗争) to describe the situation that the Party should adopt against internal and external enemies. While there is a high degree of vigilance concerning internal security and the strengthening of what are euphemistically known as the "instruments of the dictatorship of the proletariat" (无产阶级专政的工具), this has been paralleled with a similar enhancement of military capabilities to possibly combat external enemies (although China's internal security budget now exceeds its external defense budget—in itself a very telling indication of the regime's insecurity and paranoia).

Military Reforms

Since coming to power, Xi has also paid particular attention to China's military and defense establishment—probably his second priority after strengthening the Communist Party itself. He has made his mark in relatively short order on a variety of aspects of China's military modernization

Figure 6.5 Xi Jinping: People's Liberation Army Commander-in-Chief
Source: Xinhua / Alamy

and enhanced power. "I have an absolute bond with the army," Xi proclaimed in a 2019 speech.[106] First, he cleaned out (and cleaned up) the high command military leadership.[107] Then he turned his attention to deep-going structural reforms.

Xi inherited an already modernizing PLA, but he has sharply accelerated the process. In January 2016, under his new title of Commander-in-Chief of the Armed Forces, Xi launched a sweeping reorganization—the most comprehensive ever—of China's military and paramilitary forces. The restructuring is but one part of systematic efforts to build a world-class military and, in Xi's repeated exhortations, to "strengthen training under real combat conditions" and "prepare to fight and win wars."[108] In his speech to the 19th Party Congress in 2017 Xi summarized the changes as such:[109]

> Historic breakthroughs have been made in reforming national defense and the armed forces: a new military structure has been established with the Central Military Commission exercising overall leadership, the theater commands responsible for military operations, and the services focusing on developing capabilities. This represents a revolutionary restructuring of the organization and the services of the people's armed forces. We have strengthened military training and war preparedness, and undertaken major missions related to the protection of maritime rights, countering terrorism, maintaining stability, disaster rescue and relief, international peacekeeping, escort services in the Gulf of Aden, and humanitarian assistance. We have stepped up weapons and equipment development and made major progress in enhancing military preparedness. The people's armed forces have taken solid strides on the path of building a powerful military with Chinese characteristics.

Xi then proclaimed: "We will modernize our military across the board in terms of theory, organizational structure, service personnel, and weaponry. We will make it our mission to see that by 2035, the modernization of our national defense and our forces is basically completed, and that *by the mid-21st century our people's armed forces have been fully transformed into world-class forces*."[110] Indeed, under Xi, the PLA has made multiple improvements in its military hardware and software. As a result, in 2019 he advanced the target date by eight years to 2027.

The importance of the sweeping structural reorganization of the armed forces cannot be overstated. Prior to Xi's 2016 transformational initiatives, the PLA remained an organizational clone of the Soviet military (as it had been ever since the 1950s). This structure was a kind of Leninist version of military organization—rigidly vertical and stove-piped in its command and control, overconcentrated in the ground forces, with strict divisions between services, decentralized supplies and poorly coordinated logistics, powerful "general departments" at the top that were independent fiefdoms, geographically defined military regions that were based simply on carving up the country into seven regions rather than being based on the coordination of forces, communications systems that were ill-suited to high-tech warfare of the modern era, and so on. The 2016 reorganization discarded this inherited antiquated Soviet structure and replaced it with an American and NATO-style system which emphasizes coordination and joint theater commands that amalgamate and integrate control over all services in five new zones but gave each greater autonomy and responsibility for operations in their jurisdictions. The former general departments were moved, to be subsidiary organs of the Central Military Commission. Service headquarters (army, navy, air force, rocket forces) were also given greater responsibility, but within the newly integrated operational command structure. The logistics system was recentralized and streamlined. "Informationalization" (信息化) has become the watchword for digitizing communications and battlefield coordination, and a new Strategic Support Force was created to consolidate space, counter-space, cyberspace, electronic warfare, and psychological warfare capabilities. The PLA Rocket Force was upgraded to an independent service, reflecting its role as a priority in deterrence and offensive war fighting. Conventional force training and exercises have been revamped to better simulate real combat conditions. The PLA Navy has also been elevated to priority place in budgets and shipbuilding, congruent with Xi's call for China to become a "maritime strong power" (海洋强国). Further steps have been initiated to make the military more of a regional and global expeditionary force, rather than merely a peripheral force focused on the Taiwan contingency and homeland defense.[111]

These organizational reforms, which will take several years to actually implement, are all extremely important in making the Chinese military a much more capable fighting force. They can be considered the "software" of military capabilities and are actually as important as—if not more than—the "hardware" that the PLA is procuring and deploying. Here, analysts see significant across-the-board improvements in PLA weaponry. Many new state-of-the-art systems were on parade (with Xi proudly presiding) at the 70th PRC anniversary parade in 2019 in central Beijing. The weapons revealed were testimony to the rather dramatic advances that China's military-industrial complex has made in recent years (stimulated in part by another one of Xi Jinping's signature programs: "civil-military fusion"). No longer is China dependent on Russian equipment, and the gap with NATO countries has narrowed substantially, despite the continuing post-1989 arms embargo by the West on China.

Just a decade ago, the United States and other advanced militaries remained quite skeptical and even dismissive of PLA capabilities. No longer. Pentagon war games now have Chinese forces regularly defeating American forces in simulated contingencies around China's periphery—particularly with regard to Taiwan. This said, China's power projection capabilities beyond its periphery to other regions of the world still remain next to nonexistent. But this will not be the case forever. Given the progress that the PLA has made under Xi in less than a decade, one should expect significant progress to continue over the next decade in building a *global* military network of "places and bases" and deploying or rotating forces to and through them. China already has established its first base in East Africa (in Djibouti) and has established naval access agreements with a variety of countries along the Indian Ocean littoral. The PLA Navy has now deployed its second aircraft carrier (this one indigenously built), and it is not unreasonable to expect it to field two or three more by 2030. Foreign analysts believe that the goal is to have about ten carriers in total. China is becoming a global military power, and Xi Jinping is overseeing the entire process.

Foreign Policy

Since Xi Jinping's ascension to power in 2012 China has exhibited increased confidence, proactiveness, and assertiveness on the world stage. No previous Chinese leader has played a more forward-leaning role in foreign policy as has Xi. He has given more speeches on the topic and has dominated the decision-making processes more than any of his predecessors. He has convened several high-level central work conferences on foreign policy, national security, and peripheral diplomacy (周边外交). He has reorganized and centralized the foreign policy-making institutional process under his personal dominance,[112] including the establishment of a new Commission on Foreign Affairs.[113] He has been personally very active in diplomacy, visiting all continents and 69 countries on 42 trips abroad between 2012 and 2020,[114] and he regularly receives visiting foreign heads of state in the Great Hall of the People in Beijing. A perusal of these meetings and Xi's travel abroad is a real indicator of just how global in scope China's foreign relations have become. During just the last quarter of 2019, by random example, Xi met individually with the leaders of Germany, Nepal, France, Greece, Russia, India, South Africa, Brazil, El Salvador, Micronesia, South Korea, and Japan.

Xi has bombarded his country and the world with a barrage of slogans concerned with foreign relations.[115] Above all, he has replaced Deng Xiaoping's prescription for passive diplomacy—"bide time, hide brightness, do not take the lead" (韬光养晦不当头)—with his more activist dictum of "striving for achievement" (奋发有为). Xi has continually emphasized China's "great rejuvenation" (大复兴), the "Chinese Dream" (中国梦), and a "community of a shared future for mankind" (人类命运共同体). Xi has asserted that China should practice "major country diplomacy" (大国外交), and he has advocated a "new type of major power relations" (新型大国关系). Xi has notably emphasized that China should play a more prominent role in global governance (全球治理) and multilateral diplomacy (多边外交). He has also stressed the need to improve China's "external propaganda" (对外宣传) and "tell China's story well" (对外讲好中国故事) to the world. Xi proudly proclaimed to the 19th Party Congress in 2017 that "China's cultural soft power and the international influence of Chinese culture have increased significantly."[116] As a result, the budgets and worldwide efforts for external propaganda, media, united front work, and influence operations have ballooned, even if Xi's claim is not justified by an improved international image (see below).[117] Xi has even suggested that other countries should learn from the "Chinese Solution" (中国方案) of development. A campaign on "Xi Jinping Thought on Diplomacy" (a series of guidelines and principles for Chinese officials to internalize and implement) was launched at the December 2017 meeting of China's diplomatic envoys.[118] Sycophantic recitations duly followed.[119] And Xi's signature Belt and Road Initiative (一带一路) has drawn much international attention.

Despite these formulaic aphorisms, and Beijing's tendency to always paint a rosy picture of its foreign relations, China's foreign relations under Xi Jinping have actually been quite mixed and have deteriorated in a number of cases.

On the one hand, China is now truly seen as a global power. As Xi proudly proclaimed in his landmark speech to the 19th Party Congress: "The Chinese nation, with an entirely new posture, now stands tall and firm in the East and is moving to the center of the world stage. . . . The Chinese nation, which since modern times began had endured so much for so long, has achieved a tremendous transformation: it has stood up, grown rich, and is becoming strong."[120] China is also seen to be playing an increasing and more positive role in global governance (many believe replacing the United States in world affairs). China had previously (and accurately) been criticized as a "free rider" in global governance by not contributing proportionately to the global reservoir of human and financial capital. But Xi has taken a personal interest in global governance, convening several Politburo meetings to discuss it,[121] has spoken about it at numerous international forums and has directed his subordinates to increase China's involvement and contributions. As a result, China under Xi has really upped its game—contributing much more to the United Nations operating budget, global peacekeeping, overseas development assistance, and the Millennium Development Goals, while becoming more active in a range of areas from combatting climate change to public health pandemics, humanitarian and disaster relief, energy and sea lane security, counterterrorism, and anti-piracy operations in the Gulf of Aden. Yes, Beijing was criticized (particularly in Europe) in the aftermath of the COVID outbreak for asking for public acknowledgment and gratitude for its delivery of pandemic protective equipment—but nonetheless China's provision of such supplies was well received in a time of crisis. China also earned praise for distributing its Sinovac anti-COVID vaccine to many developing countries. Beijing has also created new lending institutions such as the Asian Infrastructure Investment Bank and a variety of regional organizations across Asia, the Middle East, Africa, Europe, and Latin America to promote a variety of assistance programs.[122]

On the other hand, though, China under Xi has been behaving in a much more assertive—some would say aggressive—manner abroad. Under Xi, all corners of the globe have experienced the increased presence and influence of China (bilateral and multilateral). In the South China Sea, China has built 3,200 acres of islands on seven previously submerged atolls, ignoring the 2016 ruling by the international tribunal in The Hague that China had no legal claim to these waters through its claimed expansive "nine dashed line." Military equipment is now being deployed to the islands, breaking a public promise Xi gave to President Obama in 2016 and providing China with potential power projection capability deep into Southeast Asia for the first time. Xi's signature Belt and Road Initiative,[123] while primarily economic in nature, does also have geostrategic implications for expanded Chinese influence and potential use of naval port facilities along the entire Indian Ocean littoral. As discussed above, Xi has overseen a sweeping reorganization of the People's Liberation Army—placing particular importance on building the largest navy in the world as well as other power-projection platforms.

As a consequence of the two main characteristics of Xi's foreign policy—unilateral assertiveness combined with multilateral contributions—China's international standing under Xi Jinping has been mixed overall, but has shown signs of sharp deterioration in a number of countries. Even China's increased activism in multilateralism and global governance has been viewed by skeptics as just a means to undermine the international liberal order and replace it with a Chinese (and Russian) style authoritarian order.[124] Others believe that Beijing flubbed the golden opportunity presented by the Trump administration's isolationist foreign policy.[125]

More broadly, many of China's bilateral relationships have deteriorated on Xi's watch. During his time in power, China's relations with Australia, Canada, Czech Republic, India, Japan, Norway, South Korea, Sweden, United States, United Kingdom, have reached all-time lows during the past four decades. For example, this is reflected in the October 2020 Pew Research Center's findings in a cross-section of fourteen developed countries (Fig. 6.6). Not only does this figure reveal that China's image is *the lowest ever recorded* for the countries concerned—it also clearly shows a secular trend of steady deterioration over time from 2002 to 2020. These are really rather remarkable findings and should be of serious concern to officials in Beijing (although there are no such indications).

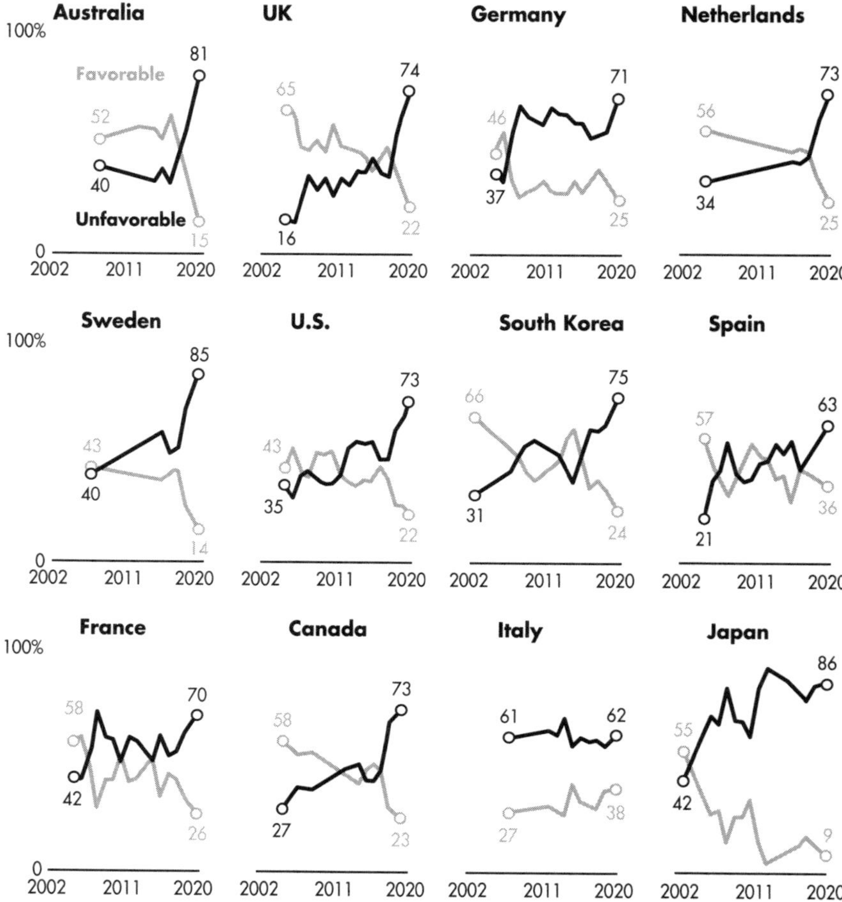

Figure 6.6 Images of China in Cross-Section of Countries, October 2020
Source: "Unfavorable Views of China Reach Historic Highs in Many Countries," Pew Research Center, Washington, DC (October 6, 2020).

The image of China has always been more positive among countries in the Global South,[126] particularly in Africa, but by 2018 surveys suggest a mixed picture across a range of individual countries and regions.[127]

Xi Jinping bears more than a little responsibility for China's deteriorating global image, owing to his increased repression at home and assertiveness abroad. As described above, he has proceeded with dramatically increased political, religious, ethnic, intellectual, and cultural repression inside China. The mass internment and brainwashing of Uighurs in prisons and detention facilities in Xinjiang, the ongoing assaults on Tibetan culture and religion, the imposition of the draconian National Security Law in Hong Kong, the creation of a mass surveillance state, the total control of information and media, the widespread detention of political dissidents, intellectuals, lawyers, and civil society activists—these actions have all shocked the world and have contributed significantly to the declining respect for China. Xi's military build-up, his hypernationalism and assertive foreign policy, his encouragement of hubristic "wolf warrior" public diplomacy by PRC diplomats and the regular diet of nationalist narratives in Chinese state media, have also contributed to global concerns. Xi himself tersely told his counterparts at the 2020 EU-China Summit, "We don't accept any lectures."[128] The economic and political coercive pressure leveraged against countries in Asia and Europe to toe China's line, and its increased "influence operations" and espionage abroad have also raised serious concerns around the world. These actions by the Xi regime have all fueled increasingly negative perceptions of China. In fact, there seems to be an inverse correlation: as China grows stronger and flexes its muscles more under Xi, a wide variety of countries are increasingly viewing China with increased suspicion.[129]

Yet, owing to rigid censorship and control of information, people inside China know nothing of these transgressions and how China is actually viewed abroad. To the people of China, Xi's diplomacy and his presence on the international stage are all viewed very positively at home. He personifies the nationalism and pride that now permeates China.

Xi Jinping on Balance

Xi Jinping has had an outsized impact on China, wider and deeper than arguably that of any Chinese leader since Deng Xiaoping. Although Deng's impact was also huge, it was primarily the result of relatively *removing* the party-state from its previously total penetration of society, economy, politics, intellectual and cultural life, and thereby unleashing sweeping forces

Figure 6.7 Xi Jinping: Emperor for Life?
Source: Xinhua / Alamy

of dynamism that transformed the country and opened it to the world. Xi's efforts have been *just the opposite*: to reinstate the party-state (particularly the Party) into *all* aspects of domestic life. Xi has also reversed one of Deng's key reforms, which established procedures for regularized political succession, by establishing himself potentially as "leader for life" (following his abolition of term limits on the presidency in 2018).[130]

While Xi's impact to date has been profound, it has also been uneven. Like all leaders, Xi's balance sheet is a mixture of pluses, minuses, mixed results and uncertain outcomes. This variegated verdict is, however, at odds with the overwhelmingly positive portrayals proclaimed in China's official media. In Beijing's rendering, Xi can do no wrong. This in itself may prove to be his Achilles heel. No leader is infallible. And people can usually see through falsely constructed narratives and images. The subterranean grousing about Xi's "imperial" leadership style now increasingly heard in

China (and from Chinese when they go abroad and speak candidly with foreigners) may be a harbinger of difficulties to come.

Having constructed a propagandistic caricature of an infallible Xi Jinping, the regime will find it very difficult—if not impossible—to deconstruct this irrational image of China's new "Great Helmsman." There are also many constituencies in China who have suffered from Xi's policies—including more than a million Party and state cadres and military officers who have lost their positions and privileges as a result of Xi's anti-corruption purges—and they may be lying in wait for him to trip up. Breaking up nepotistic corruption networks can be very disruptive to systems that depend and run on them. On the other hand, the pervasive corruption inside the Party, state, military, and business community is itself a telltale sign of regime and system decay.[131] Xi's requirement for loyalty pledges (表态) from military officers and Party members, and the routine sycophantic speeches and statements by officials and citizens alike, may mask the internal opposition to him. There is grousing among many Chinese intellectuals who interact with foreigners that Xi's breaking of the retirement rule is bad for the Party and the country.

Real indicators of cracks in Xi's monolith are difficult to identify from the outside, as the propaganda and security services have thoroughly muzzled the population and intimidated those inside the system who are disgruntled. Those individuals have no choice but to remain silent or flee the country (if they can). One high-profile individual to have done so is Cai Xia, a former professor and Party theorist at the Central Party School in Beijing. In 2018 Cai managed to get to the United States, where she has proceeded to launch searing attacks on Xi and the CCP—describing it as a "zombie party" that ritualistically obeys Xi's dictates without question.[132] It is true that the Party under Xi now behaves more like a military that receives and implements orders from above than as an institution which incorporates input from society. China's wealthy are also leaving the country in record numbers (if they can get out). According to the 2018 Hurun Research Report, a respected publication that monitors China's rich, more than one-third of those surveyed with average wealth of $4.5 million are "currently considering" emigrating to another country.[133] When a country's economic and political elite vote with their feet and seek to leave, it is a telltale sign of system discontent and decay. To prevent this the government has instituted a variety of capital and overseas travel controls to restrict Chinese from moving their personal assets abroad. Given these indications of discontent with Xi and his regime (as noted earlier in this chapter), Chinese have a pithy saying to describe situations like this: *waiying neiruan* (外硬内软)—hard on the outside, soft on the inside. Xi's strongman rule may actually belie weaknesses underneath.[134]

Xi and his regime may be facing the revolutionary challenge faced by all successful modernizing societies: the *revolution of rising expectations*. Having tasted rising incomes and other concomitant improvements in their lives, citizens stop remembering what the regime did for them yesterday, but ask rather what it will do for them today and tomorrow? Xi himself even seemed to recognize this dilemma when he told the 19th Party Congress:[135]

> The needs to be met for the people to live better lives are increasingly broad. Not only have their material and cultural needs grown; their demands for democracy, rule of law, fairness and justice, security, and a better environment are increasing. At the same time, China's overall productive forces have significantly improved and in many areas our production capacity leads the world. The more prominent problem is that our development is unbalanced and inadequate. This has become the main constraining factor in meeting the people's increasing needs for a better life.

Invariably across the world there are multiple examples of newly industrialized economies, where citizens begin demanding not only improved "public goods" (healthcare, education, environment, security, etc.)—they increasingly also seek fundamental freedoms of speech, religious practice, assembly and protest, political participation, and other expressions of individual and collective will. These are the political manifestations of the middle income trap. China has reached this point today—but instead of granting these freedoms (even relatively or incrementally), Xi Jinping has doubled down on repression. He has dramatically and cynically reversed the policies and trend of managed political and social opening pursued under his predecessors Jiang Zemin and Hu Jintao. Jiang and Hu sought to manage change, not to resist it. Xi has replaced enlightened authoritarianism with heavy-handed dictatorship. His actions reveal not a secure leader, but a profoundly insecure one. Xi's actions have not at all matched his rhetoric (see above). Xi has taken China backwards politically precisely at the time when it should be moving forward through encouraging increased freedom of expression, political participation, and civil society.

I would argue that Xi is thus *increasing, not decreasing* tensions in the system and society—tensions that will increase the possibility of eventual "eruption" and threaten far more damaging repercussions for the regime and political system than if the CCP had continued the "managed opening" of the Jiang and Hu years.[136] Atrophy is an inexorable condition of authoritarian regimes like China's—the only real questions are the *pace* of atrophy, the regime's attempts at *adaptation* to arrest the process,[137] and the precise circumstances of the ultimate *dénouement*. Through relative relaxation and opening of political participation and civil society, such regimes can more successfully *slow* the process of atrophy and possibly forestall a systemic meltdown. Yet regimes like Xi's—which seek to close rather than open the system, crack down hard through dictatorial means and institutional instruments of repression, and severely restrict rather than incrementally expand people's freedoms—such regimes are actually exacerbating, not relieving, tensions in the system. Such repressive tactics may work in the short run, but not ultimately—and certainly not in an increasingly aware, cosmopolitan, and urbanized China that now has a multitude of linkages to the outside world (despite Xi's attempts to restrict them). Xi is betting against history that he can keep these pressures (internal and external) at bay and maintain tight controls over society. Time will tell who wins the bet, but my money is on the Chinese people and their inevitable desires for greater personal freedoms.

CHAPTER 7

CHINA'S LEADERS IN CONTRAST

THE PRECEDING CHAPTERS HAVE DETAILED CHINA'S FIVE MAIN LEADERS over the past seven decades. Each was complex in his own right, and I have endeavored to provide many of the details of each leader's rule (although considerably more could have been included in every case). After all, whole *books* have been written about *each* leader. In this concluding chapter, I attempt to emerge from the detailed data and provide some overarching and contrasting summaries of each leader. In Chapter 1 I did a bit of this by examining their comparative childhoods, early adult socialization, and personality types, as well as considering typologies of leadership and some general characteristics of the political culture and institutional environment that all PRC leaders must operate in. In this concluding chapter we step back from the details of each leader's rule and attempt to summarize their overall leadership styles. Following the individual summaries, I will conclude with a brief discussion of some of the composite observations that can be drawn from contrasting these individuals and what it may mean for China's future.

Mao Zedong

Mao was an extraordinarily complex figure and leader. He is, by far, the most difficult of the five leaders to summarize. He had no singular style. He utilized differing strategies and tactics to cope with differing situations—

although his profound distrust of institutions and intrinsic populist faith in the "masses" led him to repeatedly circumvent bureaucracies and launch mass "campaigns" (运动) to mobilize them against specific targets. Mao may have been a Marxist, but he was not particularly a Leninist when it came to utilizing Party or state institutions. His deep distrust of institutions and bureaucracies led him ultimately to attack the Communist Party itself directly during the Great Proletarian Cultural Revolution (1966–1976), which almost decimated it in toto. In addition to this dramatic assault on the commanding heights, Mao's 27 years of rule (1949–1976) were punctuated by one mass campaign after another. Campaign "targets" ranged from intellectuals to peasants, to "rightists," to youth, to technocrats, and many other sub-groups. So if there was one common strand to Mao's leadership style, it was his mass mobilization "campaign style" approach to policy implementation. This was simultaneously rooted in his own personal populism and voluntarism, but also in his desire to remold Chinese society by eliminating or reshaping specific classes and groups. Campaigns were one way that Mao sought to keep the revolution going, as he did not view revolution as something that ended with the seizure of power or passed through stages. Rather, he was a believer in *perpetual revolution*. This caused great tumult during his rule. As the great Sinologist and political scientist Lucian Pye observed, "Politics in Mao's China was theater and there was constant drama. The Chairman was a master manipulator of public sentiments. Political life was an incessant stirring of emotions, as the whole society careened first in one direction and then another."[1]

Although many of these campaigns involved ideological indoctrination and "study sessions" (学习会), most also involved a large dose of brutality and "struggle sessions" (斗争会). Although estimates vary and the CCP has never released its own figures, it is (conservatively) estimated that somewhere in the neighborhood of 40 to 50 million people in *total* can be counted as having died as a result of Mao's coercive campaigns: the land reform campaign of 1950–1951, the "three anti, five anti" campaign of 1952–1953, the "suppress counterrevolutionaries" campaign of 1955, the "criticize Hu Feng" Campaign of 1955, the Anti-Rightist Campaign of 1957–1958, the Great Leap Forward of 1958–61, and the Cultural Revolution of 1966–1976. Estimates of deaths caused by the Great Leap alone range between 30 and 45 million, while land reform and *su-fan* each likely resulted in one million deaths each. The most accurate estimates for the Cultural Revolution are around 1.6 million. The Hu Feng, Anti-Rightist, and "three-anti, five-anti" campaigns each likely resulted in 100,000 or fewer deaths. While it is really impossible to find realistic figures for these campaigns, suffice to say that together with Hitler and Stalin (to a lesser extent Pol Pot), Mao was one of the great totalitarian despots and tyrants of the twentieth century. Yet, comparatively speaking, far more Chinese died at his hands than did Germans under Hitler (5.4 million Jews and 12 million non-combatants killed during the war), Russians and other nationalities under Stalin (estimated 2 or 3 million killed and 5 million who starved to death or were executed during the Ukraine famine of 1932–1933), or Cambodians who died in the "killing fields" under Pol Pot (an estimated 2 million).[2] In his most recent study, the noted historian Frank Dikötter, who has authored a searing trilogy about Mao's rule, also places him among the pantheon of the world's worst tyrannical dictators, and he astutely identifies personality disorders that Mao had in common with other despots.[3] To be certain, China has had a long history of tyrannical emperors, but Mao may rank at the top of those whose personal decisions resulted in so many deaths. As Lucian Pye (in his biography of Mao) observed: "No other Chinese ruler matched him in the number of people killed, banished from their homes to rural exile, imprisoned both in the gulags and in caste-like categories of class identities, and who starved to death in policy-produced famines."[4] This is why I describe Mao as a *populist tyrant*.

Mao was also certainly one of the great revolutionaries of the century as well. The 28-year CCP revolutionary struggle and civil war against the Nationalist (Kuomintang) regime was led by Mao. After the Zunyi Conference of January 1935 (in the midst of the Long March), Mao became the undisputed leader of the Party and the revolutionary cause. Prior to that time, he was one of the founders and key leaders of the Party, but intra-Party disputes meant that he was not in complete control. Following Zunyi, though, he was indisputably in charge. Once he and the Party gained power Mao was not content to merely preside over the nation—he wanted to change it! Mao was, above all, a transformational revolutionary leader.

Mao was also the "founding father" of the nation. On October 1, 1949, it was Mao who stood atop Tiananmen Gate and proclaimed the founding of the People's Republic of China. This put Mao in the dynastic pantheon of China's emperors, and of Sun Yat-sen (the father of the 1911 republican revolution), who had previously ruled China. Like all Chinese, Mao also much admired Sun Yat-sen, and he participated in some of his revolutionary activities in his youth. Subsequently, to this day, the CCP still reveres Sun as the father of post-imperial China (if Sun was the father of modern China, then Mao was the father of contemporary China).

Yet Mao was no ordinary head of state. For much of his time as leader he was referred to as the "Great Helmsman" (大舵手). Mao may have rebelled against the imperial system, but he was nonetheless fascinated by it and he reigned in imperial Chinese style, more like a traditional emperor than a modern statesman. Mao had an acute case of "emperor envy" and was fascinated by China's many emperors and military strategists and spent much time reading about them. This was particularly true after 1960. The "Chairman" (主席), as he was also known, even stopped attending Politburo and Central Committee meetings after 1959. His last was the fatal showdown with Defense Minister Peng Dehuai at Lushan in the summer of that year.[5] From that time on, any vestiges of collegial rule or being *primus inter pares* that Mao had previously displayed disappeared altogether—as he became increasingly isolated and adopted the characteristics of imperial rulers: ruling from "behind the curtain" (后台), acting as a monarch who would rule hundreds of millions of subjects by uttering cryptic four- or eight-character idioms drawn from classical Chinese texts (or his own contemporary "thought"), and a ruler who lived in an inner sanctum behind the high vermillion walls of the Forbidden City, interacting only with a select group of subordinates, servants, and concubines.

Thus, on one level, there was Mao the Monarch. But this is only part of the story. It is true that Mao was, for much of his rule, a disconnected leader who watched over his kingdom more than diligently ruling it. Yet, at times he was also a very hands-on and engaged figure who micro-managed certain situations. Such was usually the case with foreign policy and national security matters, as some declassified Chinese government materials attest.

Mao was also very manipulative of other senior leaders. He was certainly not collegial after the mid-1950s and was even paranoid and profoundly distrustful of his colleagues. Like many emperors he constantly feared that he was being plotted against by those who sought to usurp his rule. As a result, and like many narcissists, he regularly created "loyalty testing" exercises for others—thus always keeping colleagues and subordinates on edge, never knowing exactly where they stood in the Chairman's mind, and when he might abruptly turn against them. Mao was a master tactician and manipulator. He was also ruthless, exhibiting no loyalty to anyone (except Zhou Enlai). Colleagues could (and did) become enemies overnight. The list of his former allies-turned-victims is a long one. But before Mao went for the jugular and purged a perceived opponent, he would often erect elaborate plots to expose and entrap them (such was the case with Gao Gang, Peng Dehuai, Liu Shaoqi, Deng Xiaoping, Peng Zhen, Lin Biao, Chen Boda, and others).

Although he fancied himself an intellectual, and he went to great lengths to learn through reading and to write about various subjects throughout his life, Mao also had disdain for intellectuals. He unleashed one campaign after another to attack them—from the Yanan "rectification movement" of 1942–1945, to the Criticize Hu Feng Campaign of 1955, to the Anti-Rightist Campaign of 1957, to the Socialist Education Movement of 1964, to the Cultural Revolution of 1966–1976, to the Criticize Lin Biao and Confucius campaign of 1973–1974, to the Water Margin campaign of 1975. Mao's hate of and deep distrust for intellectuals likely grew out of his own intellectual insecurities, as well as his Marxist view that they were not reliable revolutionaries.

Although Mao himself only left China twice in his life (both trips to the Soviet Union), he was also very interested in the outside world and foreign relations. He fancied himself a geo-strategist and voraciously read Chinese ancient strategists (Sun Zi, Cao Cao, Zhu Geliang, the Three Kingdoms, etc.), and he loved to discuss geopolitics with foreign visitors. With the able assistance of Premier Zhou Enlai, Mao also took a very hands-on approach to managing China's foreign and national security policy. It was Mao who forged both the Sino-Soviet alliance and then facilitated its breakup. It was Mao who made the decision to enter the brutal Korean War against the United States. It was Mao (together with Lin Biao) who masterminded the aggressive efforts to export revolution around the world during the 1960s and 1970s. It was Mao (on the advice of Zhou Enlai and the three Marshals) who took the strategic decision to reach out to President Nixon and the Americans in 1970–1971 (Mao had in fact sent signals a year prior to Nixon). It was Mao who approved the Four Modernizations program in 1973, which initiated China's turn to the West and Japan for trade and investment. So, the Chairman was deeply involved in China's external dealings throughout his lifetime.

Mao was thus a very complicated character. His personality and leadership style have been the subject of numerous biographies, psychological and behavioral analyses, and speculations by foreign scholars and observers.[6] Chinese accounts of Mao all tend, not surprisingly, to be hagiographic. Only two, one by Mao's former secretary Li Rui and another by his former doctor Li Zhisui, go beyond standard propaganda.[7] The one by Li Zhisui, written after Mao's death and published abroad, revealed much new information and was quite critical of his patient (I drew extensively on it in Chapter 2). Mao continues to be an enigmatic puzzle to this day—but his impact on China and the world was enormous. Why would such a tyrant still be eulogized? Foreign scholars continue to publish books about Mao and Maoism.[8] Inside of China Mao continues to be revered—with his portrait hanging on Tiananmen Gate, his body resting in the center of Tiananmen Square, his face on every monetary note, his "thought" still studied, his revolutionary role still admired, and his role as father of "new China" still revered.

Deng Xiaoping

Given his enormous stature and outsized impact on China, Mao was certainly not an easy act to follow. Successors to first-generation revolutionary leaders frequently struggle to establish their own legitimacy, respect, agency, and longevity. Chiang Kai-shek and Stalin were exceptions, as they took power when the fathers of the revolution (Sun Yat-sen and Vladimir Lenin) died, not long after the success of their revolutions and creation of new states, and both ruled for long periods. More often, after the revered father of the revolution dies, a relatively short-lived caretaker successor is installed following a power struggle and brief transitional period, before another leader emerges for the longer term. Such was the case with Khrushchev's succession to Stalin, before Brezhnev muscled him aside and ruled for eighteen years (1964–1982).

Such was also the case following Mao's death, when Hua Guofeng (as Mao's personally anointed successor) took over and (ostensibly) ruled for six years (1976–1982) before Deng fully took command. Actually, as we saw in Chapter 3, Deng began to erode Hua's power base and take away his institutional positions one by one between 1978 and 1982. Thus, while the two coexisted in a kind of duumvirate for these four years, Deng effectively took control just two years after Mao's death (1978).

Deng Xiaoping is often seen as the antithesis of Mao, the anti-Mao. In many ways he was, as he explicitly rejected much that Mao had pursued after 1957, and he embarked on pragmatic reforms which overturned much of what Mao had built, destroyed, and done. This is how Deng is primarily remembered: as a *pragmatic reformer*.[9]

Unlike Mao, Deng did not rule through intimidation or coercion, terrorizing the populace through draconian repression (the 1989 Tiananmen massacre being the obvious exception). Nor did he lead the nation with great personal charisma and charm, although he certainly possessed prestige and commanded respect as the paramount leader. Nor did ideology serve as much of a tool of Deng's leadership. His Four Cardinal Principles, perhaps his most enduring ideological dicta, were not so much about Marxist ideology as they were Leninist organizational principles concerning the fundamental necessity of maintaining absolute control and monopoly of power by the Communist Party. Deng was the quintessential "organization man." For most of his career he worked in—and believed in working through—bureaucratic structures. For Deng, one thing mattered above all else: *the Party*. He worked his entire career at the organizational heart of the CCP, including years as its Secretary General, and he was dedicated to rebuilding it after Mao did his best to destroy it. Having rescued and resuscitated the Party, Deng set about trying to strengthen Party rule, using the Party to institute policies, and again making the Party legitimate in the eyes of its members and citizenry. In this respect, Deng was an *institutional politician*.

Deng was also alert to the inevitable tendency of bureaucracies to develop and pursue their own set of interests and missions, thus resisting initiatives from above and tending to ossify from within. Deng believed that all organs of the Party and state needed to have "life" (生活), agency, and responsiveness. He often exhibited intolerance of bureaucratic inertia and incompetence, championing meritocracy and streamlining bloated bureaucracy. These streamlining efforts were actually aimed at *strengthening* the bureaucracy, through making it more competent and efficient, thus enhancing the party-state's capacities rather than dismantling them. It was Mao who attacked these institutions—but it was Deng who had built them in the first place and had to rebuild them following Mao's Cultural Revolution assault. In this context, it is also important to point out that Deng's concept of "political system reform" (政治体制改革) was essentially one of *administrative reform* (行政改革). The devolution of decision-making power and the removal of the Party bureaucracy from enterprise-level economic decision-making was a centerpiece of his economic reform package. Later in life, though, like Mao, Deng became frustrated with the way that his post-1989 successors were using bureaucracy and ideology to impede his reforms. When this occurred in 1992, Deng took a page from Mao's playbook, leapfrogged the bureaucracy, and took his case straight to the people with his February 1992 "Southern Tour" (南巡). This act succeeded in kick-starting economic reforms and relaxing the post-Tiananmen draconian political controls.

Deng's position as paramount leader was widely recognized, but it never rivaled Mao's. Deng never actually sought the absolute totalitarian authority that Mao possessed and wielded, and he was convinced that Mao's dictatorial style and "cult of personality" (个人崇拜) were the principal reasons why China endured protracted economic and political crisis for much of the period after 1957. Much of Mao's workstyle deeply troubled Deng. Upon ousting Hua Guofeng and becoming *primus inter pares* himself in 1982, he was committed to ruling very differently.

One major difference between Mao and Deng as paramount leaders was the manner in which they dealt with other leaders and subordinates and made policy decisions. Deng's policy-making style was far more collective and consensus-oriented. This was partly because Deng tended to approach policy problems methodically and empirically—whereas Mao approached them rather arbitrarily and deductively, as the product of ideological dogma or his own personal whims. By contrast, Deng ruled inductively: "seek truth from facts" (实事求是) and "practice is the sole criterion of truth" (实践是检验真理的唯一标准) were two of his most memorable maxims. Another was his theory of the two cats: "It doesn't matter whether a cat is black or white, as long as it catches mice." All three aphorisms attest to Deng's pragmatism.

Another characteristic of Deng's leadership style was that he was not afraid to delegate authority, which he had done throughout his career. Mao, by contrast, avoided delegating authority and always sought to keep key decisions in his own hands. To some extent, Deng sought to make key decisions—notably in foreign policy, national security, and military affairs (like Mao)—but, on the whole, he delegated authority broadly. Nor did Deng foster tensions among subordinates and test their loyalties, as did Mao. While Deng did remove two of his personally selected designated successors—Hu Yaobang and Zhao Ziyang—he did not have to fear that either was trying to usurp his own power (as Mao did on several occasions). Hu and Zhao were removed for policy "errors" and because they had lost the confidence of other senior Politburo leaders and retired elders.

Somewhat similar to Mao, Deng appeared in public only occasionally. He preferred to operate behind the scenes. In Chapter 3 we discussed his regular daily routine, working mainly at home. Both leaders reserved their public appearances for carefully choreographed "inspection tours" of local models or appearances at Party congresses or other official meetings. Both Mao and Deng were largely invisible to the public. This is reminiscent of, and deeply entrenched in, Chinese political culture, what Lucian Pye also perceptively described as the "potency of invisibility": "Chinese political culture traditionally operated on the premise that omnipotence lies in the mystery which invisibility invokes. . . . the world of Chinese officialdom long operated on the principle that the best way to exploit such fantasies of omnipotence was to keep top leaders out of sight."[10] Pye insightfully applied this observation to Deng's leadership style:[11]

> Since Deng Xiaoping did not operate as a public figure in the open, people had to assume that his greatness lay in his ability to manipulate events from behind the scenes, much like a puppeteer. But how did he do so? Seeing the

> man in person provides no clues. He enters the room at the slow, unanimated pace in which great authority is expected to move in China, the exact opposite of the vigorous American politician or executive. He is surrounded by his assistants, all of whom seem a head taller than him. It is said that he is five feet tall, but that is surely an exaggeration. He awkwardly greets his guests; his handshake is limp, without life, almost as though the nicotine stains had taken all the strength from his fingers. As he settles into an overstuffed chair his sandaled feet barely touch the floor, and indeed hang free every time he leans forward to use the spittoon. His provincial Chinese haircut seems to bring out the contours of his skull and makes his head seem even bigger, an impression that is exaggerated as he seems to be almost without a neck. He doesn't bother to communicate any emotion. As a host he makes a feeble pass at being jovial, but he is not warm; indeed, he seems oblivious to the uses of charm. . . . He is known to rattle off statistics in the manner of Chinese cadres who strive to suggest by exaggerated precision that they are in command, or at least that they have good memories. He has an atrocious Sichuan accent, which makes his words slur together in a gargle. . . . There are few signs of liveliness of mind, of wit or humor, and no sustained, systematic pursuit of ideas—only cryptic remarks, short-hand indications of positions or opinions, or dogmatic assertions of policy positions. . . . The most lingering impression is the absence of any signs of affect, no hints as to his understanding of how emotions work—no attempt to reach out and win over others by the bonding powers of sentiment. Equally, there is no attempt to awe his audience, or to capture its imagination.

I include this lengthy description because it is one of the most insightful first-hand depictions of Deng I know of. In some of these regards, Deng was similar to Mao—notably his aloofness and penchant for cryptic philosophical remarks—but in other ways Mao's personality was much more outgoing and spontaneous than Deng's. Mao often smiled, laughed, and engaged with his interlocutors; Deng hardly ever did.

There are further contrasts between the two leaders. Until his "retirement" in 1990 Deng remained engaged—whereas Mao was more detached and withdrawn from active participation in decision-making throughout his time in power (and he never retired). Deng regularly read and commented on documents and met Party leaders (Mao did as well, but to a considerably lesser extent). Deng insisted on being informed, sought out and listened to conflicting opinions, and pressed subordinates on details. In contrast, Mao's subordinates and colleagues often remained silent in the Chairman's presence (for fear of the consequences of speaking out). Mao rarely received expert briefings and, after the 1950s, he interacted with only a handful of other leaders. Deng insisted on precision and substance from his advisors, and he was not one to waste words. As noted above, Mao stopped attending Politburo meetings after 1959, while Deng attended often. The Politburo and its Standing Committee, as well as the Central Committee Secretariat, were all important institutions of rule for Deng—whereas Mao held disdain for them, considering them to be packed with his political enemies. Deng instead tried to ensure that they contained his allies. The Central Military Commission was also of great importance to Deng (he served on it from 1954 to 1989).

There was, therefore, a certain collegiality, decisiveness, and activeness in Deng's workstyle that was absent in Mao's. Deng sought consensus when possible and was certainly more tolerant of dissenting opinions. In general, Deng protected his colleagues—while Mao attacked them. This was one of Mao's enduring lessons from the Cultural Revolution. Deng, unlike Mao, also trusted in the innate entrepreneurial spirit in Chinese society and did much to remove excessive Party and state structures from ordinary people's lives in order to unleash their entrepreneurialism. Getting government "off the backs" of average Chinese, in order to free their essential commercial instincts, will be one of Deng's most enduring legacies. To be sure, there is a certain irony here—as it was Deng (and his associates) who did much to erect the scaffold of the party-state apparatus in China, including the state planning system for the economy during the 1950s. But it is clear that Deng began to have misgivings in the early 1960s about "institutional overreach" insofar as the economy was concerned. This was likely a conclusion he drew from the 1958 commune movement and 1958–1960 Great Leap Forward—and it was Deng (along with Chen Yun, Li Xiannian, and others) who launched a broad series of economic reforms from 1962 to 1965 (which were precisely the prototypes for the reforms he re-launched during the 1980s). So, unlike Mao, who copied the Soviet planning system in toto and imposed totalitarian controls over all aspects of society in an attempt to remold the country, Deng believed that the roles of the party-state should be limited when it came to the economy, certain social and intellectual activities, and politics.[12]

There were further differences between Mao and Deng. Mao never traveled abroad (expect two trips to the Soviet Union); Deng did so with more frequency (first going abroad when he was 16). Deng also received many more foreign visitors in Beijing. Deng enjoyed talking to the foreign media; Mao never did. Mao made no effort to learn a foreign language; Deng had a good grasp of French and apparently spent some years trying to master English. Deng had a far better understanding of the intricacies of world affairs and was much more tolerant of a foreign presence in China. Deng did not mind face-to-face negotiations with foreign leaders; Mao generally eschewed them. Mao was suspicious of the West; Deng held a certain envy of it. Deng was no less nationalistic than Mao, as both were socialized with similar views of the need for a strong and dignified China, but Deng sought the West as an ally in this quest while Mao was more distrustful (even hostile). Both could be blunt, crude, even rude. Deng was no-nonsense, had no time for small talk, was often curt, chain-smoked, and spat into a spittoon. Deng was extremely confident and steady, perhaps a result of his childhood in a large more nurturing family—whereas Mao was impulsive, impatient, narcissistic, and prone to anger—all perhaps owing to his antagonistic relationship with his father and disrupted home life as a teenager.

In their personal lives, Mao sought the symbolic trappings of power; Deng lived more frugally. Mao lived like an emperor in the Zhongnanhai compound adjacent to the Forbidden City; Deng moved out and into a modest house on a lake just to the north. Mao kept concubines and ceased living with his wife Jiang Qing during the 1950s, while Deng was deeply devoted to his wife Zhou Lin and truly enjoyed family life with his numerous grandchildren. Deng played bridge (fanatically) and fraternized socially on these occasions; Mao was a loner. Both enjoyed reading, and both were apparently devotees of the *Shi Ji* (*Records of the Historian*) and other classical Chinese writings. There were thus numerous differences, with some similarities, in leadership style between Mao and Deng.

Jiang Zemin

As we saw in Chapter 4, Jiang Zemin was abruptly thrust into his national leadership position in the midst of, and on account of, the political turmoil engulfing the country in April–June 1989. Jiang assumed the position of General Secretary of the CCP on June 24, following the removal and purge of Zhao Ziyang on May 19 and the June 4 Tiananmen massacre. Prior to his unforeseen promotion, Jiang was serving as Party secretary of Shanghai, which also merited his inclusion in the ruling seventeen-member Politburo. Jiang was not a household name (even in China) when he was elevated to the top job in the country. He was therefore dismissed by many China watchers (and Chinese) as a transitional place-holding figure like Hua Guofeng. Yet, Jiang ended up ruling for thirteen years (1989–2002), longer than Deng Xiaoping. Because of his rather ordinary background as a bureaucratic functionary, Jiang was also dismissed as someone who did not possess the necessary breadth of experience, gravitas, and grasp of power politics to endure at the top of the capricious Chinese communist system. Yet Jiang surprised many and silenced his detractors—by building a diversified power base and adroitly navigating a series of challenges.

Jiang's tenure is notable for having overcome the international condemnation and isolation following the June 4 massacre; for stabilizing ties with the United States and broadening China's foreign relations; for presiding over the return of Hong Kong to Chinese rule; for implementing a series of sensitive high-level personnel changes in the leadership; for overseeing the longest stretch of sustained high-level economic growth rates in the country's history; for raising the standard of living; for managing and satisfying a variety of key bureaucratic constituencies; for setting the People's Liberation Army on a path of serious modernization; and for restarting a series of stealthy but significant political reforms (including his theory of the "Three Represents," 三个代表).

In retrospect, Jiang Zemin well out-performed the original expectations for his rule and left a legacy of substantive reforms. Yet, it was also on Jiang's watch that social inequalities deepened significantly, the gap in growth between coastal and inland China widened, corruption proliferated, low-scale protests mushroomed around the country, crime and corruption increased markedly, and a variety of systemic economic maladies became more acute. Still, on balance, Jiang's period of rule was quite successful and turned out to be far more than the brief transition many had expected. Although he was unexpectedly thrust into the position, Jiang "grew into" the role and gained confidence over time—indeed, he liked being paramount leader so much that he resisted stepping down because of mandatory retirement requirements. Even after he stepped down in 2002, Jiang clung to the chairmanship of the Central Military Commission for two more years, and he continued to exert substantial influence behind the scenes throughout the Hu Jintao period. He remains (as of this writing), at the age of 94, China's senior statesman.

Jiang's tenure was also notable for the *rise of technocrats* in Chinese elite politics.[13] This is a generation of people who were trained in engineering and the sciences during the 1950s when China was close to the Soviet Union and implementing the Soviet model of heavy industrialization and planned economy. Thousands of Chinese in their twenties and thirties were sent to the Soviet Union for specialized education in these fields, and to receive practical training in Soviet factories. University programs in engineering, industrial planning, and the sciences were also established in a number of China's universities during the 1950s. Jiang was one such person, being sent to experience the Stalin Automobile Works in Moscow following his graduation in electrical engineering from Shanghai's Jiaotong University.

Technocrats are not only specialists in the industrial arts and sciences—they have a special approach to problem-solving. Technocrats are, above all, incrementalists. That is, they approach problems and seek to solve them by breaking them down into their component parts and working on each individually and step-by-step. This is the opposite approach to how more ambitious and transformational leaders (and those trained in social sciences) approach problems: holistically and systemically, looking to address multiple issues simultaneously. Technocrats are pragmatists not ideologues, incrementalists not systemicists, are cautious not bold, are more reactive than proactive, and are problem solvers. Technocrats may not be "visionary," but they may be more effective in getting things done. Besides, following Mao and Deng, maybe China needed a little less "vision" and more practicality. While Deng was certainly a pragmatist, he was not a technocrat in the way he approached policy issues. Deng was very impatient and a man-in-a-hurry. Technocrats possess patience and work steadily over time.

Perhaps precisely because Jiang lacked the "vision thing" (to quote George H. W. Bush's self-description), his approach to rule grew directly out of his past service in the industrial bureaucracies. Jiang's approach was thus primarily *bureaucratic*—he assembled a holistic set of programs by adopting (and co-opting) individual bureaucratic constituencies. He adopted *their* agendas and made them his own. He did this with Party, state, economic, technological, foreign policy, military, and other bureaucracies. This is why I describe Jiang Zemin as a *bureaucratic politician*. In Leninist systems, people are not constituencies—bureaucratic institutions are. In the Soviet Union this became known as "USSR Inc.,"[14] or "institutional corporatism."[15] In such a system each functional bureaucracy becomes an interest group.[16] Jiang very much approached institutional bureaucracies as political constituencies—this was the essence of his rule. Jiang also favored certain geographic constituencies—namely coastal China, and particularly Shanghai and his native lower Yangzi delta region. He also promoted numerous officials from Shanghai to Beijing, thus creating what was described during his tenure as the "Shanghai Gang" (上海帮). Jiang's rule was thus very much one of *patronage politics* and *political corporatism*, where resources were provided to institutions and individuals in exchange for their loyalty, and interest group politics built around bureaucratic institutions developed. One consequence of this was that China's government institutions were strengthened during Jiang's rule; in this regard he was similar to Deng Xiaoping.

In terms of his leadership persona, however, Jiang Zemin demonstrated a very different style from Mao and Deng. Recall the penchant of both Mao and Deng to rule from behind the scenes and to be aloof when meeting foreigners. Not so with Jiang Zemin. Jiang was a true extrovert and had a big ego. He was very animated in such meetings, physically gesticulating frequently, talking incessantly, and regularly veering off-topic. When he would do so in discussions with foreign leaders, Jiang's aides would often pull their foreign counterparts aside afterwards and pass to them written "talking points" of what Jiang had meant to convey. Jiang was very spontaneous. He was also known to occasionally burst into song or recite texts he had read (for example, he had memorized Lincoln's Gettysburg address during high school and loved reciting it to American interlocutors). He also had studied English and would experiment with it with foreign visitors (but it was not very coherent and the interpreters had to correct it). His Russian was more fluent. Jiang frequently laughed in a kind of cackle. He also had the unfortunate habit of pulling a comb from his pocket and combing back his dyed jet-black hair in public. While overweight, he was fairly fashionable, wearing a variety of Western-style suits and colored ties. His oversized rectangular glasses frames dominated his face. He loved the world stage and relished attending UN, G-8, and other international summits, where he could rub shoulders with other world leaders and have his photo taken together with them. In these personal ways, Jiang was a different kind of Chinese leader from his predecessors.

Hu Jintao

Hu Jintao assumed the top twin positions of CCP General Secretary at the 16th Party Congress in November 2002 and President of the PRC at the National People's Congress in March 2003. Because Jiang Zemin did not wish to relinquish all of his power, he managed to hang on to his position as Chairman of the Central Military Commission for another year before Hu Jintao added this to his trifecta of leadership titles.

Unlike Jiang, who was suddenly elevated (the Chinese call it "helicoptering," 直升飞机) to the top in 1989, Hu Jintao had a decade to prepare for his appointments. During his last days of political activity, following the time of the 14th Party Congress in 1992, Deng Xiaoping anointed Hu to be Jiang's successor among the "fourth generation of leaders" (第四代的领袖), although Hu was never referred to as the "core" (核心) of the fourth generation. Hu was not quite 50 years old, and thus became one of the youngest members of the Politburo in CCP history. Deng designated Hu on the recommendation of elder CCP official Song Ping, who had first talent-spotted Hu when both served in Gansu province during the 1970s and early 1980s. Prior to his elevation to the Politburo Hu Jintao's career had previously been mainly spent in the provinces—working first in the hydroelectric sector and then in the Gansu provincial Communist Youth League (CYL). Hu also subsequently served in Guizhou province and Tibet.

Between assignments to Gansu and Guizhou, Hu attended the Central Party School, served as a member of the CYL Secretariat and then as CYL General Secretary during the mid-1980s. This meant that he served directly under the liberal CCP General Secretary Hu Yaobang (no relation), himself the previous leader of the CYL. This connection made many foreign China watchers (and some in China) surmise that Hu Jintao shared the progressive policy impulses of Hu Yaobang. It was not to be. Hu was no liberal in the Hu Yaobang mold. But, as we saw in Chapter 5, Hu (together with Premier Wen Jiabao) did launch a series of important intra-Party political reforms as well as reorienting the national socioeconomic policy agenda from the growth-at-all-costs orientation of Jiang Zemin to a much more socially conscious multifaceted agenda which emphasized social justice, reducing inequality, improving living standards for average people, poverty alleviation, environmental protection, and other reforms that emphasized the common citizen over business and political elites. In retrospect, Hu advanced a very progressive policy agenda.

Once Hu Jintao was elevated to Beijing in 1992 and was singled out as the likely successor to Jiang Zemin, he embarked on a decade-long apprentice period as leader-in-waiting. As I argued in Chapter 5, however, Hu did not use this time effectively, which seems odd. He could have, and should have, systematically worked in a variety of policy domains, but he did not. He only occasionally gave perfunctory speeches on non-Party subjects. His only positions of significance were as head of the CCP Secretariat and as President of the Central Party School. It was from the latter position that he seemingly did develop strong ties with the CCP Propaganda Department and system, but his decade of apprenticeship showed no other exposure to other domestic or foreign policy issue areas. Notably, he did nothing to cultivate relations with the senior brass of the PLA—indeed Hu's tenuous ties with the military were one of the noteworthy aspects of his rule. For a designated successor Hu's lack of diversity in policy portfolios was very odd. He could have used this decade-in-waiting much more effectively to cultivate a wide range of ties to different institutional stakeholders, taking a page out of Jiang Zemin's playbook. Thus, by the time he became No. 1,

Hu really only had bureaucratic ties to the Youth League, the propaganda apparatus, and expertise in intra-Party affairs—not at all a broad bureaucratic power base.

Once in power, Hu's decade of rule is generally seen as unremarkable. His lack of preparation, his own sterile personality, and little constituency-building during the previous decade may have had something to do with it. By the end, many Chinese referred to this period as the "ten lost years." In some ways, this characterization may not quite be fair—as Hu and Premier Wen Jiabao did launch a number of social policy reform initiatives during their first five-year term. Significantly, Hu also continued many of the political reforms within the Party started during Jiang Zemin's term. The common denominator in this regard was Jiang's right-hand advisor and senior leader Zeng Qinghong—who continued on in senior leadership positions during Hu's term until 2008 when he had to retire (when Zeng retired so too did political reform, to this day). These two sets of reforms—social policy and political reform—are detailed in Chapter 5. Hu also reoriented China's foreign policy from a focus on major powers and developed countries to a much greater emphasis on the Global South. He also initiated China's attention to, and subsequent obsession with gaining, "soft power."

If Hu's goal was simply to keep the train on the tracks and to keep the CCP engine running, his term as China's paramount leader (2002–2012) must be considered a success. These aforementioned reform initiatives were also significant. Yet by 2008 Hu had become a "lame duck" during his second term, Zeng Qinghong had been forced to retire, several other senior officials were making power plays of their own (notably Bo Xilai and Zhou Yongkang), and Xi Jinping loomed in the wings as Hu's successor-in-waiting. All of these reasons—plus the facts that Hu never built a diversified bureaucratic power base and did not possess a forceful personality—combined to severely constrict Hu's leadership and impact during his second five-year term. He has thus been judged as a rather ineffectual leader, although with the passage of time history may offer a more positive verdict on the Hu Jintao era.

Xi Jinping

If Hu Jintao was not particularly impactful or effective, his successor Xi Jinping has been just the opposite. In less than a decade in power Xi has put his personal and policy stamp on the nation and the world as no Chinese leader has since Mao. In Chapter 6 I described Xi as a *modern emperor*. He rules and behaves very much in ways reminiscent of China's traditional emperors: all-powerful, regal, respected, feared, sycophantically revered, in command of all organs of state power and military forces, the setter of ideological doctrine and interpreter of the past, the visionary of the future, moral exemplar, intolerant of insubordination or dissent, and a ruthless dictator.

It is actually extraordinary that in the second decade of the twenty-first century Xi Jinping has taken such full command of the continent-sized country and its 1.5 billion citizens—orchestrating and impacting their lives to a degree not experienced since the totalitarian Maoist era. Indeed, I describe the Xi period to date (he is still in power at the time of this writing with no signs of stepping down) as "neo-totalitarian." To take such full command, Xi and his regime have harnessed the full power of technology to create an unprecedented surveillance state.[17]

Xi has also significantly impacted China's posture in the world, explicitly shedding Deng Xiaoping's mandate for China to "hide its capabilities and bide its time" (韬光养晦) in favor of a far more assertive international posture. As Xi told the 19th Party Congress in 2017: "China has stood up, grown rich, and is becoming strong." As have all Chinese leaders before him, Xi has accepted the principal responsibility to make China strong and respected in the world—what he describes as the country's "Great Rejuvenation" (大复兴). This is a mandate that has been all Chinese leaders' responsibility ever since the country's decline and "century of shame and humiliation" (1840–1949), and Xi takes it extremely seriously. He is fixated on power—his own and his country's.

In less than a decade in power Xi has amassed an extraordinary amount of personal and institutional power. This process began with a sweeping purge of potential enemies, under the guise of an unprecedentedly tough anti-corruption campaign. To be certain, corruption had become a serious cancer inflicting the country and the CCP, and Xi's campaign dealt with it in an intensive and sustained fashion not seen in previous crackdowns. But it also permitted Xi to purge many in the Party, state, military, judicial, and security services—and to subsequently install officials and officers personally loyal to him. The Chinese political system thus now again evinces a real patron–client quality, to a degree not seen since at least Jiang Zemin's tenure. The sycophancy surrounding Xi has not been seen since the Mao era. I describe this as "Patriarchal Leninism."

The military (PLA) has been a particular focus of Xi's attention, in multiple dimensions: personnel, doctrine, deployments, weapons, technology, and organization. In late 2105 and into 2016 Xi initiated an unprecedented reorganization and consolidation of military structures, forces, and organs—jettisoning the six-decade-long Soviet structure for a much more flexible and modern semi-American structure. More than any Chinese leader since Deng, Xi Jinping understands military affairs and takes a very personal and hands-on approach to military modernization.

Xi has also undertaken a systematic rebuilding and restrengthening of the CCP. When he came to power in 2012, Xi was very nervous about the condition of the Party. And he was also possessed by the collapse of the Soviet Union (giving a speech about it early in his tenure). As we saw in Chapter 6, Xi has initiated numerous intra-Party reforms aimed at centralizing its organizational structures, strengthening its discipline, and increasing its all-pervasive penetration of society.

Xi also totally dominates the official discourse of the CCP and the country. Iconic images and sycophantic symbols of him are everywhere, to a degree not seen since the Maoist era. His sayings, speeches, pronouncements, and writings are widely circulated for all to read and study. There is even a Xi Jinping cell phone app that Party members and citizens must visit in order to show their allegiance and boost their "social credit" ratings. "Xi Jinping Thought on Socialism with Chinese Characteristics for a New Era" has been written into the Constitution and dominates political discourse, while his 1,782-page three-volume *The Governance of China* is mandatory reading. Xi's persona is ever-present in China today. To the extent that we can tell, Xi seems to be very popular with most citizens—although definitely not with the intelligentsia (on whom his regime has cracked down hard), not with more liberally minded Party members who would like to see a more open and less repressive CCP, and not with those who have been victims of his purges.

Xi is thus very much an emperor-like figure, but he is also a modern one—insofar as he seeks to make China's economy and technology world-class. Notwithstanding Xi's goals and accomplishments, he remains a divisive figure in China as many urbanites, intellectuals, and Party members deeply resent the strict controls and draconian repression Xi has unleashed on the country and its institutions. He is also very contentious abroad—as many countries around the world have grown very uncomfortable with China's new assertiveness in foreign affairs, its overseas "influence operations" and attempts to censor foreigners, its harassment of Chinese dissidents abroad, its coercive economic diplomacy against many states, its rapid military modernization, its island-building in the South China Sea, its hypernationalistic "wolf warrior" public diplomacy, and other steps taken under Xi that are causing rising anxieties around the world.

Thus, Xi Jinping's "report card" after nine years is mixed. He certainly has been a "transformational" leader as described by James MacGregor Burns and discussed in Chapter 1. He has had an extraordinary impact, which is perhaps even more notable in contrast with his predecessor Hu Jintao. He has worked very quickly, very methodically, and very thoroughly to implement his agenda. He is both reactive and proactive in his policies. He exudes personal confidence and exhibits an air of entitlement and sense of destiny. He possesses and has articulated a comprehensive vision for China and international affairs (although laden with hard-to-understand slogans). If there was a sense of drift in China under Hu Jintao, Xi has provided new purpose to his citizens and country. There exists a strong sense of confidence in China today. He has seemingly steamrolled any opposition in the leadership, the Party, the bureaucracies, the military and security services, and has decimated dissent in the country at large. This is actually astounding, given the size of China and its population, and the pervasiveness of social media and instant communications. While serious problems certainly lurk under the surface in Xi's China, and many do, the trajectory and momentum of the country that he has initiated is nonetheless rather remarkable. That is leadership impact.

We do not know how long Xi Jinping will rule China. His removal of presidential term limits in 2018 theoretically means he could be ruler-for-life, as there are no term limits on his Party and military positions. Inevitably the actuarial realities will catch up with him (he is 67 at the time of this writing). While there are no reports of issues with Xi's health (neither, though, does the government provide any medical reports), he is overweight, practices no known exercise regimen (it is difficult to imagine Xi on a treadmill, in a weight room, or swimming vigorous laps in a pool), and there is some speculation that he may have an occasional Parkinson's-like tremor (as he exhibited on a trip to Europe in 2019). However, as long as his health holds up, and barring a sudden *coup d'etat* and purge from power (highly unlikely but something for which there is ample precedent in Chinese politics and can never be ruled out in such authoritarian systems), Xi is likely to remain in power for some time to come. This is by no means to say that Xi has no enemies or opposition—indeed, my anecdotal conversations with a number of Chinese indicate that there is considerable subterranean discontent with Xi's rule. Yet discontent does not necessarily translate into an overthrow. Autocrats the world over have demonstrated a stubborn tenacity for sustained rule through a combination of repression and populism. Time will tell with Xi Jinping. When his time comes, then it will be time for a second edition of this book.

NOTES

Preface and Acknowledgments

1 David Shambaugh, *The Making of a Premier: Zhao Ziyang's Provincial Career* (Boulder: Westview Press, 1984).

2 Roderick MacFarquhar, *The Politics of China: Sixty Years of the People's Republic of China* (Cambridge: Cambridge University Press, third edition, 2011). Also see Jane Perlez, "Roderick MacFarquhar: Eminent China Scholar Dies at 88," *New York Times*, February 12, 2019: https://www.nytimes.com/2019/02/12/obituaries/roderick-macfarquhar-dead.html; David Shambaugh, "In Memoriam: Roderick MacFarquhar (1930–2019)": https://www.soas.ac.uk/news/newsitem138486.html.

3 Among his many impressive and insightful publications on the Mao era, see Walder's magisterial study *China Under Mao: A Revolution Derailed* (Cambridge, MA: Harvard University Press, 2015).

4 Ezra Vogel, *Deng Xiaoping and the Transformation of China* (Cambridge, MA: Belknap Press, 2013).

5 See David Shambaugh, *China's Future* (Cambridge: Polity Press, 2016).

Chapter 1

1 See Orville Schell and John Delury, *Wealth and Power: China's Long March to the 21st Century* (New York: Random House, 2014).

2 Max Weber, *Politics as a Vocation* (1919): https://web.archive.org/web/20130319092642/http://anthropos-lab.net/wp/wp-content/uploads/2011/12/Weber-Politics-as-a-Vocation.pdf.

3 James MacGregor Burns, *Leadership* (New York: Harper & Row, 1978). Burns also wrote a second volume just on transformative leadership: James

MacGregor Burns, *Transforming Leadership* (New York: Atlantic Monthly Press, 2003).

4 Ibid., p. 4.

5 Daniel Goleman, "Leadership That Gets Results," *Harvard Business Review* (March–April 2000).

6 See, for example, Tomas Chamorro-Premuzic and Michael Sanger, "What Leadership Looks Like in Different Cultures," *Harvard Business Review*, May 6, 2016.

7 Fred I. Greenstein, *The Presidential Difference: Leadership Style from FDR to George W. Bush* (Princeton: Princeton University Press, 2004).

8 See several books by Jerrold Post: *Narcissism and Politics: Dreams of Glory* (Cambridge: Cambridge University Press, 2015); *Leaders and Their Followers in a Dangerous World: The Psychology of Political Behavior* (Ithaca: Cornell University Press, 2004); *Dangerous Charisma* (New York: Pegasus Books, 2019). Also see Dean B. McFarlin and Paul D. Sweeney, *Where Egos Dare: The Untold Truth About Narcissistic Leaders—and How to Survive Them* (N.P.: Kogan Page, 2002).

9 While this argument has been made by several biographers of Mao, it is most systematically argued by Lucian Pye in *Mao Tse-tung: The Man in the Leader* (New York: Basic Books, 1976).

10 Edgar Snow, *Red Star Over China* (New York: Grove Press, 1968), p. 132.

11 Richard H. Solomon, *Mao's Revolution and the Chinese Political Culture* (Berkeley: University of California Press, 1971), chapter 2.

12 Edgar Snow, *Red Star Over China*, op. cit.

13 Ibid., p. 131.

14 Bruce Gilley, *Tiger on the Brink: Jiang Zemin and China's New Elite* (Berkeley: University of California Press, 1998), p. 10.

15 See the description of this period in Robert Lawrence Kuhn, *The Man Who Changed China: The Life and Legacy of Jiang Zemin* (New York: Crown Publishing, 2004), p. 31.

16 See Jerrold Post, *Leaders and Their Followers in a Dangerous World*, op. cit., pp. 22–23. Post draws on the work of Daniel J. Levenson, *The Seasons of a Man's Life* (New York: Knopf, 1978).

17 Jerrold Post, ibid., pp. 24–40.

18 Leon Festinger, *A Theory of Cognitive Dissonance* (Stanford: Stanford University Press, 1957).

19 In the case of Asian leaders, see Ramachandra Guha (ed.), *Makers of Modern Asia* (Cambridge, MA: The Belknap Press, 2014).

20 For studies of the CCP see Franz Schurmann, *Ideology and Organization in Communist China* (Berkeley: University of California Press, 1968, second edition); Richard McGregor, *The Party: The Secret World of China's Leaders* (New York: Harper, 2012); David Shambaugh, *China's Communist Party: Atrophy & Adaptation* (Berkeley and London: University of California Press, 2013); Bruce Dickson, *The Dictator's Strategy for Survival* (New York: Oxford University Press, 2016.

21 For the CCP Constitution see: *Constitution of the Communist Party of China*, adopted October 24, 2017: http://www.xinhuanet.com//english/download/Constitution_of_the_Communist_Party_of_China.pdf; for the PRC Constitution see: *Constitution of the People's Republic of China*, adopted March 14, 2004: http://www.npc.gov.cn/zgrdw/englishnpc/Constitution/node_2825.htm.

22 The classic works on Chinese factionalism are Lucian Pye, *The Dynamics of Chinese Politics* (Cambridge, MA: Oelgeschlager, Gunn & Hain, 1981); Andrew Nathan, "A Factionalism Model of CCP Politics," *The China Quarterly*, No. 53 (January–March 1973), pp. 34–66; Tang Tsou, "Prolegomenon to the Study of Informal Groups in CCP Politics," *The China Quarterly*, No. 65 (January 1976), pp. 98–114; Martin King Whyte, *Small Groups and Political Rituals in China* (Berkeley: University of California Press, 1974).

23 This has been a reputational problem for communist parties for decades. See, for example, Milovan Đilas, *The New Class: An Analysis of the Communist System* (New York: Harcourt Brace Jovanovich, 1957).

24 See John Burns, *The Chinese Communist Party Nomenklatura System: A Documentary Study of Party Control of Leadership Selection* (Armonk, NY: M.E. Sharpe, 1989); John Burns, "China's Nomenklatura System," *Problems of Communism* (September–October 1987); Melanie Manion, "The Cadre Management System Post-Mao: The Appointment, Promotion, Transfer, and Removal of Party and State Leaders," *The China Quarterly*, No. 102 (June 1985), pp. 203–253.

25 Mao Zedong, "Problems of War and Strategy," *Quotations from Chairman Mao* (Beijing: Foreign Languages Press, 1972), p. 61.

26 See: https://www.marxists.org/reference/archive/mao/selected-works/volume-4/mswv4_65.htm.

27 Ibid.

28 The classic study of this subject is Lyman P. Van Slyke, *Enemies and Friends: The United Front in Chinese Communist History* (Stanford: Stanford University Press, 1967).

29 See James Reardon-Anderson, *Yenan and the Great Powers* (New York: Columbia University Press, 1980).

30 For an excellent description of the role of ideology in the CCP and Chinese political system see Franz Schurmann, *Ideology and Organization in Communist China*, op. cit., chapter 1.

31 Xinhua News Agency, *Constitution of the Communist Party of China*: http://www.xinhuanet.com//english/download/Constitution_of_the_Communist_Party_of_China.pdf.

32 Lucian W. Pye, *The Mandarin and the Cadre: China's Political Cultures* (Ann Arbor: University of Michigan Center for Chinese Studies, 1988), p. 166.

33 See the discussion in my book *China's Future* (Cambridge: Polity Press, 2016), chapter 4.

Chapter 2

1 Mao Zedong, "Report on an Investigation of the Peasant Movement in Hunan," *Selected Works*, Vol. 1 (Beijing: Foreign Languages Press, 1965), p. 30.

2 Among many excellent studies, perhaps the best is Robert Bickers, *The Scramble for China: Foreign Devils in the Qing Empire, 1832–1914* (London: Penguin Books, 2013).

3 China National Bureau of Statistics, *Zhonghua Renmin Gongheguo Guomin Jingji Huifu Shi (1949–1952)* [History of the Recovery of the National Economy of the PRC, 1949–1952], (Beijing: Qiushi chubanshe, 1988). Also see A. Doak Barnett, *Communist China: The Early Years, 1949–1955* (New York: Praeger, 1964), p. 249.

4 Nicholas Lardy, "Economic Recovery and the First Five-Year Plan," *The Cambridge History of China Part I: The Emergence of Revolutionary China* (Vol. 14), (Cambridge: Cambridge University Press, 1987), p. 150.

5 N.A., "China's Grain Output Rises Nearly Six Times in 70 Years," *China Daily*, September 23, 2019.

6 Nicholas Lardy, "Economic Recovery and the First Five-Year Plan," op. cit., p. 149.

7 See *Zhonghua Renmin Gongheguo Guomin Jingji Huifu Shi*, op. cit.

8 See National Bureau of Statistics, Dept. of Comprehensive Statistics, *Xin Zhongguo Liushi Nian Tongji Ziliao Huibian* [China Compendium of Statistics, 1949–2008 (Beijing: China Statistics Press, 2010), p. 43.

9 Dharma Kumar, "The Chinese and Indian Economies from ca. 1914–1949,"

STICERD Research Program on the Chinese Economy, CP No. 22, London School of Economics, May 1992.

10 See Rana Mitter, *Forgotten Ally: China's World War II, 1937–1945* (Boston: Houghton Mifflin, 2013).

11 Andrew Walder, *China Under Mao: A Revolution Derailed* (Cambridge, MA: Harvard University Press, 2015), p. 67.

12 For an excellent first-hand set of accounts of Mao's visit by both Stalin's and Mao's aides, see CNN, "Cold War: China" (Episode 15): https://www.youtube.com/watch?v=gSPIonMrLq0&list=PL3H6z037pboGWTxs3xGP7HRGrQ5dOQdGc&index=16&t=0s.

13 See "Record of Conversation Between Comrade I.V. Stalin and Chairman of the People's Republic of China Mao Zedong," December 16, 1949, translated and available in the Woodrow Wilson Center Cold War History Project, *Cold War International History Bulletin*, Issues 6–7 (Winter 1995–1996), pp. 5–7.

14 As quoted in Alexander V. Pantsov with Steven I. Levine, *Mao: The Real Story* (New York: Simon & Schuster, 2012), p. 370.

15 Ibid., p. 371.

16 Interview with Liu Binyan, on CNN, "Cold War: China" (Episode 15), op. cit.

17 See Deborah A. Kaple, *Dream of a Red Factory: The Legacy of High Stalinism in China* (Oxford: Oxford University Press, 1994).

18 For elaboration of how the PRC was bureaucratically organized at this time see Harry Harding, *Organizing China: The Problem of Bureaucracy, 1949–1976* (Stanford: Stanford University Press, 1981); A. Doak Barnett, *Cadres, Bureaucracy, and Political Power in Communist China* (New York: Columbia University Press); Franz Schurmann, *Ideology and Organization in Communist China* (Berkeley: University of California Press, 1966).

19 See my "The Soldier and the State in China: The Political Work System in the People's Liberation Army," *The China Quarterly*, No. 127 (September 1991), pp. 527–568; and "Building the Party-State in China: Bringing the Soldier Back In," in Timothy Cheek and Tony Saich (eds.), *New Perspectives on State Socialism in China* (Armonk, NY: M.E. Sharpe, 1997).

20 See Frederick C. Teiwes, "The Chinese State During the Maoist Era," in David Shambaugh (ed.), *The Modern Chinese State* (Cambridge: Cambridge University Press, 2000).

21 For a full study of China's bureaucratic evolution during these years see Harry Harding, *Getting Organized: The Problem of Bureaucracy, 1949–1976* (Stanford: Stanford University Press, 1981).

22 Andrew Walder, *China Under Mao: A Revolution Derailed* (Cambridge: Harvard University Press, 2015), p. 65.

23 Official figures cited in Stuart Schram, *Mao Tse-tung* (Harmondsworth, UK: Penguin Books, 1966), p. 267.

24 Frank Dikötter, *The Tragedy of Liberation: A History of the Chinese Revolution, 1945–1957* (London: Bloomsbury, 2013), p. 100.

25 Figures cited in Walder, *China Under Mao*, op. cit., p. 66. For a thorough and chilling description of the origins of the labor camp system in China, and the system of "reform through labor" (劳改) and "reeducation through labor" (劳教), see Dikötter, ibid., chapter 12 ("The Gulag"). For subsequent first-hand accounts see Hongda Harry Wu, *Laogai: The Chinese Gulag* (Boulder: Westview Press, 1992).

26 Dikötter, *The Tragedy of Liberation*, op. cit., p. 89. Drawing on actual provincial archives, Dikötter details numerous cases from this reign of terror, pp. 89–100.

27 The best study of this movement remains Robert Jay Lifton, *Thought Reform and the Psychology of Totalism: A Study of 'Brainwashing' in China* (New York: W. W. Norton, 1961).

28 Quote from October 24, 1951, cited in Schram, *Mao Tse-tung*, op. cit., pp. 271–272.

29 Walder, *China Under Mao*, op. cit., p. 71.

30 See Sam Roberts, "Harriet Mills, Scholar Held in 'Brainwashing Prison' in China Dies at 95," *New York Times*, March 29, 2016: https://www.nytimes.com/2016/03/30/world/harriet-mills-scholar-held-in-brainwashing-prison-in-china-dies-at-95.html.

31 Harriet Mills, "Thought Reform: Ideological Remolding in China," *The Atlantic Monthly* (December 1959), pp. 71–77.

32 Allyn and Adele Rickett, *Prisoners of Liberation* (New York: Anchor Books, 1973).

33 The best account of this process remains Ezra Vogel, *Canton Under Communism* (Cambridge: Harvard University Press, 1980).

34 Frederick C. Teiwes, "The Establishment and Consolidation of the New Regime, 1949–1957," in Roderick MacFarquhar (ed.), *The Politics of China* (Cambridge: Cambridge University Press, third edition, 2011), p. 36.

35 Ibid., p. 37.

36 This process is described well in a variety of sources, but see Walder, *China Under Mao*, op. cit., chapter 3.

37 Among the many studies, see Max Hastings, *The Korean War* (New York: Simon & Schuster, 1988).

38 See, in particular, Chen Jian, *China's Road to the Korean War* (New York: Columbia University Press, revised edition, 1996).

39 Philip Short, *Mao: A Life* (New York: Henry Holt & Co., 1999), p. 433.

40 For an excellent account of this process in the case of Tianjin, see Kenneth G. Lieberthal, *Revolution and Tradition in Tianjin, 1949–1952* (Stanford: Stanford University Press, 1980).

41 Nicholas Lardy, "Economic Recovery and the 1st Five-Year Plan," op. cit., p. 157.

42 Frederick C. Teiwes, "The Establishment and Consolidation of the New Regime," op. cit., p. 42.

43 For the classic account of how this system functioned see Andrew G. Walder, *Communist Neo-Traditionalism: Work and Authority in Chinese Industry* (Berkeley: University of California Press, 1988).

44 Lardy, "Economic Recovery and the 1st Five-Year Plan," op. cit., p. 161–163.

45 See Frederick C. Teiwes and Warren Sun (eds.), *The Politics of Agricultural Cooperativization in China: Mao, Deng Zihui, and the "High Tide" of 1955* (Armonk, NY: M. E. Sharpe, 1993).

46 China National Bureau of Statistics, *Xin Zhongguo Liushi Nian Tongji Ziliao Huibian, 1949–2008*, op. cit.

47 This period of the mid-1950s and Mao's irrational economic impulses are well chronicled in Frederick C. Teiwes and Warren Sun, *China's Road to Disaster* (Armonk, NY: M. E. Sharpe, 1999).

48 The best account of the Gao Gang affair is Frederick C. Teiwes, *Politics & Purges in China* (Armonk, NY: M. E. Sharpe, 1993, second edition).

49 Andrew Walder, *China Under Mao*, op. cit., p. 135. For a full description of the Hu Feng affair see Merle Goldman, "The Party and the Intellectuals," in John K. Fairbank and Roderick MacFarquhar (eds.), *The Cambridge History of China*, Vol. 14, op. cit., pp. 239–242.

50 Quoted in Goldman, ibid., p. 243.

51 Cited in Roderick MacFarquhar, *The Origins of the Cultural Revolution 1: Contradictions Among the People, 1956–1957* (New York: Columbia University Press, 1974), p. 93.

52 For a good description of these and other critiques see Walder, *China Under Mao*, op. cit., pp. 139–148.

53 Many of the individual criticisms are available in Roderick MacFarquhar, *The*

Hundred Flowers Campaign and Chinese Intellectuals (New York: Praeger, 1960).

54 See *Eighth National Congress of the Communist Party of China* (Beijing: Foreign Languages Press, 1956).

55 Ibid., as cited in Frederick Teiwes, *Politics and Purges in China*, op. cit., p. 178.

56 Mao Zedong, "On the Correct Handling of Contradictions Among the People," *Selected Readings from the Works of Mao Zedong* (Beijing: Foreign Languages Press, 1971), pp. 432–479.

57 Ibid., p. 436.

58 Ibid., pp. 465–466.

59 For a good description of these see Walder, *China Under Mao*, op. cit., pp. 142–145.

60 Ibid., pp. 146–147.

61 Cited in Teiwes, *Politics and Purges*, op. cit., p. 218.

62 Cited in Dikötter, *The Tragedy of Liberation*, op. cit., p. 291.

63 The most detailed assessment of these editorials can be found in MacFarquhar, *The Origins of the Cultural Revolution 1*, op. cit., pp. 262–266.

64 Cited in Walder, *China Under Mao*, op. cit., p. 150.

65 The most thorough description of the Anti-Rightist Campaign can be found in Teiwes, *Politics & Purges in China*, op. cit., chapter 7. Also see Mu Fu-sheng, *The Wilting of the Hundred Flowers: The Chinese Intelligentsia Under Mao* (New York: Praeger, 1962).

66 Bruce Gilley, *Tiger on the Brink: Jiang Zemin and China's New Elite* (Berkeley: University of California Press, 1998), p. 42.

67 Ibid.

68 I am grateful to Robert Suettinger for this information.

69 Party History Research Center of the Central Committee of the CCP Central Committee, *History of the Chinese Communist Party, 1921–1990* (Beijing: Foreign Languages Press, 1991), pp. 264–265.

70 Mao Zedong, "The Foolish Old Man Who Removed the Mountains," *Selected Readings from the Works of Mao Zedong*, op. cit., pp. 320–323.

71 See Stuart Schram, "Mao Zedong and the Theory of Permanent Revolution," *The China Quarterly*, No. 46 (April–June 1971).

72 Stuart Schram, *The Thought of Mao Zedong* (Cambridge: Cambridge University Press, 1989), p. 131.

73 These quotations are all included in Li Gucheng (ed.), *A Glossary of Political*

Terms of the People's Republic of China (Hong Kong: Chinese University Press, 1995), pp. 40–41.

74 Cited in Roderick MacFarquhar, *The Origins of the Cultural Revolution 2: The Great Leap Forward, 1958–1960* (New York, Columbia University Press, 1983), p. 193.

75 All quotations are drawn from the text of Peng Dehuai's letter in Christopher B. Howe and Kenneth W. Walker (eds.), *The Foundations of the Chinese Planned Economy* (London: Palgrave Macmillan, 1990), pp. 88–93.

76 A first-hand account of the events at Lushan is provided by Mao's doctor. See Li Zhisui, *The Private Life of Chairman Mao* (London: Chatto & Windus, 1994), chapter 39.

77 Ibid., p. 223.

78 Ibid., p. 235. I was once shown a house on the campus of the "old" Central Party School, opposite the University of International Relations to the north-east of the Summer Palace, where I was told that Peng resided "before the Cultural Revolution."

79 As recounted by Jung Chang and Jan Halliday, *Mao: The Unknown Story* (London: Vintage Books, 2007), p. 651.

80 This information comes from Sydney Rittenberg, an American, who was also imprisoned at Qincheng at the time and would have daily access to the exercise yard, but only occasionally saw Peng Dehuai there. Discussion with Sydney Rittenberg, Ann Arbor Michigan, winter 1981. For Rittenberg's life story, see Sydney Rittenberg and Amanda Bennett, *The Man Who Stayed Behind* (New York: Simon & Schuster, 1993).

81 Quoted in CCP Central Committee Party History Research Center, *History of the Chinese Communist Party, 1921–1990*, op. cit., p. 280.

82 As cited in Nicholas Lardy, "The Chinese Economy Under Stress, 1958–1965," *Cambridge History of China*, op. cit., p. 374 (table 6).

83 See Li Zhisui, *The Private Life of Chairman Mao*, op. cit., chapter 42.

84 Ibid., p. 356. Dr. Li also recounted these in an oral interview: see CNN, "Cold War: China" (Episode 15): https://www.youtube.com/watch?v=gSPIonMrLq0&list=PL3H6z037pboGWTxs3xGP7HRGrQ5dOQdGc&index=16&t=0s.

85 Ibid., p. 356.

86 Ibid., p. 358.

87 Ibid.

88 Ji Chaozhu, *The Man on Mao's Right* (New York: Random House, 2008), p. 197.

89 For the text see: https://www.marxists.org/history/international/comintern/sino-soviet-split/cpc/leninism.htm.

90 The most significant of these were published between September 1963 and July 1964 in the form of "nine polemics." For analysis see John Gittings (ed.), *Survey of the Sino-Soviet Dispute: A Commentary and Extracts from the Recent Polemics, 1963–1967* (Oxford: Oxford University Press, 1968).

91 There are a number of good studies of the alliance and its dissolution, but perhaps the best is Odd Arne Westad (ed.), *Brothers in Arms: The Rise and Fall of the Sino-Soviet Alliance, 1945–1963* (Washington, DC and Stanford, CA: Woodrow Wilson Center Press and Stanford University Press, 1998). On the split itself, see Allen S. Whiting, "The Sino-Soviet Split," in MacFarquhar and Fairbank (eds.), *The Cambridge History of China*, Vol. 14, op. cit.; Donald S. Zagoria, *The Sino-Soviet Conflict, 1956–1961* (Princeton: Princeton University Press, 1962); Lorenz M. Lüthi, *The Sino-Soviet Split* (Princeton: Princeton University Press, 2008).

92 Of the many books on the Great Leap and its aftermath, see in particular Yang Jisheng, *Tombstone: The Great Chinese Famine, 1958–1962* (New York: Farrar, Straus, and Giroux, 2013); Frank Dikötter, *Mao's Great Famine: The History of China's Most Devastating Catastrophe, 1958–1962* (London: Bloomsbury Books, 2018).

93 National Bureau of Statistics, *Zhongguo Liushi Nian Tonji Ziliao Huibian*, op. cit., p. 37.

94 Ibid. Also see discussion of this period in Jonathan Fenby, *Modern China: The Fall and Rise of a Great Power, 1850 to the Present* (New York: Harper Collins, 2008), p. 414.

95 These documents included:

- Urgent Directive on Current Policies for Rural People's Communes (November 3, 1960).
- Urgent Directive on Guaranteeing Steel Production (December 3, 1960).
- Report on Examination of Some Problems in Propagating Mao Zedong Thought and the Revolutionary Deeds of Leaders (March 15, 1961).
- Regulations on the Work of Rural People's Communes (a.k.a. Sixty Articles on Agriculture, March 23, 1961 and revised/reissued June 12, 1961).
- Some Regulations on Improving the Work of Commerce (a.k.a. Forty Articles on Commerce, June 19, 1961).
- Regulations on Some Policies Concerning Urban and Rural Handicraft Industry (a.k.a. Thirty-Five Articles on Handicraft Industry, June 19, 1961).

- Directive and Report on Some Policy Matters in the Work of Natural Sciences (a.k.a. Fourteen Articles on Scientific Research).
- Provisional Regulations on Work in Institutions of Higher Education Directly Under the Ministry of Education (a.k.a. Sixty Articles on Work in Higher Education, September 15, 1961).
- Directive on the Question of Industry at Present (September 16, 1961).
- Regulations on the Work of State Industrial Enterprises (a.k.a. Seventy Articles Concerning Industrial Enterprises, September 16, 1961).
- Report on Improving Education and Management of Party Members (November 26, 1961).
- Suggestions on Certain Problems Concerning the Present Work in Literature and Art (a.k.a. Ten Articles on Literature and Art, April 30, 1962).
- Report on the National Conference on United Front Work (June 14, 1962).
- Outline Plan for the Development of Science and Technology (December 2, 1963).

These are all listed in CCP Central Committee Party History Research Center, *History of the Chinese Communist Party, 1919–1990*, op. cit.

96 See Mao Zedong, "Speech at the Tenth Plenum of the Eight Central Committee," in Stuart Schram (ed.), *Mao Zedong Unrehearsed: Talks and Letters, 1956–1971* (Middlesex: Penguin, 1974), pp. 188–196.

97 While the text of Mao's speech is not available, these quotations are contained verbatim in ibid., p. 301.

98 Ibid., p. 307.

99 These documents, with analysis of them, are available in Richard Baum and Frederick C. Teiwes (eds.), *Ssu-Ch'ing: The Socialist Education Movement of 1962–1966* (Berkeley: University of California Press, 1968).

100 The document was formally titled "Some Problems Currently Arising in the Course of the Rural Socialist Education Movement." See ibid., Appendix F, pp. 118–126.

101 For an excellent account of the SEM and this whole period see Maurice Meisner, *Mao's China and After* (New York: The Free Press, 1999, third edition), pp. 273–277. Also see, Frederick C. Teiwes, *Politics & Purges in China*, op. cit., chapter 11.

102 Roderick MacFarquhar and Michael Schoenhals, *Mao's Last Revolution* (Cambridge, MA: The Belknap Press, 2006).

103 Perhaps the best single compressed accounting and analysis remains Harry Harding, "The Chinese State in Crisis," in MacFarquhar and Fairbank (eds.),

The Cambridge History of China, Vol. 15 (Cambridge: Cambridge University Press, 1991), pp. 107–217. Also see Frank Dikötter, *The Cultural Revolution, 1962–1976: A People's History* (London: Bloomsbury Press, 2017).

104 See Yang Jisheng, *The World Turned Upside Down: A History of the Chinese Cultural Revolution* (Hong Kong: Cosmos Books, 2016; and New York: Farrar, Straus and Giroux, 2020). Yang Jisheng's previous monumental study *Tombstone: The Great Chinese Famine, 1958–1962*, op. cit., was also a searing and detailed examination of that catastrophe.

105 Jiang Qing, Kang Sheng, Chen Boda, Zhang Chunqiao, Wang Li, Guan Feng, Qi Benyu, and Yao Wenyuan.

106 Among the first-hand accounts available in English see Anne Thurston, *Enemies of the People: The Ordeal of the Intellectuals in China's Great Cultural Revolution* (New York: Knopf, 1987).

107 Only the Palace Museum in the Forbidden City was spared. See Jeannette Shambaugh Elliott with David Shambaugh, *The Odyssey of China's Imperial Art Treasures* (Seattle: University of Washington Press, 1997), chapter 6.

108 For further details about Chinese support for these communist insurgencies see David Shambaugh, *Where Great Powers Meet: America & China in Southeast Asia* (New York: Oxford University Press, 2021), chapter 4; William R. Heaton, "China and Southeast Asian Communist Movements: The Decline of Dual Track Diplomacy," *Asian Survey*, Vol. 22, No. 8 (August 1982).

109 Julia Lovell, *Maoism: A Global History* (New York: Knopf, 2019).

110 See Andrew G. Walder, *Agents of Disorder: Inside China's Cultural Revolution* (Cambridge, MA: The Belknap Press, 2019).

111 MacFarquhar and Schoenhals, *Mao's Last Revolution*, op. cit., p. 251.

112 Ji Chaozhu, *The Man on Mao's Right*, op. cit., p. 239.

113 For a study of the dynamics of such events see Elias Canetti, *Crowds and Power* (New York: Farrar, Straus & Giroux, 1984); Eric Hoffer, *The True Believer: Thoughts on the Nature of Mass Movements* (New York: Harper Books, 2002).

114 Ji Chaozhu, *The Man on Mao's Right*, op. cit., p. 229.

115 This and many other first-hand accounts are available in the "China in Revolution" series "The Mao Years: It is Right to Rebel! 1960–1976": https://www.youtube.com/watch?v=PJyoX_vrlns.

116 I visited Liu's cell in Kaifeng in 1984, which had been preserved as a memorial at the time. Liu's death is detailed in Jung Chang and Jon Halliday, *Mao: The Unknown Story*, op. cit., pp. 648–651.

117 See Robert F. Ash, "The Cultural Revolution as an Economic Phenomenon," in Werner Draghun and David S.G. Goodman (eds.), *China's Communist Revolutions: Fifty Years of the People's Republic* (London: Routledge Curzon, 2002).

118 State Statistical Bureau, *Zhongguo Tongji Nianjian 1998* [China Statistical Yearbook 1998] (Beijing: Tongji chubanshe, 1998), p. 57. I am grateful to Robert F. Ash for this information.

119 Ibid.

120 The *locus classicus* on the Third Front project is Barry Naughton, "The Third Front: Defense Industrialization in the Chinese Interior," *The China Quarterly*, No. 115 (Sept. 1988), pp. 351–386.

121 See Song Yongyi, "Chronology of Mass Killings During the Cultural Revolution, 1966–1976," Sciences Po, August 25, 2011: https://www.sciencespo.fr/mass-violence-war-massacre-resistance/en/document/chronology-mass-killings-during-chinese-cultural-revolution-1966–1976.

122 No Author, *A Great Trial in Chinese History: The Trial of the Lin Biao and Jiang Qing Counterrevolutionary Cliques* (Beijing: New World Press, 1981), p. 20.

123 Ji Chaozhu, *The Man on Mao's Right*, op. cit., p. 227.

124 Ibid., p. 226.

125 https://www.marxists.org/subject/china/documents/cpc/history/01.htm.

126 I have visited and been given a tour of Lin's former residence, subsequently the location of the Central Committee Compilation and Documentation Research Office (中央文献研究室).

127 For a superb accounting see Roderick MacFarquhar, "The Succession to Mao and the End of Maoism, 1969–1982," in MacFarquhar (ed.), *The Politics of China*, op. cit., pp. 265–273.

128 As cited in ibid., p. 272.

129 For a detailed account (by the daughter of one of Lin's co-conspirators) see Qiu Jin, *The Culture of Power: The Lin Biao Incident in the Cultural Revolution* (Stanford: Stanford University Press, 1999). For an unauthorized but highly detailed account (translated from Chinese) see Yao Mingle with Stanley Karnow, *The Conspiracy and Death of Lin Biao* (New York: Knopf, 1983).

130 Among the many fine studies see Margaret MacMillan, *Nixon and Mao: The Week that Changed the World* (New York: Random House, 2007).

131 Declassified "Memorandum of Conversation, February 21, 1972": https://china.usc.edu/mao-zedong-meets-richard-nixon-february-21-1972, Gerald R.

Ford Presidential Library, National Security Adviser Trip Briefing Books and Cables for President Ford, 1974–1976 (Box 19): https://digitalarchive.wilsoncenter.org/document/118064.

132 Perhaps the best compressed account is Jonathan D. Pollack, "The Opening to America," in MacFarquhar and Fairbank (eds.), *The Cambridge History of China*, Vol. 15, Part 2, op. cit., pp. 402–472.

133 For the text of the report see: https://digitalarchive.wilsoncenter.org/document/117146.pdf?v=81762c8101f0d237b21dca691c5824e4.

134 The following description derives from Li Zhisui, *The Private Life of Chairman Mao*, op. cit., chapters 80–81.

135 This description comes from Zhou and Mao's interpreter Ji Chaozhu (who may well have been the eyewitness). See Ji Chaozhu, *The Man on Mao's Right*, op. cit., p. 250.

136 Ji Chaozhu confirmed Dr. Li's account of Mao's condition, ibid., p. 254.

137 The description of Mao's health is drawn largely from Dr. Li's *The Private Life of Chairman Mao*, op. cit., chapters 82 and 84; and MacFarquhar and Schoenhals, *Mao's Last Revolution*, op. cit., pp. 413–414.

138 We will examine Hua Guofeng's role as leader in the next section, but for further information on his career up to this point see in particular Ting Wang, *Chairman Hua: Leader of the Chinese Communists* (London: C. Hurst & Co., 1980); Robert Weatherley, *Mao's Forgotten Successor: The Political Career of Hua Guofeng* (London: Palgrave Macmillan, 2010); Michel Oksenberg and Sai-cheung Yeung, "Hua Guofeng's Pre-Cultural Revolution Hunan Years, 1949–1966," *The China Quarterly*, No. 69 (March 1977), pp. 3–53.

139 The most thorough account of this period is Frederick C. Teiwes and Warren Sun, *The End of the Maoist Era: Chinese Politics During the Twilight of the Cultural Revolution, 1972–1976* (Armonk, NY: M.E. Sharpe, 2007).

140 See: https://www.youtube.com/watch?v=EKK3VeLPVR8.

141 See Roderick MacFarquhar, "The Succession to Mao and the End of Maoism," in *The Cambridge History of China*, Vol. 15, op. cit., p. 358.

142 For a first-hand account with photos, see David Zweig, "A Photo Essay on Failed Reform," *China Perspectives* (March 2016): http://journals.openedition.org/chinaperspectives/6893.

143 See MacFarquhar, "The Succession to Mao and the End of Maoism," in *The Cambridge History of China*, Vol. 15, op. cit., p. 364.

144 Mao did receive New Zealand Prime Minister Muldoon on this date, but it is unclear if he gave Hua the instructions in his presence or separately. Ji Chaozhu,

who interpreted on this occasion, makes no mention of Hua's presence or the supposed instruction to him by Mao. See Ji Chaozhu, *The Man on Mao's Right*, op. cit., p. 288.

145 Li Zhisui, *The Private Life of Chairman Mao*, op. cit., p. 623.

146 Ibid., p. 625.

Chapter 3

1 Deng Xiaoping, "How to Restore Agricultural Production," in *Selected Works of Deng Xiaoping, Volume I (1938–1965)* (Beijing: Foreign Languages Press, 1995).

2 Not surprisingly, there are a number of fine biographies in English of Deng and his career. As this chapter is a compressed account of only Deng's ten years in power, readers are directed to these other studies for fuller accounting of Deng's life and career: see Ezra Vogel, *Deng Xiaoping and the Transformation of China* (Cambridge, MA: Belknap Press, 2011); David S.G. Goodman, *Deng Xiaoping and the Chinese Revolution: A Political Biography* (London and New York: Routledge, 1994); David Shambaugh (ed.), *Deng Xiaoping: Portrait of a Chinese Statesman* (Oxford: Clarendon Press, 1995); Uli Franz, *Deng Xiaoping: China's Reformer* (New York: Harcourt, Brace, Jovanovich, 1988); David Bonavia, *Deng* (Hong Kong: Longman, 1989); Michael Dillon, *Deng Xiaoping: The Man Who Made Modern China* (London: I.B. Tauris, 2014); Alexander V. Pantsov and Steven I. Levine, *Deng Xiaoping: A Revolutionary Life* (Oxford: Oxford University Press, 2017); Richard Evans, *Deng Xiaoping and the Making of Modern China* (New York: Viking Press, 1994); Benjamin Yang, *Deng: A Political Biography* (London: Routledge, 1997).

3 See Harry Harding, *China's Second Revolution: Reform After Mao* (Washington, DC: Brookings Institution Press, 1987).

4 This is described, based on Chinese sources, by Richard Baum, *Burying Mao: Chinese Politics in the Age of Deng Xiaoping* (Princeton: Princeton University Press, 1994), p. 42 and footnote 58.

5 Party History Research Center of the Central Committee, *History of the Chinese Communist Party: A Chronology of Events, 1921–1990* (Beijing Foreign Languages Press, 1991), p. 381.

6 Vogel, *Deng Xiaoping and the Transformation of China,* op. cit., p. 199.

7 On Deng's maneuverings against Hua also see Robert Weatherley, *Mao's Forgotten Successor: The Political Career of Hua Guofeng* (London: Palgrave Macmillan, 2010), chapter 6.

8 Deng Xiaoping, "Speech to National Science Conference," March 18, 1978: http://www.china.org.cn/english/features/dengxiaoping/103390.htm.

9 See Kjeld Erik Brodsgaard, "The Democracy Movement in China, 1978–1979: Opposition Movements, Wall Poster Campaigns, and Underground Journals," *Asian Survey*, Vol. 21, No. 7 (July 1981), pp. 747–774.

10 The following summation of the plenum draws from Party History Research Center of the Central Committee (ed.), *History of the Chinese Communist Party*, op. cit., pp. 393–395.

11 Roderick MacFarquhar, "The Succession to Mao and the End of Maoism," in MacFarquhar (ed.), *The Politics of China: Sixty Years of the People's Republic* (Cambridge: Cambridge University Press, third edition, 2011), pp. 317–318.

12 "Communiqué of the Third Plenary Session of the Eleventh Central Committee of the Communist Party of China," adopted December 29, 1978, *Beijing Review*, No. 52 (August 25, 2020): http://www.bjreview.com/Special_Reports/2018/40th_Anniversary_of_Reform_and_Opening_up/Timeline/201806/t20180626_800133641.html.

13 Deng Xiaoping, "Adhere to the Party Line and Improve Methods of Work," in Central Bureau of Compilation and Translation (eds.), *Selected Works of Deng Xiaoping, Volume II (1975–1982)* (Beijing: Foreign Languages Press, 1984), p. 280.

14 Yang Zhongmei, *Hu Yaobang: A Chinese Biography* (Armonk, NY: M.E. Sharpe, 1988), pp. 120–122.

15 I am indebted to Robert Suettinger for this information. Suettinger is completing a definitive biography of Hu Yaobang.

16 See David Shambaugh, *The Making of a Premier: Zhao Ziyang's Provincial Career* (Boulder: Westview Press, 1984). Other biographies of Zhao include Zhao Wei, *The Biography of Zhao Ziyang* (Hong Kong: Educational and Cultural Press, 1989); Willy Wo-Lap Lam, *The Era of Zhao Ziyang* (Hong Kong: A.B. Books & Stationary International, 1989); Zhao Ziyang (with Adi Ignatius), *Prisoner of the State: The Secret Journal of Premier Zhao Ziyang* (New York: Simon & Schuster, 2010).

17 Zhao Wei, *Zhao Ziyang Zhuan* (赵紫阳转) [Biography of Zhao Ziyang] (Hong Kong: Wenhua jiaoyu chubanshe, 1988), chapter 4.

18 This brief description of Zhao's career is drawn from, and expanded upon in, David Shambaugh, *The Making of a Premier*, ibid.

19 Deng Xiaoping, "Remarks Made After Hearing Report from the Central

Committee's Leading Group for Financial and Economic Affairs, September 13, 1986," in *Selected Works of Deng Xiaoping, Volume III (1982–1992)*, (Beijing: Foreign Languages Press, 1994), p. 179.

20 China National Bureau of Statistics data. I am indebted to Robert F. Ash for providing these data.

21 https://www.unicef.cn/en/figure-21-gdp-capita-19782017.

22 I am grateful to David M. Lampton for noting this. See Lampton's *Following the Leader: Ruling China from Deng Xiaoping to Xi Jinping* (Berkeley: University of California Press, 2014), p. 16.

23 Deng Xiaoping, "On the Reform of the System of Party and State Leadership," *Selected Works, Vol. II (1975–1982)*: https://dengxiaopingworks.wordpress.com/2013/02/25/on-the-reform-of-the-system-of-party-and-state-leadership/.

24 See Zhang Xiaoming, "China's 1979 War with Vietnam: A Reassessment," *The China Quarterly*, No. 184 (December 2005), pp. 851–874; King V. Chen, *China's War with Vietnam* (Stanford: Hoover Institution Press, 1987).

25 Deng Xiaoping, "Streamline the Army and Raise its Combat Effectiveness," *Selected Works, Vol. II (1975–1982)*: https://dengxiaopingworks.wordpress.com/2013/02/25/streamline-the-army-and-raise-its-combat-effectiveness/.

26 For studies of the PLA during this period see David Shambaugh, *Modernizing China's Military: Progress, Problems & Prospects* (Berkeley: University of California Press, 2003); David Shambaugh (ed.), *China's Military in Transition* (Oxford: Clarendon Press, 1997); Paul H.B. Godwin (ed.), *The Chinese Defense Establishment: Continuity and Change in the 1980s* (Boulder: Westview Press, 1983).

27 Deng Xiaoping, "Answers to the Italian Journalist Oriana Fallaci," August 21 and 23, 1980: http://en.people.cn/dengxp/vol2/text/b1470.html.

28 The full indictment and trial proceedings are included in *A Great Trial in Chinese History: The Trial of the Lin Biao and Jiang Qing Counterrevolutionary Cliques* (Beijing: New World Press, 1981).

29 See Deng Xiaoping, "Remarks on Successive Drafts of the 'Resolution on Certain Questions in the History of Our Party Since the Founding of the People's Republic of China'," in Deng Xiaoping, *On Reform* (New York: CN Times Books, 2013), pp. 31–57. The quotations in this paragraph all come from ibid.

30 The full English and Chinese texts of the *Resolution* can be found at: https://

digitalarchive.wilsoncenter.org/document/121344.pdf?v=d461ad5001da989b8f96cc1dfb3c8ce7.

31 Deng Xiaoping, "Remarks Made After Hearing Report from the Central Committee's Leading Group for Financial and Economic Affairs, September 13, 1986," in *Selected Works of Deng Xiaoping, Volume III (1982–1992)*, op. cit., p. 179.

32 Deng Xiaoping, "On the Reform of the System of Party and State Leadership," *Selected Works, Vol. II (1975–1982)*, op. cit.

33 Deng Xiaoping, "Some Comments on Work in Science and Education," *Selected Works, Vol. II*, op. cit.: https://dengxiaopingworks.wordpress.com/2013/02/25/some-comments-on-work-in-science-and-education/.

34 These are best described by Richard Baum, "The Road to Tiananmen: Chinese Politics in the 1980s," in Roderick MacFarquhar (ed.), *The Politics of China*, op. cit., chapter 5.

35 Deng Xiaoping, "Adhere to the Party Line and Improve Methods of Work," *Selected Works, Vol. II (1975–1982)* (Beijing: Foreign Languages Press, 1984), p. 267.

36 Vogel, *Deng Xiaoping and the Transformation of China*, op. cit., p. 378.

37 Ibid., p. 377.

38 Deng Xiaoping, "There Is No Fundamental Contradiction Between Socialism and a Market Economy," in Deng Xiaoping, *On Reform*, op. cit., p. 90.

39 On this point see Barry Naughton, "Deng Xiaoping: The Economist," in David Shambaugh (ed.), *Deng Xiaoping: Portrait of a Chinese Statesman*, op. cit.

40 Deng Xiaoping, "Make a Success of Special Economic Zones and Open More Cities to the Outside World," excerpt from talk with leading members of the Central Committee, February 24, 1984, in *Selected Works of Deng Xiaoping, Volume III*, op. cit., pp. 61–62.

41 Julian Gewirtz, *Unlikely Partners: Chinese Reformers, Western Economists, and the Making of Global China* (Cambridge, MA: Harvard University Press, 2017).

42 See David Zweig, *Rural Restructuring in the Reform Era* (Armonk, NY: M.E. Sharpe, 1997).

43 National Bureau of Statistics, *Zhongguo Tongji Zhaiyao, 2020* [China Statistical Abstract] (Beijing: Zhongguo tongji chubanshe, 2020), p. 61.

44 *Zhongguo Xiangzhen Qiye Nianjian, 1978–1987* (Beijing: Nongye chubanshe, 1989).

45 National Bureau of Statistics, *Xin Zhongguo Liushi Nian Tongji Ziliao Huibian*, op. cit.

46 See Dorothy J. Solinger, *From Lathes to Looms: China's Industrial Policy in Comparative Perspective, 1979–1982* (Stanford: Stanford University Press, 1991).

47 *Zhongguo Tongji Nianjian, 1995* (Beijing: Tongji chubanshe, 1995), p. 263.

48 Deng Xiaoping, *Selected Works, Vol. III*, op. cit., pp. 104–106.

49 See David Shambaugh, "China's Defense Industries: Indigenous and Foreign Procurement," in Godwin (ed.), *The Chinese Defense Establishment*, op. cit.

50 Barry Naughton, *Growing Out of the Plan: Chinese Economic Reform, 1978–1993* (Cambridge: Cambridge University Press, 2010).

51 For a good discussion of enterprise reform and its impact on workers see Harry Harding, *China's Second Revolution*, op. cit., pp. 113–120.

52 Quoted in "The Sichuan Experiment with Enterprises," *Beijing Review*, No. 14, April 6, 1981.

53 Triangular debt refers to the government loaning money to one SOE which, in turn re-loaned to another, and both would be unable to repay the debt to the state.

54 Harding, *China's Second Revolution*, op. cit., p. 112.

55 Deng Xiaoping, "We Must Rationalize Prices and Accelerate the Reform," May 19, 1988, *Selected Works, Vol. III*, op. cit., pp. 257–258; Deng Xiaoping, "We Must Continue to Emancipate Our Minds and Accelerate the Reform," ibid., pp. 259–260.

56 See Dorothy J. Solinger, *China's Transition from Socialism: Statist Legacies and Market Reforms, 1980–1990* (Armonk, NY: M.E. Sharpe, 1993).

57 The best study of this is Dali L. Yang, *Remaking the Chinese Leviathan: Market Transition and the Politics of Governance in China* (Stanford: Stanford University Press, 2006).

58 See Xiaobo Lu and Elizabeth J. Perry (eds.), *Danwei: The Changing Chinese Workplace in Historical and Comparative Perspective* (Armonk, NY: M.E. Sharpe, 1997). By far, the best account of the pre-reform *danwei* system is Andrew G. Walder, *Communist Neo-Traditionalism: Work and Authority in Chinese Industry* (Berkeley: University of California Press, 1988).

59 For an excellent discussion of Deng's approach to talent cultivation see Martin King Whyte, "Deng Xiaoping: The Social Reformer," in David Shambaugh (ed.), *Deng Xiaoping: Portrait of a Chinese Statesman*, op. cit.

60 Deng Xiaoping, "On the Reform of the System of Party and State Leadership," in *On Reform*, op. cit., pp. 191–214.

61 Deng Xiaoping, "On Reform of the Political Structure" (excerpts from four talks), in *Selected Works, Vol. III*, op. cit., pp. 178–181.

62 Richard Baum, *Burying Mao: Chinese Politics in the Age of Deng Xiaoping* (Princeton: Princeton University Press, 1994), p. 145.

63 The best study of this process is Melanie Manion, *The Retirement of Revolutionaries in China: Public Policies, Social Norms, Private Interests* (Princeton: Princeton University Press, 1993).

64 Richard Baum, "The Road to Tiananmen: Chinese Politics in the 1980s," in MacFarquahar (ed.), *The Politics of China*, op. cit., p. 352.

65 Richard Baum, *Burying Mao*, op. cit., p. 139.

66 See the special symposium "The 'Singapore Model' and China's Neo-Authoritarian Dream," *The China Quarterly* (December 2018).

67 See, for example, the discussion in Baum, *Burying Mao*, op. cit., pp. 220–222.

68 For an overview of Deng's role as an international statesman and his foreign policy see in particular Michael Yahuda, "Deng Xiaoping: The Stateman," in David Shambaugh (ed.), *Deng Xiaoping: Portrait of a Chinese Statesman*, op. cit., pp. 143–164.

69 See David Shambaugh, *Where Great Powers Meet: America & China in Southeast Asia* (New York: Oxford University Press, 2021), chapter 4.

70 Deng Xiaoping, "One Country, Two Systems," in *Selected Works, Vol. III*, op. cit., pp. 68–71.

71 For further description see my "The Post-Mao State," in David Shambaugh (ed.), *The Modern Chinese State* (Cambridge: Cambridge University Press, 2000).

72 Among the many studies, I particularly recommend Michael Fathers and Andrew Higgins, *Tiananmen: The Rape of Peking* (London: The Independent, 1989); and Michel Oksenberg, Lawrence Sullivan, and Marc Lambert (eds.), *Beijing Spring 1989: Confrontation and Conflict—The Basic Documents* (London: Routledge, 1990).

73 Zhao Ziyang, *Prisoner of the State: The Secret Journal of Premier Zhao Ziyang* (New York: Simon & Schuster, 2010); Zhao Ziyang, *The Collected Works of Zhao Ziyang:1980–1989* [赵紫阳文集] (Hong Kong: Chinese University Press, 2016, 4 volumes in Chinese).

74 Deng Xiaoping, "Address to Officers at the Rank of General and Above in Command of the Troops Enforcing Martial Law in Beijing," in *Selected Works, Vol. III*, op. cit., pp. 294–299.

75 Deng Xiaoping, "A Letter to the Political Bureau of the Central Committee of the Communist Party of China," *Selected Works, Vol. III*, op. cit., pp. 312–313.

76 See David Shambaugh, "The Fourth and Fifth Plenary Sessions of the 13th Central Committee," *The China Quarterly*, No. 120 (December 1989), pp. 852–862.

77 Deng Xiaoping, "We Are Confident That We Can Handle China's Affairs Well: Excerpt from a Talk with Professor Tsung-Dao Lee of Columbia University," *Selected Works, Vol. III*, op. cit., pp. 314–317.

78 Quoted in Joseph Fewsmith (citing Hong Kong media), "Chinese Politics Since Tiananmen," in MacFarquhar (ed.), *The Politics of China*, op. cit., p. 482.

79 Ibid., p. 483.

80 Deng Xiaoping, "Excerpts From Talks Given in Wuchang, Shenzhen, Zhuhai, and Shanghai," *Selected Works, Vol. III*, op. cit., pp. 358–370.

Chapter 4

1 Jiang Zemin, "The Future of Socialism Remains as Bright as Ever (Excerpts of Remarks to Fidel Castro)," November 21–22, 1993, *Selected Works of Jiang Zemin, Vol. I*, (Beijing: Foreign Languages Press, 2010), p. 327.

2 This line of analysis and argument is best exemplified by Andrew Nathan in his classic article "China's Resilient Authoritarianism," *Journal of Democracy*, Vol. 14, No. 1 (January 2003), pp. 6–17. Nathan was not alone, though, in putting forward this argument at the time—so did I, Joseph Fewsmith, Kjeld Erik Brodsgaard, Zheng Yongnian, and other scholars of the CCP.

3 This positive retrospective perspective has become more apparent over time when contrasted with Hu's and Xi's rule. For example, even as late as 2001, as Jiang neared the end of his term, a symposium on Jiang's rule by several noted Western Sinologists did not give him very positive assessments: see the articles in *The China Journal*, No. 45 (January 2001).

4 There are two thorough biographies of Jiang Zemin: Bruce Gilley, *Tiger on the Brink: Jiang Zemin and China's New Elite* (Berkeley: University of California Press, 1998); and Robert Lawrence Kuhn, *The Man Who Changed China: The Life and Legacy of Jiang Zemin* (New York: Crown Publishers, 2004). Kuhn's biography benefitted from interviews with a number of official associates and family members. Two other volumes also provide good overviews of the Jiang period: Willy Wo-Lap Lam, *The Era of Jiang Zemin* (New York: Prentice Hall,

1999); Hung-mao Tien and Yun-han Chu (eds.), *China Under Jiang Zemin* (Boulder, CO: Lynne Rienner Publishers, 2000).

5 Cited in Gilley, ibid., p. 23.

6 China had seven ministries of machine building until the 1980s. Only the first dealt with civilian industry, the other six were all military related. For an analysis of this system see my "China's Defense Industries: Indigenous and Foreign Procurement," in Paul H.B. Godwin (ed.), *The Chinese Defense Establishment: Continuity and Change in the 1980s* (Boulder: Westview Press, 1983).

7 See *Selected Works of Jiang Zemin, Vol. I*, op. cit.

8 See Timothy Garton Ash, *The Magic Lantern: The Revolution of '89 Witnessed in Warsaw, Budapest, Berlin, and Prague* (New York: Random House, 1993).

9 Jiang Zemin, "Speech at the Fourth Plenary Session of the Thirteenth Central Committee of the Communist Party of China," *Selected Works of Jiang Zemin, Vol. I*, op. cit., pp. 54–60.

10 Jiang Zemin, "Basic Conclusions Drawn from New China's Forty-Year History," ibid., pp. 64–66.

11 Jiang Zemin, "We Chinese have Always Cherished Our National Integrity," ibid., pp. 67–70.

12 Jiang Zemin, "Strive to Make the Party into a Stauncher Vanguard of the Working Class," ibid., pp. 83–99.

13 Jiang Zemin, "Promote the Great New Undertaking of Party Building," ibid., pp. 392–401.

14 Richard Baum, *Burying Mao: Chinese Politics in the Age of Deng Xiaoping* (Princeton: Princeton University Press, 1994), p. 330.

15 See David Shambaugh, *China's Communist Party: Atrophy & Adaptation* (Washington, DC and Berkeley, CA: The Woodrow Wilson Center Press and University of California Press, 2008), particularly chapter 4. Some of the following discussion in this section draws on that earlier analysis.

16 Bo Xingxiang and Cui Zhiying, "Dong-Ou jubian de lishi jiaoxun: Tan zhizhengdang yu gongren jieji de guanxi" [The Drastic Changes in Eastern Europe and Their Historical Lessons: Discussing the Relationship Between Ruling Parties and the Working Class], *Sulian yu Dong-Ou Wenti* [Issues in the Soviet Union and Eastern Europe], No. 6 (1990), pp. 7–9.

17 See Shambaugh, *China's Communist Party*, op. cit., chapter 4 and table 4.1.

18 Andrew Nathan and Bruce Gilley, *China's New Rulers: The Secret Files* (New York: New York Review Books, 2002), p. 85.

19 The following analysis is drawn from chapter 4 in my *China's Future* (Cambridge: Polity Press, 2016).

20 See Mary Elise Sarotte, *The Collapse: The Accidental Opening of the Berlin Wall* (New York: Basic Books, 2014).

21 See Richard Baum, "The Fifteenth National Party Congress: Jiang Takes Command?" *The China Quarterly*, No. 153 (March 1998), pp. 141–156.

22 Jiang Zemin, "Hold High the Banner of Deng Xiaoping Theory for All-Around Advancement of the Cause of Building Socialism with Chinese Characteristics Into the 21st Century," report delivered to the 15th National Congress of the Communist Party of China, September 12, 1997, section VI, available at: http://www.bjreview.com/document/txt/2011-03/25/content_363499_10.htm.

23 These are elaborated in my chapter "Rebuilding the Party: The Organizational Dimension," in David Shambaugh, *China's Communist Party: Atrophy & Adaptation*, op. cit., chapter 7.

24 *Selected Works of Jiang Zemin, Vol. III* (Beijing: Foreign Languages Press, 2013), pp. 228–232.

25 See Ian Johnson, "China Stressing Civic Virtues in a New Campaign—But Many Just See Another Ploy by Jiang to Enhance His Power," *Baltimore Sun*, October 10, 1996.

26 Jiang Zemin, "Leading Cadres Must Stress Politics," *Selected Works, Vol. I*, op. cit., pp. 444–448, and "Stress Politics," pp. 503–505.

27 Jiang Zemin, "Stress Study, Politics, and Integrity," ibid., pp. 472–475; "The 'Three Stresses' is a New Endeavor to Strengthen Party Building," *Selected Works of Jiang Zemin, Vol. II* (Beijing: Foreign Languages Press, 2012), pp. 350–361.

28 Jiang Zemin, "Better Effectuate the Three Represents Under the New Historical Conditions," *Selected Works, Vol. III*, op. cit., pp. 1–5; "Always Implementing the Three Represents is the Foundation for Building the Party, the Cornerstone for its Governance, and the Source of its Strength," ibid., pp. 6–32.

29 Jiang Zemin, "Build a Moderately Prosperous Society in All Respects and Initiate a New Phase in Socialism with Chinese Characteristics," *Selected Works, Vol. III*, op. cit., pp. 511–561.

30 Jiang Zemin, "Eulogy at Comrade Deng Xiaoping's Memorial Ceremony," *Selected Works, Vol. I*, op. cit., pp. 611–624.

31 This section is adapted from my *China's Communist Party*, op. cit., pp. 111–114.

32 Jiang Zemin, "Speech at a Meeting Celebrating the 80th Anniversary of the Founding of the Communist Party of China, July 1, 2001," *Selected Works, Vol. III*, op. cit., pp. 259–293.

33 Author's interview with Liu Ji, Madrid, Spain, November 7, 2006.

34 "Investigating Work in Jiangsu, Zhejiang, and Shanghai, Jiang Zemin Stresses Going Deep into the Grass Roots, Summing Up Practice, Actively Exploring, Clearing the Way to Forge Ahead, and Building the Party in Line with the Demands of the 'Three Represents'," Xinhua, May 15, 2000.

35 Author's interview with Zheng Bijian, Washington, DC, November 12, 2003.

36 Sun Chengbin and Wang Lili, "The 'Three Represents': The CPC's Party Building Program for the New Period," Xinhua, July 2, 2000.

37 Bruce Dickson, *Red Capitalists: The Party, Private Entrepreneurs, and Prospects for Political Change in China* (Cambridge: Cambridge University Press, 2003).

38 Jane Duckett, *The Entrepreneurial State* (London: Routledge, 1998).

39 Bruce Dickson, "Beijing's Ambivalent Reformers," *Current History* (September 2004).

40 This section draws on my "China's Commander-in-Chief: Jiang Zemin and the PLA," in C. Dennison Lane et al. (eds.), *Chinese Military Modernization* Washington, DC and London: The AEI Press and Kegan Paul International, 1996); and *Modernizing China's Military: Progress, Problems, and Prospects* (Berkeley: University of California Press, 2002), chapter 2. Also see You Ji, "Jiang Zemin's Command of the Military," *The China Journal*, No. 45 (January 2001), pp. 131–138; and Ellis Joffe, "The People's Liberation Army and Politics: After the Fifteenth Congress," in Tien and Chu (eds.), *China Under Jiang Zemin*, op. cit.

41 Quoted in Li Guoqiang et al., *Zhonggong Junfang Jiangling* [High-Ranking Officers of the Chinese Communist Military] (Hong Kong: Wide Angle Press, 1992), p. 6. Author's translation.

42 Source: World Bank. See: https://www.macrotrends.net/countries/CHN/china/military-spending-defense-budget.

43 See, for example, Jiang Zemin, "The Army Needs to be Qualified Politically and Competent Militarily and Have a Fine Work Style, Strict Discipline and Adequate Logistics Support," *Selected Works, Vol. I*, op. cit., pp. 131–133; "Concerning Our Military Strategic Principle and Issues of Defense Technology," ibid., pp. 134–141; "Uphold the Absolute Leadership of the Party Over the Army," ibid., pp. 476–484; "Achieve Cross-Century Strategic Development Goals for Modernizing National Defense and the Army," *Selected*

Works, Vol. II, op. cit., pp. 82–90; "Mechanization and Informationization are Dual Historical Tasks of Army Building," *Selected Works, Vol. III*, pp. 154–164; "The Distinctly Chinese Revolution in Military Affairs," ibid., pp. 562–584; "My Heart Will Always Be With the People's Army," ibid., pp. 587–593.

44 "Jiang Zhuxi Diaocha Jiceng Budui" [Chairman Jiang Inspects Basic-Level Units], *Jiefangjun Bao*, August 2, 1993, p. 3.

45 You Ji, "Jiang Zemin's Command of the Military," *The China Journal*, op. cit., p. 136.

46 Lu Ren, "Jiang Zemin Presides Over Military Hierarchy Reshuffle," *Jing Bao* (Hong Kong), December 5, 1992, translated in FBIS-China, December 17, 1992.

47 Willy Wo-Lap Lam, *China After Deng Xiaoping* (Singapore: John Wiley & Sons, 1995), p. 214.

48 The new appointments of senior military staff are detailed in my *Modernizing China's Military*, op. cit., pp. 38–46.

49 Jiang Zemin, "The Army Must Cease All Commercial Activities," *Selected Works, Vol. II*, op. cit., pp. 175–183.

50 See David Shambaugh, "Commentary on Civil-Military Relations in China: The Search for New Paradigms," in James Mulvenon and Andrew Yang (eds.), *Seeking Truth From Facts: A Retrospective on Chinese Military Studies in the Post-Mao Era* (Santa Monica: The Rand Corporation, 2001); and "Civil-Military Relations in China: Party-Army or National Military?" in Kjeld Erik Brodsgaard and Zheng Yongnian (eds.), *Bringing the Party Back In: How China Is Governed* (Singapore: Eastern Universities Press, 2004).

51 Jiang Zemin, "Concerning China's Establishment of a Socialist Market Economy," *Selected Works, Vol. I*, op. cit., pp. 188–194.

52 Jiang Zemin, "Accelerate Economic Development of the Yangzi River Delta and Valley," ibid., pp. 195–198.

53 Jiang Zemin, "Give High Priority to Problems Facing Agriculture, Rural Areas, and Farmers," ibid., pp. 248–268.

54 Jiang Zemin, "Fully and Correctly Grasp the Situation and Maintain Steady Momentum in Economic Development," ibid., pp. 285–290.

55 These reforms are covered well in Nicholas R. Lardy, "The Challenge of Economic Reform and Social Stability," in Tian and Chu (eds.), *China Under Jiang Zemin*, op. cit.

56 The one exception was Jiang's June 26, 1995 speech "Reform State-Owned Enterprises the Chinese Way," *Selected Works, Vol. I*, op. cit., pp. 429–423.

57 See, for example, Jiang Zemin, "Encourage Original Innovation," *Selected Works, Vol. III*, op. cit., pp. 256–258; "Innovation is the Essence of Science," ibid., pp. 98–103.

58 Jiang Zemin, "Effectively Carry Out the Century Project to Develop Western China on a Large Scale," ibid., pp. 56–62; "Seize the Opportunity to Implement the Strategy of Large-Scale Development of the West," *Selected Works, Vol. II*, op. cit., pp. 331–338.

59 References to these speeches and Jiang's role in developing the "going out" policy are traced in some detail in Chen Yangyong, "Jiang Zemin 'zou chuqu' zhanlue de xingcheng jiqi zhongyao yiyi" [Jiang Zemin's "Going Out" Strategic Influence and Important Formulation], available at: http://theory.people.com/cn/GB/40557/138172/138202/8311431.html.

60 "Full Text of Jiang Zemin's Report to the 14th Party Congress," available at: http://www.bjreview.com.cn/document/txt/2011-03/29/content_363504.htm.

61 "Full Text of Jiang Zemin's Report to the Fifteenth Party Congress," available at: http://english.people.com.cn/200211/18/eng20021118_106984.shtml.

62 Chen Yangyong, "Jiang Zemin 'zou chuqu' zhanlue de xingcheng jiqi zhongyao yiyi," op. cit.

63 See David Shambaugh, *China Goes Global: The Partial Power* (New York: Oxford University Press, 2013), chapter 5.

64 World Bank data: https://data.worldbank.org/indicator/NY.GDP.MKTP.KD.ZG?locations=CN.

65 Li Shi, "Changes in Income Inequality During the Past Three Decades": https://hceconomics.uchicago.edu/sites/default/files/file_uploads/LI%20Shi%20presentation.pdf.

66 Jiang Zemin, "Establish a New Security Concept Suited to the Needs of the Times," *Selected Works, Vol. II*, op. cit., pp. 305–310; and "Promote the Disarmament Process and Safeguard World Security," March 26, 1999, available at: http://ee.china-embassy.org/eng/xnyfgk/t112774.htm.

67 Jiang Zemin, "Speech at the Fourth Plenary Session of the Thirteenth Central Committee of the Communist Party of China," op. cit.

68 "Memorandum of Conversation: Meeting Between General Secretary Jiang Zemin et al.," December 10, 1989, available on Chinafile, "U.S.–China Diplomacy After Tiananmen: Documents from the George H.W. Bush Library": https://www.chinafile.com/library/reports/us-china-diplomacy-after-tiananmen-documents-george-hw-bush-presidential-library. The specific Memcon

with Jiang can be found at: https://assets.documentcloud.org/documents/6184537/U-S-Government-Documents-Following-Tiananmen.pdf.

69 Robert L. Suettinger, *Beyond Tiananmen: The Politics of U.S.-China Relations, 1989–2000* (Washington, DC: Brookings Institution Press, 2003), pp. 181–182.

70 Thomas Friedman, "The Pacific Summit: Leaders at Summit Seek Strong Pacific Community," *New York Times*, November 21, 1993: https://www.nytimes.com/1993/11/21/world/the-pacific-summit-leaders-at-summit-seek-strong-pacific-community.html.

71 Daniel Williams, "Chinese Leader Plays to Audience at Home," *Washington Post*, November 21, 1993: https://www.washingtonpost.com/archive/politics/1993/11/21/chinese-leader-plays-to-audience-at-home/0840ca60-ed02-409f-bf6b-be7d9bdcd7a8/.

72 Suettinger, *Beyond Tiananmen*, op. cit., p. 182.

73 Ibid., p. 277.

74 "Press Conference by President Clinton and President Jiang Zemin," October 29, 1997: http://www.state.gov/www/regions/eap/971029_clinton_china2.html.

75 The White House, "Joint U.S.-China Statement," October 29, 1997, available at: http://www.state.gov/www/regions/eap/971029_usc_jtsmt.html.

76 See the description in Robert Lawrence Kuhn, *The Man Who Changed China*, op. cit., pp. 446–450.

77 Interview with Chinese Foreign Ministry official, November 12, 2001.

78 This section is drawn from my *China Goes Global*, chapter 3.

79 For a useful survey of the Sino-Russian relationship in the immediate post-Soviet era, see Jeanne L. Wilson, *Strategic Partners: Russian-Chinese Relations in the Post-Soviet Era* (Armonk, NY: M.E. Sharpe, 2004).

80 This period is well documented in Elizabeth Wishnick, *Mending Fences: The Evolution of Moscow's China Policy from Brezhnev to Yeltsin* (Seattle: University of Washington Press, 2001), chapter 8.

81 See Bobo Lo, *Axis of Convenience: Moscow, Beijing, and the New Geopolitics* (London and Washington, DC: Chatham House and Brookings Institution Press, 2008); James Bellacqua (ed.), *The Future of China–Russia Relations* (Lexington, KY: University of Kentucky Press, 2010).

82 Cited in Kuhn, *The Man Who Changed China*, op. cit., p. 451.

83 See, for example, the discussion in Willy Wo-Lap Lam, *Chinese Politics in the Hu Jintao Era* (Armonk, NY: M.E. Sharpe, 2006), pp. 15–16.
84 This process is described in detail in Lam, ibid., pp. 16–18.

Chapter 5

1 Hu Jintao, "Full Text of the Keynote Speech at the Grand Gathering Marking the 90th Founding Anniversary of the CPC," in *Selected Works of Hu Jintao* (San Bernardino, CA: Intercultural Publishing, 2012), p. 142.
2 See Hu Jintao, *Hu Jintao Wenxuan, Vol. I* (Beijing: Renmin Ribao chubanshe, 2016).
3 Kerry Brown, *Hu Jintao: China's Silent Ruler* (Singapore: World Scientific, 2012).
4 Discussion with British official, October 2009, Beijing.
5 Discussion of Hu's background and biography can be found in Cheng Li, *China's Leaders: The New Generation* (Lanham, MD: Rowman & Littlefield, 2001); Richard Daniel Ewing, "Hu Jintao: The Making of a Chinese General Secretary," *The China Quarterly*, No. 173 (March 2003), pp. 17–34; Kerry Brown, *Hu Jintao: China's Silent Ruler*, op. cit.; Willy Wo-Lap Lam, *Chinese Politics in the Hu Jintao Era* (Armonk, NY: M.E. Sharpe, 2006); David Hsieh, "A Man for All Seasons," *Asiaweek*, June 26, 1998; "Hu Jintao," *China Vitae*: https://www.chinavitae.com/biography/Hu_Jintao/full.
6 For an excellent discussion of Jiang Nanxiang's outsized impact on Tsinghua see Cheng Li, *China's Leaders*, op. cit., pp. 90–100.
7 This is well recalled in Andrew G. Walder, *Fractured Rebellion: The Beijing Red Guard Movement* (Cambridge, MA: Harvard University Press, 2009); William Hinton, *Hundred Day War: The Cultural Revolution at Tsinghua University* (New York: Monthly Review Press, 1972).
8 Willy Wo-Lap Lam, *Chinese Politics in the Hu Jintao Era*, op. cit., p. 6.
9 See my "Training China's Political Elite: The Party School System," *The China Quarterly*, No. 196 (December 2008), pp. 827–844.
10 See the discussion in Daniel Ewing, "Hu Jintao: The Making of a Chinese General Secretary," op. cit., p. 20.
11 https://www.youtube.com/watch?v=3uQcGcGGepw.
12 As reported in Willy Wo-Lap Lam, *Chinese Politics in the Hu Jintao Era*, op. cit., p. 9.

13 As quoted in Ewing, "Hu Jintao," op. cit. Also see David Holley, "Tibet Expels Foreigners, Intensifies Crackdown," *Los Angeles Times*, March 10, 1989: https://www.latimes.com/archives/la-xpm-1989-03-08-mn-257-story.html.

14 "Hu Jintao Says Martial Law Does Not Change Policy on Tibet," Xinhua, March 17, 1989, as reported in BBC *Summary of World Broadcasts*, cited in Ewing, ibid.

15 Hu Jintao, "Jiwang kailai, tuanjie fendou, zhenxing Xizang" [Carry Forward the Cause and Forge Ahead into the Future, United in the Struggle, and Rejuvenate Tibet], Speech on the Occasion of Celebrating the Thirty Year Anniversary of the Implementation of Tibet's Ethnic Reform, April 20, 1989, in *Hu Jintao Wenxuan, Vol. I*, op. cit., pp. 20–38.

16 Ibid., p. 28.

17 Hu Jintao, "Ba Xizang fan fenlie douzheng jinxing daodi" [Incessantly Carry Forward to the End Tibet's Anti-Separatist Struggle], in ibid., pp. 39–44.

18 See, for example, Party Building Institute of the CCP Central Organization Department (ed.), *Dangjian Yanjiu Zengheng Tan, 2000–2001* [Comprehensive Research on Party Building, 2000–2001] (Beijing: Dangjian duwu chubanshe, 2001).

19 This is discussed at length in my *China's Communist Party*, op. cit., pp. 134–137.

20 See *Hu Jintao Wenxuan, Vol. I*, op. cit., pp. 104–128, 138–144, 161–187, 262–269, 466–471, 472–481, 545–543.

21 Ibid., pp. 55–61, 62–64, 73–76, 77–83, 216–221.

22 Ibid., pp. 84–89, 131–136, 156–160, 222–230, 253–261, 453–459, 492–499.

23 Ibid., pp. 188–191, 464–465.

24 Ibid., various pages.

25 Ewing, "Hu Jintao," op. cit., p. 28.

26 Ibid.

27 Parts of this chapter are adapted from my books *China's Communist Party*, op. cit., chapters 6–7; and *China's Future* (Cambridge: Polity Press, 2016), chapters 3–4.

28 For further analyses of the 16th Party Congress see Li Cheng and Lynn T. White III, "The Sixteenth Central Committee of the Chinese Communist Party: Hu Gets What?" *Asian Survey*, Vol. 43, No. 4 (July–August 2003). For further analysis of the fourth-generation leadership see Cheng Li, *China's Leaders*, op. cit.; David M. Finkelstein and Maryanne Kivlehan (eds.), *Chinese Leadership in the 21st Century: The Rise of the Fourth Generation* (Armonk, NY:

M.E. Sharpe, 2002); and Joseph Fewsmith, "Generational Transition in China," *Washington Quarterly*, Vol. 25, No. 4 (Autumn 2002).

29 Willy Wo-Lap Lam, *Chinese Politics in the Hu Jintao Era*, op. cit., p. 61.

30 Noted in Joseph Fewsmith, "Promoting the Scientific Development Concept," *China Leadership Monitor*, No. 11 (2004).

31 See Pan Yuanzheng (ed.), *Dangdai Zhongguo Kexue Fazhanguan* [Contemporary China's Scientific Development] (Beijing: Zhongyang Dangxiao chubanshe, 2004).

32 Hu Jintao, "Comprehensively Implement and Fulfill the Scientific Development Concept," *Qiushi*, No. 1 (2006).

33 I discuss this in depth in my book *China's Future*, op. cit., chapters 1 and 2.

34 See Hu Jintao, "Gojian shehuizhuyi hexie shehui," *Hu Jintao Wenxuan, Vol. II* (Beijing: Renmin ribao chubanshe, 2016), pp. 300–305; Hu's speech was also summarized in "Hu Jintao Emphasizes the Necessity of Gaining a Thorough Understanding of the Great Importance of Building a Socialist Harmonious Society and Earnestly Doing a Good Job in Vigorously Promoting Social Harmony and Unity, at the Opening Session of a Seminar for Provincial and Ministerial Principal Leading Cadres on the Special Topic of Increasing the Ability to Build a Socialist Harmonious Society," Xinhua News Agency, February 19, 2005.

35 Ibid.

36 Ibid.

37 Wang Weiguang, "Under the Premise of Giving Priority to Efficiency, Give Consideration to Fairness in a Better Way," *Xuexi Shibao* (Study Times), August 15, 2005.

38 See Bruce Dickson, *The Dictator's Dilemma: The Chinese Communist Party's Strategy for Survival* (New York: Oxford University Press, 2016).

39 David Shambaugh, *China's Future*, op. cit.; Minxin Pei, *China's Trapped Transition: The Limits of Developmental Autocracy* (Cambridge, MA: Harvard University Press, 2008).

40 Richard McGregor, "Data Show Social Unrest on the Rise in China," *Financial Times*, January 19, 2006; Joseph Kahn, "Pace and Scope of Protest in China Accelerated in '05," *New York Times*, January 20, 2006.

41 The full text of Charter '08 can be found on Chinafile: http://www.chinafile.com/chinas-charter-08.

42 See "CCP Central Committee Proposal on Formulating the Eleventh Five-Year Plan for National Economic and Social Development," Xinhua News

Agency, October 21, 2005; "The Eleventh Five-Year Plan: Pushing Forward the Building of a Socialist Harmonious Society," Xinhua News Agency, March 6, 2006.

43 Ibid.

44 "Communiqué of the Sixth Plenum of the Sixteenth Central Committee," Xinhua News Agency, October 11, 2006.

45 Alice Miller, "Demands of Globalization and Governance," in Roderick MacFarquhar (ed.), *The Politics of China* (Cambridge: Cambridge University Press, third edition, 2011), p. 586.

46 Xinhua, "Premier: China Confident in Maintaining Growth," March 16, 2007: http://news.xinhuanet.com/english/2007-03/16/content_5856569.htm.

47 "Communiqué of the Fifth Plenum of the 17th Central Committee of the Communist Party of China," October 18, 2010: http://english.mofcom.gov.cn/aarticle/translatorsgarden/famousspeech/201011/20101107250865.html.

48 I am indebted to a former member of the Central Party School for alerting me to this distinction.

49 See Alice L. Miller, "Hu Jintao and the Party Politburo," *China Leadership Monitor*, No. 9 (Winter 2004); "Party Politburo Processes Under Hu Jintao," ibid., No. 11 (Summer 2004); "More Already on Politburo Procedures Under Hu Jintao," ibid., No. 17 (Winter 2006).

50 Hu Jintao, "Jiaqiang dang de zhizheng nengli jianshe" [Accelerate the Party's Ruling Capacity Building], *Hu Jintao Wenxuan, Vol. II*, ibid., pp. 242–246.

51 "Hu Jintao's Speech at the June 30 Rally to Mark the 85th CPC Founding Anniversary and to Sum Up the Results of the Educational Drive Launched for Maintaining Communist Party Members' Advanced Nature," Xinhua, June 30, 2006.

52 Hu Jintao, "Hold High the Great Banner of Socialism with Chinese Characteristics and Strive for New Victories in Building a Moderately Prosperous Society in All Respects," Report to the 17th Party Congress, October 15, 2007, section XII; Hu Jintao, *Selected Works of Hu Jintao, 2001–2012* (San Bernardino, CA: Intercultural Publishing, 2012).

53 Central Propaganda Department (ed.), *Dang de Shiliuju Sizhong Quanwei "Jueding"* [The Decision of the 16th Party Congress Fourth Plenary Session] (Beijing: Xuexi chubanshe and Dangjian duwu chubanshe, 2004).

54 Author's discussion with knowledgeable individual, October 25, 2020.

55 "Chinese Communist Party Publishes Key Policy Document on Governance

Capability": http://www.english.peopledaily.com.cn/200409/26/eng20040926_158378.html.

56 *Dang de Shiliuju Sizhong Quanwei "Jueding,"* op. cit.

57 Ibid.

58 Zeng Qinghong, "Jiaqiang dang de zhizheng nengli jianshe de ganlingxing wenzhai" [Programmatic Materials for Strengthening the Party's Ability to Govern] in Central Propaganda Department (ed.), *Dang de Shiliuju Sizhong Quanwei "Jueding,"* op. cit., pp. 31–63.

59 Ibid.

60 Ibid.

61 Ibid.

62 See, for example, Chen Daichang, *Jiaqiang Dang de Zhizheng Nengli Jianshe de Diaocha yu Yanjiu* ([Investigation and Research on Enhancing the Party's Governing Ability Construction] (Beijing: Zhongyang dangxiao chubanshe, 2004).

63 The following discussion is drawn from my *China's Future*, chapter 4.

64 "Wen Jiabao Promises Political Reform in China," *The Daily Telegraph*, October 4, 2010: http://www.telegraph.co.uk/news/worldnews/asia/china/8040534/Wen-Jiabao-promises-political-reform-for-China.html.

65 "China's Wen Jiabao Calls for 'Urgent' Political Reform," *The Daily Telegraph*, March 14, 2012: http://www.telegraph.co.uk/news/worldnews/asia/china/9142333/Chinas-Wen-Jiabao-calls-for-urgent-political-reform.html.

66 "China Needs Political Reform to Avert 'Political Tragedy'," *The Guardian*, March 14, 2012: http://www.theguardian.com/world/2012/mar/14/china-political-reform-wen-jiabao.

67 Hu Jintao, "Tigao dangnei minzhu jianshe zhiliang he shuiping" [Raise and Build the Quality and Level of Intra-Party Democracy], *Hu Jintao Wenxuan, Vol. III* (Beijing: Renmin Ribao chubanshe, 2016), pp. 222–226.

68 Hu Jintao, "Full Text of the Keynote Speech at a Grand Gathering Marking the 90th Founding Anniversary of the CPC," op. cit., p. 138.

69 See Bruce Dickson, "No Jasmine for China," *Current History*, No. 110 (2011), pp. 211–216.

70 My sense of this bureaucratic coalition and its preferences derives in large part from discussions I had with numerous individuals in Chinese academic circles, the media and propaganda system, and the military during the winter of 2009–2010 (when I was a resident visiting scholar at the Chinese Academy of Social Sciences Institute of World Politics and Economics).

71 China National Bureau of Statistics, *Zhongguo Tongji Zhaiyao* (Beijing: Tongji chubanshe, 2020), p. 28.

72 See Srikanth Kondapalli, "Regional Multilateralism with Chinese Characteristics," in David Shambaugh (ed.), *China & the World* (New York: Oxford University Press, 2020).

73 Hu Jintao, "Wo jun zai xin shiji xin jieduan de lishi shiming" [Our Military's New Century New State Historical Mission], *Hu Jintao Wenxuan, Vol. I*, op. cit., pp. 256–262.

74 For more on this subject see, for example, my *China Goes Global: The Partial Power* (New York: Oxford University Press, 2013), chapter 6; and "China's Soft Power Push: The Search for Respect," *Foreign Affairs* (July–August 2015), 99–107.

75 See Hu Jintao, "Nuli jianshe chijiu heping gongtong fanrong de hexie shijie," [Strive to Build a Harmonious World of Lasting Peace and Common Prosperity], *Hu Jintao Wenxuan, Vol. II*, op. cit., pp. 350–356.

76 The text of Zheng's concept first appeared in *Foreign Affairs*, Vol. 84, No. 5 (2005) and is reprinted in David Shambaugh (ed.), *The China Reader: Rising Power* (New York: Oxford University Press, 2016), pp. 20–23.

77 See, for example, Michael D. Swaine, "Perceptions of an Assertive China," *China Leadership Monitor*, No. 32 (2010), available at: http://media.hoover.org/sites/default/files/documents/CLM32MS.pdf.

78 See Alastair Iain Johnston. "How New and Assertive is China's New Assertiveness?" *International Security*, Vol. 37. No. 4 (Spring 2013), pp. 7–48.

Chapter 6

1 Xi Jinping, "Secure a Decisive Victory in Securing a Moderately Prosperous Society in All Respects and Strive for the Great Success of Socialism with Chinese Characteristics in the New Era," October 18, 2017, Xinhua, November 3, 2017: http://www.xinhuanet.com/english/download/Xi_Jinping's_report_at_19th_CPC_National_Congress.pdf.

2 See David Shambaugh, "Don't Expect Reform from China's New Leaders," *Washington Post*, November 15, 2012: https://www.washingtonpost.com/opinions/dont-expect-reform-from-chinas-new-leaders/2012/11/15/82cd4402-2f47-11e2-9f50-0308e1e75445_story.html.

3 "Full Text: China's New Party Chief Xi Jinping's Speech," BBC, November 15, 2012: https://www.bbc.com/news/world-asia-china-20338586.

4 See, for example, Liza Lin, "Xi's China Crafts Campaign to Boost Youth Patriotism," *Wall Street Journal*, December 31, 2020: https://www.wsj.com/articles/xi-china-campaign-youth-patriotism-propaganda-11609343255.
5 "Full Text: China's New Party Chief," op. cit.
6 Gary Shih, "In China, Investigations and Purges Become the New Normal," *Washington Post,* October 22, 2018.
7 See Minxin Pei, "From Tiananmen to Neo-Stalinism," *Journal of Democracy*, Vol. 31, No. 1 (January 2020), pp. 155–156. These figures are drawn from Pei's detailed study *China's Crony Capitalism: The Dynamics of Regime Decay* (Cambridge, MA: Harvard University Press, 2016).
8 Xinhua, "Xi Highlights National Goal of Rejuvenation," *China Daily*, November 30, 2012: https://www.chinadaily.com.cn/china/2012-11/30/content_15972687.htm.
9 See my *China's Communist Party: Atrophy & Adaptation* (Berkeley and Washington, DC: University of California Press and Woodrow Wilson Center Press, 2013).
10 Ibid., p. 61 (which cites many of the Chinese analysts who argued this position).
11 For a full description of this school of thought and line of analysis see ibid., chapter 4.
12 See Shi Jingyue, "Xi Jinping zai Guangdong kaocha shi de jianghua" [Xi Jinping's Speech on Investigation Tour of Guangdong], in *Zhonggong Ban Mimi Baogao: Xi Jinping Nan Er Meng—Jiu Dang* [Secret Reports of the Chinese Communist Party: Xi Jinping's Incessant Dream—Save the Party] (New York: Mirror Media Group, 2014); and Richard McGregor, *Xi Jinping: The Backlash* (Sydney: Lowy Institute, 2019), p. 20.
13 See "Leaked Speech Shows Xi Jinping's Opposition to Reform," *China Digital Times*, January 27, 2013: https://chinadigitaltimes.net/2013/01/leaked-speech-shows-xi-jinpings-opposition-to-reform/.
14 Quoted in Graham Allison and Robert D. Blackwill, with Ali Wyne, *Lee Kuan Yew: The Grand Master's Insights on China, the United States, and the World* (Cambridge, MA: MIT Press for the Belfer Center for Science and International Affairs, 2012), p. 17.
15 Wu Ming, *A Biography of Xi Jinping* (Hong Kong: CNHK Publications, 2012), pp. 20–21.
16 Ibid., p. 22.
17 Ibid., p. 23.

18 Kerry Brown, *CEO, China: The Rise of Xi Jinping* (London: I.B. Tauris, 2016), p. 53.

19 Wu Ming, *A Biography of Xi Jinping*, op. cit., p. 32.

20 See François Bougon, *Inside the Mind of Xi Jinping* (London: C. Hurst & Co., 2018), p. 96.

21 Quoted in Robert Lawrence Kuhn, *How China's Leaders Think* (Singapore: John Wiley & Sons, 2011), p. 61.

22 Wu Ming, *A Biography of Xi Jinping*, op. cit., p. 32.

23 Ibid., pp. 34–35.

24 See, for example, "Changing the Guards," *The Economist*, January 9, 2021, p. 73.

25 Wu Ming, *A Biography of Xi Jinping*, as quoted on p. 49.

26 Ibid., pp. 58–59; Kerry Brown, *CEO, China*, op. cit., p. 56.

27 I am grateful to Professor Joseph Torigian (who is completing a comprehensive biography of Xi Zhongxun) for this information.

28 There is a photo of Xi immediately following his return in Xi Jinpijng, *The Governance of China, Vol. I* (Beijing: Foreign Languages Press, 2014), photo follows page vi.

29 See George C. Wilson, "New Military Relationship with China is Developing," *Washington Post*, May 29, 1980: https://www.washingtonpost.com/archive/politics/1980/05/29/new-military-relationship-with-china-is-developing/8d1c8405-df48-4d50-a675-1bee188e85cb/.

30 Jeremy Page, "Xi's Autocratic Turn Rooted in His Past," *Wall Street Journal*, December 24, 2020.

31 See "Plagiarism and Xi Jinping," *Asia Sentinel*, September 24, 2013: https://www.asiasentinel.com/p/plagiarism-and-xi-jinping; Tom Hancock and Nicolle Liu, "Top Chinese Officials Plagiarized Doctoral Dissertations," *Financial Times*, February 26, 2019: https://www.ft.com/content/2eb02fa4-3429-11e9-bd3a-8b2a211d90d5.

32 "Fujian is My Second Home Says Chinese President Xi Jinping," *China Daily*, November 4, 2014: http://www.chinadaily.com.cn/china/2014-11/04/content_27651018.htm.

33 Gary Cheung, "Xi Jinping's Former Father-in-Law, Diplomat Ke Hua, Dies in Beijing at Age 103," *South China Morning Post*, January 3, 2019: https://www.scmp.com/news/hong-kong/article/2180598/chinese-president-xi-jinpings-former-father-law-diplomat-ke-hua-dies.

34 Wu Ming, *A Biography of Xi Jinping*, op. cit., p. 181.

35 Elisabeth Rosenthal, "China Sentences Eleven to Death in Smuggling Scandal," *New York Times*, January 9, 2000: https://www.nytimes.com/2000/11/09/world/china-sentences-11-officials-to-death-in-smuggling-scandal.html.

36 "Smuggling Show in Xiamen Draws Visitors," *People's Daily*, January 29, 2002: http://en.people.cn/english/zhuanti/Zhuanti_75.html.

37 Quoted in Wu Ming, *A Biography of Xi Jinping*, p. 249.

38 This is all recounted in Wu Ming, ibid., pp. 273–279.

39 Ibid., pp. 308–309.

40 See Martin Stuart-Fox, *A Short History of China and Southeast Asia: Tribute, Trade, and Influence* (Crow's Nest, Australia: Allen & Unwin, 2003); Wang Gungwu, *The Nanhai Trade* (Singapore: Times Academic Press, 1998); David Shambaugh, *Where Great Powers Meet: America & China in Southeast Asia* (New York: Oxford University Press, 2021), chapter 4.

41 Wu Ming, *A Biography of Xi Jinping*, op. cit., p. 290.

42 Ibid., p. 298.

43 National Bureau of Statistics, *Zhongguo Tongji Zhaiyao* (Beijing: Tongji chubanshe, 2020), p. 31.

44 Wu Ming, *A Biography of Xi Jinping*, op. cit., 285.

45 Ibid., pp. 324–325.

46 For a good analysis of Xi's factional network see Neil Thomas, "Ties That Bind: Xi's People on the Politburo," *Macro Polo*, June 17, 2020: https://macropolo.org/analysis/the-ties-that-bind-xi-people-politburo/.

47 Xi Jinping, "Secure a Decisive Victory," op. cit.

48 Xi Jinping, "Secure a Decisive Victory," ibid.

49 Minxin Pei, "China: From Tiananmen to Neo-Stalinism," op. cit.

50 Xi Jinping, "Secure a Decisive Victory," op. cit.

51 Xi Jinping, "Secure a Decisive Victory," op. cit.

52 Kai Strittmatter, *We Have Been Harmonized: Life in China's Surveillance State* (New York: Harper Collins, 2020), pp. 136–137.

53 See Susan L. Shirk, "China in Xi's 'New Era': The Return to Personalistic Rule," *Journal of Democracy*, Vol. 29, No. 2 (April 2018).

54 Parts of this section are drawn from my book *China's Future* (Cambridge: Polity Press, 2016), chapter 2.

55 See, for example, Asia Society Policy Institute and Rhodium Group, "The China Dashboard": https://chinadashboard.gist.asiasociety.org/china-dashboard/.

56 Xi Jinping, "Secure a Decisive Victory," op. cit.

57 See the discussion in Barry Naughton, "Economic Rebalancing," in Jacques deLisle and Avery Goldstein (eds.), *China's Challenges* (Philadelphia: University of Pennsylvania Press, 2015).

58 See: https://data.worldbank.org/indicator/NY.GDP.PCAP.CD.

59 See Wing Thye Woo, "The Major Types of Middle Income Trap That Threaten China," in Wing Thye Woo, Ming Lu, Jeffrey D. Sachs, and Zhao Chen (eds.), *A New Economic Growth Engine for China: Escaping the Middle Income Trap by Not Doing More of the Same* (London and Singapore: Imperial College Press and World Scientific Publishing, 2012).

60 Development Research Center of the State Council Medium to Long-Term Growth Project Team, *China's Next Decade: Rebuilding Economic Momentum and Balance* (Hong Kong: CLSA Books, 2014).

61 For an excellent description of innovation under Xi see Elizabeth Economy, *The Third Revolution: Xi Jinping and the New Chinese State* (New York: Oxford University Press, 2018), chapter 5.

62 Deng Yaqing, "Leaping into the First Echelon," *Beijing Review*, April 23, 2015; "Route to a New Frontier," *Beijing Review*, June 4, 2015.

63 "Leaping into the First Echelon," ibid., p. 13.

64 See Regina M. Abrami, William C. Kirby, and F. Warren McFarlan, *Can China Lead? Reaching the Limits of Growth and Power* (Cambridge, MA: Harvard Business School Press, 2014).

65 See CSIS China Power Project, "Is China a Global Leader in Research and Development?": https://chinapower.csis.org/china-research-and-development-rnd.

66 See, in particular, Daniel Breznitz and Michael Murphree, *Run of the Red Queen: Government, Innovation, Globalization, and Economic Growth in China* (New Haven: Yale University Press, 2011); and Michael T. Rock and Michael A. Toman, *China's Technological Catch-Up Strategy* (New York: Oxford University Press, 2015).

67 For the Plenum communiqué see: http://www.xinhuanet.com/2020-10-29/c_1126674147.htm.

68 See James MacGregor, *No Ancient Wisdom, No Followers: The Challenges of Chinese Authoritarian Capitalism* (N.P.: Prospecta Press, 2012).

69 Lingling Wei, "China Approves Push to Merge State Firms," *Wall Street Journal*, September 8, 2015.

70 Xi Jinping, "Confidently and Self-Assuredly Build Stronger, Better, and Bigger

State-Owned Enterprises," Xinhua, July 4, 2016: www.xinhuanet.com//politics/2016-07/04/c_1119162333.htm.

71 No author, "China's Auditor Says State Firms Falsified Revenue and Profit," *Bloomberg Business*, June 28, 2015.

72 Patricia Cheng and Marco Yau, *China Banks* (Hong Kong, CLSA Ltd., 2015), p. 1.

73 This process has been traced in detail in Nicholas R. Lardy's *The State Strikes Back: The End of Economic Reform in China?* (Washington, DC: The Peterson Institute for International Economics, 2019).

74 Cited in David Zweig, "China's Political Economy," in William A. Joseph (ed.), *Politics in China* (New York: Oxford University Press, second edition, 2014), p. 268.

75 Cited in Minxin Pei, "China: From Tiananmen to Neo-Stalinism," op. cit., p. 150.

76 Ibid.

77 "Full Text of Foreign Minister Wang Yi's News Conference at Second Session of 13th NPC 2019," Xinhua, March 8, 2019.

78 Jonathan E. Hillman, *The Emperor's New Road: China and the Project of the Century* (New Haven: Yale University Press, 2020), p. 9.

79 Ibid., p. 14.

80 See David Shambaugh, *Where Great Powers Meet: America & China in Southeast Asia*, op. cit., chapters 5 and 6. For other various other regions see Hillman, ibid., and Joshua Eisenman and Eric Heginbotham, "China's Relations with Africa, Latin America, and the Middle East," in David Shambaugh (ed.), *China & the World* (New York: Oxford University Press, 2020).

81 See US Library of Congress, *Government Responses to Disinformation on Social Media Platforms: China*, July 24, 2020: https://www.loc.gov/law/help/social-media-disinformation/china.php.

82 Kai Strittmatter, *We Have Been Harmonized*, op. cit., p. 187.

83 See Edward Wong, "CCP News Alert: Chinese Media Must Serve the Party," *New York Times*, February 16, 2016; "Xi Jinping Asks for 'Absolute Loyalty' From State Media," *The Guardian*, February 19, 2016: https://www.theguardian.com/world/2016/feb/19/xi-jinping-tours-chinas-top-state-media-outlets-to-boost-loyalty.

84 Ibid.

85 See Editorial Board, "China's Pathetic Crackdown on Civil Society," *Washington Post*, April 22, 2015: https://www.washingtonpost.com/opinions/

chinas-pathetic-lockdown/2015/04/22/bddf8fdc-e548-11e4-905f-cc896d379a32_story.html; "Beijing's Secret Memo and the Jailing of Gao Yu," *Wall Street Journal*, April 23, 2015: https://www.wsj.com/articles/beijings-secret-memo-1429841508; Tania Branigan, "US and EU Protest Chinese Journalist's Jailing for 'Leaking State Secrets'," *The Guardian*, April 17, 2015: https://www.theguardian.com/world/2015/apr/17/gao-yu-and-document-no-9-china-jails-journalist-for-leaking-state-secrets.

86 See "Communiqué on the Current State of the Ideological Sphere," translation on Chinafile, November 8, 2013: https://www.chinafile.com/document-9-chinafile-translation.

87 Hua Xia, "Xi Stresses Carrying Forward Great Spirit of Resisting Aggression," Xinhua, September 4, 2020: http://www.xinhuanet.com/english/2020-09/04/c_139340869.htm.

88 Xi Jinping, "Secure a Decisive Victory," op. cit.

89 Human Rights Watch, "China: Events of 2018," *World Report 2019*: https://www.hrw.org/world-report/2019/country-chapters/china-and-tibet#.

90 Austin Ramzy, "Beijing's Repression of Muslims, Explained," *New York Times*, January 21, 2021.

91 See Tania Branigan, "China Locks Down Western Province After Ethnic Riots Kill 140," *The Guardian,* July 6, 2009: https://www.theguardian.com/world/2009/jul/06/china-uighur-urumqi-riots.

92 "China Steps Up Surveillance in Xinjiang," BBC, July 2, 2009: https://www.bbc.com/news/10485129; "China Puts Urumqi Under Full Surveillance," Associated Press, January 25, 2011: https://www.theguardian.com/world/2011/jan/25/china-urumqi-under-full-surveillance.

93 Austin Ramzy and Chris Buckley, "'Absolutely No Mercy': Leaked Files Expose How China Organized Mass Detentions of Muslims," *New York Times*, November 16, 2019: https://www.nytimes.com/interactive/2019/11/16/world/asia/china-xinjiang-documents.html.

94 Xinhua, "Xi Calls for Building 'Great Wall of Iron' for Xinjiang's Stability," Xinhuanet, March 10, 2017: http://www.xinhuanet.com//english/2017-03/10/c_1361119256.htm.

95 As cited in Jonathan Hillman, *The Emperor's New Road*, op. cit., pp. 206–207.

96 See Maya Wang, "More Evidence of China's Horrific Abuses in Xinjiang," Human Rights Watch, February 20, 2020: https://www.hrw.org/news/2020/02/20/more-evidence-chinas-horrific-abuses-xinjiang#; Emma

Graham-Harrison, "China Has Built 380 Internment Camps in Xinjiang, Study Finds," *The Guardian*, September 23, 2020: https://www.theguardian.com/world/2020/sep/24/china-has-built-380-internment-camps-in-xinjiang-study-finds; Australia Strategic Policy Institute, *The Xinjiang Data Project*: https://xjdp.aspi.org.au.

97 See Austin Ramzy, "He Needed a Job. China Gave Him One: Locking Up His Fellow Muslims," *New York Times*, March 2, 2019: https://www.nytimes.com/2019/03/02/world/asia/china-muslim-detention-uighur-kazakh.html.

98 Human Rights Watch, "China: Events of 2018," op. cit.

99 See Adrian Zenz, *Sterilizations, IUDs, and Mandatory Birth Control: The CCP's Campaign to Suppress Uighur Birthrates in Xinjiang* (Washington, DC: The Jamestown Foundation: 2020): https://jamestown.org/wp-content/uploads/2020/06/Zenz-Sterilizations-IUDs-and-Mandatory-Birth-Control-FINAL-27June.pdf?x71937.

100 U.S-China Economic and Security Review Commission, *2020 Report to Congress* (Washington, DC: US Government Printing Office), p. 341.

101 Human Rights Watch, "China: Events of 2018," op. cit.

102 Gilles Sabrie, "Inside China's Dystopian Dreams: A.I., Shame, and Lots of Cameras," *New York Times*, July 8, 2018: https://www.nytimes.com/2018/07/08/business/china-surveillance-technology.html.

103 Strittmatter, *We Have Been Harmonized*, op. cit., pp. 191–192.

104 See Mirjam Meissner, *China's Social Credit System* (Berlin: MERICS, 2017): https://merics.org/en/report/chinas-social-credit-system; Samantha Hoffman, *Social Credit* (Canberra: Australian Strategic Policy Institute, 2018): https://www.aspi.org.au/report/social-credit.

105 Strittmatter, *We Have Been Harmonized*, op. cit., p. 7.

106 Quoted in Jeremy Page, "Xi's Autocratic Turn Rooted in His Past," op. cit.

107 See You Ji, "How Xi Jinping Dominates Elite Party Politics: A Case Study of Civil-Military Leadership Formation," *The China Journal*, No. 84 (July 2020).

108 Among many such exhortations by Xi, see "Xi Stresses Military Training to Raise Capability of Winning Wars," Xinhua, November 25, 2020: http://www.xinhuanet.com/english/2020-11/25/c_139542743.htm.

109 Xi Jinping, "Secure a Decisive Victory," op. cit., p. 5.

110 Ibid., p. 48.

111 These changes are all very well described and analyzed in Phillip C. Saunders et al., *Chairman Xi Remakes the PLA: Assessing Chinese Military Reforms* (Washington, DC: National Defense University Press, 2019). Also see Andrew

Scobell et al., *China's Grand Strategy: Trends, Trajectories, and Long-Term Competition* (Santa Monica: RAND Corporation, 2020), especially chapter 5.

112 This is well described in Suisheng Zhao, "China's Foreign Policy Making Process: Players and Institutions," in David Shambaugh (ed.), *China & the World*, op. cit.

113 Xi Jinping, "Strengthen CCP Central Committee Leadership Over Foreign Affairs," *The Governance of China, Vol. III*, op. cit., pp. 493–494.

114 https://en.wikipedia.org/wiki/List_of_international_trips_made_by_Xi_Jinping.

115 Shaun Breslin offers a superb cataloguing and discourse analysis of Xi's narratives in his book *China Risen: Studying Chinese Global Power* (Bristol, UK: Bristol University Press, 2021).

116 Xi Jinping, "Secure a Decisive Victory, Section 1, op. cit.

117 See, for example, David Shambaugh, "China's Soft Power Push: The Search for Respect," *Foreign Affairs* (July–August 2015): https://www.foreignaffairs.com/articles/china/2015-06-16/chinas-soft-power-push.

118 Xi Jinping, "China's Diplomacy in the New Era," *The Governance of China, Vol. III* (Beijing: Foreign Languages Press, 2020), pp. 489–492.

119 See Yang Jiechi, "Studying General Secretary Xi Jinping's Thought on Diplomacy," *Qiushi* (November/December 2017): http://english.qstheory.cn/2017-11/28/c_1122007258.htm.

120 Xi Jinping, "Secure a Decisive Victory," op. cit.

121 See Xi Jinping, "Improve Our Ability to Participate in Global Governance: Speech at the 35th Study Session of the Political Bureau of the 18th CPC Central Committee," in *The Governance of China, Vol. II* (Beijing: Foreign Languages Press, 2017), pp. 487–490.

122 See Srikanth Kondapalli, "Regional Multilateralism with Chinese Characteristics," in David Shambaugh (ed.), *China & the World*, op. cit.

123 See Jonathan Hillman, *The Emperor's New Road*, op. cit.; David M. Lampton et al., *Rivers of Iron: Railroads and Chinese Power in Southeast Asia* (Berkeley: University of California Press, 2020); Eyck Freymann, *One Belt One Road: Chinese Power Meets the World* (Cambridge: Harvard University Press, 2021).

124 See Nadège Rolland, *China's Vision for a New World Order* (Seattle: National Bureau of Asian Research, 2020), p. 48.

125 See Mark Magnier, "China's Fumble: Beijing Dropped the Ball After Donald Trump's US Left the Global Stage, Analysts Say," *South China Morning Post*, December 25, 2020: https://www.scmp.com/news/china/diplomacy/art

icle/3115280/chinas-fumble-why-xi-jinping-dropped-ball-after-trumps-us-left.

126 See, for example, Xinhua, "China's Image Better Among Developing Countries: Survey," October 18, 2019: http://www.xinhuanet.com/english/2019-10/18/c_138482489.htm.

127 CSIS China Power Project, "How Are Global Views of China Trending?": https://chinapower.csis.org/global-views/.

128 Drew Hinshaw, Sha Hua, and Laurence Norman, "Pushback on Xi's China Vision Spreads Beyond U.S.," *Wall Street Journal*, December 28, 2020: https://www.wsj.com/articles/pushback-xi-china-europe-germany-beyond-u-s-11609176287.

129 The global backlash against Xi's China has been summarized in Richard McGregor, *Xi Jinping: The Backlash*, op. cit. Also see Hinshaw, Hua, and Norman, "Pushback on Xi's China Vision Spreads Beyond U.S.," op. cit.

130 See "Xi's Not Going," *The Economist*, October 31, 2020.

131 See Minxin Pei, *China's Crony Capitalism: The Dynamics of Regime Decay*, op. cit.

132 See Cai Xia, "The Party That Failed: An Insider Breaks with Beijing," *Foreign Affairs* (January/February 2021).

133 Hurun Report Releases Immigration and the Chinese HNWIs 2018, June 30, 2018: https://hurun.net/en-US/Info/Detail?num=670D27DA6723; Robert Frank, "More Than a Third of Chinese Millionaires Want to Leave China: Here's Where They Want to Go," CNBC, June 6, 2018: https://www.cnbc.com/2018/07/05/more-than-a-third-of-chinese-millionaires-want-to-leave-china.html.

134 See Sarah Cook, "Behind Xi Jinping's Steely Façade, a Leadership Crisis is Smoldering in China," *The Diplomat*, October 9, 2020: https://thediplomat.com/2020/10/behind-xi-jinpings-steely-facade-a-leadership-crisis-is-smoldering-in-china/. This is also the main argument in Carl Minzer's insightful book *End of an Era: How China's Authoritarian Revival is Undermining its Rise* (New York: Oxford University Press, 2018); and George Magnus' *Red Flags: Why Xi's China is in Jeopardy* (New Haven: Yale University Press, 2018).

135 Xi Jinping, "Secure a Decisive Victory," op. cit.

136 This was the core argument of my 2015 article (and I still believe it), "China's Coming Crack-up," *Wall Street Journal*, March 6, 2015: https://www.wsj.com/articles/the-coming-chinese-crack-up-1425659198.

137 See David Shambaugh, *China's Communist Party: Atrophy & Adaptation*, op. cit.;

Bruce Dickson, *The Dictator's Dilemma: The Chinese Communist Party's Strategy for Survival* (New York: Oxford University Press, 2016).

Chapter 7

1 Lucian W. Pye, "An Introductory Profile: Deng Xiaoping and China's Political Culture," in David Shambaugh (ed.), *Deng Xiaoping: Portrait of a Chinese Statesman* (Oxford: Clarendon Press, 1995), p. 4.
2 See Timothy Snyder, "Hitler vs. Stalin: Who Was Worse?" *New York Review of Books*, January 27, 2011: https://www.nybooks.com/daily/2011/01/27/hitler-vs-stalin-who-was-worse/.
3 See Frank Dikötter, *How to Be a Dictator: The Cult of Personality in the Twentieth Century* (London: Bloomsbury Books, 2019).
4 Lucian Pye, "An Introductory Profile," op. cit.
5 Mao did preside over the Ninth CCP Congress and Politburo in 1969.
6 The main biographies of Mao are: Stuart Schram, *Mao Tse-tung* (Harmondsworth, UK: Penguin Books, 1966); Dick Wilson (ed.), *Mao Tse-tung in the Scales of History* (Cambridge: Cambridge University Press, 1977); Lucian W. Pye, *Mao Tse-tung: The Man in the Leader* (New York: Basic Books, 1968); Clare Hollingworth, *Mao* (London: Triad Paladin Grafton Books, 1987); Alexander V. Pantsov with Steven I. Levine, *Mao: The Real Story* (New York: Simon & Schuster, 2007); Philip Short, *Mao: A Life* (New York: Henry Holt, 1999); Jung Chang and Jon Halliday, *Mao: The Unknown Story* (New York: Knopf, 2005); Zhong Wenxian (pseud.), *Mao Zedong: Biography, Assessment, Reminiscences* (Beijing: Foreign Languages Press, 1986).
7 Li Rui, *Mao Zedong: Zhengrong Suiyue* (Beijing: Joint Publishing Co., 2013); Li Zhisui, *The Private Life of Chairman Mao* (London: Chatto and Windus, 1994).
8 Recent examples include Julia Lovell, *Maoism: A Global History* (New York: Knopf, 2019); Andrew G. Walder, *China Under Mao: A Revolution Derailed* (Cambridge, MA: Harvard University Press, 2017).
9 The following discussion draws on my "Deng Xiaoping: The Politician," in David Shambaugh (ed.), *Deng Xiaoping: Portrait of a Chinese Statesman*, op. cit., pp. 49–82.
10 Lucian Pye, "An Introductory Profile," in David Shambaugh (ed.), *Deng Xiaoping: Portrait of a Chinese Statesman*, op. cit., pp. 7–8.
11 Ibid., pp. 8–9.
12 See Martin King Whyte, "Deng Xiaoping: The Social Reformer," and Barry

Naughton, "Deng Xiaoping: The Economist," in David Shambaugh, *Deng Xiaoping: Portrait of a Chinese Statesman*, op. cit.

13 For a good discussion of technocrats in Chinese politics see Cheng Li, *China's Leaders: The New Generation* (Lanham, MD: Rowman & Littlefield, 2001), chapter 2.

14 See, for example, Alfred G. Meyer, "USSR, Incorporated," *Slavic Review*, Vol. 20, No. 3 (October 1961), pp. 369–376; Allen Kassof, "The Administered Society: Totalitarianism without Terror," *World Politics*, Vol. 16, No. 4 (July 1964), pp. 558–575.

15 See Jerry F. Hough and Merle Fainsod, *How the Soviet Union is Governed* (Cambridge: Harvard University Press, 1979); Valerie Bunce and John M. Echols III, "Soviet Politics in the Brezhnev Era: 'Pluralism' or 'Corporatism'?" in Donald R. Kelley (ed.), *Soviet Politics in the Brezhnev Era* (New York: Praeger, 1980); Valerie Bunce, "The Political Economy of the Brezhnev Era," *British Journal of Political Science*, Vol. 13, No. 2 (April 1983), pp. 129–158.

16 See H. Gordon Skilling, "Interest Groups and Communist Politics," *World Politics* (April 1966) pp. 435–451; H. Gordon Skilling and William Griffiths (eds.), *Interest Groups in Soviet Politics* (Princeton: Princeton University Press, 1971).

17 See Kai Strittmatter, *We Have Been Harmonized: Life in China's Surveillance State* (New York: Harper Collins, 2020).

INDEX

Page numbers in *italics* refer to figures and tables.